IC³® Internet and Computing Core Certification Global Standard 4

Standard 4

Study Guide

Ciprian Adrian Rusen

SYBEX®
A Wiley Brand

Senior Acquisitions Editor: Ken Brown
Development Editor: Tom Cirtin
Technical Editor: Vlad Falon
Production Editor: Dassi Zeidel
Copy Editor: Linda Recktenwald
Editorial Manager: Mary Beth Wakefield
Production Manager: Kathleen Wisor
Associate Publisher: Jim Minatel
Supervising Producer: Rich Graves
Book Designers: Judy Fung and Bill Gibson
Proofreader: Kim Wimpsett
Indexer: Ted Laux
Project Coordinator, Cover: Brent Savage
Cover Designer: Wiley
Cover Image: ©Getty Images, Inc./Jeremy Woodhouse

About the Author

Ciprian Adrian Rusen is a recognized Windows Consumer Expert – Microsoft Most Valuable Professional (MVP). He has published several books about Windows and Microsoft Office, and he's also a very active tech blogger at http://www.7tutorials.com.

On his website you can find many tutorials about Windows 7, Windows 8.1, and Windows 10. He and his team of editors also publish how-to guides about other Microsoft products like Windows Phone and Xbox One. If you would like to keep up to date with the latest Microsoft consumer products, you should subscribe to his blog.

Contents at a Glance

Contents

Table of Exercises

Introduction

Welcome to the *IC3: Internet and Computing Core Certification Global Standard 4 Study Guide* for the IC3 Digital Literacy Certification. The purpose of this book is to help you prepare for the certification exams, which cover the following three areas:

Computing Fundamentals   Computing Fundamentals covers subjects needed for a good basic understanding of computing, including knowledge and use of computer hardware, software, and operating systems.

Key Applications   Key Applications covers four major types of applications: word processing, spreadsheet, presentation, and database software. You will learn the common features of these types of applications, how to perform all kinds of tasks (opening and saving files, formatting them, printing them, and so on), and how to collaborate with others to create all kinds of business documents and files.

Living Online   Living Online covers aspects of working in an Internet or networked environment, including basic knowledge of networks and the Internet, skills in specific applications such as email software and web browsers, skills required to find and evaluate information, and an understanding of issues related to computing and the Internet being used at work, home, and school (ergonomics, security, ethics, Internet "netiquette," and the like).

The book contains all of the information you need to pass the required exams. It also includes notes and warnings from the author to help reduce issues you may be experiencing in your own environment. By studying for and passing this exam, you will gain insight that will make you more valuable in your current position and will make you more likely to be recognized.

In the remainder of this section we will look at some of the facts about the exam, give some commonsense tips for taking the exam, and review the process for registering for the exam.

Exam Facts

Individuals seeking IC3 certification are required to take and pass all three IC3 exams: Computing Fundamentals, Key Applications, and Living Online. Here are some facts about them:

- The IC3 exams are administered by Certiport and are taken at Certiport Authorized Testing Centers.
- The exams are based on Microsoft Windows 7 and Microsoft Office 2010.
- There are 45 multiple-choice questions for each exam.
- There is a time limit of 50 minutes for each exam.
- Each exam has a maximum score of 1000.
- The minimum passing score could range from 620 in difficult tests to 720 on easier tests.
- There is a short survey before the exam begins (taking the survey does not use any of the available 50 minutes).

- If you do not pass the exam, you can retake it as many times as you want, but you must wait 24 hours before taking the exam a second time. If you do not pass the exam again, a two-day waiting period will be imposed for each subsequent exam retake.

Tips for Taking the IC3 GS4 Exams

Here are some general tips for improving the odds of passing your certification exam:

- Read each question carefully. Although the test is not written to be confusing, there are times when the obvious choice is not the correct choice.

- Make sure you answer each question. Any unanswered questions are considered wrong, so you are better off making an educated guess than leaving a question unanswered.

- For any questions where you are unsure of the correct answer, use a process of elimination to remove any obviously incorrect answers first. Once you have eliminated the obviously incorrect answers, make an educated guess from the remaining answers.

- If you are unsure about a question, select the answer you think is most likely to be correct, mark it for review, and come back to it at a later time.

- Get a good night's sleep the night before the exam. This will help you to be more alert and think clearly during the exam.

Exam Registration

Take the following steps to register for the IC3 exams:

1. Using a browser navigate to the Certiport website: http://www.certiport.com.
2. To register with Certiport, click the Register link in the top-right corner and provide all the required personal information.
3. Once the registration process is complete, select that you would like to take an exam or prepare for an exam and click Next.
4. Register for the IC3 certification.
5. Locate a Certiport Authorized Testing Center (CATC) near you.
6. Once you have found a CATC, you should then contact the Testing Center directly to confirm that they offer the exam(s) you wish to take, determine their prices and fees, set up a date and time to take the exam, and find out what exam preparation resources/courses they offer.

You can find the exam policies that you must abide by at this web page: http://www.certiport.com/PORTAL/desktopdefault.aspx?page=common/pagelibrary/LiveApp.htm.

IC3 requires certification candidates to accept the terms of a nondisclosure agreement before taking certification exams.

Who Should Read This Book?

This book is intended for individuals who want to earn their IC3 GS4 certification. For both the student and the job-seeker, IC3 provides the foundation of knowledge needed for success, and it is a well-respected and internationally recognized credential that reflects the most relevant skills needed in today's academic and business environments.

What's Inside?

Here is a glance at what's in each chapter:

Part I: Computing Fundamentals

Chapter 1: Understanding Operating Systems   This chapter introduces basic concepts like hardware, software, and operating systems and explains how they work together. It also explains the basics of managing files on a computer and customizing an operating system.

Chapter 2: Understanding Hardware   This chapter goes into more detail about hardware and provides more information about different types of hardware, what they are used for, and how to measure their performance.

Chapter 3: Understanding Software   This chapter demonstrates how to install, uninstall, and reinstall various software. It explains the different licensing models and the basics of using several types of software.

Chapter 4: Troubleshooting Problems with Your Computer   This chapter describes the most common types of problems you may encounter when dealing with both software and hardware and how to deal with them.

Part II: Key Applications

Chapter 5: Exploring Common Application Features in Microsoft Office   This chapter explains the basics of using the applications that are included in the Microsoft Office 2010 suite: how to format files, copy and paste data, print it, and so on.

Chapter 6: Using Microsoft Word   This chapter focuses on using Microsoft Word 2010 for tasks like configuring the layout of your documents, organizing data, and so on.

Chapter 7: Using Microsoft Excel   This chapter focuses on using Microsoft Excel 2010 for tasks like navigating among worksheets, workbooks, tables, and cells; formatting data; sorting it; adding formulas and functions; and inserting charts and graphs.

Chapter 8: Using Microsoft PowerPoint   This chapter focuses on using Microsoft PowerPoint 2010 for tasks like creating presentations, changing their design, adding multimedia files, and creating animations and transitions between slides.

Chapter 9: Using Microsoft Access   This chapter focuses on using Microsoft Access 2010 for tasks such as adding data to a database, finding data in a database, and using queries and reports for filtering and displaying data.

Chapter 10: Collaborating with Others When Working in Microsoft Office   This chapter focuses on collaboration while creating files and documents in Microsoft Office applications. You will learn how to track changes, leave and review comments, and share your work with others.

Part III: Living Online

Chapter 11 Using the Internet   This chapter introduces the basics of the Internet and the World Wide Web. In this chapter you will learn what a web browser is and how to use it to navigate web pages, download files, and more.

Chapter 12: Understanding Networking and Its Most Important Concepts   This chapter delves into complex network topics and tools like the different types of networks that are available, network addressing, security, and the performance of Internet connections. It also shares the basic tools for troubleshooting problems.

Chapter 13: Communicating Online with Others   In this chapter you will learn the basics of communicating online with others, using services like email, text messaging, audio- and videoconferencing, social networks, blogs, and more.

Chapter 14: Being a Responsible Digital Citizen   This chapter discusses ethics, Internet "netiquette," censorship, piracy, and common piracy-prevention tools and recommendations.

Chapter 15: Maintaining Your Health and Safety While Using Computers   This chapter shares several recommendations about how to protect your identity when online, how to remove data from your computer, and how to secure your computer. It also provides recommendations on how to maintain your health while using computers for a long time.

Chapter 16: Searching the World Wide Web   In the last chapter of this book you will learn how to use search engines to search for information, how to find information online, and how to evaluate its truthfulness.

What's Included with the Book

This book includes many helpful items intended to prepare you for the IC3 GS4 certification.

Assessment Test   The Assessment Test at the conclusion of the book's introduction can be used to quickly evaluate where you are with your general computing knowledge and skills that prove your competency in digital literacy. This test should be taken prior to beginning your work in this book, and it should help you identify areas in which you are either strong or weak. Note that these questions are purposely simpler than the types of questions you may see on the exams.

Objective Map and Opening List of Objectives   At the start of this book is a detailed exam objective map showing you where each of the exam objectives is covered in this book. In addition, each chapter opens with a list of the exam objectives it covers. Use these to see exactly where each of the exam topics is covered.

Exam Essentials   The end of each chapter provides a brief overview of the concepts covered in the chapter. We recommend reading through these sections carefully to check your recollection of each topic and returning to any sections of the chapter you're not confident about having mastered.

Chapter Review Questions   Each chapter includes review questions. The material for these questions is pulled directly from information that was provided in the chapter. These questions are based on the exam objectives, and they are similar in difficulty to items you might actually encounter on the IC3 GS4 exams.

Interactive Online Learning Environment and Test Bank

The interactive online learning environment that accompanies *IC3 GS4 Study Guide* provides a test bank with study tools to help you prepare for the certification exams—and increase your chances of passing it the first time! The test bank includes the following:

Sample Tests   All of the questions in this book are provided: the Assessment Test, which you'll find at the end of this introduction, and the Chapter Tests that include the Review Questions at the end of each chapter. In addition, there are six Practice Exams. Use these questions to test your knowledge of the study guide material. The online test bank runs on multiple devices.

Flashcards   Questions are provided in digital flashcard format (a question followed by a single correct answer). You can use the flashcards to reinforce your learning and provide last-minute test prep before the exam.

Practice Files   Many exercises in this book use practice files that were created specifically for this book. You can find them online, in the Other Study Tools section of the interactive learning environment that was created for this book. Before going through all the exercises that are offered, please register and download all the practice files.

Other Study Tools   A glossary of key terms from this book is available as a fully searchable PDF.

 Go to http://sybextestbanks.wiley.com to register and gain access to this interactive online learning environment and test bank with study tools.

How to Use This Book

If you want a solid foundation for preparing for IC3 GS4 exams, then look no further. We've spent a lot of time putting this book together with the sole intention of helping you to pass the exam!

This book is loaded with valuable information. You'll get the most out of your study time if you follow this approach:

1. Take the Assessment Test immediately following this introduction. (The answers are at the end of the test, but no peeking!) It's okay if you don't know any of the answers— that's what this book is for. Carefully read over the explanations for any question you get wrong, and make note of the chapters where that material is covered.

2. Study each chapter carefully, making sure you fully understand the information and the exam objectives listed at the beginning of each one. Again, pay extra-close attention to any chapter that includes material covered in questions you missed on the Assessment Test.

3. Answer all the review questions related to each chapter. Specifically note any questions that confuse you, and study the corresponding sections of the book again. And don't just skim these questions—make sure you understand each answer completely.

4. Test yourself using all the electronic flashcards. This is a brand-new and updated flash-card program to help you prepare for the latest IC3 GS4 exam, and it is a really great study tool.

Learning every bit of the material in this book is going to require applying yourself with a good measure of discipline. So try to set aside the same time period every day to study, and select a comfortable and quiet place to do so. If you work hard, you will be surprised at how quickly you learn this material. If you follow the steps listed here and study with the review questions, practice exams, and electronic flashcards, you will increase your chances of passing the exam.

How to Contact Sybex

Sybex strives to keep you supplied with the latest tools and information that you need for your work. Please check the website at http://sybextestbanks.wiley.com.

IC3 GS4 Exam Objectives

IC3—Module 1: Computing Fundamentals

Objective Number	Objectives and Skill Sets	Chapter
1.0	Operating System Basics	1
1.1	What is an OS and what does it do?	
1.1.1	Explain the differences between software applications and operating systems and demonstrate their uses.	

Objective Number	Objectives and Skill Sets	Chapter
1.1.2	Common OS features, explain each of their uses: Power On/Power Off Log on/log off/switch user Lock/Unlock Differences between common OSs	1
1.1.3	Explain how hardware can influence the Operating System and software and vice versa.	
1.1.4	Software updates, security fixes, bugs, adaption to new hardware. Demonstrate how to update software, using manual and automatic settings.	
1.2	Manage computer files and folders.	
1.2.1	Directory and folder hierarchy and structure: Menu, Toolbar, and Window Navigation Expand and Collapse Folder views	
1.2.2	File/Folder management: Keyboard shortcuts Copy Paste Delete Move Rename Create shortcuts Search	
1.2.3	Identify file extensions and their associations such as .docx, .xlsx, .pdf, .mp3, etc.	
1.3	Manage computer configuration, Control Panel, OS, and drivers.	
1.3.1	Basic Desktop Customization Visual options Languages Date and Time Accessibility options	

continues

Objective Number	Objectives and Skill Sets	Chapter
1.3.2	Describe the various states of operation available in a typical consumer-level OS. Include Shutdown, hibernation, standby, fully awake, etc.	1
1.3.3	User accounts and rights: Group policy (specifically mobile) Read/Write Administrative vs. standard user rights File and Directory Permissions	
2.0	Computer hardware and concepts	2
2.1	Common computer terminology	
2.1.1	Define the terms and explain the differences between input/output devices and hardware and peripherals. Processing: Gigahertz, Hertz, CPU Input/Output: Monitor and Projector, Mice, Keyboards, Stylus, Microphone, Speakers, Touchpad Printers	
2.1.2	Explain the different types of memory (Volatile, Nonvolatile). Volatile - RAM Nonvolatile - SSD drive, Magnetic hard drive, ROM, Flash drives (USB, Jump, Thumb, etc.) Units of measurement: Mega, giga, tera, peta Explain the difference between Bit vs. Byte.	
2.2	Types of devices	
2.2.1	Explain these different types of computers. Compare and contrast uses and capabilities. Server Desktop Laptop Tablet Smartphone	
2.3	Computer performance	

Objective Number	Objectives and Skill Sets	Chapter
2.3.1	Specify criteria that could be used to evaluate the pros and cons of various computing devices and peripherals, Focus on performance issues.	2
2.3.2	Processing vs. memory vs. storage: Describe the concepts of Processing capacity, Processing speed, Memory capacity, Memory speed, Storage capacity, and Storage speed including how each interacts with the other to determine overall computing capacity, speed and power.	
3.0	Computer software and concepts	3
3.1	Software management	
3.1.1	Describe how to install, uninstall and reinstall various kinds of software, including application software, drivers and system software, upgrades and patches, on various types of personal computers and configure the environment for use.	
3.2	Licensing	
3.2.1	Understand the various licensing models used for computer software such as operating systems, application programs, system software, databases, browsers, etc. Freeware, shareware, open-source, premium applications.	
3.2.2	Demonstrate an understanding of the legal and ethical obligations associated with EULAs and the user's responsibilities, commitments, and benefits that can be derived by entering into a typical computer industry EULA.	
3.2.3	Demonstrate an understanding of the concept of a single seat and site License options, how each party benefits, restrictions, obligations, etc.	
3.3	Software Usage	
3.3.1	Describe the dependencies and constraints that exist between hardware and software operation.	
3.3.2	Demonstrate an understanding of the similarities and differences between a basic, consumer-level relational database management system and a typical spreadsheet program, including an understanding of which situations would be better suited to which product.	

continues

Objective Number	Objectives and Skill Sets	Chapter
3.3.3	Describe what desktop publishing is, how and when desktop publishing software should be used, and the general feature set included in a representative desktop publishing program.	3
3.3.4	Describe what a Presentation program is, its purpose, how it is used, and the general feature set included in a typical consumer-level presentation program.	
3.3.5	Demonstrate how to use templates, default settings, and quick start aids to rapidly generate usable application user data.	
3.3.6	Describe the purpose and use of a personal computer-based entertainment program. List the features that could be expected to be found in such a program and explain how they work.	
3.4	Software tools Explain what file compression is and how it works with various file types. Explain how files are stored on a Hard Disk. Demonstrate how to organize, compress, defragment, and otherwise optimize a computer's hard disk performance. Explain the danger posed by viruses and malware and how virus and malware scanning software work. List several common/popular brands and types of virus and malware scanning software.	
3.4.1	Install/uninstall applications	
4.0	Troubleshooting	4
4.1	Software	
4.1.1	Explain the concepts associated with version control of Operating System (OS) software. Further explain how the OS version can affect the compatibility of other software on the PC.	
4.1.2	Demonstrate how to identify and remove a virus or other malware from an infected PC.	
4.1.3	Explain what 'safe mode' is in popular PC operating systems (OSs), and how and when it should be used when troubleshooting problems on a personal computer system.	
4.1.4	Explain where and how to find information beyond that stored on the PC to help troubleshoot problems on a PC. List popular Knowledge base, forums, and self-help web sites and explain how to use them for troubleshooting.	

Objective Number	Objectives and Skill Sets	Chapter
4.1.5	Demonstrate how to invoke and interpret the information available in a PC's Task, Process, or Application Manager. Further demonstrate how to use this tool when troubleshooting a problem on the affected PC.	4
4.2	Hardware	
4.2.1	Explain how different versions of firmware affect performance of hardware subsystems on a PC and how that information may be used in troubleshooting a problem on a PC.	
4.2.2	Explain the role of Cables and other connectors that connect the various parts of a computer together and what can happen when one or more cable or connector does not make the proper connection.	
4.3	Devices and Peripherals	
4.3.1	Explain how different versions of firmware can affect performance of peripheral devices and hardware attached to a PC and how that information may be used in troubleshooting a problem on a PC.	
4.3.2	Explain what a device driver is, how it fits into the operating system architecture, and how incompatibilities may lead to problems. Further explain how this information may be used in troubleshooting a problem on a PC.	
4.4	Backup / Restore	
4.4.1	Demonstrate how to backup and then restore software and data to: Safe offsite location. External drive Cloud	
4.4.2	Explain the implications of versioning and re-cycling of backups in an incremental backup system. Explain how to properly restore from an incremental backup system.	

continues

IC3—Module 2: Key Applications

Objective Number	Objectives and Skill Sets	Chapter
1.0	Common Application Features	5
1.1	Common Features and Commands	
1.1.1	Demonstrate the use of keyboard shortcut keys or "hot keys" to invoke application features in an application such as a word processor, spreadsheet, presentation package, database manager, or other software application product.	
1.1.2	Demonstrate how to move, copy, and paste user data within an application such as a word processor, spreadsheet, presentation package, database manager, or other software application product.	
1.1.3	Demonstrate how to reveal or hide user data from view within an application such as a word processor, spreadsheet, presentation package, database manager, or other software application product.	
1.1.4	Demonstrate how to print user data from within an application such as a word processor, spreadsheet, presentation package, database manager, or other software application product and control the configuration in which the data is presented or printed as listed in the objective.	
1.1.5	Demonstrate how to check spelling within user data, find and replace portions of user data, and use the Undo and Redo features to alter user data within an application such as a word processor, spreadsheet, presentation package, database manager, or other software application product.	
1.1.6	Demonstrate how to move user data using the Drag and Drop features within an application such as a word processor, spreadsheet, presentation package, database manager, or other software application product.	
1.1.7	Preferences, resets, customization. Demonstrate how to control presentation and configuration of user data within an application such as a word processor, spreadsheet, presentation package, database manager, or other software application.	

Objective Number	Objectives and Skill Sets	Chapter
1.1.8	Identify the various sources of help, built-in, online, context-sensitive, help lines, chat services, coworkers, help desks, etc. available to get assistance in learning how to use an application such as a word processor, spreadsheet, presentation package, database manager, or other software application product. Describe how each source of help is accessed, what kind of help can be found at each source, and which resources are available when.	5
1.1.9	Selecting Demonstrate how to select user data using the features listed in the objective within an application such as a word processor, spreadsheet, presentation package, database manager, or other software application product. Demonstrate how to sort user data using the features built into an application such as a word processor, spreadsheet, presentation package, database manager, or other software application product.	
1.2	Formatting	
1.2.1	Demonstrate how to organize, configure, and/or format user data from within an application such as a word processor, spreadsheet, presentation package, database manager, or other software application product using a 'Styles' or 'Styles-like' feature in such a way as to control the look, feel, and other display characteristics with which the data is presented on-screen or printed.	
1.2.2	Demonstrate how to control the font face display features listed in the objective from within an application such as a word processor, spreadsheet, presentation package, database manager, or other software application product in such a way as to control the look, feel, and other display characteristics with which the user data is presented on-screen or printed. Basic text formatting	
1.3	Navigating	

continues

Objective Number	Objectives and Skill Sets	Chapter
1.3.1	Demonstrate how to launch and terminate an application such as a word processor, spreadsheet, presentation package, database manager, or other software application product. Further demonstrate how to open an application data file and make it available for editing within an application program and how to close an application data file so that it is no longer immediately available to an application such as a word processor, spreadsheet, presentation package, database manager, or other software application product.	5
1.3.2	Demonstrate how to save user data in an application data file using the same and/or different file names and path information from within an application such as a word processor, spreadsheet, presentation package, database manager, or other software application product.	
1.3.3	Demonstrate how to create a new empty application data file, either blank, or using an available templates provided with the application from within an application such as a word processor, spreadsheet, presentation package, database manager, or other software application product.	
1.3.4	Demonstrate how to manipulate OS and application windows to automatically resize while using an application such as a word processor, spreadsheet, presentation package, database manager, or other software application product.	
1.3.5	Describe how to search for specific subsets of user data within a larger set of user data in an application such as a word processor, spreadsheet, presentation package, database manager, or other software application product.	
1.3.6	Demonstrate how to display user data from within an application such as a word processor, spreadsheet, presentation package, database manager, or other software application product and control the size, orientation, portion of data displayed and other display configuration settings in which the data is presented as listed in the objective, including ways to save, change, and delete those settings. Views	
1.4	Working with multimedia files	

Objective Number	Objectives and Skill Sets	Chapter
1.4.1	Demonstrate how to adjust the display of pictures, videos, audio, or other multimedia content within an application such as a word processor, spreadsheet, presentation package, database manager, or other software application product according to the action listed in the objective.	5
1.4.2	Demonstrate how to incorporate and display pictures, videos, audio, or other multimedia content within an application such as a word processor, spreadsheet, presentation package, database manager, or other software application product according to the action listed in the objective.	
2.2.1	Page Layout Demonstrate how to arrange user data and set options within a word processor so as to cause those text and data to display and print in a particular format or layout. Within that context control the attributes and structures listed in the objective to display and print as specified, including ways to save, change, and delete those saved configurations.	
2.0	Word Processing Activities	6
2.1	Organizing data	
2.1.1	Demonstrate how to organize text and data into tables within a word processor. Further demonstrate the ability to add columns, rows, merge and split cells within those tables. Demonstrate how to move, copy, and paste user data within an application such as a word processor, spreadsheet, presentation package, database manager, or other software application product.	
2.1.2	Demonstrate how to organize text and data into lists within a word processor. Further demonstrate the ability to order and re-order those lists according to various criteria (alphabetize, lowest-to-highest, by date, etc.).	
2.2	Layout	
2.2.2	Demonstrate how to set line and paragraph spacing within a word processor.	
2.2.3	Demonstrate how to indent text within a word processing program.	

continues

Objective Number	Objectives and Skill Sets	Chapter
3.0	Spreadsheet Activities	7
3.1	Spreadsheet Layout	
3.1.1	Insert/delete Demonstrate how to add, insert, remove, delete rows and columns in a spreadsheet environment.	
3.1.2	Demonstrate how to adjust the size of cells and the amount of data displayed in a cell within a spreadsheet.	
3.1.3	Demonstrate how to adjust the alignment and positioning of cells and the positioning and orientation of data as displayed in cells within a spreadsheet.	
3.1.4	Navigation	
3.1.5	Demonstrate how and when to merge or un-merge cells within a spreadsheet, including how to preserve, manage, and arrange data within the merged or un- merged cells.	
3.2	Data Management	
3.2.1	Filter and sort	
3.2.2	Formulas and Functions	
3.2.3	Number format	
3.2.4	Cell format	
3.2.5	Charts, graphs	
4.0	Presentation Activities	8
4.1	Inserting content	
4.1.1	Demonstrate how to insert text into a presentation application so as to display properly and effectively in the desired font face, size and style in a slide show.	
4.1.2	Demonstrate how to insert a table into or create a table and insert text into it in a presentation application so as to display properly and effectively in the desired font face, size and style in a slide show.	
4.1.3	Demonstrate how to insert an audio, video, animations, and other media clips into a presentation application so as to display properly and effectively with the desired timing and control in a slide show presentation.	

Objective Number	Objectives and Skill Sets	Chapter
4.1.4	Demonstrate how to insert a chart into or create a chart and insert text, numbers, and shapes into it in a presentation application so as to display properly and effectively in the desired colors, layout, and format in a slide show presentation.	8
4.1.5	Demonstrate how to insert shapes, graphics, and pictures of various formats, file formats, sizes, palettes, etc. into or create shapes and graphics and insert content into them in a presentation application so as to display properly and effectively in the desired colors, layout, and format in a slide show presentation.	
4.2	Slide Management	
4.2.1	Demonstrate how to add slides into or create slides within a presentation application.	
4.2.2	Demonstrate how to delete slides from or remove slides from within a presentation application.	
4.2.3	Describe how to alter the presentation order of slides or move them around within a presentation application.	
4.3	Slide Design	
4.3.1	Layout	
4.3.2	Animations	
4.3.3	Transitions	
5.0	Basic Database Interactions	9
5.1	Record Managements	
5.1.1	Run Reports	
5.1.2	Search and use stored queries	
5.1.3	Input data (records)	
6.0	Collaboration	10
6.1	Comments	
6.1.1	Review comments	
6.1.2	Accept or Reject	
6.1.3	Add comments	
6.2	Sharing files	

continues

Objective Number	Objectives and Skill Sets	Chapter
6.2.1	Share using e-mail	10
6.2.2	Network storage	
6.2.3	Cloud	

IC3—Module 3: Living Online

Objective Number	Objectives and Skill Sets	Chapter
1.0	Browsers	11
1.1	Internet vs. Browsers vs. WWW	
1.1.1	Explain the concepts of: Internet, Browsers, WWW.	
1.1.2	Explain the differences between: Internet, Browsers, WWW.	
1.1.3	Demonstrate how to use each: Internet, Browsers, WWW.	
1.2	Navigation	
1.2.1	Domains	
1.2.2	Explain how hyperlinks function in a web browser environment.	
1.2.3	Demonstrate how and why you would want to set a homepage.	
1.2.4	Demonstrate how to move back, forward and refresh in a variety of browsers. Identify universal symbols used for each term.	
1.2.5	Explain why favorites/bookmarks are helpful. Describe how to establish, save, invoke, and delete a bookmark.	
1.2.6	Explain what a plugin is and its function. Describe how to find, install, configure, use, disable, enable, and delete a plugin.	
1.2.7	Explain how the History function of a browser works and how to use it. Describe how to clear history.	
1.2.8	Demonstrate how to search using an internet browser, including the use of advanced features such as using basic Boolean logic including, Or, And, plus sign +, quotation marks ", etc.	
1.2.9	Tabs	
1.2.10	Downloading/Uploading	

Objective Number	Objectives and Skill Sets	Chapter
2.0	Networking concepts	**12**
2.1	Internet Connection	
2.1.1	Speed Explain the units of measurement associated with an internet connection and what they mean – mbps, kbps. Explain the things that can limit or increase speed: multiple browsers open, wireless connection, etc.	
2.1.2	Explain the differences between Dial up and broadband connections and the process each uses to establish a connection.	
2.1.3	Wireless	
2.1.4	Security	
2.2	Network types and features, capabilities	
2.2.1	Explain the concepts associated with the Publicly switched networks.	
2.2.2	Explain the concepts associated with DNS (Domain Name Server).	
2.2.3	Explain the concepts associated with Addressing.	
2.2.4	Explain the concepts associated with and the difference between LAN vs. WAN.	
2.2.5	Explain the concepts associated with VPN.	
2.3	Network troubleshooting	
2.3.1	Demonstrate the ability to solve simple networking connectivity problems in various settings.	
2.3.2	Explain methods of identifying common network problems.	
2.3.3	Explain the concepts associated with Define IP Addressing.	
3.0	Digital Communication	13
3.1	E-mail communication	
3.1.1	E-mail Account Settings	
3.1.2	Appropriate use of e-mail	
3.1.3	Managing e-mail communications	
3.2	Real-Time-communication	
3.2.1	Text communication:	

continues

Objective Number	Objectives and Skill Sets	Chapter
3.2.2	Audio Visual communication	13
3.2.3	Social Media	
4.0	Digital Citizenship	14
4.1	Communication Standards	
4.1.1	Explain the difference between personal and professional communication and the importance of spelling and use of abbreviations in each type of communication.	
4.1.2	All capitals vs. standard capitalization	
4.1.3	Verbal vs. Written, Professional vs. Personal communication	
4.1.4	Explain the terms: Spamming, flaming, bullying and the harm that each can cause. Explain how they are not faceless, harmless electronic actions.	
4.1.5	Explain the terms Libel and Slander and the real life legal consequences of each.	
4.2	Legal and responsible use of computers	
4.2.1	Explain what censorship is. Contrast its benefits and drawbacks.	
4.2.2	Explain what filtering is. Contrast its benefits and drawbacks.	
4.2.3	Explain Intellectual Property, its real value and the implications of its misuse.	
4.2.4	Explain Piracy, how to protect yourself from it and the ethical issues surrounding it.	
4.2.5	Explain what a copyright is, how it is obtained, the legal ramifications surrounding a copyright and its value to its holder.	
4.2.6	Licensing	
4.2.7	Explain what Creative Commons is, the licensing availability and legal issues surrounding it, as well as the benefits to the community.	
5.0	Safe Computing	15
5.1	Secure online communication or activity	
5.1.1	Identity Protection	

Objective Number	Objectives and Skill Sets	Chapter
5.1.2	Explain Data Protection including the following: Explain how to completely remove data from hard drives, portable memory, digital devices. Explain how to secure the data on your computer and keep it updated by backing up data to other sources – cloud, backup hard drives. Describe how to use protection programs and the value of these services. Also describe the harm that can come from not using these products and services.	
5.2	Ergonomics	
5.2.1	Explain and demonstrate proper ergonomics. Problems that come from improper ergonomics in relation to monitor height and angle.	
5.2.2	Explain and demonstrate proper ergonomics. Problems that come from improper ergonomics in relation to mouse and keyboard shapes and use.	
5.2.3	Explain the ergonomics around proper chair height and settings, arms, lumbar support, etc.	
5.2.4	Explain the issues around poor lighting, short term and long term eye problems.	
5.2.5	Explain the physical issues surrounding poor body posture, especially with prolonged time in the same position(s).	
6.0	Research Fluency	16
6.1	Using Search Engines	
6.1.1	Explain how to use search engines to acquire information. The value of the resources available on the internet.	
6.1.2	Demonstrate how to use search engines to answer questions and solve problems by using good search terms to get specific information from reputable sources.	
6.2	Evaluate search results	
6.2.1	Forums Explain the value and problems with internet forums.	

continues

Objective Number	Objectives and Skill Sets	Chapter
6.2.2	Explain that ads are paid messages from companies that want to interest you in their products. Messages are not necessarily factual.	
6.2.3	Explain that sponsored links are a form of advertising and not to be relied on as an informational resource.	
6.2.4	Explain that a knowledge base is a collection of data around a particular subject. Include examples like Help menus available from software and hard good manufacturers.	
6.2.5	Explain how to determine the validity of various sources, including but not limited to domain names/domain, published journals, government sites and documents vs. forums, blogs, personal websites.	
6.2.6	Explain that articles can be both factual and made up. Articles are created for a number of reasons including, reviews of products that may or may not have been given to the reviewer, personal opinion, or well researched documenting of fact.	
6.3	Using advanced features of search engines	
6.3.1	Search types	

Assessment Test

IC3—Module 1: Computing Fundamentals

1. What is the keyboard shortcut for the Copy command?
   - **A.** Ctrl+V
   - **B.** Ctrl+Z
   - **C.** Alt+F4
   - **D.** Ctrl+C

2. Which of the following is an operating system?
   - **A.** Bing
   - **B.** Facebook
   - **C.** Android
   - **D.** Skype

3. Which of the following are characteristics of modern operating systems? (Choose all that apply.)
   - **A.** They are real-time.
   - **B.** They are multitasking.
   - **C.** They are impossible to learn.
   - **D.** They can be used for a limited time.

4. For how long does an operating system holds the information from the Clipboard?
   - **A.** Until you update the operating system
   - **B.** Until you press Alt+F4 on your keyboard
   - **C.** Until you use a search engine to copy that information
   - **D.** Until you use the Paste command

5. What is Windows Update?
   - **A.** A tool that keeps Android up to date
   - **B.** A Windows virus
   - **C.** A tool that keeps Windows up to date
   - **D.** A data-recovery tool for Windows

6. What does the processor of a computer do?

   A. Stores your data in the form of files and folders

   B. Carries out the instructions sent by the software you run

   C. Processes and generates the image that is displayed by your computer

   D. Connects a computer to a network

7. What are peripherals?

   A. The internal hardware components of a computer

   B. A type of software

   C. A type of search engine

   D. External hardware components that can be connected to a computer

8. What is a laptop?

   A. A mobile phone with advanced computing capabilities

   B. A portable computer that is suitable for mobile use

   C. A specialized business computer that is intended to be used at a single controlled location

   D. A type of software

9. Which of the following units of measure do you use for measuring the storage space available on a hard disk?

   A. GHz

   B. GB

   C. Number of cores

   D. SSD

10. What is open source?

   A. A commercial license for software

   B. A type of hardware

   C. A type of software license

   D. A web browser

11. Which of the following is a presentation program?

   A. Microsoft Word

   B. Mozilla Firefox

   C. Google

   D. Microsoft PowerPoint

12. Which of the following activities can be performed with a personal entertainment application? (Choose all that apply.)

    A. Write documents

    B. Listen to music

    C. Create databases

    D. Watch movies

13. Which of the following programs can you use to view the applications that are running on your Windows computer?

    A. Windows Update

    B. Windows Media Player

    C. Task Manager

    D. Control Panel

14. What is firmware?

    A. A driver

    B. An operating system

    C. The first software to run on a hardware device when it is powered on

    D. A web browser

15. What is Safe Mode?

    A. A networking protocol

    B. A Windows error message

    C. The process of updating the firmware on a hardware device

    D. A different way of starting Windows that loads only the barest essentials that are required for Windows to function

IC3—Module 2: Key Applications

1. What is the keyboard shortcut for closing any Windows application?

    A. Ctrl+V

    B. Windows+Tab

    C. Alt+F4

    D. Alt+Tab

2. Which of the following is a good way of opening a Microsoft Word document?

   A. Open Windows Explorer, navigate to its location, and double-click it.

   B. Open Windows Explorer, navigate to its location, and right-click it.

   C. Open Windows Explorer, navigate to its location, and press Delete.

   D. Open Windows Explorer, navigate to its location, and press Shift+Delete.

3. Which of the following Microsoft Office tools do you use to identify and correct spelling and grammar mistakes?

   A. Track changes

   B. The indent

   C. Spell checker

   D. The ruler

4. What is the keyboard shortcut for accessing the printing options in Microsoft Office?

   A. Ctrl+V

   B. Alt+P

   C. Alt+F4

   D. Ctrl+P

5. What is the keyboard shortcut for selecting all the text in Microsoft Word document?

   A. Ctrl+A

   B. Shift+A

   C. Alt+F4

   D. Ctrl+P

6. Which of the following types of lists can you create in Microsoft Word? (Choose all that apply.)

   A. Hexadecimal

   B. Numbered

   C. Bulleted

   D. Infinite

7. Which of the following is a place where you *cannot* add page numbers in a Microsoft Word document?

   A. On the bottom of each page

   B. On the margins of each page

   C. On the top of each page

   D. On the ribbon

8. Which keyboard shortcut do you use to move to the next cell in a Microsoft Excel worksheet?

   A. Alt

   B. Tab

   C. Up arrow

   D. Down arrow

9. What does the (*fx*) symbol represent in Microsoft Excel?

   A. The ruler

   B. The size of the selected cell

   C. The formula bar

   D. A worksheet

10. What is the keyboard shortcut for adding a new slide in a Microsoft PowerPoint presentation?

    A. Alt+F4

    B. Alt+Tab

    C. Ctrl+P

    D. Ctrl+M

11. Which tool can you use to quickly format the tables in a Microsoft PowerPoint presentation?

    A. Table styles

    B. The ruler

    C. Shapes

    D. Transitions

12. To which of the following elements can you add transitions in Microsoft PowerPoint presentations?

    A. Pictures

    B. Slides

    C. Text

    D. Video

13. What is a database?

    A. An organized collection of data

    B. An organized collection of slides

    C. A type of software

    D. A type of hardware

14. Which of the following Microsoft Office applications can be used to access and manage databases?

   A. Microsoft Word

   B. Microsoft Outlook

   C. Microsoft PowerPoint

   D. Microsoft Access

15. Which Microsoft Word feature allows you to track the changes that were made to a document?

   A. Slideshow

   B. Spell checker

   C. Track Changes

   D. Accept And Move To Next

IC3—Module 3: Living Online

1. What does WWW stand for?

   A. Wild Wild West

   B. World Wide WAN

   C. World Wide Web

   D. World Wide Fund for Nature

2. What is the Web?

   A. The whole of the Internet

   B. A system of websites connected by links

   C. A networking protocol

   D. A type of software

3. Which of the following is an example of a URL?

   A. john.smith@email.com

   B. #twitter

   C. ☺

   D. http://www.microsoft.com

4. Which of the following is an example of a web browser?

   A. Internet Explorer

   B. Skype

   C. OneDrive

   D. Microsoft Word

5. How do you save a website so that you quickly access it later?

    A. Save it as a document.

    B. Save it as a favorite.

    C. Send an email.

    D. Print it.

6. What does LAN stand for?

    A. Local area network

    B. Wide area network

    C. Legal area network

    D. Local area nature

7. Which of the following is an example of a WAN?

    A. The network in your home

    B. FTP

    C. The network in your office building

    D. The Internet

8. Which of the following commands can you use to test the connection between two devices on the network?

    A. ping

    B. FTP

    C. ipconfig

    D. Google

9. Which of the following is an example of an email address?

    A. http://www.microsoft.com

    B. #hashtag

    C. Instagram

    D. John.Smith@example.com

10. Which of the following applications can you use to make audio and video calls on the Internet?

    A. Bing

    B. FTP

    C. Skype

    D. Google

11. Which of the following is an example of a social network?

   A. Google

   B. Facebook

   C. #hashtag

   D. Blog

12. Which of the following is an example of an emoticon?

   A. Luv u

   B. @twitter

   C. #hashtag

   D. ☹

13. What is piracy?

   A. The whole phenomenon of copyright infringement

   B. A licensing model

   C. A DRM tool

   D. Open source software

14. What is the keyboard shortcut for deleting a file that you select on your computer?

   A. Alt+Tab

   B. Ctrl+C

   C. Del

   D. Shift

15. What are search operators when referring to search engines?

   A. Symbols that can be added to searches to help narrow down your results

   B. Quotes that can be added to searches to help narrow down your results

   C. Mathematical functions that can be added to searches to help narrow down your results

   D. Words that can be added to searches to help narrow down your results

Answers to Assessment Test

IC3—Module 1: Computing Fundamentals

1. **D.** The keyboard shortcut for Copy is Ctrl+C.

2. **C.** Android is the only operating system in the list.

3. **A, B.** Modern operating systems execute applications and commands in real time, and they allow multiple applications to run at the same time (multitasking).

4. **D.** The Clipboard holds information temporarily until you opt to paste it somewhere else.

5. **C.** Windows Update is a tool that keeps Windows up to date.

6. **C.** The processor is the "brains" of a computer. The CPU is what carries out the instructions sent by the software you run.

7. **D.** Peripherals are external hardware components that can be connected to a computer.

8. **B.** A laptop is a portable computer that is suitable for mobile use.

9. **B.** The amount of storage space is measured in bytes and its multiples. Modern computers tend to have large hard drives with lots of storage space. It is very common to have a hard disk in your computer with 500 GB of storage space or even 1 TB.

10. **C.** Open source is a type of software license.

11. **D.** The most popular examples of presentation programs are Microsoft PowerPoint (included in Microsoft Office) and Impress (included in LibreOffice).

12. **B, D.** Personal entertainment applications allow you to do fun things on your computer, like listening to music or watching movies.

13. **C.** Task Manager shows a list of all the applications that are running on your computer.

14. **C.** Firmware is a very basic piece of software that contains only the instructions that are required for the hardware to work as intended. It is the first software to run on a device when it is powered on.

15. **D.** Safe Mode is a different way of starting Windows that loads only the barest essentials that are required for Windows to function.

IC3—Module 2: Key Applications

1. C. You can press Alt+F4 on your keyboard to close any application.

2. A. Browse your computer using Windows Explorer and double-click the file that you want to open.

3. C. When you use the spell checker in Microsoft Office, each mistake is highlighted, and one or more solutions are suggested for fixing it.

4. D. You can access the printing options by pressing Ctrl+P on your keyboard.

5. A. Select all the text in a document by pressing Ctrl+A on your keyboard.

6. B, C. In Microsoft Word you can create bulleted, numbered, and multilevel lists.

7. D. You cannot add page numbers on the ribbon; they need to be added in the pages of a document.

8. B. Press Tab on your keyboard to move to the next cell.

9. C. The formula bar is labeled with the function symbol (*fx*).

10. D. You add a new slide by pressing Ctrl+M on your keyboard.

11. A. Microsoft PowerPoint offers table styles that can be used to quickly change the looks of your tables.

12. B. You can set transitions, which are similar to animations, to slides, but they affect only what happens when moving from one slide to the next.

13. A. Databases are organized collections of data.

14. D. Microsoft Access was designed to access, use, and manage databases.

15. C. When Track Changes is turned on, all the changes that are made to the document are kept and can be viewed at any time, as long as no one deactivates this feature.

IC3—Module 3: Living Online

1. C. WWW is an abbreviation for World Wide Web.

2. B. The Web, or the World Wide Web, is a system of websites connected by links.

3. D. `http://www.microsoft.com/` is an example of a URL.

4. A. Internet Explorer is a web browser.

5. B. You can set a website as a favorite and create a link that you can use to access it quickly later on.

6. A. LAN is an abbreviation for local area network.

7. D. The Internet is an example of a WAN.

8. A. The ping tool allows you to test the connection between two devices on the network.

9. D. John.Smith@example.com is an example of an email address.

10. C. Skype is an example of an application that can be used for both audio- and videoconferencing.

11. B. Facebook is a social network.

12. D. ☺ is an emoticon.

13. A. Piracy is the whole phenomenon of copyright infringement.

14. C. Del or Delete is the keyboard shortcut for deleting files.

15. D. Search operators are words that can be added to searches to help narrow down your results.

IC³® Internet and Computing Core Certification Global Standard 4
Study Guide

Computing Fundamentals

PART

I

Chapter

1

Understanding Operating Systems

THE FOLLOWING IC3 GS4: COMPUTER FUNDAMENTALS EXAM OBJECTIVES ARE COVERED IN THIS CHAPTER:

✓ **What Is An OS And What Does It Do?**

- Explain the differences between software applications and operating systems and demonstrate their uses.

- Common OS features, explain each of their uses:

  - Power On/Power Off

  - Log on/log off/switch user

  - Lock/Unlock

  - Differences between common OSs

- Explain how hardware can influence the Operating System and software and vice versa.

- Software updates, security fixes, bugs, adaptation to new hardware. Demonstrate how to update software, using manual and automatic settings.

✓ **Manage Computer Files and Folders**

- Directory and folder hierarchy and structure

  - Menu, Toolbar, and Window Navigation

  - Expand and Collapse

  - Folder views

- File/Folder management

  - Keyboard shortcuts

  - Copy

  - Paste

  - Delete

- Move
- Rename
- Create shortcuts
- Search
- Identify file extensions and their associations such as .docx, .xlsx, .pdf, .mp3, etc.

✓ **Manage Computer Configuration, Control Panel, OS, and Drivers**

- Basic Desktop Customization
  - Visual options
  - Languages
  - Date and Time
  - Accessibility options
- Describe the various states of operation available in a typical consumer-level OS. Include Shutdown, hibernation, standby, fully awake, etc.
- User accounts and rights
  - Group policy (specifically mobile)
  - Read/Write
  - Administrative vs. standard user rights
- File and Directory Permissions

Modern computers and devices like smartphones and tablets consist of numerous components, even though some devices are really small. First, there are plenty of specialized hardware components like video cards or sound cards, each of which has its own role to play. Then there are the operating system (e.g., Windows) and the programs (e.g., Microsoft Office) that make the device useful to users. Without them, any piece of hardware, no matter how powerful, cannot be used. That's why, in this chapter, we will start by discussing the role each component plays in a modern computer and the basics of how they work together. Then we will focus on the operating system, what it does, how it works, and how to personalize it.

Operating Systems and Their Roles When Using Computers and Devices

We will start by defining hardware, software, and operating systems so that you have a good understanding on what they are and what their role is. As you will see, the relationship between them is quite delicate and very important. Any computer or device cannot function and cannot be used productively without these three elements working well together. That's why we will start by discussing them and by explaining all the key concepts that are involved.

What Is Hardware?

Any computer or device is composed, at a physical level, of *hardware*. For example, a computer almost always has a monitor, a mouse and keyboard, a hard disk or flash memory, a graphics card, a sound card, some memory, a motherboard, a network card, a case, and a power supply.

If you look inside a smartphone and a tablet, you will find similar components. The most important difference is their size, since they need to fit into a person's hand. Also, the display is touch sensitive, and mobile devices have a battery built in.

Each hardware component is specialized to perform a set of specific tasks. For example, the sound card is in charge of providing sound to the user, the graphics card takes care of processing the image and sending it to display, the network card is in charge of connecting to the network and the Internet, and so on.

What Is Software?

Software is a set of machine-readable instructions that direct a computer or device to perform specific operations. Software is not physical like hardware is. It is ephemeral, in the sense that it is anything that can be stored electronically on the hardware of a computer or device.

There are many types of software, the most important being these two:

System Software   This software is designed to directly operate the hardware of a computer or device. Such software provides all the basic functions that allow users and other software to control the device's hardware. The most common types of system software are the operating system, drivers (which control a specific hardware component), and system utilities (which assist users in the maintenance of their computers).

Application Software   This is specialized software the users can employ to perform certain tasks. For example, Microsoft PowerPoint lets users create presentations. Antivirus software like Norton Antivirus or Kaspersky Antivirus keeps your computer safe from threats and so on. This type of software is also referred to as applications, programs, or apps (when working with mobile devices). In order to function, application software needs to run on top of both the system software and hardware. Applications are either provided by the operating system (for example, Paint is an application offered by Windows) or installed by users on top of the operating system.

To help you understand these concepts better, let's take a look at each of these two types of software in more detail.

What Is an Operating System?

An *operating system* is a special type of software that manages all the communications between the user, the software applications, and the hardware in a computer or device. It is the most important piece of software that runs on a device because without it interactions with that device would be impossible. Operating systems perform important tasks like recognizing the hardware components of a device, controlling them, taking input from devices such as the keyboard or the touch screen (in the case of tablets and smartphones), managing the file system on that device, taking input from the user or from other software applications, and sending it to the hardware.

The most popular operating systems are Windows, Linux, Mac OS X, Android, iOS, and Windows Phone. Some are designed to work on computers and laptops (Windows, Linux, or Mac OS X), while others are designed to work on mobile devices like smartphones and tablets (Android, iOS, Windows Phone).

Operating systems have many characteristics that allow them to be classified in multiple ways. The most important characteristics are these:

- Modern operating systems are real-time.

  They execute applications and commands in real time. The benefit of being real-time is that the operating system delivers a quick and predictable response to the commands issued by the user or by the applications they are using.

- Modern operating systems are multitasking.

  They allow multiple applications to run at the same time. Hardware resources are allocated and managed automatically by the operating system and shared among all the programs and services that are running.

- Operating systems can be multiuser or single-user.

  For example, Windows and other operating systems that are designed to run on computers are multiuser. This means that you can create multiple user accounts on the same computer and have them share that computer's hardware and software resources. Single-user operating systems allow only one user account. Generally, these operating systems are found on mobile devices like smartphones and tablets. However, even these types of devices will have multiuser operating systems in the future.

- Some operating systems can be embedded.

  This means that they are designed to be used in small devices like cash registers, ATMs, and so on. These devices are very compact and have limited resources. Embedded operating systems are optimized to run on limited hardware resources, and they generally provide a small and specialized set of services and interactions.

How Do They All Work Together?

When you start a computer or a device like your smartphone, the operating system loads first. Once that is loaded, you will interact with both the application software that is installed on it and the operating system. For example, when you use an application like Microsoft Word to write a document, the application sends your input and commands to the operating system. The operating system then communicates with the hardware, and it automatically manages the resources used by Microsoft Word in order to deliver the desired results.

Users can also work directly with the operating system. For example, in Windows, you can access the files and folders that are stored on your computer and open them. You can also browse the storage on your computer, using the operating system and its features, without needing to install other applications.

Figure 1.1, which shows how the operating system and system software are layered on a typical computer, should help you understand this more clearly. The arrows indicate how the information flows.

FIGURE 1.1 The flow of information among the user, software applications, the operating system, and the hardware

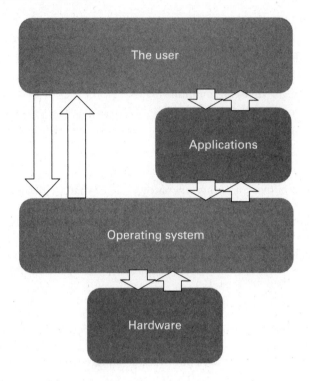

 Real World Scenario

Which Computer Operating System Is Best?

There is a never-ending debate about which is the best operating system for your computer. Is it Windows? Is it Mac OS X? Is it Linux? The truth is that modern operating systems are not that different anymore, at least not when it comes to what you can do with them. You can use any of them to write a document, deliver a presentation, play games, watch movies, surf the Internet, and so on. Very few features are unique to one operating system. The differences between them are mostly in the way the user interface works.

Choosing one operating system versus another is mostly a matter of personal preference. If you like how a Mac looks and feels, you might purchase a Mac and use Mac OS X. If you are a great believer in free software, then you might prefer to use Linux on your computer. If you want to have access to the greatest number of applications, devices, and learning resources, then you will go for Windows.

Accessing and Locking the Operating System

When you press the power button on a computer or other device, the operating system is loaded, and you're asked to sign in if you've set up a password or *personal identification number (PIN)*. Regardless of the device, the basic idea is the same: you need to power up your computer or device, wait for the operating system to load, and then authenticate yourself in order to use it.

If you have only one user account on your computer and no password set for it, it is enough to press the power button on your computer and wait for Windows 7 to start and automatically sign you in. However, not having a password makes your computer a lot less secure, and we recommend that you always set a password for your user account.

Let's do an exercise together in which you'll learn how to power on your computer and sign into Windows 7 (Exercise 1.1).

EXERCISE 1.1

Signing into Windows 7

1. Press the power button on your computer.

2. Wait for the operating system to start.

   When that process is finished, you are shown the sign-in screen (Figure 1.2), where you can see the user accounts that exist on your computer.

FIGURE 1.2   The Windows log-in screen showing the user accounts that exist on your computer

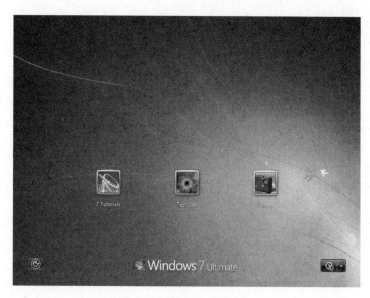

EXERCISE 1.1 *(continued)*

3. Select your user account and then type your password.

   If you have only one user account on your Windows 7 computer, you are directly prompted for your password, without having to go through this step. Also, if you have no password set for your account, then you won't be asked to type one.

4. Click the sign-in button, which is an arrow pointing to the right (Figure 1.3).

FIGURE 1.3   The sign-in screen for your user account

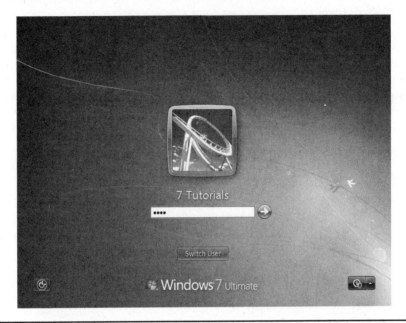

Once you log into Windows 7, you can start using the software applications that are installed on it and do your work. When you have finished working on the computer, you can do the following:

Switch User   You can switch to another user account that exists on your computer so that someone else can use it. When you do this, your account remains active in the background and so do all your running applications. They will be available to you in the state in which you left them when you switch back to your user account. Be aware that other users can turn off the computer, and your unsaved work will be lost if that happens.

Log Off   All your applications and files are closed. The computer and the operating system remain turned on, and other users can log in with their accounts and continue using the computer.

Lock   Your user account remains active in the background as well all your running applications. Windows 7 displays the sign-in screen and requests your user account password. You can unlock your account by typing your password, and you will be able to resume your work exactly where you left off. No one else can use your account and your running applications unless they type your password and unlock your account.

Restart   All your applications and files are closed. The operating system is shut down and then your computer and the operating system are restarted. When the restarting procedure is over, you are back to the sign-in screen, where you can log back into Windows.

Sleep   Sleep is a low-power mode that saves significantly on power consumption. Your user account gets locked, Windows stores your work in memory, and then it places itself into stand-by mode. When you press the power button, Windows resumes from sleep and allows you to sign in and resume your work, exactly where you left off. Resuming from sleep is generally faster than powering on your computer.

Shut Down   First, all your applications and files are closed. Then the operating system turns itself off as well as the computer. When shut down, the computer does not use electrical power because it is no longer running.

To access all these options, click the Start button to open the Start menu. On the right side you will see the Shut Down button and a small arrow near it. Clicking the Shut Down button will obviously power off your computer, as mentioned earlier. Clicking the small arrow near it will give you access to the additional options that were mentioned earlier, as shown in Figure 1.4.

FIGURE 1.4   Options for switching the user, logging off, locking the computer, restarting it, or putting it to sleep

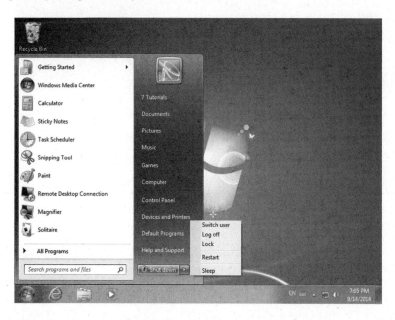

To learn more, let's do this small exercise, which teaches you how to put Windows 7 to sleep and then resume from sleep (Exercise 1.2).

EXERCISE 1.2

Putting Your Computer to Sleep and Then Resuming Your Work

1. Click the Start button in Windows 7, on the bottom-left corner of the screen.

2. Click the small arrow near the Shut Down button to reveal other options (Figure 1.5).

FIGURE 1.5   The Sleep button

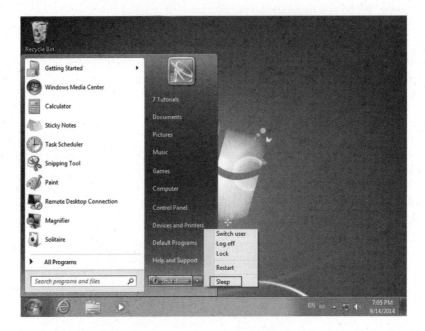

3. Click Sleep and wait for Windows 7 to turn off the screen and put itself into sleep mode.

4. Wait a couple of seconds, press the power button, and then wait for Windows 7 to resume from sleep.

5. At the sign-in screen, type your user account password and click the Sign In button.

Software and System Updates

Most applications and operating systems receive updates on a regular basis. Windows receives updates through the Windows Update service, whereas software applications receive updates through their own update services, if their manufacturer provides them. For example, Internet browsers made by companies other than Microsoft (e.g., Google Chrome, Mozilla Firefox, Opera) have their own update service. They are updated on a monthly basis because they require continuous improvement in order to keep up with the needs of their users and the evolution of the Internet. Other applications may not have their own update service, so users need to manually download and install newer versions when they become available. Most applications are like this, including popular ones like the 7-Zip file archiver or the GOM multimedia player.

Luckily, Microsoft also offers updates to popular software like Microsoft Office or Windows Essentials through the Windows Update service, if you set it to deliver them.

Software updates are created for many reasons:

- To fix problems of any kind, ranging from security issues to bugs that don't allow the software run as it was intended.

- To add new features and characteristics that make the product more useful to its users.

- Some operating system updates also provide new driver versions that allow the operating system to better use and manage the hardware components of your computer.

By default, Windows is set to automatically check for updates and install them when they are available. However, you can also install them manually. Exercise 1.3 details how to check for updates and install those that are available.

EXERCISE 1.3

Manually Installing Windows Updates

1. Click Start and then Control Panel.

2. Click System And Security and then Windows Update (Figure 1.6).

FIGURE 1.6 The System And Security section in Control Panel

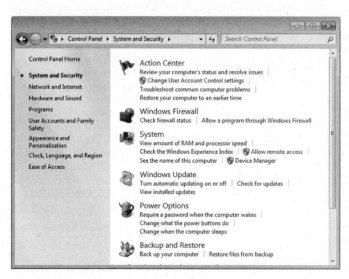

3. In the column on the left, click Check For Updates (Figure 1.7).

FIGURE 1.7   The Windows Update window

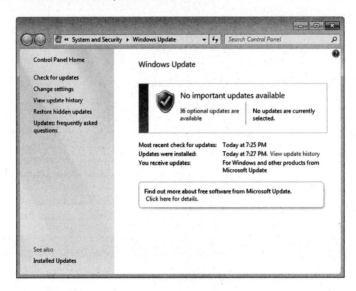

4. Wait for Windows to check for updates and let you know whether there are any updates available to be installed.

5. If updates are available, click Install Updates (Figure 1.8) and wait for them to be installed.

    When the process is finished, you are informed that the updates were successfully installed.

FIGURE 1.8   Windows Update informing you how many updates are available

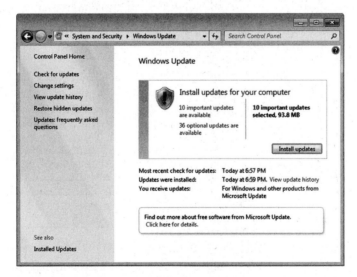

6. It is possible that Windows will recommend that you restart your computer in order to install those updates. If that is the case, click Restart Now (Figure 1.9). Otherwise, close the Windows Update window.

FIGURE 1.9 Windows Update informing you that updates were successfully installed

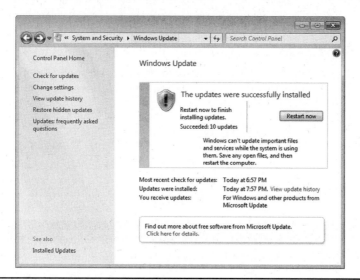

 Real World Scenario

Always Keep Windows Update Turned On

On some technical forums or blogs you may encounter a recommendation to disable Windows Update. Some recommend this because they think that it improves general system performance. Others recommend this because using Windows Update on pirated copies of Windows will install updates that figure out whether users are using an illegal copy of Windows and try to inform them about this problem and educate them on how to purchase a legal copy of Windows.

Disabling Windows Update is a very bad practice that only creates problems for users. For starters, your Windows installation will not benefit from the many security updates provided by Microsoft. Therefore, it will be vulnerable to all kinds of security threats. Also, you won't benefit from bug fixes and performance improvements. Also, some updates add new features to Windows that may be useful to you. That's why you should always check and confirm that Windows Update is enabled on your computer and that it installs updates automatically.

Windows Update can be set to work in four different ways:

- Install Updates Automatically (Recommended)

  Every day, Windows automatically checks for updates and installs them in the background when they are available. If a computer restart is required in order to finalize their installation, it will request it from the user. This is the default setting for Windows Update.

▪ Download Updates, But Let Me Choose Whether to Install Them

Windows Update automatically checks for updates and downloads them in the background when they are available. The user is prompted to install them, when appropriate.

▪ Check For Updates, But Let Me Choose Whether to Download and Install Them

Windows Update automatically checks for updates in the background, and it informs the user when they available for download and installation. It doesn't download any updates without the user's prior consent.

▪ Never Check For Updates (Not Recommended)

This means that Windows Update is turned off and not working. Windows is not kept up to date, and it becomes vulnerable to all kinds of problems.

When setting up your Windows computer for the first time, it is a good idea to double-check that Windows Update is turned on and working well. Exercise 1.4 shares how to do this.

EXERCISE 1.4

Confirming That Windows Update Is Turned On

1. Click Start and then Control Panel.

2. Click System And Security and then Windows Update.

3. In the column on the left, click Change Settings.

4. In the Important Updates section, select Install Updates Automatically (Recommended) (Figure 1.10).

FIGURE 1.10 Where you change the Windows Update settings

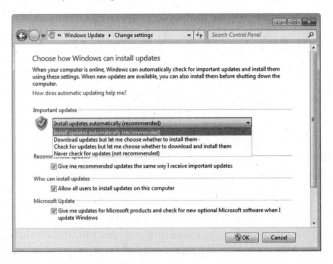

5. Click OK.

6. Close the Windows Update window.

Working with Files, Folders, and Libraries

When you work on a computer, you will create files and folders to store your work and use it later on. A file is a resource for storing information that can then be opened and used with the help of a computer program. To make it simpler, imagine the file to be the digital counterpart of a paper document. Similarly, a folder is the digital equivalent of the file folder used in offices. *Libraries* are a new concept that was introduced in Windows 7 and used in all subsequent versions of Windows. A library is a virtual collection of folders on your computer.

Files   *Files* can store any kind of data. For example, Word files will store documents created with Microsoft Word. Documents can include text, graphics, tables, and so on. Images are also files—the digital counterpart of pictures. Images can be opened with programs that are designed to deal with images and render them on the screen. Videos and movies are also stored as files, and they can be viewed with specialized programs that render them on the screen.

Files can be created by the user, by the applications they are using, and by the operating system. They are generally stored in folders with different names and sizes.

Folders   *Folders* are a way of organizing files and other folders on your computer. You can think of a folder as a collection of references to other files and folders that are inside it. Some people also refer to them as directories. Folders always have a hierarchical tree-like structure. One folder contains several files and other folders (also named subfolders). Its subfolders have their own files and subfolders, and so on (Figure 1.11).

Libraries   Libraries do not exist as actual folders on the computer but only as references to one or more folders and the files stored inside them. Libraries are named using the type of files and folders they tend to store: Documents, Pictures, Music, and Videos. The Documents library will link to the folders where you store your documents, the Pictures library will link to the folders where you store your pictures, and so on.

Libraries are useful because they have direct shortcuts throughout the operating system, and you can easily access them. Also, their content is automatically indexed by Windows so that you can quickly search for the files you are looking for. Searching for files that are not part of a library generally takes longer than when searching for files that are part of a library.

FIGURE 1.11   A folder and its contents displayed by Windows Explorer

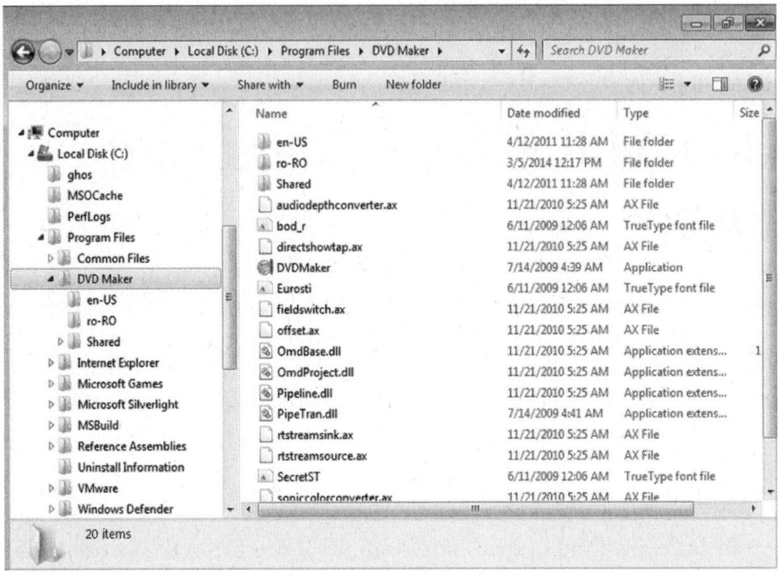

Accessing Your Files and Folders

All operating systems provide an easy way for you to access your files and folders. In Windows 7, you can use Windows Explorer. To open this program, click the folder icon on the taskbar—the transparent bar that runs across the bottom of the screen. You can see the folder icon in Figure 1.12.

FIGURE 1.12   The shortcuts on the Windows taskbar, including the one for Windows Explorer

The left side of Windows Explorer is named the Navigation pane. There you will see several sections and shortcuts to different locations on your computer. Whatever is selected in the Navigation pane determines what is shown on the right pane (Figure 1.13).

By default, Libraries is selected. There you will see the four default libraries that exist in Windows 7: Documents, Music, Pictures, and Videos. To make things easy for you, it is best to save your documents in the Documents library, your pictures in the Pictures library, and so on.

In order to successfully navigate through your computer's files and folders, you have to learn how Windows Explorer works. First, let's take a look at its window and each of its elements, as they are highlighted in Figure 1.14.

FIGURE 1.13   The Windows Explorer window

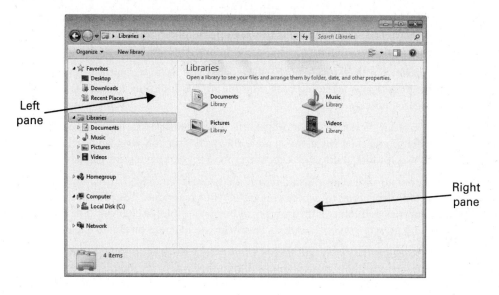

Left pane

Right pane

FIGURE 1.14   The different navigation elements of the Windows Explorer window

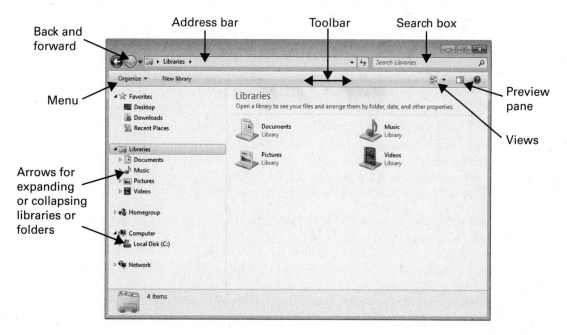

Back and forward

Address bar

Toolbar

Search box

Menu

Preview pane

Views

Arrows for expanding or collapsing libraries or folders

Now let's discuss them one by one:

Address Bar   On the very top of the Windows Explorer window you will see a bar that initially says Libraries. As you navigate through your computer, this bar will always tell you where you are on your computer.

Back and Forward   On the left side of the address bar you have two buttons pointing left and right. The left button is for going back, and the right is for going forward through the folder structure in your computer.

Search Box   On the right side of the address bar is a box that you can use to quickly search for a file or folder. If you enter the name of a file and press Enter on your keyboard, Windows will start searching for files and folders that correspond to the search term you are using.

Toolbar   The toolbar is displayed just beneath the address bar. This bar includes contextual buttons depending on where you are on your computer. You will notice that as you browse your files and folders, the number of buttons available changes. The toolbar tries to adapt and present you with options that help you be more productive depending on what you are doing.

Menus   On the left side of the toolbar you will find the Organize menu. As you can see, this menu has an arrow pointing downward. Each time you see that arrow for an item on the toolbar, it means that it is a menu that can be opened.

Views   On the right side of the toolbar you will notice another button with an arrow pointing downward, signaling that it is actually a menu. If you click it, you will be able to change the way you view the files and folders displayed in the right pane. Your files and folders remain the same; only the way they are presented here changes, depending on which view you select. We will discuss views in more detail shortly.

Preview Pane   On the right side of the toolbar, near the Views menu, you will find the button for enabling or disabling the Preview pane. When it's enabled, a third pane is displayed on the right side of the Windows Explorer window. When you select a file in the middle pane, you can see a preview of its content in this Preview pane. If you have a larger screen that can accommodate this pane, it is a good idea to enable it because it can be useful when navigating the files on your computer.

Arrows   In the Navigation pane on the left side of the Windows Explorer window you will notice that many elements have a small arrow to the left of their name. You can use these arrows to expand or collapse the element. For example, if you click the arrow for Libraries, it will collapse them. Click it again and it will expand them.

Your computer stores not just your data but also lots of files and folders that are installed by the operating system and the applications that you are using. All this data is always stored in the Local Disk (C:) drive on your computer. You will always find this drive in the Navigation pane. Please note that the C: drive may have a different name because it can be easily customized, but on most computers it is named Local Disk.

When navigating this drive, you will see plenty of folders with names like Windows (this is where Windows is installed), Program Files (this is where applications are installed), or Users (this is where your user files and folders are stored as well as those of other users on the same computer). You can double-click any of these folders and explore their content. However, you should refrain from deleting or changing anything. Most of your work should be done in the Users folder. If you open it, you will see a subfolder for each user that has been created on your computer, and one of them will be yours. If you open your subfolder, then you will see your Documents, Pictures, and Music folders, and so on.

We mentioned earlier the concept of views. They are just different ways of viewing your files and folders. The views you can use in Windows Explorer are the following, as shown in Figure 1.15:

FIGURE 1.15   The views that are available in Windows Explorer

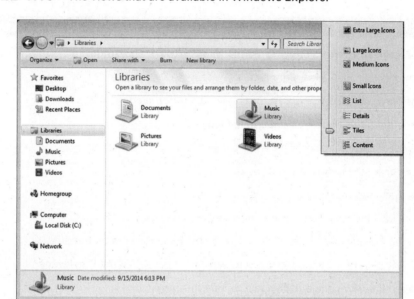

Extra Large Icons   Displays the contents of your libraries and folders using very large icons. This view is generally useful for people with vision disabilities.

Large Icons   Displays the contents of your libraries and folders using large icons. This view is useful when you want to see the pictures found on your computer and you want to see a preview of them instead of a small icon.

Medium Icons   Displays the contents of your libraries and folders using medium icons.

Small Icons   Displays the contents of your libraries and folders using small icons.

List   Displays the contents of your libraries and folders in a list that contains only the name of each file and its respective icon.

Details   Displays the contents of your libraries and folders by providing detailed information about each item, including its name, the date when it was last modified, its type, its size, and so on. This view is very useful when you want to learn more about each file and folder before opening it.

Tiles   This view displays medium-sized icons for each file and folder, as well as information about their type and size.

Content   When using this view, each file and folder are placed on a separate row. Each row has detailed information about each file and folder: the date when it was last modified, its size, its author, and so on.

You should definitely experiment with each view and learn how they work (Exercise 1.5) so that you can use them effectively depending on what you want to do.

EXERCISE 1.5

Using Views and the Preview Pane in Windows Explorer

1. On the taskbar, click the Folder icon.

2. In the Navigation pane, click Pictures in the Libraries section.

3. In the right pane, double-click Sample Pictures.

4. Click the Views menu and click Extra Large Icons.

    Notice how the pictures are now displayed.

5. Click the Views menu again and then Details.

    Notice how the way pictures are displayed has changed.

6. Click the Preview pane button. Note that a new pane appears on the right.

7. Click any picture in the middle pane to see a preview of it in the Preview pane.

8. Click the Preview pane button again to hide this pane.

9. Click the Views menu and choose Large Icons.

10. Click the X in the top-right corner of the Windows Explorer window to close it.

Understanding File Types

When working on your computer, you will create many types of files: documents, spreadsheets, presentations, music files, and so on. When you save a file, you are prompted to give a name to the file and choose a file type. If you get the file from somewhere else, it has already been assigned a file type.

When browsing your files in Windows Explorer, you can see the file type of each file when you are using the Content, Tiles, and Details views. The file type is generally denoted by a three- or four-letter extension that follows the filename and also by the icon used by Windows Explorer to display that file. For example, document·docx means a file named document with the extension ·docx. The dot separates the name of the file from its extension. The file extension is hidden by default in Windows when viewing files, but it is added automatically when saving them.

You can opt to change the file type when multiple options are available and change from the default file extension to something else. In Figure 1.16 you can see Paint open and the options that are available for saving a file. To save a file, click the Save As option, choose a file type, and then type the name of the file. If you make changes to the same file later, you need only click Save.

FIGURE 1.16 The Save As options that are available in Paint

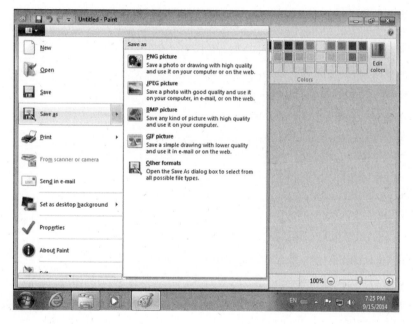

Some of the most common types of files are the following:

- Microsoft Office files
    - Microsoft Word (.doc and .docx)
    - Microsoft PowerPoint (.ppt and .pptx)
    - Microsoft Excel (.xls and .xlsx)
    - Microsoft Publisher (.pub and .pubx)
    - Microsoft OneNote (.one)

- Picture files
  - JPEG files
  - GIF files (`.gif`)
  - Bitmap files (`.bmp`)
  - PNG files (`.png`)
  - TIFF files (`.tif` and `.tiff`)
  - RAW files (`.raw`)
- Music files
  - Windows audio files (`.wav`)
  - MP3 audio files (`.mp3` and `.m3u`)
  - Windows Media audio files (`.asx`, `.wm`, `.wma`, and `.wmx`)
  - Free Lossless Audio Codec files (`.flac`)
  - AAC files (`.aac`)
- Video files
  - Audio Video Interleaved files (`.avi`)
  - Motion JPEG files (`.avi` and `.mov`)
  - Windows Media files (`.wm`, `.wmv`, and `.asf`)
  - Matroska multimedia files (`.mkv`)
  - Apple QuickTime files (`.mov` and `.qt`)
  - MPEG Movie files (`.mp4`, `.mov`, `.m4v`, `.mpeg`, `.mpg`, `.mpe`, `.m1v`, `.mp2`, `.mpv2`, `.mod`, `.vob`, and `.m1v`)

Other types of popular files are the following:

Executable Files (`.exe`)   Executable files can be run with a double-click.

Text Files (`.txt`)   Simple text documents without any kind of formatting.

Portable Document Format Files (`.pdf`)   A very popular type of files that is generally used for sharing non-editable documents that need to look the same on all the devices on which they are used, no matter what operating system is used.

OpenOffice and LibreOffice Documents (`.odt`, `.ott`, `.oth`, and `.odm`)   Documents created using free open-source office applications like OpenOffice and LibreOffice.

Managing Your Files and Folders

While working on your computer, it is better that you organize your work so that you will have an easier time finding the files you need later on. For starters, use the libraries provided by Windows 7 to store your files depending on their type. Save your pictures in the Pictures library, your documents in the Documents library, and so on.

Once things get too crowded, you will want to create your own folders and subfolders, move files around, and delete those that you do not need. Let's take each file and folder management activity and see how it is done:

Create a File   You can create files from applications like Microsoft Office, but you can also create empty files directly from Windows Explorer. To do so, follow these steps:

1.   Open the folder where you want to store the file.

2.   Right-click anywhere in the available empty space and select New and then one of the available file types, as shown in Figure 1.17.

3.   Type the name of the file and press Enter on your keyboard.

FIGURE 1.17   The types of files that can be created using the context menu in Windows Explorer

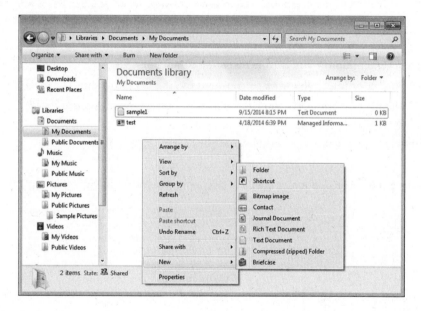

A new file is created, with the name and type you have provided. However, the file is empty because it has no contents. If you double-click it, you can open it and edit it in the appropriate application for files of that type. Don't forget to save your edits so that they are stored inside the file.

Create a Subfolder   Subfolders are helpful when you want to better organize your files. You can create subfolders with different names and then move files into them, according to your way of organizing things. To create a subfolder, do the following:

1.   Navigate to the desired parent folder and click New Folder on the Windows Explorer toolbar.

2.   Type a name for the folder and press Enter on your keyboard.

Alternatively, you can use the keyboard shortcut Ctrl+Shift+N or right-click somewhere in the available empty space and select New and then Folder.

Copy   You may want to copy a file or folder to another location. Here's how it is done:

1. Select the file or folder that you want to copy somewhere else.

2. Use the Copy command to copy it to a part of memory called the Clipboard.

> The Clipboard holds this information temporarily so that you can paste it somewhere else. You'll want to use the Paste command immediately after you use the Copy command. This is because the Clipboard can hold only one thing at a time. If you copy another item, the previous one is removed from the Clipboard. When you use the Copy command, the original file or folder stays where it is and is not moved. When you use Paste after the Copy command, a copy of that item is created in the desired location.

There are several options for accessing the Copy command:

- Click the file or folder you want to copy and use the keyboard shortcut Ctrl+C.
- Click the file or folder you want to copy and from the Organize menu in Windows Explorer click Copy.
- Right-click the file or folder to copy and click Copy (Figure 1.18).

FIGURE 1.18   The options available in the context menu when right-clicking a file

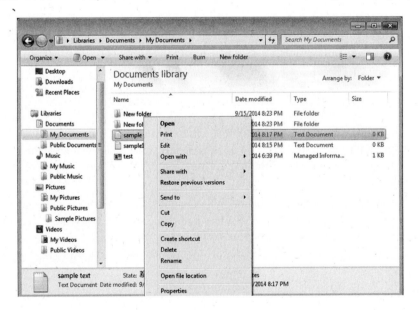

Paste   Once you've copied something to the Clipboard, using one of the methods shared earlier, you can use the Paste command to perform the actual task of copying the item to its new location.

1. Navigate to the location where you'd like to paste the file or folder.

    This might be a new subfolder you created, a library, or even the Desktop.

2. Then use one of the following options:

    - Use the keyboard shortcut Ctrl+V.

    - Click the Organize menu in Windows Explorer and then click Paste.

    - Right-click the empty area inside the folder or on the Desktop and click Paste (Figure 1.19).

FIGURE 1.19   The Paste option in the context menu

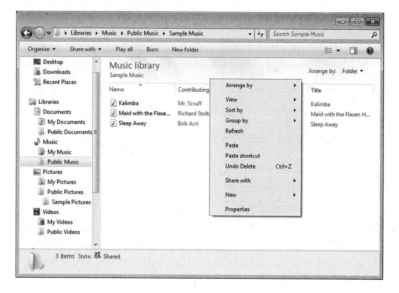

Cut   This command works like the Copy command, except that the selected file or folder is removed from its original location and can be moved to the new one. Be careful when using Cut and make sure that you use Paste immediately after. The problem with using Cut is that if anything fails during the moving process (after you use Paste), then you will lose the selected file or folder. That's why it is better to use the Copy command instead and then delete the selected file or folder from the original location once its copy has been made in the new location. There are several options for accessing the Cut command:

- Click the file or folder to cut and use the keyboard shortcut Ctrl+X.

- Click the file or folder to cut and from the Organize menu in Windows Explorer click Cut.

- Right-click the file or folder to cut and click Cut.

Move Here   You can use the Move Here command to move a file or folder. It works like Cut and Paste; the item will be moved, and the original item will no longer appear in its original location. To use this command, follow these steps:

1. Right-click the file or folder to move, and hold down the right mouse button while you drag the file on top of its new location, in the Navigation pane.

2. Let go of the right mouse button and click Move Here (Figure 1.20).

FIGURE 1.20   The Move Here option

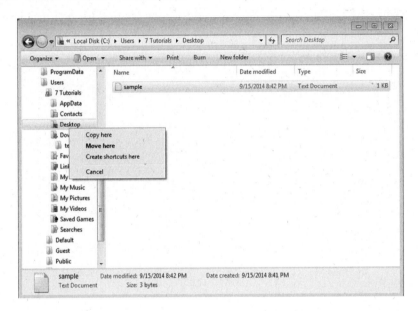

Alternatively, you can use the Cut and Paste commands for the same effect.

Rename   You can rename both files and folders. This can be done in several ways:

▪   Select the item by clicking it. Press the F2 key on the keyboard. Type the new name.

▪   Click the item one time, wait a second or two, and then click it again. Type the new name.

▪   Right-click the item to rename and click Rename. Type the new name.

Delete   You can remove both files and folders from your computer. This can be done in several ways. Here's one method:

1. Select the item by clicking it.

2. Press the Delete key on the keyboard and confirm that you want to delete that item.

    The item is moved to the Recycle Bin and can be recovered in case you decide that you need it again.

You can also do the following:

1. Right-click the item to delete.
2. Click Delete and confirm that you want to delete that item.

Alternatively, you can drag the item to the Recycle Bin using the mouse.

To delete an item without moving it to the Recycle Bin, follow these steps:

1. Select the item by clicking it.
2. Then, hold down the Shift key and the Delete key.

But be aware that this way the item cannot be recovered if you need it again.

Create a Shortcut　If you need to access a file or folder from another location but you do not want to copy or move it, you can create a shortcut. You can tell which files are shortcuts because they have an arrow in their icon and Shortcut included in the filename. Shortcuts are only references to other files and folders and do not hold any data except for what's required to point their target location. The option to create a shortcut is available from the options that appear when you right-click the item. There are several ways of creating a shortcut. Here's the first way:

1. Right-click the item you want to create a shortcut for.
2. Click Create Shortcut.

    The shortcut is created in the same location.

3. You can now cut and paste that shortcut to another location like the Desktop.

 The original file should be kept in its initial location; otherwise the shortcut won't work.

You can also do the following:

1. Right-click the file or folder.
2. Click Send To and then click Desktop (Create Shortcut), as shown in Figure 1.21.

    A shortcut is created for that item on the Desktop.

And finally, you can use this method:

1. Press and hold down Ctrl+Shift while you drag that item to the location you want to create a shortcut to.
2. Release the item in the location where you want to create a shortcut for it.

Search for a File　There are many ways to search for a specific file, provided you know something about it. One way is to use the Search box on the top-right of the Windows Explorer window:

1. Select the library or folder where you want to perform the search.
2. Click inside the Search box (Figure 1.22) and type the name of the file you are looking for.

FIGURE 1.21   The Send To menu in Windows Explorer

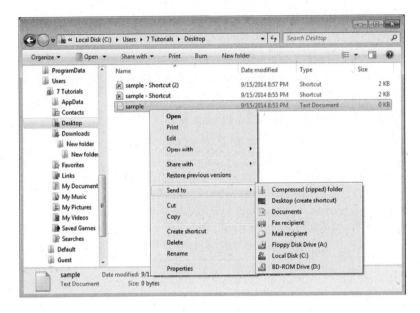

FIGURE 1.22   The Search box in Windows Explorer

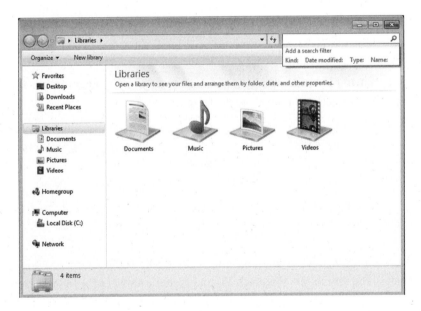

If you want to search for a file on the whole computer, do this:

1. Select Local Disk (C:) in the Computer section of the Navigation pane.

2. Then use the Search box.

Here's another way:

1. Close Windows Explorer and press the F3 key on the keyboard.

2. This brings up a Search window where you can type the name of the file (Figure 1.23).

If you don't know the filename, you can search based on the date you believe it was created, by the kind of file it is, by the type, and other criteria. Your search will be made across your whole computer.

FIGURE 1.23   The Search window that is accessed by pressing F3

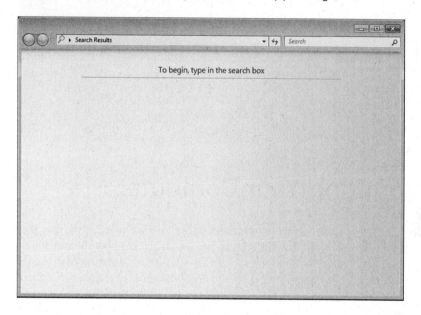

You can also click the Start button on the Desktop and start typing the name of the file (Figure 1.24). Searches are performed automatically as you type but only in locations that are indexed by Windows, like your libraries. To access a file or folder, click it in the list of results. If you want to perform a computer-wide search, the previous methods work better.

Although we provided the necessary keyboard shortcuts that you can use while working with files and folders in Windows, there are many more keyboard shortcuts for you to discover. You can find a complete list of keyboard shortcuts on Microsoft's Knowledge Base, here: http://support.microsoft.com/kb/126449. Don't hesitate to consult it and learn how each keyboard shortcut works. They will surely make you more productive when using Windows.

FIGURE 1.24   The Start menu search

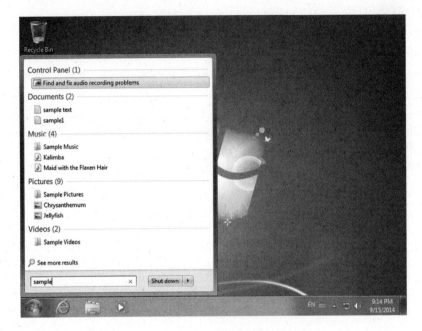

Customizing Your Computer

All modern operating systems give you plenty of options for configuring the way they look and how you use them. The most basic customizations are about changing the way the operating system looks. For example, in Windows 7, you can change the resolution of the screen, the Desktop background, the theme, and so on. Obviously, you can go into a lot of detail and customize more advanced settings, but there's no need to, unless you have very specific needs.

When you first use a computer, most probably you will want to change the way Windows looks, the language used for typing, the time and the date, and how accessible the computer is, in case you have a disability.

Another aspect that you might want to customize is how many user accounts there are on your computer and who is allowed to use it and who the administrator is.

Let's look at the most common types of customizations that are performed on a computer and see how they are done.

Customizing the Desktop

All the visual customization options that are available in Windows are found in the Control Panel. To access them, click Start ➢ Control Panel ➢ Appearance And Personalization, as shown in Figure 1.25.

FIGURE 1.25   The Appearance And Personalization section in the Control Panel

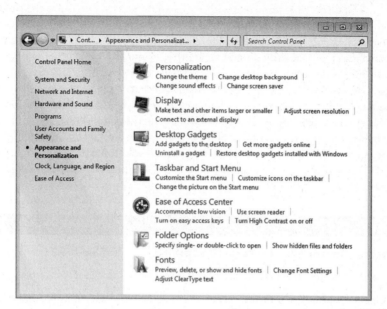

In this panel you will find that Windows offers lots of visual customizations:

- You can change the theme used by Windows, the Desktop background, sound effects, and the screensaver.

- You can change the resolution of the screen and make text and other items larger or smaller.

- You can add gadgets to the Desktop, which provide additional information like weather data or the calendar. Please note that this feature of Windows has been discontinued, and Microsoft doesn't provide any new gadgets except those already found in Windows 7.

- You can customize the icons on the taskbar and the items that are displayed by the Start menu.

- You can improve the level of accessibility and turn on features like High Contrast or a screen reader, in case you have disabilities that do not allow you to use your computer without help.

- You can install new fonts, view those that are installed, and adjust their settings.

- You can also set how files and folders are displayed when using Windows Explorer.

Customizing the Screen Resolution

The display of any computer or device has a specific size that is measured in inches (for example, 9″, 24″, and so on). This number tells you the diagonal measurement of the screen, measured from the bottom-left corner to the top-right corner.

All displays are split into really small squares that are used to display color. Think of the image on your display like a puzzle with really small pieces. Pixels are the smallest squares that could be manufactured and used to display color. How many pixels are on the screen depends on the size of the screen. The total number of pixels is communicated using the screen resolution. It is usually quoted as width × height, with the units in pixels; for example, 1366×768 means the width is 1366 pixels and the height is 768 pixels.

The bigger the resolution, the clearer the image is because there's more room for displaying small details on the screen. When you increase the resolution, items on the screen appear smaller. The opposite happens when you lower the screen resolution. Computer displays have a maximum resolution that can be set, depending on their size and the actual number of pixels available. However, their resolution can be lowered if needed. Exercise 1.6 demonstrates how to change the screen resolution so that items on the screen appear bigger, if you need them to.

EXERCISE 1.6

Changing the Resolution of Your Screen

1. Click the Start button and then click Control Panel.

2. Click Appearance And Personalization and then Adjust Screen Resolution, under Display.

3. Click the drop-down list next to Resolution and use the slider to set a lower resolution like 1024×768, if it is available, as shown in Figure 1.26.

FIGURE 1.26   The Resolution slider from the Screen Resolution window

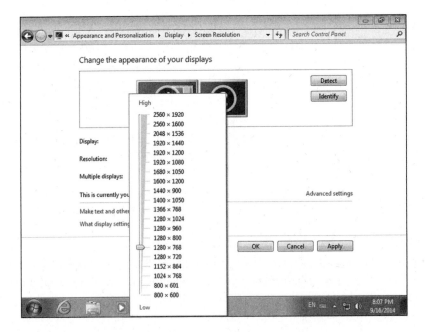

4. Click Apply.

5. If you like the new resolution, click Keep Changes. Otherwise, click Revert and repeat steps 3 and 4.

6. Click OK.

If you want to make the text and other items larger than they are and you do not want to change the resolution, you can do that. Exercise 1.7 shows you how.

EXERCISE 1.7

Changing the Size of the Items on Your Screen

1. Click the Start button and then click Control Panel.

2. Click Appearance And Personalization and then Display.

3. Change the size you want for the text and other items. You can choose Smaller, Medium, or Larger (Figure 1.27).

FIGURE 1.27 The Display window

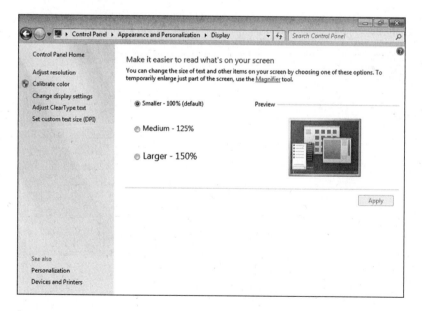

4. Click Apply.

5. You are asked to log off your computer to apply these changes. Make sure that you do not have any unsaved work and then click Log Off Now.

6. Log back into Windows.

Customizing the Desktop Appearance

Windows allows you to change the background image that is displayed on the screen as well as the general visuals and the sounds that are used through the operating system. To make things simpler and easier to manage, Microsoft uses the concept of themes in its Windows operating system. A *theme* is the collection of all the visual settings and sounds that are used by Windows: the Desktop background, the color used to display the user interface, the sounds that are played when messages are displayed, and the screensaver that is displayed when you have kept your computer turned on but you are not using it.

For starters let's see how to change the Desktop background in Windows. Exercise 1.8 demonstrates everything you need to know.

EXERCISE 1.8

Changing the Desktop Background

1. Click the Start button and then click Control Panel.

2. Click Appearance And Personalization and then Personalization (Figure 1.28).

FIGURE 1.28 The Personalization window

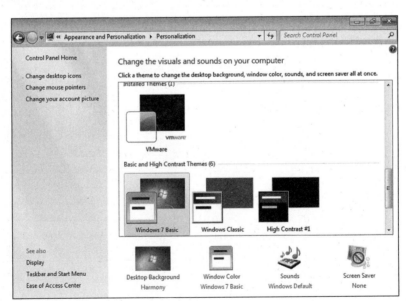

3. Click Desktop Background and choose one of the available images (Figure 1.29).

FIGURE 1.29   The Desktop Background window

4. Set the picture position and then click Save Changes.

5. Close the Personalization window in order to see the new Desktop background.

Themes can also be changed from the Personalization window. They are displayed in the center of the window and are split into categories like My Themes, Aero Themes, and Basic And High Contrast Themes. Browse through the available themes and select the one that you want to apply. You will notice that each theme uses a different Desktop background, different visuals, and so on. When you have found a theme that you are happy with, close the Personalization window.

Customizing the Language You Are Using

Windows 7 offers you the ability to change both the language that you use for typing (the keyboard input language) as well as the language used to display everything on the screen (the display language). Changing the keyboard input language can be done in all versions of Windows 7. Unfortunately, changing the display language is possible only in the more expensive versions of Windows 7: Windows 7 Ultimate and Windows 7 Enterprise. Affordable versions like Windows 7 Home and Windows 7 Professional do not include this useful feature.

First, you'll learn how to change the language used for typing, using the instructions shared in Exercise 1.9.

EXERCISE 1.9

Adding a New Keyboard Input Language

1. Click the Start button and then click Control Panel.

2. Click Clock, Language, And Region and then Region And Language.

3. Select the Keyboards And Languages tab (Figure 1.30).

FIGURE 1.30   The Keyboard And Languages tab in the Region And Language window

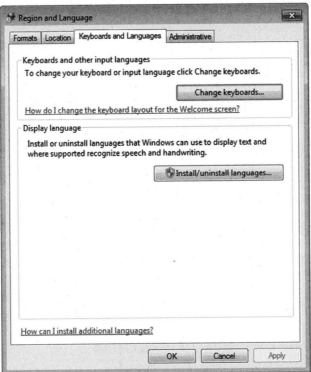

4. Click the Change Keyboards button.

5. In the new Text Services And Input Languages window, click Add.

6. Double-click the keyboard input language that you want to add, to expand it (Figure 1.31).

FIGURE 1.31   The Add Input Language window where you can add a new input language

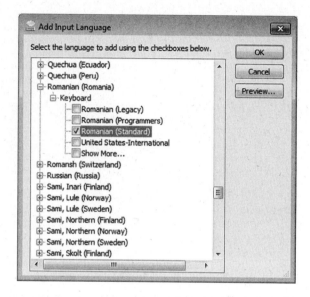

7. Then double-click Keyboard and select the type you want to add.

8. Click OK and then click OK again in the windows that remain open.

You can add as many keyboard input languages as you wish and then switch between them. This is very helpful if you are a multilingual person who works using more than one language.

You can switch between languages for typing at any time during your work. All you have to do is to click the two-letter language code near the keyboard icon that is shown on the taskbar (the bar on the bottom of the screen) and select the language that you want to use (Figure 1.32). You can also use the keyboard shortcut Alt+Shift for the same effect.

If you have Windows 7 Ultimate or Windows 7 Enterprise, you can also change the display language that is used. Exercise 1.10 shows how.

FIGURE 1.32 The keyboard input language switcher

EXERCISE 1.10

Adding a New Display Language

1. Click the Start button and then click Control Panel.

2. Click Clock, Language, And Region and then Region And Language.

3. Select the Keyboard And Languages tab.

4. Click the Install/Uninstall Languages button.

5. In the new Install Or Uninstall Display Languages window, click Install Display Languages (Figure 1.33) and then Launch Windows Update.

6. In the Windows Update window, click the link that says how many optional updates are available (Figure 1.34).

7. Scroll down to Windows 7 Language Packs and select the display language that you want to install (Figure 1.35).

FIGURE 1.33 The Install Or Uninstall Display Languages Wizard

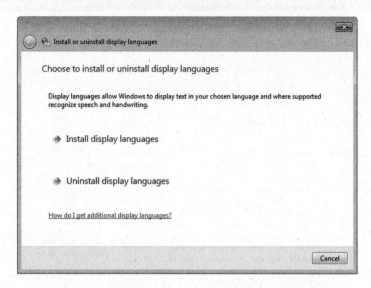

FIGURE 1.34 Windows Update displaying the number of optional updates available

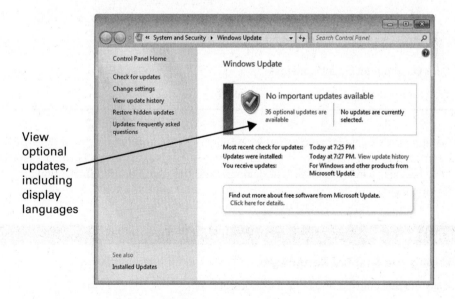

FIGURE 1.35 A list of the optional updates that are available

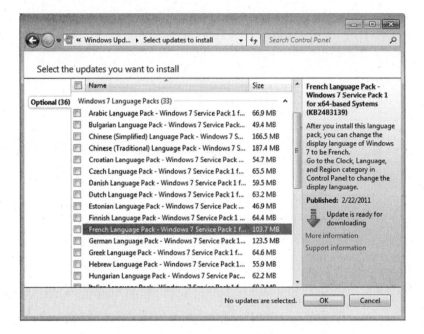

8. Click OK and then Install Updates.

9. Wait for the display language to be installed.

Changing the display language used by Windows 7 is relatively easy, but it does take more steps than changing the keyboard input language. Also, there's no keyboard shortcut available for this switch. Exercise 1.11 demonstrates the steps involved in changing the display language.

EXERCISE 1.11

Changing the Display Language

1. Click the Start button and then click Control Panel.

2. Click Clock, Language, And Region and then Region And Language.

3. Choose the Keyboard And Languages tab.

4. In the Display Language section, click the Choose A Display Language drop-down list and select the language that you want to use.

5. Click OK, and you will be notified that you need to log off. Close any files that you have open and then click Log Off Now.

6. Log back into Windows 7 and you will see the selected display language used.

Changing the Date and Time

When you set up a new computer or when you have just installed Windows 7, the date and the time might be incorrect. Fortunately, changing them is very easy, and it takes only a few clicks. Exercise 1.12 shows how it is done.

EXERCISE 1.12

Changing the Date and the Time

1. Click the Start button and then click Control Panel.

2. Click Clock, Language, And Region and then Date And Time.

3. Click the Change Date And Time button.

4. Change the date using your mouse and the calendar that is shown on the left in Figure 1.36.

FIGURE 1.36   The Date And Time Settings window

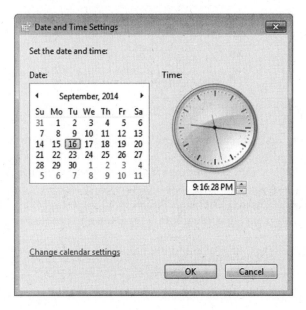

EXERCISE 1.12 *(continued)*

5. Change the time by selecting the hour or the minute and then typing the correct values.

6. When finished, click OK and then click OK again.

Making the Computer More Accessible

If you have a disability that makes it difficult to hear, see, or physically use the computer, there are options and features available that you can configure to make things easier for you. These options are found in the Control Panel by selecting Appearance And Personalization and then Ease Of Access Center, as shown in Figure 1.37.

FIGURE 1.37   The Ease Of Access Center in the Control Panel

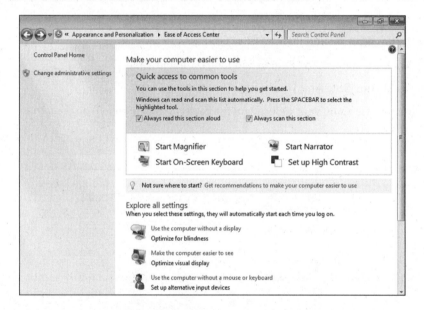

The easiest way to understand what features you should enable is to work through the wizard that is available by clicking the link "Get recommendations to make your computer easier to use." Work through it on your own and select the statements that apply to you. Upon completion, you'll see options to enable features that Windows 7 deems appropriate, based on your answers (Figure 1.38).

Here are some of the items that you might be prompted to enable based on the answers you give:

High Contrast   When this option is turned on, you change how the computer displays information on the screen. The colors used to display everything will have a very high contrast so that you have an easier time figuring out the different elements that are displayed.

FIGURE 1.38   The settings recommended by the Ease Of Access Center

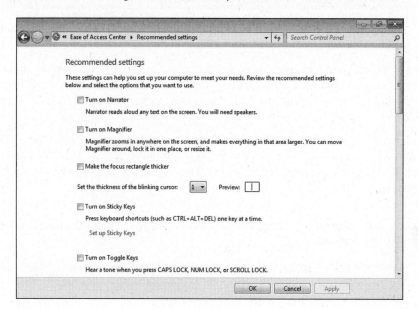

Narrator   Reads aloud the text that appears on the screen.

Speech Recognition   Once you set it up, you can use speech commands like "Open Control Panel" to control the computer, if you have a microphone available. You can also use it to dictate text.

Magnifier   Zooms in on areas of the screen that you select. In its default form, you use it like a magnifying glass.

On-Screen Keyboard   Lets you type words using a keyboard that appears on the screen. You can type on the keyboard using the mouse or another pointing device.

Understanding User Accounts

In order to use Windows, you need a user account and a password set for it. A *user account* is a collection of settings that Windows uses for understanding your preferences and for controlling the files and folders you access, the tasks you are allowed to perform, the devices and resources you are allowed to use, and so on. User accounts are also used to separate the people that use the same computer and make sure that they can keep their personal files private (like the ones stored in their libraries) and that they do not change each other's settings.

In the Windows 7 operating system there are three types of user accounts that you can choose from (Figure 1.39).

Administrator   User accounts of this type have complete control over the operating system, its applications, and its settings. It is the only type of user account that can install or uninstall applications in Windows. Administrators can also manage other user accounts and create new user accounts.

Standard   A limited type of user account that can use only existing software applications and cannot install or uninstall applications. Also, this user account cannot modify system settings that affect other users. Standard user accounts can change only their own settings.

Guest   A limited type of user account. There is only one Guest user account on a Windows device, and it has no password. It is meant only for temporary access to the PC, and it can be used only for running existing applications. This user account type cannot modify any system settings.

FIGURE 1.39   The Manage Accounts window where you can see the user accounts existing on your computer

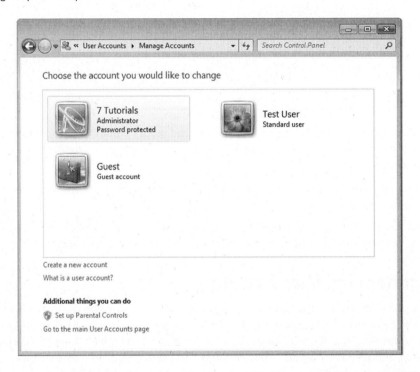

In Windows 7, the first person to create a user account is the administrator. When you create other user accounts, you can choose their type. Also, the Guest account exists by default in Windows 7. It only needs to be enabled in order for it to be used. But first, you'll learn how to create a user account using the instructions in Exercise 1.13.

EXERCISE 1.13

Creating a Standard User Account

1. Click Start and click Control Panel.

2. Under User Accounts And Family Safety, click Add Or Remove User Accounts.

3. Click Create A New Account.

4. Type a name for the account, leave Standard User selected, and click Create Account, as shown in Figure 1.40.

FIGURE 1.40   The Create New Account window

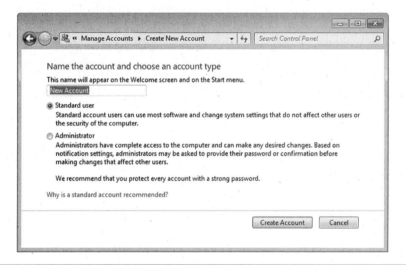

Sharing Folders with Other Users

User accounts are also important when you want to share your work with others. For example, you might share the same computer with another person, and you may want to give the other person access to one of your folders. Or, your computer is connected to a network, and you may want to share a folder with others on the network. Before you do that, you will need to understand one more concept: permissions.

If you want to share a folder with another person (on the same computer or on the same network), you need to set the level of permissions assigned to that person for that folder. The permissions you can give another person are as follows:

Read   The other person can only read the files and subfolders that are found in the folder you are sharing. They cannot modify them or delete them.

Read/Write The other person can read the files and folders that are found in the folder you are sharing. They can also modify them and delete them.

You will see these two options in Windows each time you try to share anything with someone else.

To simplify sharing on small networks like the one in your home or in a small company, Microsoft has introduced the concept of Homegroup. The Homegroup is a group of Windows computers and devices that share content and devices with each other, in the same network. What is shared with the Homegroup is not available to other computers that are on the same network but are not part of the Homegroup. The Homegroup can be joined by Windows 7 and Windows 8 computers and devices.

By design, there's no limit to the number of computers that can join a Homegroup. The Homegroup is protected by a password that you share with the users who want to participate in it. This password is requested only when a new computer joins the Homegroup. You create or join a Homegroup from Control Panel under Network And Internet.

In Windows Explorer, you can easily share a folder by first opening it and then clicking the Share With menu on the toolbar. There you will see several options, including Homegroup (Read) and Homegroup (Read/Write), as shown in Figure 1.41. Read and Read/Write are the permissions you want to assign to the Homegroup for that shared folder.

FIGURE 1.41 The Share With menu in Windows Explorer

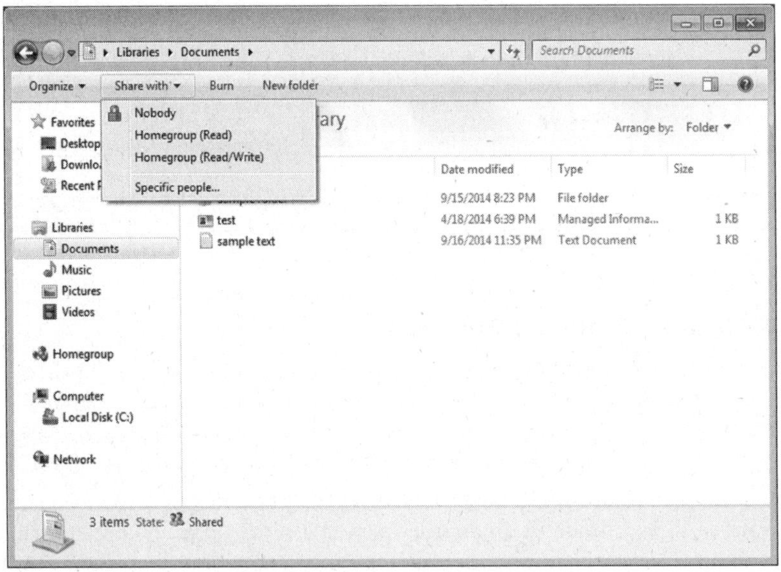

You can also share a folder with another person who has a user account on the same computer. Exercise 1.14 shows you how it is done.

EXERCISE 1.14

Sharing a Folder with Another User Account

1. Open Windows Explorer and select your Documents library.

2. Click the Share With menu on the toolbar and then select Specific People.

3. Click the arrow pointing downward and select the user with whom you want to share your documents (Figure 1.42).

FIGURE 1.42   Choosing with whom to share in the File Sharing Wizard

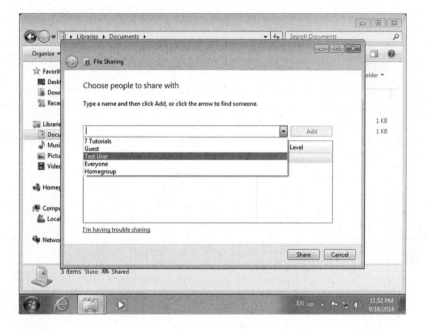

4. Click Add.

5. Click the arrow beside Read, on the line for the new user.

6. If desired, click Read/Write. If not, leave Read selected.

7. Click Share.

The person with whom you are sharing that folder can access it by opening Windows Explorer and double-clicking Local Disk (C:), Users, and then the name of your user account.

To stop sharing that folder with the user you initially shared it with, repeat steps 1 and 2 from Exercise 1.14, click the name of the user to remove, and then click Remove. Lastly, click Share to update with whom you are sharing that folder.

Managing Permissions in Large Businesses

So far, with regard to creating user accounts and sharing data, we've been focused on small networks like the one in your home or in a small business. In large enterprises, user accounts and permissions are managed differently. Consider what would happen if there were thousands of users who each had their own computer. Think about how hard it would be and how long it would take to create all those user accounts and share data among them, using the aforementioned methods, on every one of those computers and for every one of those users. It just isn't manageable.

To make things more manageable, enterprises create a network domain, and they hire network administrators who create all the network users on a computer called a server. Users' data is saved to this server or others. Because users and their data are centralized, one network administrator can manage all users and all data sharing and assign all permissions to the data and resources that are shared, from a single location.

The set of permissions that the network administrator applies is created and managed through the Group Policy. Just as it sounds, permissions are created for entire groups of users, and those permissions make up a policy that those users are restricted by. So, a network administrator can create a Group Policy that restricts all users in a specific group (say Accountants, Guests, or Marketing), to efficiently place limits on what members of that group can access on the network and what they can do on their own computers.

 Real World Scenario

How Organizations Assign Permissions Using Group Policy

In some colleges, users are placed into groups that represent the job they do. There are groups for adjunct faculty, full-time faculty, administrators, human resources, marketing, and so on. There are groups for mobile users too, namely those people who access data remotely from home or on the road. Permissions are assigned to these groups and thus are also applied to the users who are in those groups. This makes it easy to manage access to resources while limiting what users can do once they're connected to that organization's network.

As an example, users in the adjunct faculty group are allowed to access the student database for the purpose of finding a student's phone number or address or to look up a grade for a specific class, but they cannot change this information. Users in the faculty group can do all of these things too, but they also have the ability to change a student's grade in a course. They do not have the ability to change a student's phone number or address. Users in the human resources group have permission to access and alter a student's phone number or address but not their grade. Mobile users might be assigned specific permissions that apply only to them, perhaps to protect access to sensitive data over an unprotected network such as the Internet. These permissions are easy to manage because they have to be applied only to the group and not the individual users.

Additionally, when new employees are hired, it is easy for the network administrator to add a new user account to the group in which that employee belongs. That user is automatically assigned the permissions for that group. When an employee is laid off or retires, it is equally easy to remove that person from a group. Because the user is no longer a member of the group, they cannot access the group's resources.

Often, users are assigned to more than one group. For the most part, users' permissions are cumulative. So if a user has permission to read one resource in one group and also write to it in a second, the user can both read and write to the resource. Users can also be denied access to specific resources should they be found to abuse them. For example, if a user is overusing the printer, they may be blocked from accessing it.

Summary

Before you can use a computer effectively, you must know a little about what makes it work. A computer must have an operating system and applications. Without those essential elements no work can be done. These two types of software are updated by their manufacturers on a regular basis so that they are kept safe from security problems, their problems are fixed, and new features are introduced.

Once your computer is powered on, you can log on and start using all the applications that are available to create and save data. This data is stored in files, each with its own type and file extension. In order to keep track of your files, the operating system has a file system that allows you to view your files, use them, and manage them as you see fit. In this chapter you learned all the basic commands for working with files in Windows.

In order for users to be truly productive, operating systems on modern computers allow multiple users to use the same computer. Each user should have an individual user account so that each person's data, applications, and settings are kept separate. Obviously, this data can be shared at any time with other users on the same computer or with other users on the network. In this chapter you also learned how to share your folders with others.

Finally, it is important to be able to customize your computer so that it better meets your needs. In this chapter we showed how to customize the way the operating system looks, how to change the language you are using, how to modify the date and time (in case the operating system has the wrong information), and how to improve its accessibility if you have a disability that makes using the computer difficult.

In the next chapter will talk in more detail about hardware and the different hardware components of a typical computer. We will also talk about different types of computers and how to measure and compare their relative performance.

Exam Essentials

Understand the difference between the operating system and software applications.   An operating system is the most important software that runs on a device, because without it, interactions with that device would be impossible. The operating system is what makes communication between the user, software applications, and the internal hardware possible. Applications are either included with the operating system or installed on top of the operating system. Applications allow you to create data and use your computer more productively. You should know the differences between the operating system and software applications.

Understand how to power on and power off your computer.   In order to use a computer, you should understand how to log into Windows with your account, switch users, log off, and shut down the computer. You should also know that logging off closes all applications and windows, while switching users, locking the computer, or putting the computer to sleep only pauses those things so that you can get to work more quickly when you return.

Know how to browse your computer's files and folders.   You cannot be a productive user unless you know what Windows Explorer is and how to use it to browse the files and folders that are found on your computer. Learn how to work with the views that are available and understand the differences between them.

Know how to manage your files and folders.   Understand how to organize your files and folders, depending on their type. Use the libraries that are available in Windows to keep things organized, and know how to move your data around. Also, you should learn the keyboard shortcuts for useful commands like Copy, Cut, Paste, Rename, and so on. They will make things easier when working with your files.

Know how to customize Windows 7.   There are too many customization options available to discuss them all here. Thus, you'll need to work through all of the options on your own. Know how to change the theme and the Desktop background and how to update the date and the time if your computer is using the wrong data. Knowing this will allow you to personalize your computer and have it look and work the way you want it to. Also, you should understand the basic Accessibility options that are available and how they can help people with disabilities.

Key Terms

Before you take the exam, be certain you are familiar with the following terms:

files	operating system
folders	personal identification number
hardware	software
libraries	

Review Questions

1. What does an operating system such as Windows do?

   A. Manages the files and folders on my computer

   B. Displays the image on the screen of my computer

   C. Allows communication between the user, software applications, and the internal hardware of my computer

   D. Powers on the computer when I need to use it and powers it off when I'm finished working

2. Which of these are operating systems? (Choose all that apply.)

   A. Windows

   B. Hardware

   C. Microsoft Office

   D. Android

3. You need to leave your computer unattended for a couple of minutes, and you want to secure it. You do not want to have to close all of your applications or save your work because on your return you want to get back to work quickly, right where you left off. Which of the following options will enable you to do this? (Choose all that apply.)

   A. Log off

   B. Lock the computer

   C. Use the Switch User command

   D. Shut down

4. You want to move a folder to another location. Which two commands do you use to perform this task? (Choose all that apply.)

   A. Copy

   B. Cut

   C. Move

   D. Paste

5. Which views in Windows Explorer allow you to learn the type of each file? (Choose all that apply.)

   A. Content

   B. List

   C. Tiles

   D. Details

6. What two keyboard shortcuts can you use to copy and paste a file to another location?

    A. Ctrl+C and Ctrl+V

    B. Ctrl+X and Ctrl+P

    C. Ctrl+X and Ctrl+V

    D. Ctrl+C and Ctrl+X

7. If everything on the screen is too small to see, what can you do? (Choose all that apply.)

    A. Use the Magnifier.

    B. Decrease the screen resolution.

    C. Increase the screen resolution.

    D. Opt to make text and other items larger from the Display window.

8. Where do you go in Windows 7 in order to change the Desktop background or the theme?

    A. Start ➤ Control Panel ➤ Appearance And Personalization ➤ Display

    B. Start ➤ Control Panel ➤ Clock ➤ Language ➤ Region

    C. Start ➤ Control Panel ➤ Appearance And Personalization ➤ Personalization

    D. Start ➤ Control Panel ➤ Appearance And Personalization ➤ Desktop Gadgets

9. Which of these user accounts has the permission to manage other users?

    A. Homegroup users

    B. Standard users

    C. Homegroup members

    D. Administrators

10. Which sharing permission allows a user to access and view a file but not make any changes to it?

    A. View

    B. Read/Write

    C. Delete

    D. Read

Chapter

2

Understanding Hardware

THE FOLLOWING IC3 GS4: COMPUTER FUNDAMENTALS EXAM OBJECTIVES ARE COVERED IN THIS CHAPTER:

✓ **Common Computer Terminology**

- Define the terms and explain the differences between input/output devices and hardware and peripherals.
  - Processing
    - Gigahertz
    - Hertz
    - CPU
  - Input / Output
    - Monitor and Projector
    - Mice
    - Keyboards
    - Stylus
    - Microphone
    - Speakers
    - Touchpad
  - Printers
- Explain the different types of memory.
  - Volatile
    - RAM
  - Nonvolatile]
    - SSD drive
    - Magnetic hard drive
    - ROM
    - Flash drives (USB, Jump, Thumb, etc.)

- Units of measurement
  - Mega, giga, tera, peta. Explain the difference between Bit vs. Byte

✓ Types of Devices

- Explain these different types of computers. Compare and contrast uses and capabilities:
  - Server
  - Desktop
  - Laptop
  - Tablet
  - Smart Phone

✓ Computer Performance

- This objective may include, but is not limited to, the following topics:
  - Specify criteria that could be used to evaluate the pros and cons of various computing devices and peripherals, Focus on performance issues.
  - Processing vs. memory vs. storage:
    - Describe the concepts of Processing capacity, Processing speed, Memory capacity, Memory speed, Storage capacity, and Storage speed including how each interacts with the other to determine overall computing capacity, speed and power.

In Chapter 1, "Understanding Operating Systems," we mentioned that computers generally have software components and a hardware component. Now that we have explained important concepts like software, operating systems, and applications, it is time to take a look at the physical components of a computer: the hardware.

We will start by talking about the components that make up a computer and what they do. Then we will talk about external components that can be connected to a computer in order to increase its capabilities and usefulness.

Since computers are just as diverse as the components they are made of, we will also discuss the most common types of computers and devices that are used today and their properties.

Then we will talk about how information is sent inside your computer and how it is represented. Knowing that will also help you understand the characteristics of a computer and its components, as well as how to evaluate its performance. There's a lot of ground to cover and lots of interesting things to share, so let's get started.

The Internal Hardware Components of a Computer

Hardware is the term that is used to describe the physical components of a computer or device. While software and operating systems are ephemeral and nontangible, hardware is always physical and tangible. You may never see or touch the hardware inside your computer, but that doesn't mean the components don't exist. Hardware is generally protected by a case, to keep it safe from damage, from dust, and from other things that might stop it from working.

Hardware components are specialized for the jobs they do. For example, one component handles the sound that is played by the computer, another handles the image displayed on the screen, another handles the connection to the network, and so on. Generally, inside the case of a computer you will find the following hardware components:

Processor Also known as the *CPU* (central processing unit), it is the "brains" of a computer. The CPU is what carries out the instructions sent by the software you run. It's the most important hardware component in a computer. You cannot have a running device without a processor.

RAM RAM means random access memory, and it is a volatile and very fast form of memory that allows data to be read and written in roughly the same amount of time. Software uses RAM to carry out calculations and operations as quickly as possible. When an application is closed, it no longer uses a portion of the available RAM, and it frees it up for other applications. RAM can't be used for long-term storage, however, because all data in RAM disappears when a computer is restarted or shut down.

Disk Storage   There are two types of disk storage solutions that are commonly used in computers:

Hard Disk   This is the data storage device in your computer that is used for storing and retrieving information. Unlike RAM, a hard disk stores data permanently, and it can hold large amounts of information. Also, it is slower at writing and reading data. On a hard disk, data is usually read faster than it is written. In many modern computers, traditional hard disks are replaced with devices named SSDs.

SSD   Solid-state disks (SSD) are also data storage devices, but they use different circuitry and methods for storing your data as well as fewer moving parts. They are much faster than traditional hard disks and consume less power when running. Generally, SSDs are at least five times faster than traditional hard disks. Due to their benefits and continuously lowering prices, they will ultimately replace hard disks.

Graphics Card   This is the hardware that processes and generates the image that is displayed by your computer. It is also known as a video card, video adapter, or graphics adapter. A graphics card is always directly connected to the monitor; otherwise, the image would not get displayed. Due to the advances in technology, graphics cards can also be small chips that are built into the motherboard.

Sound Card   This is the hardware that processes and generates sound. Without a sound card you would not be able to listen to music and hear the sounds played by the operating system and the applications that you are running. With the help of a microphone, sound cards can also take sound input from outside the computer and turn it into audio recordings. Just like graphics cards, sound cards can also be small chips that are built into the motherboard.

Network Card   Also known as a network interface controller (NIC) or network adapter, it is the hardware that connects a computer to a network and manages the data transfers between the network and the computer. Network cards can use either network cables or wireless signals to connect to the network but never both at the same time. You will need two separate network cards for that: one for network cables and one for wireless signals. Due to the advances in technology, network cards can also be small chips that are built into the motherboard.

DVD Drive   This device can read and write to a digital video disc (DVD) that is used to store all kinds of data, from movies to games and all types of files.

Blu-ray Drive   This is a device that can read Blu-ray discs. Blu-ray is the modern alternative to the DVD and is slowly replacing it. Blu-ray discs are similar in shape and size to DVDs, but they store a lot more data. Typically, Blu-ray discs store six times more data than DVDs. Blu-ray drives can also read DVDs, so you won't need both a Blu-ray drive and a DVD-ROM drive in your computer.

Motherboard   This is the main board in a computer. It holds all the crucial hardware components of the computer, like the processor and the RAM. All the internal hardware components of a computer are connected to it in some way. This is because the motherboard acts as the hub that manages all the communication between hardware components. Without a motherboard, the hardware components of a computer would not be able to interact and cooperate with each other. Many modern motherboards integrate chips that replace other hardware components like a sound card, network card, or graphics card.

Power Supply Unit   This manages the alternating current from the wall socket and transforms it into direct current, which is necessary for your computer to run. It is one of the most important components of a computer since it provides the necessary electrical power for all other components.

Computer Cooling   All the hardware components of a computer generate heat. If any component gets overheated, it will malfunction and stop working. All computers and devices, no matter how big or small, have some form of cooling built in. In a typical computer, cooling is provided through the use of small fans to reduce temperature by actively exhausting hot air.

All these components make up all computers, including laptops and mobile devices like smartphones and tablets. Because mobile devices are smaller so that they can be easily carried, their hardware components are much smaller than on traditional computers. Also, they are optimized to consume as little energy as possible and release as little heat as possible. Desktop computers are bigger because their components are more powerful. They deliver more performance while consuming more power and requiring more cooling and ventilation.

 Real World Scenario

Volatile vs. Nonvolatile Memory

We mentioned that RAM is volatile memory. *Volatile* means that it can store data only while powered on. When it's powered off, data stored in RAM is lost. This is why this type of memory is used only for making real-time calculations in a computer and not for storing files and other data that needs to be used on a long-term basis.

Nonvolatile memory can store data even when powered off. Obviously, you cannot use the data from nonvolatile memory if it is powered off, but the data will never be lost unless the memory is physically damaged. Nonvolatile memory can come in many forms and shapes. The most common types of nonvolatile memory are hard disks, SSDs, DVDs, Blu-ray discs, external hard disks, and USB flash drives.

Peripheral Devices That Can Be Connected to a Computer

Previously we listed the internal hardware components of a computer. There are also external hardware components that can be connected to the computer; see Figure 2.1. These are called *peripherals*. Here are the types of peripherals you can connect to a computer.

Monitor   This is the visual display for the computer. It takes the data sent by the graphics card and displays it to the user. On small devices like laptops, tablets, and smartphones, the monitor is built into the device, and therefore it is not considered a peripheral but an internal hardware component of that device. Modern devices like tablets and smartphones have more evolved displays that include sensors for touch gestures. They are called touchscreens. Users can use the touchscreen to react to what is displayed and control how it is displayed. Touchscreens generally replace mice and keyboards.

FIGURE 2.1   A desktop computer and several peripherals that are connected to it: printer, scanner, and projector

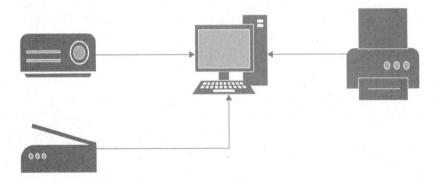

Mouse   A mouse is a pointing device that detects motion relative to the surface you place it on. This motion is translated into a pointer that is shown on the display of your computer. The pointer can be used to control what is displayed and how it is displayed.

Keyboard   This device is similar to a typewriter. It has characters engraved or printed on its keys, and each press of a key corresponds to the single written symbol on top of it. It is the most commonly used device for providing data input to computers.

Speakers   Speakers produce the sound in response to the data sent by the sound card of a computer.

Microphone   This device converts the sound in air into an electrical signal that can be sent to the sound card and later on processed and used by the computer.

Webcam   A webcam is a video camera that takes the image in real time and sends it to the computer that it is connected to. The resulting video can be viewed, saved, streamed, or sent to others. Webcams generally include a microphone so that they can record both the sound and the image from their area.

Printer   This is a device that prints graphics or text on paper and other similar media.

Scanner   This device optically scans images, printed text, and handwriting and converts it to a digital image. It is the opposite of a printer: whereas the printer takes digital input and turns it into physical output like text on paper, the scanner takes the physical input (the text on paper) and turns it into a digital image.

Flash Drives   These devices use nonvolatile flash memory (a type of memory that can be erased and reprogrammed with electrical signals) for storing data. They are similar to SSDs when it comes to the types of memory used for storage, but they have less advanced circuitry, chips, and so on. The most common examples of flash drives are the USB flash drive and the Secure Digital (SD) cards. USB flash drives are plugged into a computer via USB ports, and they are used to easily store and carry data between computers. They are used for the same purposes as a DVD or Blu-ray disc. SD cards are used in the same ways as USB flash drives. However, they are smaller in size and are optimized for use in portable devices like smartphones, digital cameras, and tablets.

Stylus   This device is used to assist in navigating or providing more precision when using touchscreens. A stylus generally looks like a pen. They are especially useful with smaller screens or touchscreens that have less precision and sensitivity. You can use a stylus to accurately navigate through menus and windows, send messages, and write on your touch screen.

Projector   This optical device projects the images it receives from your computer onto a surface like walls or projection screens.

Peripherals complement the internal hardware of a computer. For example, you can do more with a sound card if you have a microphone connected to it. Some peripherals are also mandatory in order to use a computer. For example, if you have a desktop computer, you must have a monitor attached to it in order to view the image. The mouse and keyboard are also mandatory on a desktop computer because without them you cannot control the computer.

On the other hand, laptops have a monitor built in and do not need an external monitor in order to be used successfully. Also, mobile devices like tablets and smartphones don't need a mouse and keyboard because they have touchscreens that use touch input from the user to control those devices.

 Real World Scenario

Peripherals vs. Internal Hardware Components

With each new generation of mobile devices, more and more hardware components get included in each device. For example, in classic desktop computers, the monitor is a peripheral because it is not inside the computer case. In a smartphone, the monitor is included in the device itself and is no longer a peripheral. It is a core part of the device. Also, the display of a smartphone includes touch sensors that allow you to control it with your fingers. As a result, you don't need a mouse and keyboard like you do to control a desktop computer. Speakers and microphones are also an internal part of more computers and devices. This trend will only continue with time. You will see even more devices that move from being an external peripheral to an integral hardware component of a computer or device.

Peripherals are generally split in two types:

Input Devices   These peripherals are used to provide data and control commands to the computer they are connected to. For example, the keyboard is an input device because you use it to enter text and send commands to the computer. The mouse is an input device because you use it to control what is displayed on the screen. The scanner is another input device that takes images, printed text, and handwriting and converts it to a digital image. Other examples of input devices are the webcam, the stylus, and the microphone.

Output Devices   These peripherals are used to communicate the outcome of the data processing that was carried out by the computer to the user. The monitor is an output device because it displays the image on the screen, based on the commands sent by the user. Other examples of output devices are the speakers, the printer, and the projector.

Some peripherals can be both input and output devices. For example, there are multifunctional printers that are both a printer and a scanner, and you can use them for inputting data to the computer through the use of the scanner and outputting data from it through the use of the printer. Let's go through Exercise 2.1 and help you identify input and output devices, based on the definitions that were shared earlier.

EXERCISE 2.1

Separating Output Devices from Input Devices

Beside each entry write either "Input" or "Output" to denote the type of device:

1. Printer

2. Scanners

3. Speakers

4. Mouse

5. Multifunctional printer

The answers to Exercises 2.1, 2.2, and 2.3 are found at the end of this chapter before the summary.

The Most Common Types of Computers and Devices

Computers and devices now have increasingly different forms and properties; see Figure 2.2. Some are big, powerful, less mobile, and less power efficient. Others are more power efficient and mobile while being less powerful in terms of performance. In general, we use the following types of devices:

Desktop Computers   A desktop computer is a personal computer that it is intended to be used at a single location, usually on a desk or a table. Desktop computers generally require many peripherals like a monitor, a keyboard and mouse, speakers, and more. Also, they need an external power source in order to function. Their components are generally placed in a case that is an upright tower or horizontal desktop. Performance-wise, desktop computers tend to be more powerful than laptops and other mobile devices, but they have higher energy requirements.

Servers   A server is a specialized business computer that is intended to be used at a single controlled location. Servers generally have powerful hardware (like faster processors, increased storage capacity, and so on), and they require more energy than other types of computers. They are run using special software that provides services to other computers on a network.

A server can be used to store data from a company's network, manage users, manage printers, and so on. There are print servers, data servers, email servers, and more. An enterprise generally uses one or more servers to manage a domain, which allows network administrators to manage hundreds or thousands of users and their data effectively.

Laptops   A laptop is a portable computer that is suitable for mobile use. Laptops, sometimes called *notebook* computers, include a display, speakers, a keyboard, and a pointing device combined into a single unit. Most modern laptops also come with an integrated webcam and microphone. Laptops can be powered by using a built-in rechargeable battery as well as an external power supply. They are easy to carry around and can be used in many locations and on different surfaces.

FIGURE 2.2   A desktop computer on the left and a laptop on the right

Tablets   A tablet is a mobile computer with the display, its battery, and all its other components in a single unit. They may include physical buttons (like On/Off and/or volume switches), but they do not always include an external keyboard, although a virtual keyboard is included in the operating system. You control them by using your fingers or a stylus to touch their display. Tablets are highly mobile devices due to their small size, energy efficiency, and long battery life.

Hybrid Devices   These are newer types of devices that combine the properties of two different devices. They are growing both in the number of devices available and in popularity. One example of hybrid devices is all-in-ones: desktop computers that integrate all their hardware components in the same case as the display. Also, the screen can include touch sensors, making it easy to control with your fingers. Such devices are more mobile than traditional desktop computers, and they require less space.

Another example of hybrid devices is convertibles. They are mobile devices that generally mix the properties of a tablet with those of a laptop. For example, Microsoft Surface devices are tablets to which you can magnetically attach a keyboard. They also have a kickstand, which allows you to place them on your desk and use them as laptops. However, when you are on the go, you can detach the keyboard and use the device as a tablet.

Smartphones   Smartphones are mobile phones with advanced computing capabilities. They combine the features of a computer with those of a mobile phone. Just like a computer, they have an operating system installed, and you can install applications (which are called apps). You can use them to browse the Internet, take pictures, view documents, and so on. You can also use them to call other people or send them text messages. Some smartphones are nearly large enough to double as a tablet, such as Apple's iPhone 6 Plus.

An average person may own and use a reasonably large number of devices. You may have a smartphone to keep in touch with others while on the go, a desktop computer at home with a large monitor so that you can have fun with your family, and a laptop at work that you also take with you on business trips.

In Exercise 2.2 we will ask you to distinguish between examples of operating systems, applications, and types of computers.

EXERCISE 2.2

Distinguishing among the Operating System, Applications, and Types of Computers

Specify the category of each of the following items. Choose from Operating System, Application, or Type of Computer:

1. Windows 7

2. Laptop

3. Microsoft Office

4. Android

5. Server

When purchasing a new computer or device, you should take into consideration its price, its performance, and how well it meets your needs. But before you do that, you need to know how information flows inside a computer and how you can evaluate the performance of the devices that you are considering.

How Information Is Transmitted inside a Computer

Computers are electronic devices, and they can interpret and produce only two kinds of input: on or off. Like electricity traveling through a light switch, which is either a complete circuit (light is on) or a broken circuit (light is off), data and instructions are transmitted in the same manner through a computer, via electrical circuits found on the computer's motherboard. Because of that, data must be offered to the computer with only two types of symbols to represent it. Those symbols are 1 and 0: 1 is on; 0 is off. These are called *bits*.

Each 1 and each 0 is a single bit. A bit is the smallest unit of storage. A bit isn't anything on its own, but when you combine 8 bits, you get a *byte*, and a byte is something much more important. In fact, 1 byte can represent a letter, such as A, B, C, or D. If you think about spelling out a single word, then you can imagine that several bytes are created to represent that word.

So, moving on from a single byte, note the following:

- A kilobyte (KB) is 1,024 bytes (2^{10}).
- A megabyte (MB) is 1,024 kilobytes.
- A gigabyte (GB) is 1,024 megabytes.
- A terabyte (TB) is 1,024 gigabytes.
- A petabyte (PB) is 1,024 terabytes.

To get an idea of how much data these entries represent, consider that a CD holds about 700 MB of data, which is around 80 minutes of music or 60 minutes of video. Seven minutes of high-definition television (HDTV) video is about 1 GB of data; 100,000 digital pictures taken with a 6-megapixel camera comes to about 500 GB.

To help you remember all these units of measure and the differences between them, let's go through Exercise 2.3.

EXERCISE 2.3

Converting Bits and Bytes

Fill in the blanks:

1. A byte = _____ bits.

2. A kilobyte = _____ bytes.

3. A terabyte = _____ gigabytes.

How to Evaluate the Performance of a Computer or Device

In order to evaluate the performance of any computer or device, you first need to know its most important characteristics and understand what they mean. For example, when buying a new computer or laptop, you will encounter terms like *number of cores*, *processor speed*, *storage space*, and so on. If you don't know what these terms mean, you won't have an idea of how well the device will perform and whether it will meet your needs.

Let's take the most important components of a computer and discuss their most important properties:

The Processor (CPU)   Most computer manufacturers mention the speed of the processor using a unit of measure named *hertz* (Hz). A hertz is one computing cycle per second. A cycle is described as one computer instruction; 100 Hz means 100 cycles per second or 100 computer instructions. Modern computers have really fast processors, and they can run millions of cycles per second. To make it easier to express their speed, multiples are used: KHz (kilohertz, 10^3 Hz), MHz (megahertz, 10^6 Hz), and GHz (gigahertz, 10^9 Hz). The most common multiplier used when expressing a processor's speed is GHz; 1 GHz means one billion hertz. The bigger the number of gigahertzes, the faster the processor is.

Early processors had one physical computing component named core. Since the early 2000s, processors started including more than one core. Because of the improvements in the technology used to build processors, manufacturers can now add more cores into a processor without making it bigger in size. Therefore, we have dual-core, quad-core, hexa-core, and eight-core processors and so on. Each core has the same speed as the others (measured in hertz), and each core can process its own computer instructions in parallel with the other cores. Therefore, the more cores available, the higher the performance of that processor.

RAM   When referring to the random-access memory of a computer, one of the most important properties is how much is physically installed. The more RAM you have, the greater the amount of data that can be stored in it. You will often see RAM described using GBs; a computer might have 2 GB, 4 GB, 8 GB, or more of installed RAM. When a computer has 8 GB of RAM, it means that it can fill up to 8 GB of data in the RAM to perform calculations. The more RAM you have, the better your computer will perform.

Hard Drive   The amount of storage space is also measured in bytes. Modern computers tend to have large hard drives with lots of storage space. It is very common to have a hard disk in your computer with 500 GB of storage space or even 1 TB. However, if you are using an SSD inside a computer, it will most probably have a smaller amount of storage space, due to the fact that SSDs are more expensive to manufacture than traditional hard disks. That's why you will often see SSDs having only 64 GB or 128 GB of storage space.

Display Size   One of the most important properties of a monitor is its size. This is described by the length of its diagonal, which is the distance between opposite corners. This distance is measured in inches. The size of the display differs from device to device. For example, a tablet may be 9 or 10 inches in diagonal, a laptop may have a screen with a diagonal from 11 inches to 17 inches, while a desktop computer may have a screen with a 24-inch diagonal.

Obviously these are not the only properties of a computer; there many other characteristics that you can use to get an idea of what it has to offer. For example, weight is an important factor when choosing a mobile device like a laptop or a tablet. If you buy a desktop computer, you may want one with a powerful graphics card and so on.

You can get a better view of the performance delivered by a computer by using the operating system and the information shared by tools like Task Manager or the Windows Experience Index. For example, you can use Task Manager to see how your computer's resources are currently being used and if there are any bottlenecks, as explained in Exercise 2.4.

EXERCISE 2.4

Determining the Available Hardware Resources Using Task Manager

1. In Windows 7, open Task Manager by pressing Ctrl+Alt+Esc on your keyboard.

2. Click the Performance tab and wait for a couple of seconds (Figure 2.3).

FIGURE 2.3   The Performance tab in Task Manager

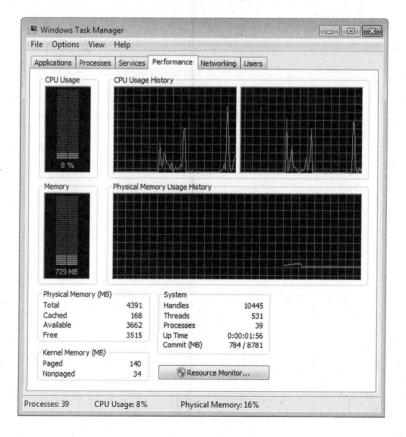

3. Look at the CPU Usage graph to learn how much of the CPU processing power is currently being used.

4. Look at the CPU Usage History graph to learn how much of your CPU's processing power was used in the last couple of minutes. If you are using a computer that has a CPU with multiple cores, you will see an individual graph for each core.

5. Look at the Memory graph to learn how much RAM is in use.

6. Look at the Physical Memory Usage History graph to learn how much RAM was used in the last couple of minutes.

7. Close Task Manager by clicking the X in the top-right corner of the window.

Another tool that you can use to interpret the performance that is delivered by a Windows computer or device is the Windows Experience Index, as explained in Exercise 2.5. This is Microsoft's measurement of how well a computer can run Windows. A computer with a base score of 2.0 has the ability to run general computing tasks, but it would not be powerful enough to run advanced multimedia features in Windows 7 or Windows 8. A computer with a base score of 3.0 can run many Windows features at a basic level, but it might have issues running higher-level functions, such as playing high-definition content. Most computers running Windows 7 should have a score of at least 4. A score of 7 and above generally means a higher-end computer with powerful hardware.

To calculate a computer's Windows Experience Index score, Windows rates certain components and gives them a subscore. Those components are defined by the following areas:

Processor   Calculations per second

Memory (RAM)   Memory operations per second

Graphics   Desktop graphics performance for Windows features

Gaming Graphics   The performance delivered when running games that are demanding from a visual perspective or when running image-editing applications

Primary Hard Disk   Disk data transfer rate for the hard disk where the operating system is installed

The base performance score of your computer is the lowest subscore in any of the areas just mentioned. For example, if your computer has a processor subscore of 7 and a graphics subscore of 3, the base performance score will be 3 and not the average of all the individual subscores. These subscores will help you identify which hardware component is the weakest part of your computer. You may use this information when deciding which component is worth replacing with a better one. For example, there's no point in changing the processor if the primary hard disk is the component receiving a very low subscore.

EXERCISE 2.5

Determining the Windows Experience Index of Your Computer

1. Click Start and then Control Panel.

2. Click System And Security and then System (Figure 2.4).

FIGURE 2.4   The System And Security section in Control Panel

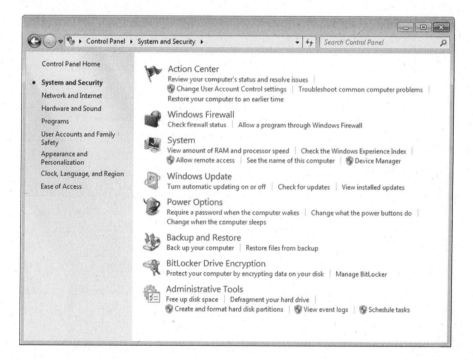

3. In the System window, look for the Rating line in the System section. There you will see the base score for your computer (Figure 2.5).

4. Click the Windows Experience Index link to see a list with all the individual subscores for each component.

5. Note the component with the highest subscore and the one with the lowest (Figure 2.6).

FIGURE 2.5 The System panel

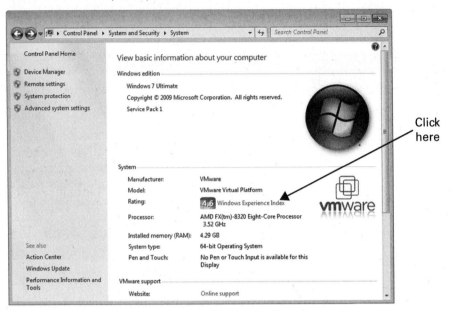

Click here

FIGURE 2.6 The Performance Information And Tools window

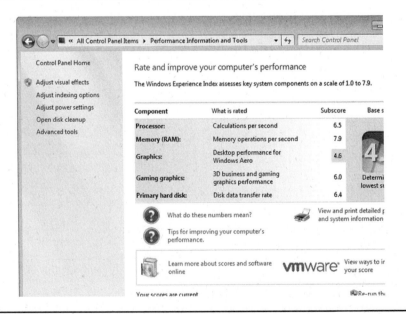

Answers to Exercises 2.1–2.3

Answers to Exercise 2.1
1. Output
2. Input
3. Output
4. Input
5. Input and output

Answers to Exercise 2.2
1. Operating system
2. Type of computer
3. Application
4. Operating system
5. Type of computer

Answers to Exercise 2.3
1. 8
2. 1024
3. 1024

Summary

There are many different types of computers (servers, laptops, tablets, and so on), and each has several internal hardware components that allow it to work. You can't have a computer without a motherboard, a processor, RAM, a hard disk, and so on. Also, external hardware devices can be connected to a computer to allow you to do more with it. For example, connecting a printer to your computer allows you to print your work on a piece of paper, which wouldn't be possible otherwise.

Every piece of hardware has its own unique properties, and some hardware is faster than other hardware, or can store more data, and so on. The sum of the properties of each hardware device that makes up a computer determines its overall performance and what you can do with it. That's why, before purchasing a new computer or device, it is recommended that you look at its most important properties in order to understand if it offers what you need.

Now that you understand the basics about software and hardware in a computer, in the next chapter we will start to go more in depth about software, how to install and uninstall various kinds of software, the licensing models used for software, and the most important types of software applications that you can use to do your work.

Exam Essentials

Understand the role of each hardware component.   Make sure you know what hardware is used for what type of task so that you have a good understanding of how computers work. Know that the CPU is for processing computer instructions, RAM is for storing data temporarily, and the hard disk is for storing data in the long term.

Understand the difference between peripherals and internal hardware.   Know what kinds of devices are considered peripherals, what they do, and how they expand what a computer can do. You should also know the difference between input and output devices and be able to distinguish the type of each commonly used peripheral device.

Know the units of measurement used with hardware.   Learn what a bit is, what a byte is, and the various extensions of these (MB, GB, and so on). Be able to convert, or at least state, how many bits are in a byte and perform similar conversions.

Understand the most important properties for the most important components that make up a device.   Learn how processor speed is measured and how the number of cores available impacts performance. Know how storage space is measured as well as the amount of available RAM. Also, you should know how the display size is measured.

Know how to evaluate performance.   Task Manager can help you understand how your computer's hardware resources are used and how many resources are available. The Windows Experience Index will help you evaluate the overall performance of your system and identify the components that have lower performance than others.

Key Terms

Before you take the exam, be certain you are familiar with the following terms:

Blu-ray drive	Mouse
Computer cooling	Network card
CPU	Power supply unit
Desktop computers	Printer
Disk storage	Processor

DVD drive

Flash drives

Graphics card

Hybrid devices

Keyboard

Laptops

Microphone

Monitor

Motherboard

RAM

Scanner

Servers

Smartphones

Sound card

Speakers

Stylus

Tablets

Webcam

Review Questions

1. Which of these are considered internal hardware? (Choose all that apply.)

    A. RAM

    B. Mouse

    C. CPU

    D. Printer

2. Which of these types of memory are nonvolatile? (Choose all that apply.)

    A. SSD

    B. RAM

    C. DVD

    D. USB flash drive

3. Which of these hardware components are peripherals for a desktop computer? (Choose all that apply.)

    A. SSD

    B. Speakers

    C. Webcam

    D. Sound card

4. Which of these devices are considered output devices? (Choose all that apply.)

    A. Monitor

    B. Speakers

    C. Microphone

    D. Keyboard

5. Which type of computer has very powerful hardware and is used to provide specialized services to other computers on the network?

    A. Laptop

    B. Tablet

    C. Smartphone

    D. Server

6. How are bits related to bytes?

    A. 1 bit = 8 bytes

    B. 1 byte = 8 bits

    C. 1 bit = 2 bytes

    D. 1 bit = 24 bytes

7. What can you represent with a single byte?

     A. A letter like A or Z

     B. A single picture

     C. A single video

     D. You can't represent anything with a single byte. You have to group 8 bytes together to represent something.

8. What unit of measurement is generally used to denote the amount of RAM installed in a computer?

     A. GHz

     B. MB

     C. GB

     D. MHz

9. You want to use Task Manager to view RAM usage and usage history. What tab in Task Manager offers a graph that details this?

     A. Processes

     B. Services

     C. Resource Monitor

     D. Performance

10. What does 1 hertz stand for when measuring a processor's speed?

     A. One bit per second

     B. One computer instruction per second

     C. One computer instruction per minute

     D. One computing cycle per minute

Chapter 3

Understanding Software

THE FOLLOWING IC3 GS4: COMPUTER FUNDAMENTALS EXAM OBJECTIVES ARE COVERED IN THIS CHAPTER:

✓ **Software Management**

- Describe how to install, uninstall and reinstall various kinds of software, including application software, drivers and system software, upgrades and patches, on various types of personal computers and configure the environment for use.

✓ **Licensing**

- Understand the various licensing models used for computer software such as operating systems, application programs, system software, databases, browsers, etc. Freeware, shareware, open-source, premium applications.

- Demonstrate an understanding of the legal and ethical obligations associated with EULAs and the user's responsibilities, commitments, and benefits that can be derived by entering into a typical computer industry EULA.

- Demonstrate an understanding of the concept of a single seat and site License options, how each party benefits, restrictions, obligations, etc.

✓ **Software Usage**

- Describe the dependencies and constraints that exist between hardware and software operation.

- Demonstrate an understanding of the similarities and differences between a basic, consumer-level relational database management system and a typical spreadsheet program, including an understanding of which situations would be better suited to which product.

- Describe what desktop publishing is, how and when desktop publishing software should be used, and the general feature set included in a representative desktop publishing program.

- Describe what a Presentation program is, its purpose, how it is used, and the general feature set included in a typical consumer-level presentation program.

- Demonstrate how to use templates, default settings, and quick start aids to rapidly generate usable application user data.

- Describe the purpose and use of a personal computer-based entertainment program. List the features that could be expected to be found in such a program and explain how they work.

✓ Software Tools

- Explain what file compression is and how it works with various file types.

- Explain how files are stored on a Hard Disk. Demonstrate how to organize, compress, defragment, and otherwise optimize a computer's hard disk performance.

- Explain the danger posed by viruses and malware and how virus and malware scanning software work. List several common/popular brands and types of virus and malware scanning software.

In order to use a computer or device as productively as possible, you shouldn't stick to using only the operating system and the tools and applications that are built into the system. You should consider installing other kinds of software applications that allow you to do many things ranging from creating documents and presentations to doing your work and to having fun.

When dealing with software applications, you should first understand what requirements they have and how to install them and remove them when you no longer need them. We will start this chapter by explaining the concept of system requirements and demonstrating how to install and remove applications in Windows 7.

When installing software applications, you will often encounter a step where you have to accept the license agreement, which is the contract between you as the user and the publisher of the software that you are installing. There are many types of software license agreements, and each has its rights and limitations for the user. We will discuss the most important types of licenses and how they affect your use of the software that you are installing.

Then we will move on and discuss the most common types of software applications that you are likely to install on your computer and share what you can do with them.

Finally, we will discuss common software tools like file-compression applications, tools that can optimize your computer's performance, and applications that can help you keep it safe from digital threats like computer viruses.

The Dependencies between Hardware and Software

In order to be used efficiently, software needs certain hardware components or other software resources to be present on the computer or device where you want to use it, prerequisites that are called system requirements. They are often shared by the publisher of the software you are using and serve as a guideline. Some software, especially computer games, has two sets of system requirements: minimum and recommended. The minimum system requirements are the minimum hardware and software components you should have in order to run that software, even though its performance and responsiveness might not be great. The recommended software requirements are what you need in order to run that software with optimal performance and responsiveness.

The most important system requirements are those of the operating system that you want to use. Any operating system needs to be installed on a computer or device with a minimum hardware configuration that allows it to run correctly. For example, Microsoft says that Windows 7 needs at least the following:

- A computer with a processor running at 1 GHz
- 1 GB of RAM
- 16 GB of free space on its hard disk

Obviously, if your computer has a faster processor, more RAM, or more free space on its hard disk, Windows 7 will run faster and better.

Applications also have system requirements that must be met in order to run. For example, Microsoft Office 2010 has the following hardware requirements:

- A processor running at 500 MHz, with 256 MB of RAM
- 3 GB of free space on your hard disk
- A computer display with a minimum resolution of 1024 × 768 pixels

Applications might have software requirements as well. For example, Microsoft Office 2010 works only when using the following operating systems:

- Windows Vista
- Windows 7
- Windows 8
- Windows 8.1

Microsoft Office 2010 doesn't work on older Windows versions like Windows XP, which was discontinued by Microsoft.

The same goes for mobile apps. For example, if you have an Android smartphone, some apps will work only with the latest version of Android and not with older versions. Other apps may require your device to have at least 512 MB of RAM, while others (especially mobile games) may require several gigabytes of free space in order for you to download, install, and use them.

Before purchasing and installing any software, it is best to check its system requirements and consider whether your computer or other device meets them. If it meets the minimum hardware and software configuration that's requested by the publisher, then it is OK to use that software. If it doesn't, then you should reconsider.

Installing, Removing, or Reinstalling Software

In order to take full advantage of your computer and use it for as many things as possible, you will need to install many kinds of software on it:

Applications   Software that you install in order to perform specialized tasks. For example, if you want to create documents or presentations, you will want to install Microsoft Office or LibreOffice. If you are a graphic designer, you may need to install advanced photo-editing applications like Adobe Photoshop.

Drivers   Software that operates and controls particular hardware devices connected to your computer. Drivers ensure that your operating system takes full advantage of your hardware. Operating systems come with generic drivers, but for full access, you often need specific drivers.

For example, if you install the driver for your computer's video card, Windows will be able to identify it correctly and fully use all its features. Either drivers are installed automatically by Windows for the hardware components it identifies and knows or you need to install them separately, just like any other program. Generally, many components bundle a disc with drivers that you can use when installing them on your computer.

Installing any Windows application is generally a quick and simple process. The steps involved are similar from application to application, and their flow is generally the same:

1.   You start the setup program and confirm that you want to install the application.

2.   You select whether you want a quick installation or a slower custom installation.

     It is better to go for the lengthier, custom installation process because you can control where the application is installed, which shortcuts are installed, and what features are enabled, and you can prevent unwanted things from being installed or activated on your computer.

3.   Commercial applications that cost money generally ask you to enter an activation code or serial number that proves that you have purchased them from a legitimate source.

4.   You select the folder where you want to install the application and which features and modules you want installed.

5.   The installation is performed. The process takes longer for larger applications with lots of files. A smaller application like a web browser generally installs itself in seconds.

6.   Once the setup program finishes the installation, you close it, and you can then use the application.

The way the setup program looks is different from application to application, and the steps involved may not always be in the same order as mentioned here. However, the basic principles are the same when installing all applications.

Installing drivers for your hardware components is very similar to installing applications. The only difference is that the setup program includes fewer steps and offers fewer customization options. Also, you may be asked to restart your computer so that the operating system can load the driver and use it to manage the hardware component it was made for. When downloading a driver, you need to pay attention and make sure that you download the driver that's appropriate for your specific hardware component. You must download and install the driver that was created by the manufacturer of the hardware component you are using and for its exact model name and number.

 Real World Scenario

Things to Pay Attention to When Installing Free Software Applications

When installing a free software application, it is very important that you go for a lengthier custom installation process in which you pay attention to all the details that are displayed. That's because it is very likely that the developers of that free application will try to take advantage of your installation to make some money. There are two common methods that they could use for monetizing their free applications:

- They display ads that run during the installation, encouraging you to download other applications. In Figure 3.1, you can see an example of an ad that is displayed when installing a popular application named KMPlayer. If you click the link for PandoraTV, you will be taken to a web page from which you can download and install the application recommended by that ad.

FIGURE 3.1   The installation for the popular KMPlayer application

- They recommend that you install software applications made by other companies, which you may not need or want. For example, the popular avast! free antivirus software recommends that you install both Google Chrome and the Google Toolbar, as shown in Figure 3.2. If you do not pay attention and you do not uncheck the two boxes that allow the installation of these two additional applications, you will end up installing three software applications instead of just one.

FIGURE 3.2   The installation for avast! free antivirus

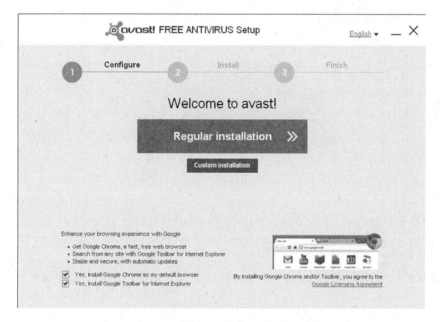

- Such practices are so widespread that if you automatically choose the quick installations, you will end up with all kinds of applications you don't want or need. These additional programs lower your computer's responsiveness and performance. Some of these additional programs may also expose your computer to security risks.

To help you get a better understanding of the steps involved when installing an application, work through Exercise 3.1 and install a popular free Internet browser, Mozilla Firefox.

EXERCISE 3.1

Installing an Application Like Mozilla Firefox

1. Download Mozilla Firefox from https://www.mozilla.org/.

   You will download an executable setup file that includes the words *Firefox Setup* in its name.

2. Open Windows Explorer and navigate to where you have downloaded the Firefox Setup file and double-click it. Generally you will find it in the Downloads folder.

3. In order to do a custom installation, click Options, as shown in Figure 3.3.

FIGURE 3.3   The Mozilla Firefox installation program

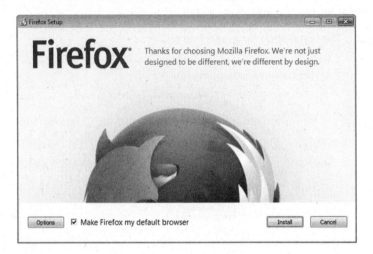

You can now choose the shortcuts that are created for Firefox, select the destination folder where Firefox is installed, and configure the settings that control how it works.

4. Customize the installation as you prefer and click Install, as shown in Figure 3.4.

FIGURE 3.4   Customizing the Mozilla Firefox installation

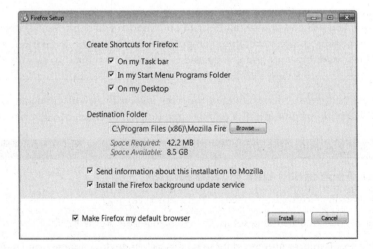

5. Wait for the Firefox Setup to download and install the necessary files.

6. When the installation is complete, you are asked whether you want to import settings and data from other installed browsers. Select Don't Import Anything and click Next (Figure 3.5).

FIGURE 3.5   The Mozilla Firefox Import Wizard

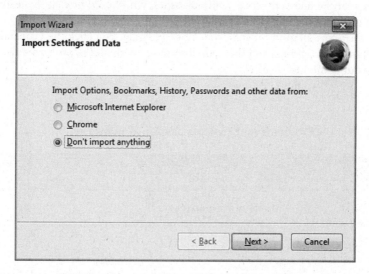

Firefox is now started, and you can start using it. Most probably you will also be asked whether you want Firefox to be set as your default browser (Figure 3.6).

FIGURE 3.6   The Mozilla Firefox browser

7. Answer whether you would like to make it your default browser and then close the Mozilla Firefox window.

Removing an application from your computer is somewhat similar to installing it. The steps involved are almost the same, but some options will be different from application to application. Also, the uninstall program will look different from application to application. To make sure that the uninstall works without issues, you should first close the application that you want to remove from your computer.

You start the uninstallation process from Control Panel. You click the Uninstall A Program link under Programs, and then you'll see a list with all the programs that are installed on your computer (Figure 3.7).

FIGURE 3.7   The Programs And Features panel in Windows

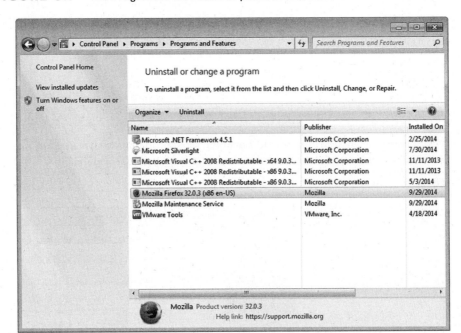

If you select each installed program one by one, you will notice that the toolbar at the top of the list displays different buttons for each application:

Uninstall   Triggers the uninstall program for the application that you have selected.

Change   Triggers the setup program that allows you to change how the selected application is installed on your computer (Figure 3.8).

Repair   Triggers the setup program that allows you to repair the selected application. A typical repair reinstalls the application and all its files and settings (Figure 3.9).

FIGURE 3.8   The Change button in the Programs And Features panel

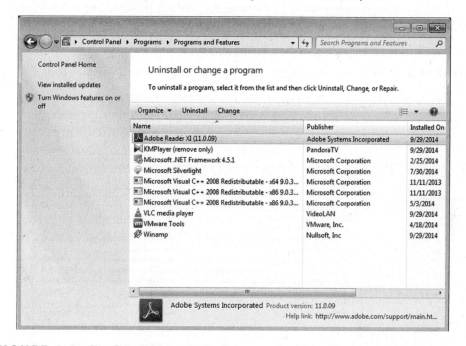

FIGURE 3.9   The Repair button in the Programs And Features panel

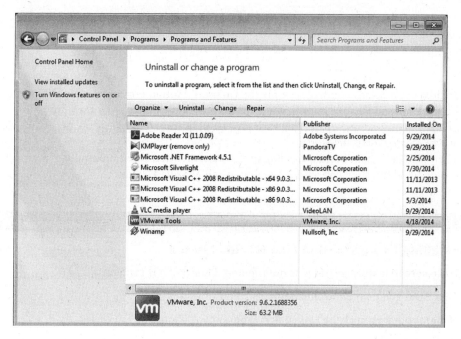

Uninstall/Change   Triggers the uninstall program for the application that you have selected, which allows you to remove it or change the way it is installed on your computer (Figure 3.10).

FIGURE 3.10   The Uninstall/Change button in the Programs And Features panel

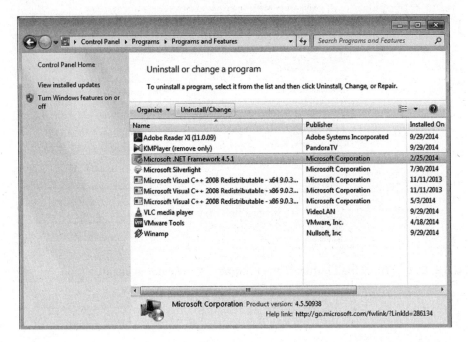

For most applications you will see only the Uninstall button. For some applications you will see the Uninstall/Change button, while for others you will see two or three buttons: Uninstall, Change, and/or Repair. This varies from application to application, depending on how it was created by its developer.

To help you get a better understanding of the steps involved when uninstalling an application, work through Exercise 3.2 and uninstall Mozilla Firefox.

EXERCISE 3.2

Uninstalling an Application Like Mozilla Firefox

1.   Make sure that Mozilla Firefox is not running. Close it if it is running.

2.   Click Start and then Control Panel.

3.   Under Programs, click the Uninstall A Program link (Figure 3.11).

FIGURE 3.11   Control Panel

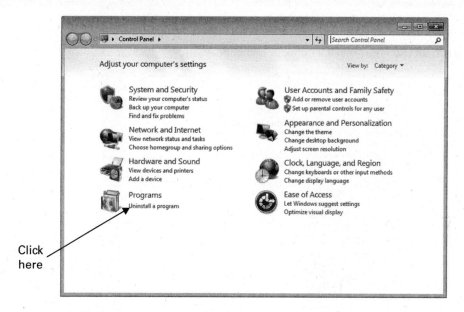

Click
here

4.   In the Programs And Features window, select Mozilla Firefox (Figure 3.12).

FIGURE 3.12   The Programs And Features panel

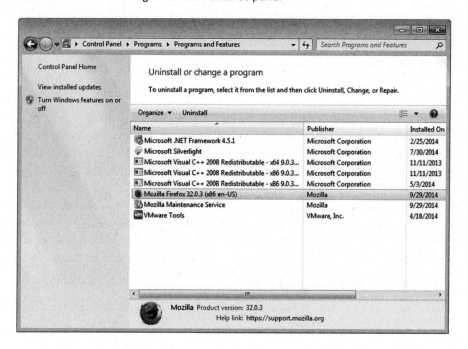

5. Click Uninstall. The Mozilla Firefox Uninstall Wizard is now started (Figure 3.13).

FIGURE 3.13 The Mozilla Firefox Uninstall Wizard

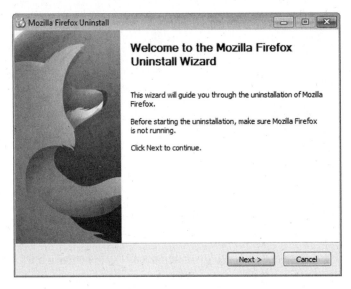

6. Click Next.

7. You are informed that Firefox will be uninstalled from the location where it is currently installed. Click Uninstall (Figure 3.14).

FIGURE 3.14 The Mozilla Firefox uninstall location

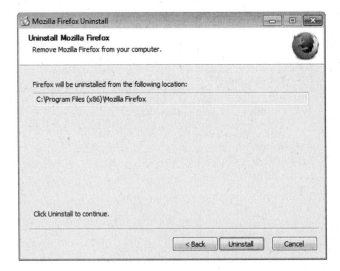

8. When you are informed that Mozilla Firefox has been uninstalled from your computer, click Finish (Figure 3.15).

FIGURE 3.15   Finalizing the Mozilla Firefox uninstall process

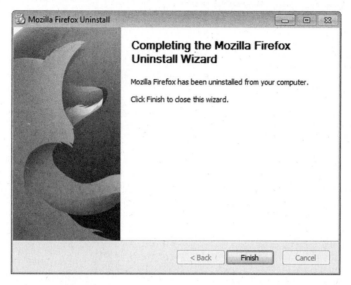

One thing you may notice when installing drivers for your computer's hardware components is that they tend not to be listed in the Programs And Features window from which you uninstall software applications. This is because once a driver is installed, it is best to leave it installed so that the operating system can use it. If a new version of a driver is available for a hardware component, you can simply install it and the old driver version will be automatically replaced by the newer version.

Software Licensing and Its Implications

Each time you install a software application or driver, you will go through a step that requires you to read and accept the end-user license agreement (EULA) or software license agreement. This step is mandatory when dealing with software installations because the *EULA* is the contract between the company that published the software you want to use and you, the user. The EULA communicates the license used by the application you are installing. It gives you the right to use the application in some manner while also stating the restrictions that are imposed by the software publisher. In the screen capture shown in Figure 3.16, you can see a portion of the EULA for the popular Winamp music player.

FIGURE 3.16   The Winamp license agreement

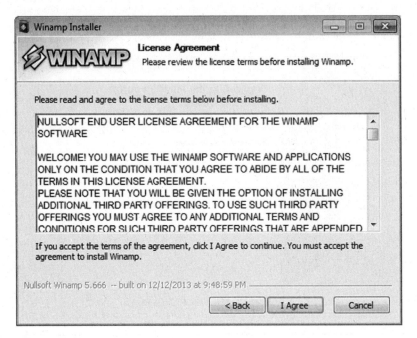

EULAs are not legally binding contracts. The software publisher seeks the user's agreement to its requirements prior to installing and using the software. When the user agrees to the specified terms, they are purchasing or renting a license from the software publisher. Without accepting the EULA, the user cannot install and use the software.

Does Anyone Read EULAs?

One of the most criticized aspects of end-user license agreements is the fact that they are often too long and users don't take time to read them. Sometimes they are also filled with legal jargon that may be hard to understand for a person without any legal background or studies. That's why most users blindly accept the EULA for the software they want to install and use, and they do not know their rights and limitations when using it.

An important caveat of EULAs is that they tend not to protect the user, only the software publisher that owns the copyright. Also, EULAs are not designed to be any kind of warranty. Most software sold at retail disclaims any warranty on the performance of the software and limits liability for any damages to the purchase price of the software.

When dealing with software license agreements, you will encounter three major types of licenses:

Proprietary Licenses   The software publisher grants the use of one or more copies of its software under the end-user license agreement, but the ownership of those copies remains with the software publisher. The user can use the software only under certain conditions and is restricted from modifying, sharing, or redistributing the software. Here are some of the most common restrictions that are imposed by proprietary licenses:

- Only a specific number of installations may be allowed per user. For example, the software may be licensed for use on only one computer, and the user may install it as many times they want on that computer. However, installing it on a second or third computer requires the purchase of another license. Retail versions of Microsoft Office generally have such restrictions.

- Only a specific number of users are allowed to use the software. Licenses that involve this type of restriction are called *per-seat licenses*. This type of licensing and restrictions is common for products used by specialized professionals in industrial settings: designers, chemists, biologists, researchers, and the like. For example, an institution may purchase a 10-seat license for a specialized software application, which means that a maximum of 10 users can use it. A user may be a person, another application, or a device accessing that application.

- Only a specific group of users can use the software. This type of licensing is typically applied to business, government, and educational institutions. An organization purchases a volume license or a site license of a software application. The organization is allowed to install the software in its sites or facilities, and the license restricts the use of that application to only the users who are part of that organization. The Windows operating system is generally licensed this way to organizations.

- The user can use the software for free for a limited time, and in order to continue using it, they must pay the license fee. This type of software is called *shareware*, and its purpose is to give potential users the opportunity to try out the application on a limited basis, for a limited time, and to judge its usefulness before purchasing a license for the full version. Once the free trial period has passed, the application may stop running until a license is purchased or may continue to run with limitations (for example, the inability to save your work) until a license is purchased. The most popular example of shareware is computer games. Many games have a shareware version that's available for free so that users can try it and see if they enjoy playing it before purchasing the full version.

- The user can use the software only after paying a subscription fee. It is sometimes referred to as software as a service (SaaS) or on-demand software. Many business applications are licensed this way as well as an increasing number of consumer applications. This type of licensing involves a monthly or annual subscription fee. When the subscription expires, the user has to renew it and pay another fee in order to continue using the software. The best known example of such software is Office 365, from Microsoft. Most proprietary licenses are perpetual, meaning that there is no time limitation involved when using the software. The advantage of subscription-based licensing is that the monthly or annual fee is a lot more affordable than traditional perpetual licenses. Users have to pay for software only for as long as they need to use it.

Proprietary licenses can combine multiple types of restrictions. For example, some software licensing may involve restrictions for both time and number of users. Other licensing may involve restrictions for both number of users and number of installations.

Freeware   This type of license doesn't involve any monetary cost for the user but restricts the usage rights in ways that are similar to proprietary licenses. For example, some freeware software is fully functional for an unlimited time but doesn't allow the user to modify it or redistribute it. Other freeware has only basic functions enabled, but fully functional versions are available commercially, under typical proprietary licenses. The software publisher may also restrict the user from copying, distributing, modifying, or making derivative works of that software. One of the most popular examples of freeware is the Google Chrome web browser.

Open-Source Licenses   Either these types of licenses have minimal requirements that affect how the software can be redistributed to other users or they don't involve monetary costs for their users or they preserve the freedoms that are given to the users. The most popular free software licenses are the following:

GPL (GNU General Public License)   This free software licensing guarantees end users the freedoms to use, study, share, and modify the software they are using. The most popular example of GPL software is the Linux operating system. Many distributions like Ubuntu Linux and Linux Mint are distributed using a GPL.

MIT License   This license originated at the Massachusetts Institute of Technology (MIT), and it permits reuse within proprietary software provided all copies of the licensed software include a copy of the MIT license terms and the copyright notice. Many software development tools are licensed using an MIT license.

🌐 Real World Scenario

Free Software vs. Commercial Software

There is a never-ending debate about whether people should use free and open-source software instead of commercial software with proprietary licenses. Unfortunately there is no clear-cut answer, and choosing the software that you want to use depends on a mix of factors like financial costs, the level of support you receive, the alternatives that you have, and so on.

Free and open-source software has the advantage that it doesn't require a direct monetary cost for the user in order to use it. Also, it tends to protect the user's rights a lot more than proprietary software, at least from a licensing perspective. Open-source software tends to adopt new trends and technologies faster than commercial software with proprietary licenses. Because open-source software is free, it means that it is developed by a community that's not interested in making money from the software but rather in developing the product as much as possible, as fast as possible. This is the reason why you will encounter many great open-source applications like the Mozilla Firefox web browser, many different versions and distributions of the Linux operating systems, or office applications like LibreOffice.

There are also disadvantages to using open-source products instead of proprietary software. For example, some open-source applications are of lower quality than proprietary alternatives because they are developed and maintained by a small number of people, with limited time and resources available. Large companies may develop higher-quality software because they can involve more people and resources in their software development process.

When using open-source software, there's no company responsible for the product that you are using. This means that if you encounter problems and issues, there's no company to go to and ask for help. You are dependent on the community that is developing that software, and it may or may not help you. This is generally a problem for business environments, and many companies prefer proprietary software for this reason.

Another argument against using open-source software, especially in business environments, is that while it doesn't incur monetary costs to install and use it, that doesn't mean that it is free. Because open-source software is not so widely used as proprietary software and it is generally developed by small communities of software developers, you may not have access to complete product documentation, training materials, or support services. Having all of these elements in place involves costs for the company, which sometimes may be higher than when using proprietary software.

As you can see, there is no right answer to which type of software you should use. Before making a decision, you must balance your needs as a user with the alternatives that are available and the costs involved when choosing one type of software versus another.

The Most Common Types of Office Applications

Whether you are at home or at work, in order to use your computer productively, you will need to install and use a suite of office applications. The most popular suite is Microsoft Office, and it includes a diverse number of applications, depending on the exact version you are using. Most office suites will include the following types of applications:

Word Processing Program   These applications allow users to compose, edit, format, and print written documents. Modern word processors permit the use of specific fonts, can perform spell checking and grammar checking, and include automatic text correction and other advanced features. The most popular examples of word processors for Windows are Microsoft Word (included in Microsoft Office) and Writer (included in LibreOffice).

Presentation Program   These applications allow users to display information in the form of a slide show. They permit users to insert formatted text, images, videos, and sound and arrange everything into a slide-show system to display this content. The most popular examples of presentation programs are Microsoft PowerPoint (included in Microsoft Office) and Impress (included in LibreOffice).

Desktop Publishing Application   These applications generate layouts and produce typographic-quality text and images that are comparable to traditional typography and printing. This type of application allows users to produce a wide variety of materials ranging from magazines to books to promotional posters. Some of the most popular desktop publishing applications are Adobe InDesign, CorelDraw, and Microsoft Publisher (included in some versions of Microsoft Office).

Spreadsheet Program   These applications can be used to organize, analyze, and store data in tabular form, using rows and columns. They are computerized simulations of paper accounting worksheets. Modern spreadsheet programs can have multiple interacting sheets filled with data and can display the data as text, numerals, or graphics. When using spreadsheet programs, it is very easy to perform mathematical, statistical, or financial operations. The most popular examples of spreadsheet programs are Microsoft Excel (included in Microsoft Office) and Calc (included in LibreOffice).

Database Management System   Any company will use one or more databases to collect and store data about its operations. Databases are organized collections of data. They are created to collect large quantities of information; in order to use the data in a meaningful way, a database management system is required. This system provides an interface between the users and the database. There are many types of databases and database management systems. Two examples of database management systems are Microsoft Access (included in most versions of Microsoft Office) and Base (included in LibreOffice).

Personal Information Manager   These are applications that function as a personal organizer. They allow users to store, organize, and share different types of personal information: documents, address books, significant calendar dates (birthdays, meetings, and appointments), reminders, email messages, fax communications, and more. The most popular application of this type is Microsoft Outlook (included in some versions of Microsoft Office).

Other suites of office applications may include applications for making diagrams and flowcharts (for example, Microsoft Visio, LibreOffice Draw) or for managing projects (for example, Microsoft Project).

 Real World Scenario

Databases vs. Spreadsheets—Which Is Best at What?

Although the tables in a database look similar to spreadsheets in the way they are organized, they are not the same, and they should be used for different purposes.

First of all, databases are used to store raw data, while spreadsheets are used to store formatted data. There is no need to format the information in a database table. In order to view the information from a database, you must create reports, which then display the data in a human-readable format. Spreadsheets are formatted during the data-entry process so that users can understand and use them as soon as they are created.

Databases are optimized for entering, storing, and managing large amounts of data. Doing the same with spreadsheets is unmanageable. Spreadsheets are best used when working with limited data sets that one person can easily manage.

Another important difference is that databases make it easy to maintain data, but doing the same with spreadsheets is difficult and requires lots of manual intervention.

One advantage of spreadsheets over databases is that spreadsheets allow quick analysis and the creation of what-if scenarios that simulate what will happen in different situations based on existing data. Such analysis can be done when working with databases, but it generally requires custom tools and reports that are built specifically for that database. Spreadsheets are created and optimized for performing quick analysis and calculations for all kinds of data sets.

Finally, databases allow multiple users to work with them at the same time and perform different tasks ranging from data entry to data maintenance and reporting. Although it is possible to work collaboratively on spreadsheets, it is a lot more difficult for concurrent users to use the same spreadsheet.

Using Templates to Get Started with an Application

Many applications offer a variety of predefined templates that allow you to be more productive and create needed documents, spreadsheets, or presentations faster than if you had started from scratch.

For example, Microsoft Excel has plenty of templates for creating things like budgets, inventories, invoices, reports, time sheets, and so on. You browse through the available choices, select the predefined template that you want to use, wait for it to download, and then start creating your spreadsheet. The great thing about templates is that they are preformatted and populated with standard fields of data. You just enter your own data, make some minor adjustments, and you are finished. You don't have to create everything from scratch.

The same goes for Microsoft Word, PowerPoint, and other applications in the Microsoft Office suite. To give you one last example, Microsoft Word has templates for things like agendas, cards, certificates, contracts, letters, job descriptions, memos, resumes, and so on.

To help you get a better understanding of templates and how they work, go through Exercise 3.3 and use a resume template in Microsoft Word to help you create your resume faster.

EXERCISE 3.3

Using a Template in Microsoft Word

1. Click Start and then All Programs.

2. Click Microsoft Office and then Microsoft Word 2010 (Figure 3.17).

3. In the Microsoft Word window, click File and then New. A list of all the available templates is now loaded.

4. Scroll down until you find Resumes And CVs and click it (Figure 3.18).

5. Click Basic Resumes and then double-click Chronological Resume (Traditional Design). The selected template is downloaded into Microsoft Word (Figure 3.19).

6. Scroll down the document, and notice how this template includes the necessary sections and fields for completing your resume.

7. Enter your personal data into the appropriate fields.

   The resume is organized and formatted for you (Figure 3.20).

8. Close Microsoft Word by clicking the small X on the top-right side of the window.

FIGURE 3.17   The Start menu

FIGURE 3.18   Creating new documents in Microsoft Word

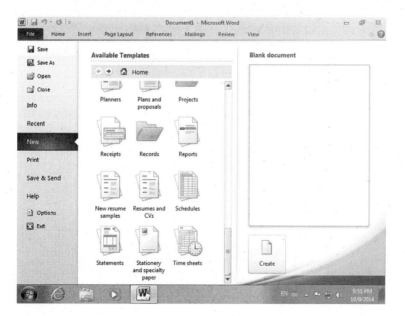

FIGURE 3.19 Choosing a template in Microsoft Word

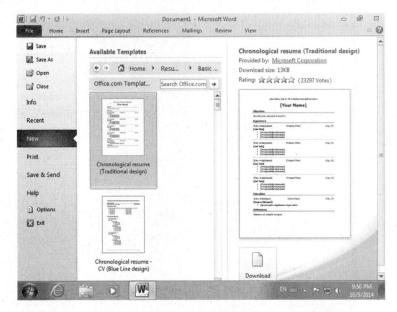

FIGURE 3.20 A new document in Microsoft Word

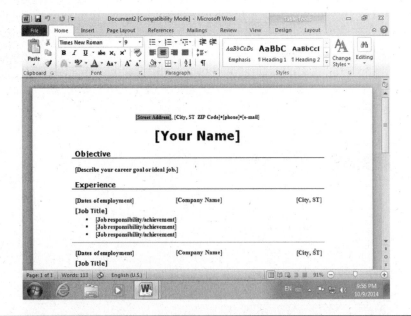

Personal Entertainment Applications

We use computers and devices not only to work but also to have fun. And having fun means different things to different people. That's why you will encounter lots of entertainment software of all kinds.

For example, if you want to listen to music or watch movies, you may want to use a media player like Winamp, Windows Media Player, or VLC Media Player. You may want to use your computer to view and record live television. You can do so by using programs like Windows Media Center.

Many people have fun playing games on their computers. That's why there are thousands of games developed each year. Yes, Windows does include some casual games like Solitaire, Chess, or Minesweeper, but you may want to play different games, including some with very advanced graphics. You can purchase and install all kinds of games as long as your computer meets their minimum system requirements.

Compressing Files to Save Space

When dealing with large files that take up a lot of disk space, it is a good idea to compress or archive those files so that they take fewer bits than in their original representation. Compression is useful because it helps reduce the space occupied on the hard disk as well as reduce the time it takes to transfer the file from a source to another.

There are two types of compression:

Lossless   Some data compression algorithms allow you to compress data without losing information, so you can easily return a file to its uncompressed state. There are many formats and file types for storing compressed data in a lossless way. For example, the PNG and BMP file formats are used for storing images in a compressed, lossless manner. When compressing files of diverse types, they are usually compressed into archives with formats like ZIP or RAR. However, compressing them into these formats requires specialized applications like 7-Zip, WinZip, or WinRAR.

Lossy   Such compression algorithms generally drop nonessential data from the source in order to save storage space. This type of compression reduces the file size using approximations of data, and the files are not reversible. However, the compressed file is close enough to the original to make this type of compression worth using. Lossy compression is generally used when working with multimedia files like pictures, videos, and music. For example, JPEG is the most popular lossy compression type for images that allows you to save a lot of space while still having an image that's close enough to the original that your eye won't notice the differences without analyzing it in detail. When working with audio files, MP3 is the most popular type of lossy compression, and when working with video, MPEG is the most popular.

When storing and transferring documents of all kinds, if you want to save space and make file transfers faster, it is a good idea to compress them into one or more archives with a popular format like ZIP. While creating such archives requires you to install specialized software like the popular 7-Zip, extracting their contents is easily done by Windows, without having to install any file-compression application. Exercise 3.4 shares how to extract the contents of any archive in Windows 7. In order to complete this exercise, please download the documents.zip practice file to your computer.

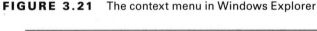

EXERCISE 3.4

Extracting the Contents of a ZIP File Archive

1. Navigate to the location of the documents.zip file that you want to extract.

2. Right-click that file and then click Extract All (Figure 3.21). The Extract Compressed (Zipped) Folders Wizard appears.

FIGURE 3.21   The context menu in Windows Explorer

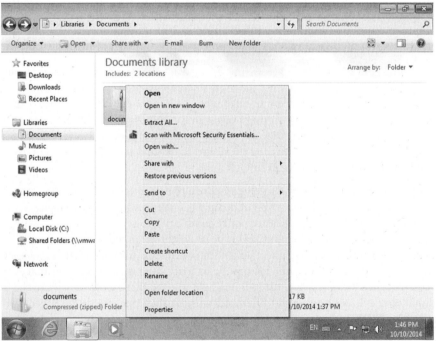

3. Click Extract (Figure 3.22).

The contents of the archive are extracted and shown. You can now use the files that were inside the archive and modify them as you wish.

FIGURE 3.22   The Extract Compressed (Zipped) Folders Wizard

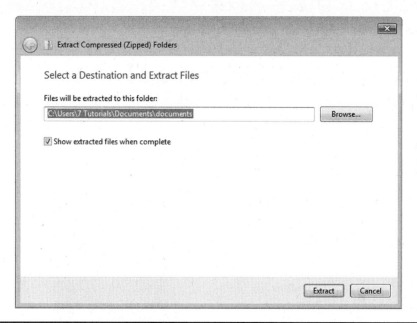

Optimizing Your Computer's Hard Disk Performance

When you use your computer, the operating system and your applications generate all kinds of temporary files that are stored in special folders designated for this task. For example, if you browse the Internet and visit several websites, your browser will copy temporary files like images and all kinds of data from those websites. If you work on a document in Microsoft Word, temporary copies of it are stored on the disk so that they can be used in case something goes wrong and you are in danger of losing your data. When installing Windows Updates or new applications, log files are created. You get the idea: when doing any kind of work on your computer, chances are that many temporary files and folders are created, for all kinds of purposes both by Windows and by your applications.

The trouble with these files is that some of them are never deleted from your computer so, as time goes by, you will have less disk space available. In order to help with this problem, Windows 7 includes an application named *Disk Cleanup*. With it, you can remove unnecessary files from your computer: temporary Internet files, deleted files from the Recycle Bin, setup log files, error reports, user file history, and so on. In Exercise 3.5 you will learn how to use it to clean up unnecessary files and save space on your hard disk.

EXERCISE 3.5

Freeing Up Disk Space with Disk Cleanup

1. Click Start and then All Programs.

2. Click Accessories ➢ System Tools ➢ Disk Cleanup (Figure 3.23).

   Disk Cleanup automatically scans your computer for files that can be deleted. When finished, it displays what it finds.

FIGURE 3.23   The Start menu

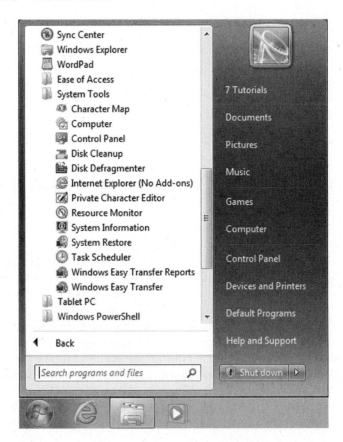

3.   Select the types of files that you want to delete and click OK (Figure 3.24).

You are asked to confirm that you are sure you want to permanently delete those files.

FIGURE 3.24   Disk Cleanup

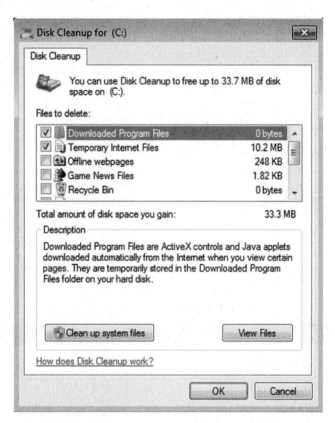

4.   Click Delete Files and wait for Disk Cleanup to remove them (Figure 3.25).

When finished, the Disk Cleanup application will close itself automatically.

FIGURE 3.25   Confirmation dialog for Disk Cleanup

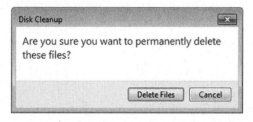

Another common issue with computers is in the way files are stored on traditional hard disks. Because of the way hard disks work, when you save a file on your computer, it is stored in a specific location on the hard disk. When you make changes to it, those changes end up being saved in a different physical place on the hard disk. This doesn't change where the file appears in Windows, only where the bits of information that make up the file are stored on the hard disk. As you work with more and more files, they get more and more fragmented. This fragmentation may degrade the performance of your computer. In order to help with this problem, Windows 7 includes an application named *Disk Defragmenter*. With it, you can consolidate all fragmented data on your hard disk. It rearranges the data on your hard disk and reunites the fragmented data so that your computer can run more efficiently.

Depending on how Windows is set up, this tool may run automatically, once every few days. On other computers it may not. That's why it is best to run it manually at least one time and see whether the disk is fragmented or not.

Exercise 3.6 shows how to use Disk Defragmenter in Windows 7 to improve your computer's performance.

EXERCISE 3.6

Using Disk Defragmenter

1. Click Start and then All Programs.

2. Click Accessories ➤ System Tools ➤ Disk Defragmenter (Figure 3.26).

   The application opens, and you can see the status of the disks that are found inside your computer.

3. Select the disk that you want to defragment and click Defragment Disk (Figure 3.27).

   The disk is analyzed and then defragmented, if necessary. When finished, Disk Defragmenter will show you the percentage of fragmentation that's left at the end of its work.

4. Close Disk Defragmenter.

FIGURE 3.26   The Start menu

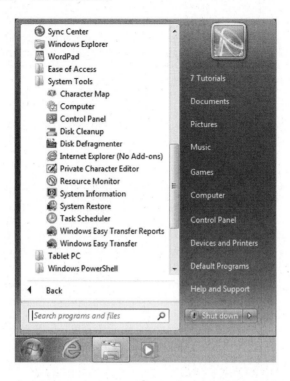

FIGURE 3.27   Disk Defragmenter

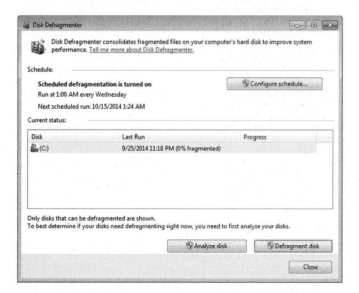

> It is very important to note that fragmentation affects only traditional hard disks because of the way they store data. Modern SSD drives are not affected by fragmentation because they have a different way of storing data. This is why Disk Defragmenter doesn't work on computers and devices with SSD drives. If you force the defragmentation process on an SSD drive, you will lower its life expectancy.

Now that you know the basics of optimizing your computer's performance, let's talk a bit about protecting it from security threats.

Protecting Yourself from Malware

When you use any computer or device and connect it to the Internet, you will expose yourself to all kinds of security threats. Those threats are referred to using all kinds of names, the most popular being *malware* and *viruses*.

Malware is the broadest term when referring to security threats, and it includes any software that is used to disrupt the operation of your computer, to gather sensitive information, or to gain access to private computers. Malware can appear in all kinds of forms and in all kinds of places. It evolves at a very fast pace, and new forms are invented each year. However, when referring to different types of malware, you will most probably encounter terms like the following:

Viruses   Viruses are malware applications that, when executed, replicate themselves. They often do harmful things like stealing private information, corrupting data, sabotaging other computers, displaying humorous messages on your screen, or logging your keystrokes. The defining characteristic of viruses is that they self-replicate without the user's consent.

Spyware   Spyware is software that aids in gathering information about a person or organization without their knowledge. This software will send the information it collects to another entity without the user's consent.

Keyloggers   These are software that records the keystrokes on your keyboard. Generally this type of software is installed without the user's consent, and its purpose is to actively monitor what the user does.

Rootkits   This is a stealthy type of malicious software that hides its existence from normal methods of detection in order to run with privileged access to a computer. Rootkits are hard to detect, and they generally gain full control over the infected computer. They are used for all kinds of malicious purposes, from corporate espionage to attacking other computers and systems.

Trojans   These are a non-self-replicating type of malware that, when executed, carries the actions that were determined by its creator. Trojans generally mask themselves as legitimate software applications. Once installed, they can be used for all kinds of purposes, including corrupting data, stealing personal information, watching the user's screen and/or webcam, controlling the system remotely, and so on.

To protect yourself from malware, you need to install specialized security software that's used to prevent, detect, and remove malicious software. This type of software is called antivirus, and it provides protection from all kinds of malware.

An antivirus program actively monitors what is going on with a computer, and if it detects any unusual activity, it blocks it or informs the user. Antivirus software also regularly scans your computer for malware, and if it finds any infected files, it removes them.

Antivirus software can be either free or cost money. Generally, free antivirus software offers only the basics in terms of malware protection, things like real-time scanning of your system, manual scans, and malware detection and removal. Commercial antivirus software tends to be more advanced and, alongside the features offered by free antivirus software, includes things like advanced behavioral analysis and rootkit protection.

To keep your computer as safe as possible, you should install at least a free antivirus product. Some of the most popular free antivirus applications are Microsoft Security Essentials, avast! antivirus, and AVG Antivirus Free. If you are willing to purchase a commercial antivirus product, you will have plenty of options to choose from. You should consider products like Kaspersky Anti-Virus, Bitdefender Antivirus, Norton AntiVirus, ESET NOD32 Antivirus, or Webroot SecureAnywhere Antivirus.

Summary

In order to be productive when using a computer, you will need to install all kinds of software applications. The most common type of applications that are installed on computers worldwide is office suites, like Microsoft Office. It is important to learn what each application from this suite does and what it is good at.

When you install software, you first need to make sure that your computer meets its system requirements. If it doesn't have the necessary minimum in terms of hardware and software, it won't run correctly. Then, during the installation process, you will encounter the end-user license agreement. If you don't agree with its terms and conditions, then you won't be able to install and use that software. That's why you should have a good understanding of those terms before purchasing and installing any kind of software.

Obviously, you will also want to use your computer to have fun. You should consider installing a multimedia player on your computer if you want to listen to music and watch videos. Games are also another way you can have fun on your computer, but before installing them, you should make sure that your computer meets the minimum system requirements. Games tend to be more demanding than other types of software, and paying attention to their system requirements is very important for a good experience.

While you work on your computer, both your applications and the operating system will generate all kinds of temporary files that are not always cleaned up automatically. Also, files will become more and more fragmented. That's why you will end up having less disk space available on your computer, and its general performance may decrease in time. With the help of tools like Disk Cleanup and Disk Defragmenter, you can increase the space available on your disk and improve your computer's performance.

Finally, it is very important to understand the risks that you expose your computer to when connecting it to the Internet. There are all kinds of security threats and malware that can infect it and do harm in one way or another. It is important to install an antivirus application on your computer so that you keep it as safe and secure as possible.

Now that you understands the basics of installing and using software, we will discuss ways to troubleshoot and fix problems with your computer. In the next chapter you will learn how to remove malware from your computer, how to figure out what's causing problems on your computer, and how to create your own backup system in Windows.

Exam Essentials

Understand the dependencies between hardware and software.   Know what system requirements are and their role in your decision of whether to purchase and install software on your computer.

Know how to install or remove applications.   You will need to install plenty of applications on your computer in order to use it more productively. You should know how to install an application and how to remove it when you no longer need it.

Understand the basics of software licensing.   Software licensing is a bit tricky, and it is important to know the basics on this subject. You should understand the differences between open-source software and proprietary software as well as the advantages offered by the most important types of licenses.

Know the most important types of office applications.   In order to use your computer productively, it is very likely that you will need to install and use an office suite of applications like Microsoft Office. You should know the types of applications that are generally included in such suites and what they are used for.

Know how to save space on your computer and maintain its performance.   Over time, you will have less space available on your computer's hard disk. Knowing how to save space using file compression or tools like Disk Cleanup will be very useful. Also, disk fragmentation may lower your computer's performance levels, especially after you have used it for a long time. Knowing how to defragment your files will help you keep its performance at normal levels for a longer time.

Key Terms

Before you take the exam, be certain you are familiar with the following terms:

Applications

Database management system

Desktop publishing application

Disk Cleanup

Disk Defragmenter

Drivers

EULA

Freeware

GPL (GNU General Public License)

Malware

MIT license

Open-source licenses

Per-seat licenses

Personal information manager

Presentation program

Proprietary licenses

Shareware

Spreadsheet program

Viruses

Word processing

Review Questions

1. What do system requirements tell you?

    A. The hardware configuration your computer should have in order to run an application with maximum performance

    B. The minimum hardware configuration and other software resources your computer should have in order to run an application

    C. The best configuration your computer should have in order to run an application

    D. The minimum software configuration your computer should have in order to run an application

2. What are the things you can generally customize when installing an application? (Choose all that apply.)

    A. The installation folder

    B. The EULA

    C. When to remove the application

    D. Which shortcuts are installed

3. Where do you remove installed applications from?

    A. Start ➢ Control Panel ➢ System And Security

    B. Start ➢ Default Programs

    C. Start ➢ Control Panel ➢ Uninstall A Program

    D. Start ➢ Control Panel ➢ Programs

4. What is a EULA? (Choose all that apply.)

    A. The end-user license agreement

    B. The end-user legal advisor

    C. The contract between the company that has published the software that you want to use and you, the user

    D. The contract between the developers of the software that you want to use and you, the user

5. Which of the following is an open-source license? (Choose all that apply.)

    A. Freeware

    B. GPL

    C. Shareware

    D. MIT License

6. Which are the characteristics of spreadsheet programs? (Choose all that apply.)

A. It is easy for multiple users to work on the same data set at the same time, performing different types of operations.

B. They are used to store raw data.

C. They make it easy to perform mathematical, statistical, or financial operations.

D. They are computerized simulations of paper accounting worksheets.

7. What are the differences between a desktop publishing program and a word processing program?

A. Word processing programs allow you to compose written documents, whereas desktop publishing programs allow you to produce typographical-quality text and images.

B. Word processing programs allow you to produce books, and desktop publishing programs allow you to create promotional posters.

C. Word processing programs cannot work with images, whereas desktop publishing programs can work with images.

D. Word processing programs allow you to edit words, whereas desktop publishing programs allow you to edit images.

8. Which is an example of a presentation program? (Choose all that apply.)

A. Microsoft Publisher

B. Microsoft PowerPoint

C. LibreOffice Impress

D. Microsoft Word

9. How you can increase the amount of free space available on your computer's hard disk? (Choose all that apply.)

A. Compress large files

B. Delete the files you no longer need

C. Install an antivirus program

D. Run Disk Cleanup

10. What is the main characteristic of a virus?

A. It can corrupt data on your computer.

B. It can log your keystrokes.

C. It can monitor your webcam.

D. It self-replicates without the user's consent.

Chapter

4

Troubleshooting Problems with Your Computer

THE FOLLOWING IC3 GS4: COMPUTER FUNDAMENTALS EXAM OBJECTIVES ARE COVERED IN THIS CHAPTER:

✓ **Software**

- Explain the concepts associated with version control of Operating System (OS) software. Further explain how the OS version can affect the compatibility of other software on the PC.

- Demonstrate how to identify and remove a virus or other malware from an infected PC.

- Explain what 'safe mode' is in popular PC operating systems (OSs), and how and when it should be used when troubleshooting problems on a personal computer system.

- Explain where and how to find information beyond that stored on the PC to help troubleshoot problems on a PC. List popular Knowledge base, forums, and self-help web sites and explain how to use them for troubleshooting.

- Demonstrate how to invoke and interpret the information available in a PC's Task, Process, or Application Manager. Further demonstrate how to use this tool when troubleshooting a problem on the affected PC.

✓ **Hardware**

- Explain how different versions of firmware affect performance of hardware subsystems on a PC and how that information may be used in troubleshooting a problem on a PC.

- Explain the role of Cables and other connectors that connect the various parts of a computer together and what can happen when one or more cable or connector does not make the proper connection.

✓ **Devices and Peripherals**

- Explain how different versions of firmware can affect performance of peripheral devices and hardware attached to a PC and how that information may be used in troubleshooting a problem on a PC.

- Explain what a device driver is, how it fits into the operating system architecture, and how incompatibilities may lead to problems. Further explain how this information may be used in troubleshooting a problem on a PC.

✓ **Backup/Restore**

- Demonstrate how to backup and then restore software and data to: Safe offsite location, External drive, Cloud.

- Explain the implications of versioning and re-cycling of backups in an incremental backup system. Explain how to properly restore from an incremental backup system.

When you use computers on a regular basis, you will encounter problems of all kinds. Some applications might stop working correctly, while others may use way too many resources. Your computer may get infected with malware, putting your data in danger. Windows might suddenly stop working and you won't know what to do to fix it. Hardware components might start to fail or perhaps have bugs that can be fixed only by installing new firmware or drivers. Let's face it: you can encounter problems with computers just as you can with any other tool.

In this chapter we will cover all the basic things you need to know in order to troubleshoot problems at both a software level and a hardware level. Finally, you will learn about several methods that you can use to keep your data safe so that no matter what happens with your computer, you never lose your data. Let's get started.

Dealing with Problems Caused by Software

When you use a computer, you get to install lots of software applications that can be used for all kinds of tasks. Since software is so diverse, chances are that some things might not work as you expect them to. For example, you may want to use an old application that is not compatible with your operating system, or you may use another application that consumes too many of your computer's resources, making it slow down dramatically. Or, while browsing the Internet or checking your email, you may get your computer infected with some harmful virus. The kinds of problems you may encounter are as diverse as the number and types of applications you are installing on your computer.

To give you a hand and help you understand what is going on and how to deal with software-related problems, we will cover several common scenarios that most users deal with at some point when using computers. First, we'll explain how to deal with incompatibilities between the operating system and the applications that a user may attempt to install.

Dealing with Incompatibilities between the Operating System Version and Your Applications

Each new version of any operating system introduces all kinds of changes and advancements. Sometimes, newer versions also introduce problems that did not exist in the previous versions, as well as incompatibilities with older applications. This is why it is very important to keep both your operating system and your installed applications up to date. Both the operating system and the applications you are using need to improve and evolve over time so that you have access to the latest features, bug fixes, and productivity and security improvements.

When you install a new version of Windows on your computer, most of your applications will keep working as they did in the past. However, some of your older software might stop working. These applications just might be too old and outdated, and the new version of Windows introduces enough changes that the old version doesn't work anymore. If this happens, then you need to check for newer versions of those applications that work with your new version of Windows.

While this is OK for home users who install mostly free or affordable software that's easily upgradable on their computers, businesses might have some issues. Applications that are designed for business tend to be more expensive, and upgrading them on a regular basis may incur very high costs for the company. That's why, before upgrading to a new version of Windows, each company must evaluate the compatibility of its applications with that version. To help you with this evaluation, Microsoft has created a website named *Windows Compatibility Center*. You can find it at this address: `http://www.microsoft.com/en-us/windows/compatibility/CompatCenter/Home`.

If you prefer a shorter address that is easier to type, use this address: `http://bit.ly/19fq1xr`.

When you visit this website, follow these steps:

1. Type the name of the application for which you want to check the compatibility with a certain version of Windows.

2. Press Enter on your keyboard.

3. Select it from the list of results.

4. Select the version of Windows you are interested in.

The Windows Compatibility Center will tell you whether this application is compatible with the version of Windows you selected and whether you need to take any kind of action (see Figure 4.1).

If you cannot upgrade a specific application to a newer version that works on your new version of Windows, there's another solution that might help: the *Compatibility Mode* feature that's included in every version of Windows. It allows you to edit the properties of the application that is causing you trouble and set Windows to run it in compatibility mode with an older version of Windows. When you do that, Windows tries to adjust its settings and simulate an environment that is similar to the older version of Windows you selected. In certain scenarios this helps you run older applications that otherwise would refuse to run correctly.

FIGURE 4.1   The Windows Compatibility Center

In Exercise 4.1 you will learn how to set the compatibility mode for any application that is installed on your Windows computer.

EXERCISE 4.1

Setting the Compatibility Mode for Any Windows Application

1.   Click Start and then Computer.

2.   Browse your computer's C: drive and find the executable (.exe) file of the application that is not working.

Applications are generally installed in the Program Files folder.

EXERCISE 4.1 *(continued)*

3. Right-click the executable file of that application and select Properties (Figure 4.2).

FIGURE 4.2 The context menu for an executable file

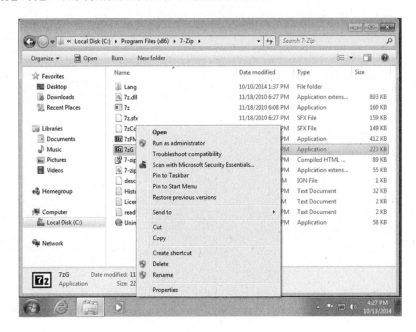

4. In the Properties window of that file, click the Compatibility tab.

5. Check the box that says "Run this program in compatibility mode for" (Figure 4.3).

FIGURE 4.3 The Compatibility tab in the Properties window

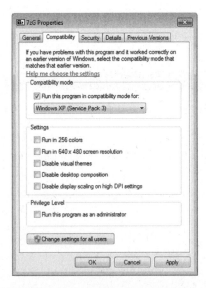

6. Select the older Windows version on which this application used to work (Figure 4.4).

FIGURE 4.4   Selecting the compatibility mode for a file

7. Click OK.

The next time you run the selected application, it will run in an environment that is similar to the older version of Windows that you selected at the previous step.

Dealing with Unresponsive Applications

While you are using applications on your computer, some may become unresponsive at some point, for all kinds of reasons. For example, the antivirus might scan a file you have opened with another application and the file gets locked out and unusable for a while by that application, causing it to stop working. Or, you may be using an application that requires an Internet connection and the Internet connection drops, causing the application to stop working. This lack of response may last only a few seconds, or it may be permanent. That's why if you notice that an application is no longer responding to your commands, it is best to first wait for a couple of seconds. If nothing changes, then you need to take action.

The reasons why an application may stop working vary. What's common to most unresponsive applications is that they tend to slow your computer down until you force them to close. With the help of the Task Manager, you can force any application to stop and close.

When you open the *Task Manager* and select the Applications tab (Figure 4.5), you will see all the applications that you have started.

FIGURE 4.5 The Task Manager in Windows 7

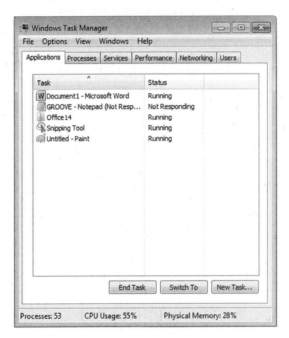

The Task column lists the name of each application, while the Status column shows whether each application is running or not responding. If an application is marked as Not Responding, you won't be able to continue using it, and in order to fix this problem, you need to use the Task Manager to stop it.

In Exercise 4.2 you will learn how to use the Task Manager in Windows to identify applications that are not responding and how to make them stop and close.

EXERCISE 4.2

Identifying Nonresponsive Applications and Ending Their Functioning

1. When you are using an application that is no longer responding, press Ctrl+Shift+Esc on your keyboard to open the Task Manager.

2. Click the Applications tab and identify the application that is no longer responding.

3. Select it and then click End Task (Figure 4.6).

FIGURE 4.6   Closing an application with the Task Manager

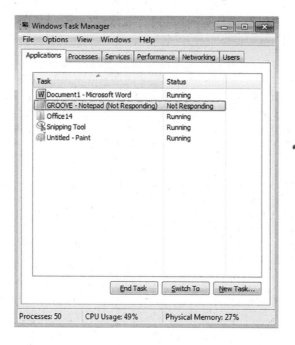

4. Windows 7 will tell you that the selected application is not responding, and you can select what you want to do. Select Close The Program (Figure 4.7).

FIGURE 4.7   The warning shown when a program is not responding

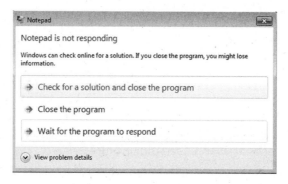

Now that you know how to deal with unresponsive applications, let's discuss another scenario that's likely to happen when you use a computer on a regular basis.

Dealing with Applications That Consume Too Many Resources

Some applications may consume a big percentage of your computer's resources. They won't become unresponsive, but if you want to run other applications at the same time, those other applications will have limited hardware resources at their disposal, and they will work slower than usual. If you open several applications at the same time, your computer will become slow to respond, and all your commands will take a long time to work.

If you are dealing with this scenario, Task Manager is again the tool that can help you. If you open it and select the Processes tab, you will see all the processes that are running. They include both applications that you have started and processes that are run automatically by Windows. In this tab there are several columns with information:

Image Name   The name of the process that is running. The process is always named using the name of the file that it is running. When you run an application, you will not see its name but the name of that application's executable file (with .exe at the end of its name).

User Name   The name of the user account that started the process.

CPU   The percentage of your computer's processor power used by the process.

Memory   The amount of RAM used by that process. This is generally measured in kilobytes.

Description   A description of the process. In the case of applications, you will see the name of the application that started the process.

By default, Task Manager displays only the processes that you have started or that Windows has started automatically for your user account. If you want to see all the processes that are running on your computer, including those started by other users, click the Show Processes From All Users button (see Figure 4.8). Task Manager will now display all running processes, from all user accounts.

If you want to identify the process that is using the biggest share of your computer's processor power, follow these steps:

1. Click the CPU column to sort it in descending order (see Figure 4.9).

   You will first see the processes that are using the most of your computer's processor.

2. Click this column again, and you will sort it in ascending order with the processes that use the fewest resources listed first.

3. If you want to identify the applications that are using the most RAM, click the Memory column once to sort it in descending order.

4. Look at the Description column to learn the name of the application that is consuming the most memory.

5. Close that application and notice how your computer's resources are freed and other applications become more responsive.

FIGURE 4.8   The Task Manager showing running processes

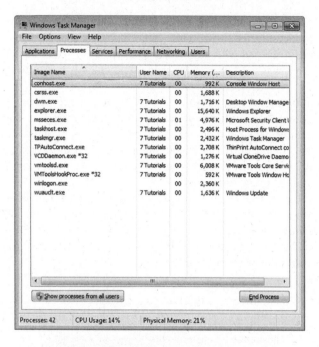

FIGURE 4.9   The Processes tab in the Task Manager, sorted by CPU use

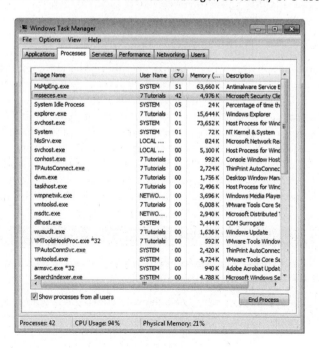

Dealing with Malware Infections

Another problem you may encounter when using your computer is malware infections. You may try to download an infected file from the Internet, from an untrusted source. You may have received a malicious email with an infected attachment, or you may have plugged in a USB memory stick that was used on another computer, which was infected with some form of malware.

If you have an antivirus program installed, its real-time protection engine should be able to identify the threat and block it before it gets the chance to infect your computer and cause harm. For example, when you download a new file to your computer, it should be automatically scanned by the antivirus. If you plug in a USB memory stick, the antivirus should automatically scan it. If it doesn't, you should scan it yourself to make sure that you are not exposing yourself to security problems.

If a security problem is detected, the antivirus program will inform you about it and should be able to automatically deal with it. For example, in Figure 4.10, *Microsoft Security Essentials* (the free antivirus provided by Microsoft for Windows 7 users) informs the user that detected threats are being cleaned and that no action is needed from the user after a malicious file was downloaded from the Internet.

FIGURE 4.10   A Microsoft Security Essentials prompt

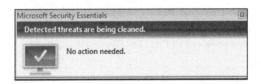

While other antivirus software will look different and display different prompts with more or less information being revealed, its real-time protection engine should work in a similar way.

We recommend that you regularly scan your computer for malware at least once a month. You can perform the scan manually or you can set your antivirus to do that for you, automatically. However, some free antivirus products like Microsoft Security Essentials don't include any scheduling features, and you will have to perform the scans yourself. In Exercise 4.3 we will demonstrate how to perform a full-system scan on your computer with Microsoft Security Essentials and how to deal with the infected files that it detects.

EXERCISE 4.3

Scanning Your Computer for Malware with Microsoft Security Essentials and Removing Infected Files

1.   Click Start and then All Programs to see a list with shortcuts to your programs (Figure 4.11).

FIGURE 4.11   The Start menu in Windows 7

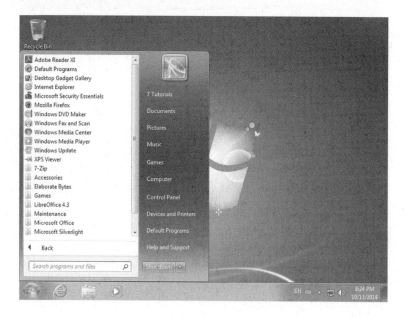

2. Click Microsoft Security Essentials to start this antivirus program.

3. In the Home tab, select Full as the scan option and then click Scan Now (Figure 4.12).

FIGURE 4.12   Microsoft Security Essentials

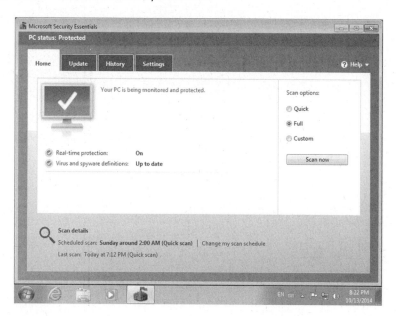

4. Wait for the scan to end and then look at the results displayed.

5. If threats are detected, click Clean PC (Figure 4.13).

FIGURE 4.13   Potential threats detected by Microsoft Security Essentials

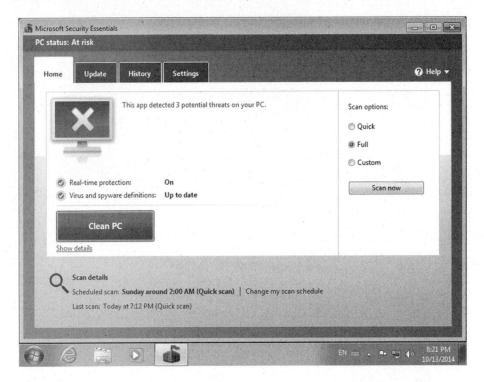

6. Wait for Microsoft Security Essentials to deal with them. When it has finished, click Close (Figure 4.14).

FIGURE 4.14   Threats removed by Microsoft Security Essentials

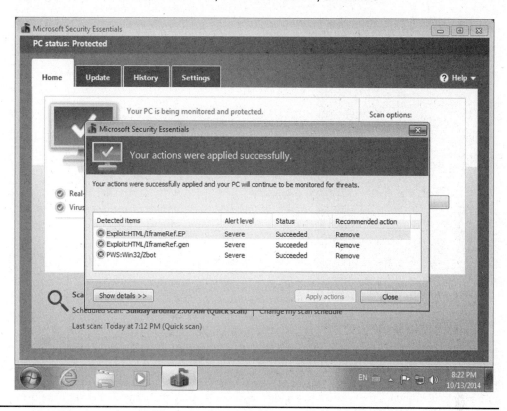

Using Safe Mode to Fix Problems with Windows

If you have problems with the way Windows works, then one quick way to fix it is to start it using the Safe Mode feature. *Safe Mode* is a different way of starting Windows that loads only the barest essentials that are required for Windows to function. For example, most drivers are not loaded, and most Windows services are not started. Also, the applications that are normally set to run at startup are not loaded. When in Safe Mode, Windows will run using the lowest possible graphics and the minimum resolution that is supported—800 × 600 pixels (see Figure 4.15).

Because Safe Mode is a minimal way of running Windows, it should be used only for diagnosing computer problems and for fixing them.

Safe Mode can start in one of three ways:

Safe Mode   Normal Safe Mode loads only the bare essentials that are required for Windows to function.

Safe Mode with Networking   This way also loads the drivers for your computer's network card so that you can access the network or the Internet.

FIGURE 4.15   Safe Mode

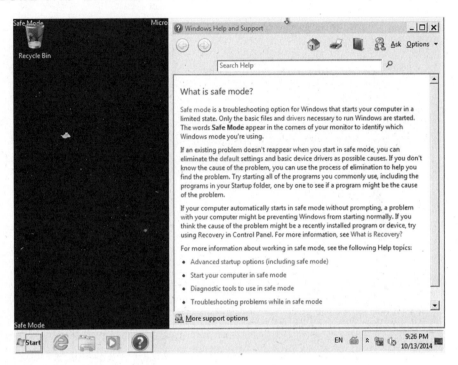

Safe Mode with Command Prompt   When you start Windows using this mode, it automatically launches the command prompt without displaying other elements of the user interface, such as the Start button. This mode is useful only to IT professionals who know how to use command-line utilities to administer Windows.

You can use Safe Mode to solve all kinds of problems, including but not limited to the following:

▪ Disk corruption problems that do not allow Windows to start or run normally

▪ Instability caused by malfunctioning drivers that need to be removed

▪ Incompatible applications that cause Windows to malfunction

▪ Malware infections that are hard to remove

In Exercise 4.4 you will learn how to start Windows 7 in Safe Mode.

EXERCISE 4.4

Starting Windows 7 in Safe Mode

1. Shut down your Windows 7 computer.

2. Press the power button to start your computer and then press the F8 key on your keyboard.

3. Keep the F8 key pressed until you see the Advanced Boot Options screen shown in Figure 4.16.

FIGURE 4.16   Advanced Boot Options

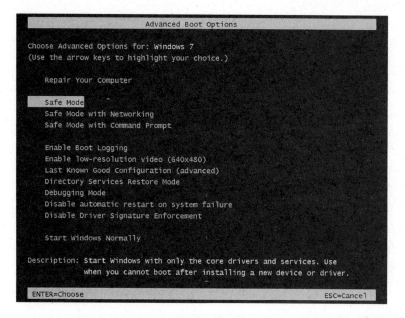

4. Using the arrow keys on your keyboard, move the cursor to one of the Safe Mode boot options and then press Enter.

5. Wait for Windows 7 to start in Safe Mode and then log in with your user account, if required.

    Windows 7 is now started using Safe Mode.

Finding Help Online

If you have a computer problem that you can't fix using any of the methods shared earlier in this chapter, then your best choice is to search for help online. On the Internet you will find plenty of websites, knowledge bases, forums, and technical communities where you can find solutions to your problems or ask for help from others.

One of the best places to get started is Microsoft's *Fix It Solution Center*. It is a portal where you can find information to help you fix all kinds of problems. When you visit it, you are asked to select the problem area and what you were trying to do. Then you are given a list of documented problems and their solutions. For some problems you can download and run a specially crafted file that will help you fix the problem that you have. You can access the Fix It Solution Center by entering in your browser either of the following two addresses:

```
http://support.microsoft.com/fixit/
http://bit.ly/1cjQQlU
```

You can also try online communities like *Microsoft Answers*, where you can get help from Microsoft's employees, technical experts who are active in that community, or other users like yourself. When visiting this community, select the product you are having trouble with, and then you will see all the available discussion threads or wikis with documentation. You can access Microsoft Answers by entering in your browser either of the two following addresses:

```
http://answers.microsoft.com
http://bit.ly/1peZGaz
```

There are many other communities where you can ask for help from others, even though they are not managed by Microsoft. An example of a great technical community is superuser.com. Also, you can find plenty of websites with lots of how-to articles and guides that show you how to best use Windows and its applications and how to fix problems. Two such great websites are 7tutorials.com and howtogeek.com. Don't hesitate to visit them and read their articles. You will definitely learn more about using your computer, and you will find plenty of help for fixing your technical problems.

Dealing with Problems Caused by Hardware

Hardware can also cause problems from time to time. You may have to deal with simple issues like your monitor not powering on or more complex issues like never-ending crashes and continuous restart loops. Since hardware components are very diverse, the problems that they may cause are just as diverse.

To help you understand how to deal with hardware-related problems, we will cover several common scenarios that most users deal with at some point. We will start with the simplest of issues, which are caused by cables and connectors not being plugged in correctly.

Dealing with Problems Caused by Cables and Connectors

When you use a computer, you may encounter small incidents that will stop it from working correctly. These are most often caused by minor issues like cables and connectors not being plugged in correctly.

For example, if you try to type something and the computer seems to ignore your key presses, then the first thing you should do is to check the cable that connects the keyboard to the computer. Take a look at it and see whether it is still plugged into the back of your computer. Maybe the keyboard is no longer plugged correctly into the USB or PS/2 port. The same goes for the mouse—if all of a sudden it stops registering your commands, then most probably the cause for this issue is that its cable is no longer plugged in correctly. If you have wireless mice and keyboards that run using batteries and they don't work, you should also check whether their batteries are empty or whether they are correctly inserted into the appropriate slots.

The same principle applies each time your computer suddenly ignores your input or when it no longer provides the expected output. For example, if you press the power button on your computer and the computer doesn't start, then maybe it no longer is receiving power. Check that the power cable is correctly plugged into your computer, that the power is on, and that the power supply unit is turned on. Most power supplies generally have an On/Off switch on their back, and it might be set to Off.

Another issue that may happen is for your monitor to stop displaying the image on the screen. It just stays black, no matter what you do. In this case, there are three things that you can check:

- Check whether the monitor is plugged correctly into the power socket.
- Check whether the monitor is correctly connected to the computer.
- Check whether the monitor is turned on.

Chances are that one of these situations is the cause of your problem and you can fix it quickly.

The same principles apply also when dealing with peripherals like printers or webcams. If a printer no longer prints anything, check that it is turned on, that it is receiving power, and that it is connected correctly to your computer.

Obviously, it may happen that all cables and connectors are plugged in correctly and your computer still doesn't work because some hardware component is broken and needs to be fixed or replaced. But in most cases, simple things like these are the cause of your issues.

Upgrading the Firmware for Your Computer's Components and Peripherals

In order to function, every piece of hardware has some small permanent software that is programmed into its memory. Because it is not really software in the classic sense and it exists at the boundary between hardware and software, it is named *firmware*.

Generally, firmware is a very basic piece of software that contains only the instructions that are required for the hardware to work as intended. It is the first software to run on a device when it is powered on. Without it, the hardware would be impossible to use. Even though it is not evident, you will find firmware in all kinds of products, from washing machines to the individual components that make up a computer to peripherals like printers, portable music players, scanners, and so on.

Changing the firmware of a device may rarely or never be done during its lifetime; some firmware memory devices are permanently installed and cannot be changed after they are produced. Examples of such devices are USB memory sticks, CPUs, and network cards. However, for some hardware components, updating the firmware is possible and advisable because it can help fix annoying bugs or add new features. The most common component in a computer for which it is advisable to upgrade the firmware is the motherboard. Also, many mobile devices like tablets and smartphones get regular firmware updates that fix problems or add new features.

In the motherboard of a computer or device, the firmware is named *BIOS*, meaning Basic Input/Output System. The term was coined in 1975, and it has been used ever since when referring to the firmware of a motherboard or a computer. It has a different name from other firmware because motherboards are more complex hardware that manages the interaction among all kinds of hardware that make up a computer.

The BIOS is one of the most advanced forms of firmware. It is in charge of initializing and testing all the hardware components of a computer, providing the necessary power for other hardware, including the cooling devices found inside a computer, and it is also responsible for loading the operating system. From the BIOS you can configure the way your computer's motherboard works.

The BIOS is the only form of firmware that has a visual interface, which you can access by pressing a key on your keyboard immediately after starting your computer. The key that you have to press varies from computer to computer. In Figure 4.17 you can see the user interface for a typical BIOS. Please keep in mind that the number of configuration options displayed varies from computer to computer, and on your computer things will be different than in this figure.

FIGURE 4.17   The BIOS

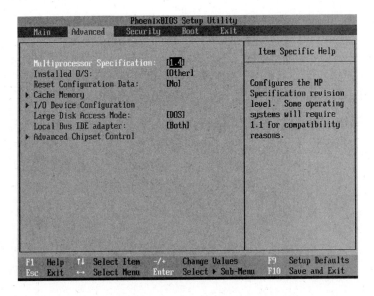

The upgrade process for the firmware is called *flashing*, and it involves overwriting the existing firmware and data on that device. Flashing the firmware of any computer or device is done using specialized software for this task. This software works differently and looks different for each component and manufacturer. In Figure 4.18 you can see the HP System BIOS Update Utility that is used to update the BIOS on HP computers.

FIGURE 4.18   The HP System BIOS Update Utility

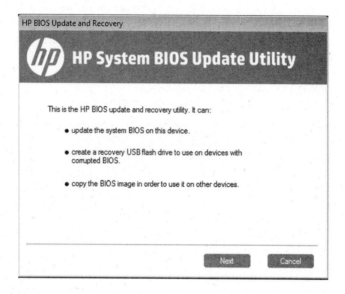

It is very important that this process runs without problems and that the device remains powered on through the duration of its flashing. If the process is interrupted in any way, the device becomes unusable because it no longer has the firmware necessary to function. It has only a partial copy of the firmware that's not able to work on its own.

The firmware for any hardware device is always found on its manufacturer's website. You have to be careful and look for the firmware that's created specifically for your hardware component's name and model number. If you try to install the firmware that was created for another model number or another component, you will damage that component, and it will stop working, possibly for good.

Dealing with Drivers for Your Computer's Hardware

We first introduced the concept of *drivers* in Chapter 3, "Understanding Software," and we said that they are software that operates and controls particular hardware devices attached to your computer. They ensure that your operating system takes full advantage of your hardware. Operating systems come with some generic drivers, but for full access you often need specific drivers. Drivers can be a problem, and they can cause performance and stability issues if they are not handled correctly.

Windows has a large database of hardware components and drivers for them. If your computer has commonly used hardware, chances are that Windows automatically detects it and installs the appropriate drivers through the Windows Update service. When that happens in Windows 7, you will see a notification like the one shown in Figure 4.19, stating that Windows is installing device driver software. Wait for the installation to finish prior to using that device. This prompt is most often encountered when you connect peripherals to your computer like USB memory sticks, external hard disks, webcams, or printers.

FIGURE 4.19 Windows 7 installing device driver software

Drivers are also required for peripherals. For example, if you want to use a printer or a scanner, you have to install the drivers that are found on its installation disk or on the manufacturer's website. Again, download the drivers for your exact printer or scanner, and make sure that they are compatible with the operating system version you are using.

Before installing a driver you need to double-check the following:

That it is made for the exact hardware component you are using.   You need to make sure that it was made for the exact model and model number of that component and not for another one. This is especially true when dealing with drivers for more complex hardware like the graphics card or the sound card. If you don't install the appropriate driver, your component will not work, and you will almost certainly cause instability or performance issues.

That the driver is compatible with the exact version of the operating system you are using.   This is a big problem when you want to upgrade an older computer or laptop to a newer version of Windows. Even though the latest version of Windows theoretically works on your computer's hardware configuration, some of your computer's components might not have drivers available for this version of Windows. That's why you should always check before upgrading to a newer version of Windows whether your computer's hardware components have drivers for it.

If, by mistake, you install drivers that were made to work on another version of Windows, chances are that your computer will crash and stop working normally. In the section "Dealing with Incompatibilities between the Operating System Version and Your Applications" earlier in this chapter, we mentioned the Windows Compatibility Center website, which can help you evaluate whether the software that you want to use is compatible with your version of Windows. Luckily this website also includes many hardware components in its database, so you can use it to check whether your computer's components are compatible with the latest version of Windows before upgrading to it (Figure 4.20).

FIGURE 4.20   The Windows Compatibility Center

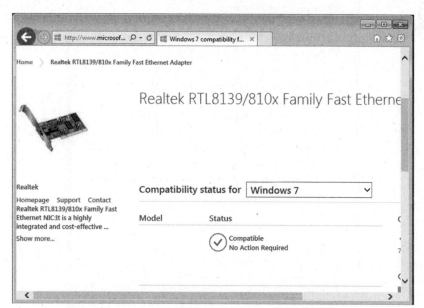

Type the name of the hardware component that you want to check, click Search, and look through the results that are returned. You can find the Windows Compatibility Center at either of these two addresses:

```
http://www.microsoft.com/en-us/windows/compatibility/CompatCenter/Home
http://bit.ly/19fq1xr
```

After installing Windows on a computer and adding the appropriate drivers for its hardware, you should double-check that you have installed all the necessary drivers and that you did not forget anything. This check can be quickly performed using a tool named Device Manager that's found in Windows. Exercise 4.5 demonstrates how to use it to check whether there are any hardware components for which you are missing drivers.

EXERCISE 4.5

Checking Whether There Are Any Missing Drivers in Windows

1. Click Start and then type the word device in the search box.

2. Click the Device Manager search result (Figure 4.21), and the tool will open.

FIGURE 4.21   The Device Manager shortcut

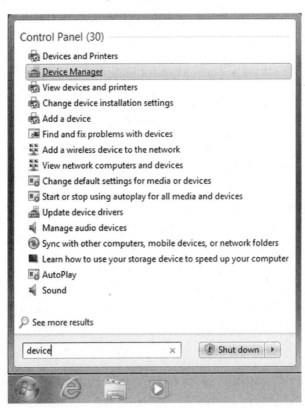

Here you can see all the hardware components that are inside your computer as well as the peripherals that are connected to it.

3. In the Device Manager window, look for a section named Other Devices (Figure 4.22). If you find it, there you will see at least one device for which Windows does not have the appropriate drivers.

FIGURE 4.22 The Device Manager window

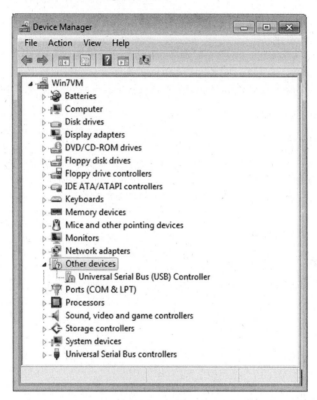

4. Write down the information that is displayed by the Device Manager for each device in the Other Devices category, and use it to find the missing drivers that need to be installed on your computer.

If you find at least one device listed in the Other Devices section of the Device Manager, it means that you have not installed all the necessary drivers for your computer. If this category does not exist in Device Manager, it means that all the necessary drivers have been installed and there's no need to worry.

With this information in hand, you should look on the website of your computer's manufacturer for any devices that you may have missed in your search for drivers. You will surely find a driver that's available for download that you did not install.

Creating Your Own Backup System

In order to have a safe computing experience, it is very important to have some sort of backup system in place so that you won't lose your data if your computer has problems or gets stolen. Backups can be done in many ways, using different kinds of tools and storage media. First of all, you can use tools that are included in Windows 7, like Backup and Restore, or you can use third-party software that is designed for this task.

In terms of the media where you can back up your data, you have the following options:

External Drive   You can use an external hard drive that is connected to your computer, multiple DVDs, or one or more Blu-ray discs, if you have a drive that can burn this type of disk with data.

Network Location   You can store your backup on a shared folder on another computer in your network or on a network server that's used by your company for backing up user data. Generally companies tend to have their own automated backup systems that users don't control. In business environments, the network administrator handles the data backup, the backup server, and when and how the data is backed up for each user.

Cloud Storage   The cloud is a model of data storage where your data is stored on multiple physical servers that are owned and managed by a company that specializes in storing and securing user data. Users buy or lease storage capacity from the providers of this type of service. There are many cloud storage services. The most popular are Dropbox, OneDrive from Microsoft, Google Drive, and Box. While all of them are commercial services that require a paid subscription, they all have a free plan with limited storage included.

In terms of data safety, the safest storage solution is the cloud because your data is stored in specialized data centers that are actively maintained and administered by specialized companies. Also, your data has copies so that it doesn't get lost if a specific server crashes. Your data won't be lost even if your computers are lost or a natural disaster takes place in your area.

In this section we will discuss how to back up your data on all three kinds of media. We will also share how to restore your data when required.

Backing Up Your Data with Backup and Restore

While there are many software applications that you can use to make backups of your computer and your data, many prefer to use the *Backup and Restore* tool that's included in Windows 7. That's because it is free and it is relatively easy to use.

With it, you can back up your entire operating system, its settings, and all your data. You can allow Windows 7 to choose what to back up, or you can select individual folders, libraries, and the disk drives that you want backed up. When you use this tool for the first time, you can set it to run on an automatic schedule and make sure that it backs up your data regularly, without you having to do it manually. Backup and Restore is able to keep track of your files and folders automatically, and it adds only your new or modified files to your recurring backups so that it doesn't waste space.

With this tool you can back up your data on all kinds of media: an external hard drive that's connected to your computer, on DVDs or Blu-Ray discs, or on network locations like shared folders on other computers. During the backup procedure, all you have to do is select the desired location for your backup, and Backup and Restore will take care of the necessary transfers for you. When you store your backup in a network location, you have to provide the network location and the necessary credentials if you need to authenticate yourself in order to access that location, as shown in Figure 4.23.

FIGURE 4.23   The Set Up Backup Wizard

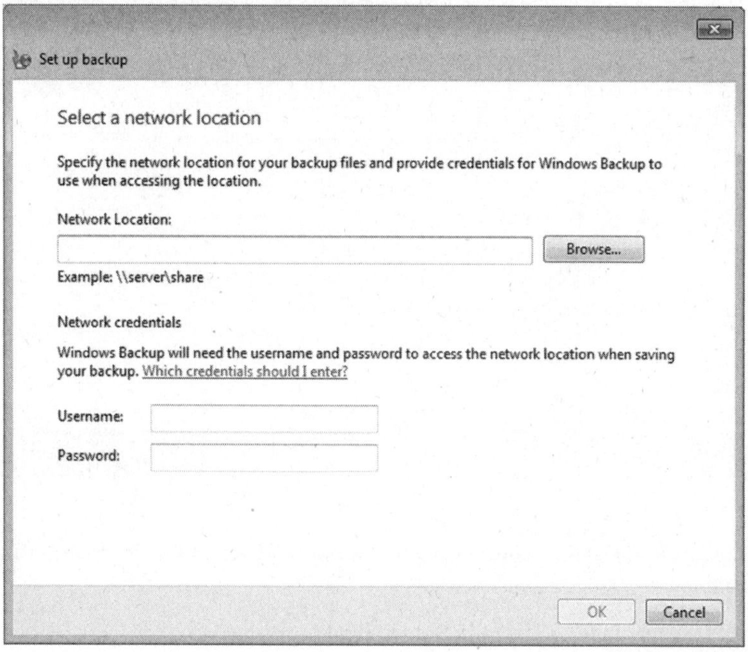

In Exercise 4.6 you will learn how to back up your computer with Backup and Restore on an external hard disk. Before you start this exercise, make sure that you plug an external hard disk into your computer and wait for it to be detected and installed by Windows.

EXERCISE 4.6

Backing Up Your Data with Backup and Restore

1. Click Start and then Control Panel.

2. Click System And Security and then Backup And Restore (Figure 4.24).

FIGURE 4.24   The Backup And Restore entry in the Control Panel

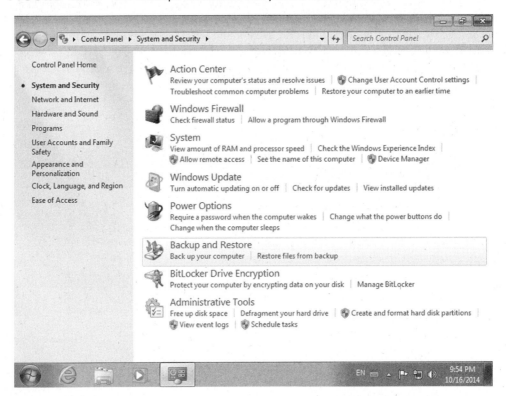

3. In the Backup And Restore window, click the Set Up Backup link in the top right (Figure 4.25).

    Windows takes a while to start the Set Up Backup Wizard.

FIGURE 4.25   The Backup And Restore window

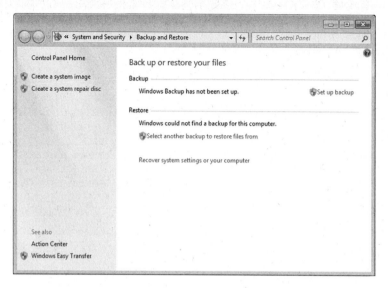

You are asked to select where the backup is to be saved.

4.   Select the external hard disk that is connected to your computer and click Next (Figure 4.26).

FIGURE 4.26   Selecting where to save your backup

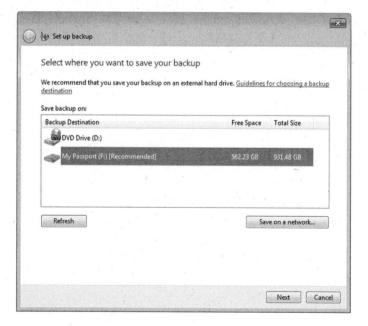

EXERCISE 4.6 *(continued)*

5.   You are asked what to back up. Select Let Windows Choose (Recommended) and click Next (Figure 4.27).

FIGURE 4.27   Selecting what you want to back up

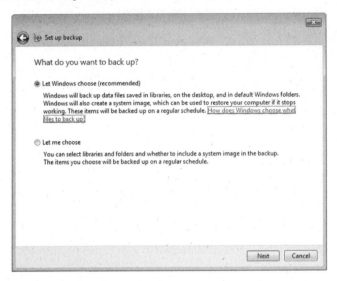

The Set Up Backup Wizard shares its settings and what it will back up.

6.   Read the information displayed and click Save Settings And Run Backup (Figure 4.28).

FIGURE 4.28   Reviewing your backup settings

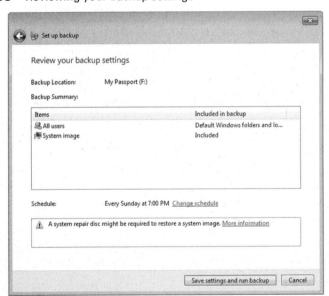

You return to the Backup And Restore window, where you can see the progress of the backup process (Figure 4.29). Wait for it to finish.

FIGURE 4.29   The backup in progress

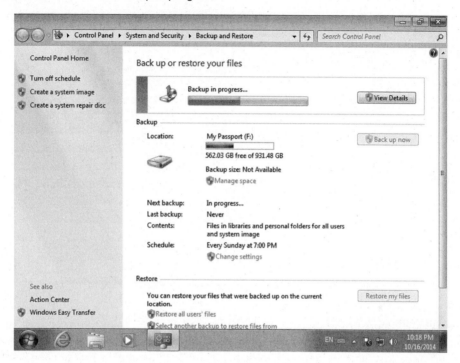

When the backup is finished, you are shown the date and time when it was done as well as the schedule of the next automatic backup.

7. Close the Backup And Restore window.

Restoring Your Data with Backup and Restore

You can also use the Backup and Restore tool from Windows to restore your backups. You can restore all the files of all the user accounts that are on your computer, or you can restore only your own files from the latest backup.

If you choose to restore your own files, the easiest way to restore them is to select Browse For Folders (Figure 4.30) and select the folders that you want to restore.

FIGURE 4.30   The Restore Files Wizard

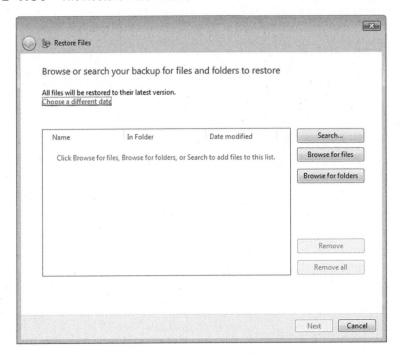

During the restore process you are also asked where you want to restore your files. You can restore them to their original location, in which case you will have to overwrite the ones that currently exist there, or you can choose to restore them to another location like another folder or an external hard disk.

In Exercise 4.7 you will learn how to use Backup and Restore in Windows 7 to restore some of your files from the latest backup.

EXERCISE 4.7

Restoring Your Backed-Up Data with Backup and Restore

1. Click Start and then Control Panel.

2. Click System And Security and then Backup And Restore.

3. Click the Restore My Files button found at the bottom of the Backup And Restore window (Figure 4.31).

FIGURE 4.31   The Backup And Restore window

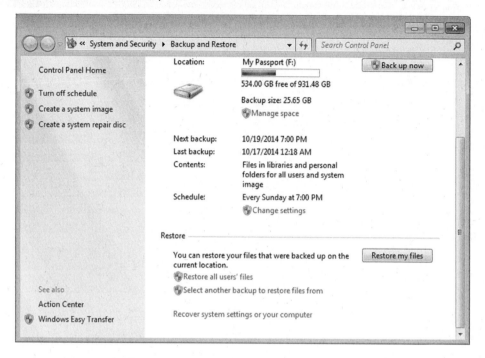

4. You need to select which files will be restored to their latest version. Click Browse For Folders (Figure 4.32).

FIGURE 4.32   The Restore Files Wizard

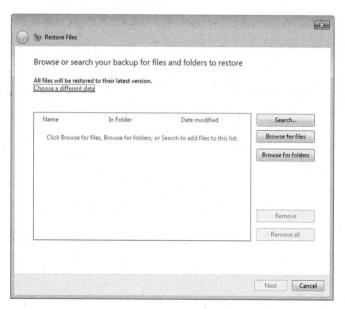

EXERCISE 4.7 *(continued)*

5. Browse the folders found inside your latest backup and select the folder that you want to restore. Click Add Folder (Figure 4.33).

FIGURE 4.33   The Browse The Backup For Folders Or Drives dialog

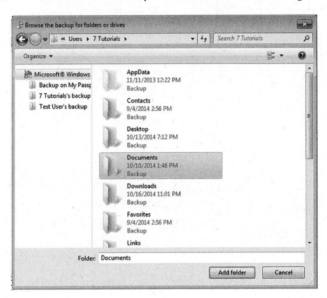

6. In the Restore Files Wizard, click Next (Figure 4.34).

FIGURE 4.34   The folders that will be restored

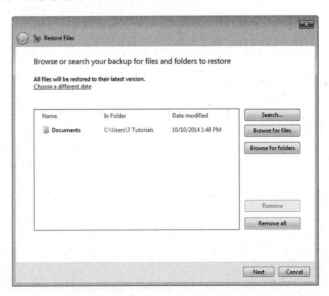

7. You are asked where you want to restore your files. Choose In The Original Location and click Restore (Figure 4.35).

FIGURE 4.35   Selecting where to restore your files

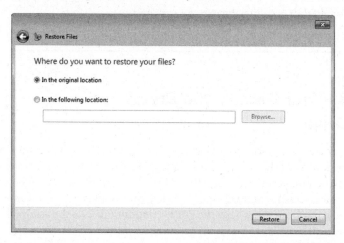

Your files are copied from the backup to their original location. During this process you are asked whether you want the files from the backup to replace the files found currently in that location.

8. Check the box that says Do This For All Conflicts as shown in Figure 4.36, and then click Copy And Replace.

FIGURE 4.36   The Copy File dialog

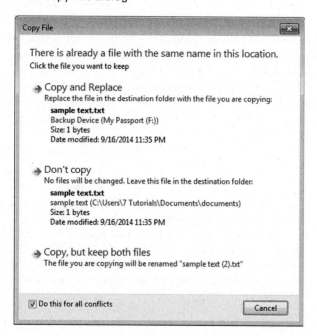

EXERCISE 4.7 *(continued)*

When the backup files from the selected folder are copied to their original location, you are informed that your files have been restored.

9. Click Finish.

Backing Up Your Data to the Cloud with OneDrive

There are many cloud storage solutions that you can use to back up your data, and while they look and work differently, the basic principle is the same: they are services that allow you to back up and access your data from any device with an Internet connection. Even if your computer crashes and no longer works, your data is safe and can easily be accessed and recovered from anywhere. The only condition is that you know the necessary credentials to authenticate yourself as a user of that service.

Another advantage of cloud storage solutions is that they are more reliable in the sense that they always update your latest files automatically, as long as the backup and synchronization application runs in the background. Windows tools like Backup and Restore run once every couple of days, so you may lose a few days' worth of files or at least a few hours' worth if something bad happens. Cloud storage solutions diminish the risk of losing your work. Also, storing your files on several physical servers of a specialized company makes your data harder to lose than with traditional backup systems.

One of the most popular cloud storage services is *OneDrive* from Microsoft. With it, you can back up your data on any of your computers and devices, including smartphones and tablets. You can also have it synchronized across all of them and be able to also access it by using the OneDrive website.

In order to use OneDrive, you need to have a Microsoft account, meaning an account that's registered with Microsoft, with an email address and password. You can create your own Microsoft account by going to https://signup.live.com/ and following the instructions displayed on the screen.

Some people prefer to enable two-step verification, meaning that in order to log in, they need to provide not only their email and password but also a temporary code that's shared with them via email, SMS, phone, or an app for their smartphone. This helps protect their accounts from unauthorized people who might learn their password through various methods and then try to access their accounts without their approval.

If you are using Windows 7, you need to download the OneDrive application and install it on your computer. This application is found by going to https://onedrive.live.com.

Once you download it, you need to install and configure OneDrive. Exercise 4.8 demonstrates how this is done.

EXERCISE 4.8

Installing and Setting Up OneDrive on Your Windows 7 Computer

1. Open File Explorer and navigate to the location where you downloaded the OneDriveSetup.exe file. Then double-click it.

   The OneDrive setup process starts.

2. Click the Get Started button shown in Figure 4.37.

FIGURE 4.37   The Microsoft OneDrive setup program

You are asked to sign in with your Microsoft account.

3. Type your username and password and click Sign In (Figure 4.38).

FIGURE 4.38 Signing in to OneDrive

Depending on how you have set up your Microsoft account, you may be asked to enter a code to verify your identity. If that happens, the code will be generated by a special Authenticator app on your smartphone.

4. Enter that code and click Submit (Figure 4.39). If you are not asked for this code, skip to the next step.

FIGURE 4.39   Entering your two-step verification code

You are informed that the OneDrive folder will be created in your user account.

5.   Click the Next button shown in Figure 4.40.

FIGURE 4.40   The location of your OneDrive folder

You are asked what you want to synchronize.

6.   Select All Files And Folders On My OneDrive (Figure 4.41) and click Next.

FIGURE 4.41   Selecting what you want to sync

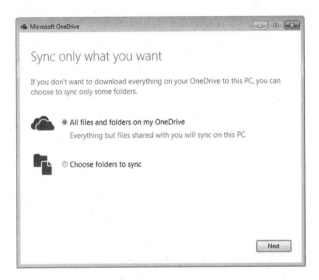

You can then select whether you want OneDrive to allow you to fetch any of your files from this PC from anywhere on the Internet.

7.   Leave the box checked and click Done (Figure 4.42).

FIGURE 4.42   Setting the fetch feature in OneDrive

OneDrive is now installed, and Windows Explorer is opened directly to your OneDrive folder (Figure 4.43).

FIGURE 4.43   The OneDrive folder

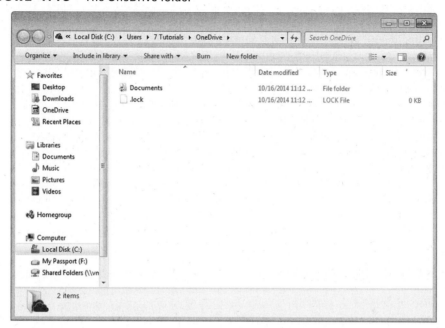

8. Copy the files and folders that you want to back up in the cloud to this folder.

9. When finished, close Windows Explorer.

Once OneDrive is installed on your Windows 7 computer, you can access it using the shortcuts from Windows Explorer. OneDrive works just like any other folder. You can cut, copy, paste, and delete any file or folder just as you would normally do. Anything that's found inside the OneDrive folder is automatically synchronized to the cloud and with other devices and computers where you are using OneDrive with the same Microsoft account.

If Windows crashes and you need to reinstall it, your data is safely stored in the cloud. After reinstalling Windows, all you have to do is to reinstall OneDrive, and all of your backedup files will be automatically downloaded to your computer. You can also access those files at any time from the OneDrive website by using the OneDrive apps for tablets and smartphones. Once a file is synchronized with this server, it is never lost, no matter what happens, unless you delete it from OneDrive.

Summary

As you have seen in this chapter, there are plenty of computer issues you may have to deal with, and the list doesn't stop at what we managed to cover in this chapter. We discussed only the most common types of issues that are caused by hardware and software components, not all of the issues that you may encounter.

Knowing how to troubleshoot common computing problems is very useful in your everyday work, and not having to call tech support for every simple problem will save you some frustration, time, and sometimes even money.

Finally, building your own backup system is a great way to ensure that your data is always safe, no matter what happens. Computers and devices are perishable, and at some point they will stop working for various reasons, including old age. Having a backup system in place ensures that you won't lose your precious data when your computer stops working. While you may be able to afford to replace a hardware component or buy a new computer, you may not be able to afford to lose your work and your personal files. A backup will always help you recover your files when you need them and restore them on other computers, if your own is no longer working.

Exam Essentials

Learn how to identify applications that are not compatible with your operating system and learn how to deal with them.   When upgrading to a newer version of Windows, you may encounter old applications that don't work with that version. It is important to know how to identify incompatible applications and what you can do in order to use them.

Know how to end unresponsive applications.   While using a computer, some applications may stop working, causing your computer to slow down. It is good to know how to end those applications that have stopped working and find those applications that are consuming a big percentage of your computer's hardware resources.

Know how to remove malware from your computer.   If your computer is connected to the Internet, then you will encounter all kinds of malware that may or may not infect your computer, depending on the effectiveness of your antivirus application. Knowing how to remove viruses and other malware from your computer is crucial for having a secure computing experience.

Know how to deal with simple hardware-related problems.   While using a computer, you may have to deal with simple issues that are caused by cables and connectors not being plugged in correctly. Your keyboard may stop working suddenly, your computer may not start when you press the power button, and so on. It is very good to know how to deal with these kinds of issues and fix them quickly.

Understand the role of firmware and drivers when dealing with hardware. In order for a computer to run well, its components must have up-to-date firmware and drivers installed. These types of software have a big impact on your computer's performance and on the way you are using the computer. That's why you should have a good understanding of these concepts and the role they play when using a computer.

Know how to set up your own backup system. Your work and your data are even more important than your computer, and you should always have a system to keep it safe. Setting up your own backup system is vital to a good computing experience, and having a way to recover your data when something goes wrong will save you lots of frustration, time, and money.

Key Terms

Before you take the exam, be certain you are familiar with the following terms:

Backup and Restore	Microsoft Answers
BIOS	Microsoft Security Essentials
Compatibility Mode	OneDrive
Drivers	Safe Mode
Firmware	Task Manager
Fix It Solution Center	Windows Compatibility Center
Flashing	

Review Questions

1. What tool you can use to check whether an application is compatible with your Windows version?
   - **A.** Microsoft Fix It Solution Center
   - **B.** Compatibility Mode
   - **C.** Safe Mode
   - **D.** Windows Compatibility Center

2. What tool you can use to close applications that are not responding?
   - **A.** Windows Defender
   - **B.** Microsoft Security Essentials
   - **C.** Task Manager
   - **D.** Microsoft Word

3. Which of the following are ways of preventing malware infections? (Choose all that apply.)
   - **A.** When downloading a new file on your computer, you scan it with an antivirus.
   - **B.** When plugging a USB memory stick into your computer, you scan it with an antivirus.
   - **C.** Boot into Safe Mode.
   - **D.** You use your antivirus to scan your computer for malware regularly, at least once a month.

4. What is Safe Mode? (Choose all that apply.)
   - **A.** Windows loading only the barest essentials that are required for it to run
   - **B.** Windows loading without a user interface
   - **C.** A way of loading Windows that allows you to troubleshoot and fix problems with the operating system
   - **D.** Windows loading without a desktop background

5. Which of the following are resources where you can get help from Microsoft? (Choose all that apply.)
   - **A.** Microsoft Word
   - **B.** Microsoft Answers
   - **C.** Yahoo! Answers
   - **D.** Fix It Solution Center

6. When your computer's monitor remains black after turning on the computer, what should you do to fix this problem? (Choose all that apply.)

   A. Check whether the monitor is turned on.

   B. Check whether the monitor is correctly connected to the computer.

   C. Check whether the monitor is full of dust.

   D. Check whether the monitor is plugged correctly into the power socket.

7. What should you check before installing a driver for a hardware component? (Choose all that apply.)

   A. That it was released in the last 30 days

   B. That it is compatible with the exact version of the operating system you are using

   C. That it is made for the exact hardware component that you are using

   D. That it was created by the manufacturer of your hardware's component

8. What is the BIOS? (Choose all that apply.)

   A. Firmware with a user interface

   B. Software that runs when the operating system is started

   C. The firmware that is in charge of initializing and testing all the hardware components of a computer

   D. Basic Input/Output System

9. Why should you back up your data? (Choose all that apply.)

   A. To lose it when your computer crashes

   B. To be able to recover it when your computer crashes

   C. To be able to recover it when your computer gets stolen

   D. To have it in the cloud

10. Which of the following are characteristics of cloud storage? (Choose all that apply.)

   A. Your data is stored on multiple physical servers.

   B. Your data can be accessed from different computers and devices with an Internet connection as long as you have the correct credentials to access it.

   C. Your data can be recovered from anywhere at any time.

   D. Your data can be recovered only for a limited time.

Key Applications

PART II

Chapter

5

Exploring Common Application Features in Microsoft Office

THE FOLLOWING IC3 GS4: KEY APPLICATIONS EXAM OBJECTIVES ARE COVERED IN THIS CHAPTER:

✓ **Common Features and Commands**

- Demonstrate the use of keyboard shortcut keys or "hot keys" to invoke application features in an application such as a word processor, spreadsheet, presentation package, database manager, or other software application product.

- Demonstrate how to move, copy, and paste user data within an application such as a word processor, spreadsheet, presentation package, database manager, or other software application product.

- Demonstrate how to reveal or hide user data from view within an application such as a word processor, spreadsheet, presentation package, database manager, or other software application product.

- Demonstrate how to print user data from within an application such as a word processor, spreadsheet, presentation package, database manager, or other software application product and control the configuration in which the data is presented or printed as listed in the objective.

- Demonstrate how to check spelling within user data, find and replace portions of user data, and use the Undo and Redo features to alter user data within an application such as a word processor, spreadsheet, presentation package, database manager, or other software application product.

- Demonstrate how to move user data using the Drag and Drop features within an application such as a word processor, spreadsheet, presentation package, database manager, or other software application product.

- Demonstrate how to control presentation and configuration of user data within an application such as a word processor, spreadsheet, presentation package, database manager, or other software application.

- Identify the various sources of help, built-in, online, context-sensitive, help lines, chat services, coworkers, help desks, etc. available to get assistance in learning how to use an application such as a word processor, spreadsheet, presentation package, database manager, or other software application product.

- Describe how each source of help is accessed, what kind of help can be found at each source, and which resources are available when.

✓ Selecting

- Demonstrate how to select user data using the features listed in the objective within an application such as a word processor, spreadsheet, presentation package, database manager, or other software application product.

- Demonstrate how to sort user data using the features built into an application such as a word processor, spreadsheet, presentation package, database manager, or other software application product.

✓ Formatting

- Demonstrate how to organize, configure, and/or format user data from within an application such as a word processor, spreadsheet, presentation package, database manager, or other software application product using a 'styles' or 'styles-like' feature in such a way as to control the look, feel, and other display characteristics with which the data is presented on-screen or printed.

- Demonstrate how to control the font face display features listed in the objective from within an application such as a word processor, spreadsheet, presentation package, database manager, or other software application product in such a way as to control the look, feel, and other display characteristics with which the user data is presented on-screen or printed.

- Basic text formatting

✓ Navigating

- Demonstrate how to launch and terminate an application such as a word processor, spreadsheet, presentation package, database manager, or other software application product.

- Further demonstrate how to open an application data file and make it available for editing within an application program and how to close an application data file so that it is no longer immediately available to an application such as a word processor, spreadsheet, presentation package, database manager, or other software application product.

- Demonstrate how to save user data in an application data file using the same and/or different file names and path information from within an application such as a word processor, spreadsheet, presentation package, database manager, or other software application product.

- Demonstrate how to create a new empty application data file, either blank, or using an available templates provided with the application from within an application such as a word processor, spreadsheet, presentation package, database manager, or other software application product.

- Demonstrate how to manipulate OS and application windows to automatically resize while using an application such as a word processor, spreadsheet, presentation package, database manager, or other software application product.

- Describe how to search for specific subsets of user data within a larger set of user data in an application such as a word processor, spreadsheet, presentation package, database manager, or other software application product.

- Demonstrate how to display user data from within an application such as a word processor, spreadsheet, presentation package, database manager, or other software application product and control the size, orientation, portion of data displayed and other display configuration settings in which the data is presented as listed in the objective, including ways to save, change, and delete those settings.

- Views

✓ Working with multimedia files

- Demonstrate how to adjust the display of pictures, videos, audio, or other multimedia content within an application such as a word processor, spreadsheet, presentation package, database manager, or other software application product according to the action listed in the objective.

- Demonstrate how to incorporate and display pictures, videos, audio, or other multimedia content within an application such as a word processor, spreadsheet, presentation package, database manager, or other software application product according to the action listed in the objective.

In this chapter we will spend a lot of time demonstrating and explaining how to create your first Microsoft Office files. They can be documents, presentations, worksheets, or databases, and even though the user interface of the different applications that you have to use is not always the same, some basic principles, features, and tools are the same across all of them.

We will begin by showing how to start the Microsoft Office application that you want to use and how to create your first empty file. You will then learn how to save your work and how to work with multiple Microsoft Office windows at the same time.

Then we will take a deep dive into more complex aspects of working with data: selecting it, copying it, and moving it around your files. You will learn how to find a specific subset of your data, how to replace it, how to improve the spelling of your files, and how to change the way you view them. Then we will demonstrate how to print your files when you have finished working with them.

The next portion of this chapter will be about formatting your files and improving the way they look so that you can communicate more effectively when you share them with others.

Finally, we will demonstrate the basic ways you can add multimedia files to your Microsoft Office documents and presentations, along with the adjustments you can make so that your multimedia files will display to their best advantage. There's a lot of ground to cover, so let's get started.

Creating New Empty Documents with Microsoft Office

The first step you need to go through when creating any Microsoft Office file is to learn how to start the Microsoft Office application that you want to use and how to create an empty file. Then you can start working with it. When you have finished, you need to know how to save your work so that it is not lost.

Chances are that you will need to work with multiple files at the same time and use data from multiple sources. That's why it is good to know how to work with multiple application windows at the same time so that you can easily switch among them.

When you have finished your work, you need to know how to close the Microsoft Office applications that you are using so that your computer's resources are released for other applications. In the following sections of this chapter we will demonstrate how to do all these things, one by one.

Starting and Closing Microsoft Office Applications

In order to use any application, you need to start it. As you will see in this chapter, starting any Microsoft Office application is very easy. All you have to do is to use the shortcuts that are available in the Start menu (Figure 5.1).

FIGURE 5.1   The Microsoft Office shortcuts found in the Start menu

Closing any application, including those from the Microsoft Office suite, is just as easy. You can use the mouse and click the small red X icon that is shown in the top-right corner of any application window, or you can press Alt+F4 on your keyboard to close the application window.

In Exercise 5.1 we demonstrate how to start and then close the following Microsoft Office applications: Microsoft Word and Microsoft Excel.

EXERCISE 5.1

Starting and Then Closing Microsoft Office Applications

1. Click Start and then All Programs.

2. Click Microsoft Office and then Microsoft Word 2010. Microsoft Word is now started.

3. Click the small X icon in the top-right corner of the application to close it.

4. Click Start ➢ All Programs ➢ Microsoft Office ➢ Microsoft Excel 2010. Microsoft Excel is now started.

5. Press Alt+F4 on your keyboard to close the application.

Now that you know how to start and close Microsoft Word and Microsoft Excel, repeat these steps and start Microsoft Access and Microsoft PowerPoint.

Opening and Closing Microsoft Office Files

Opening Microsoft Office files can be done in the following ways:

- You can start the Microsoft Office application that can open the file that you want to work with and open the file from that application.

- You can browse your computer using Windows Explorer and double-click the file that you want to open in Microsoft Office. The file will be opened using the appropriate application for its type.

When you close a file, Microsoft Office will first check to see if you have made any changes to it. If you did, it will prompt you to save your changes before closing your file (Figure 5.2). If you choose to save them, they will be saved. If you do not, your changes will not be saved, and the file will be closed in the form that it had when you first opened it.

FIGURE 5.2   Notification to save changes made to a Microsoft Word document

In Exercise 5.2 you will learn how to open Microsoft Office files. In order to complete this exercise, please download the `Presentation1.pptx` and `Sample1.docx` practice files to your computer.

EXERCISE 5.2

Opening and Closing Microsoft Office Files

1. Click Start and then Computer.

2. Browse to the location of the Presentation1 PowerPoint presentation and double-click it.

    It will be opened with Microsoft PowerPoint.

3. Close Microsoft PowerPoint by clicking the small X button on the top-right corner of the window.

4. Start Microsoft Word 2010.

5. Click File and then Open.

6. In the Open dialog (Figure 5.3), browse to the location where you saved the Sample1.docx file on your computer, select it with the mouse, and click Open.

FIGURE 5.3 The Open dialog

7. The selected file is opened in Microsoft Word, and you can view its contents.

8. Close Microsoft Word by clicking the small X button on the top-right corner of the window.

Creating New Empty Files with Microsoft Office

When you start a Microsoft Office 2010 application like Microsoft Word, Microsoft Excel, or Microsoft PowerPoint, it automatically creates an empty file that you can work on and then save.

Newer versions of Microsoft Office (such as Microsoft Office 2013) first ask you to select whether you want to create a new empty file or choose one of the available templates.

When using Microsoft Office 2010, the only exception to this rule is Microsoft Access. Because it is a database management system in which you can create and manage all kinds of databases, it first asks you to select which type of database you want to create. You can choose from several templates, including one named Blank Database, provide a name for the database, and then create it.

In Exercise 5.3 you will learn how to create a blank database in Microsoft Access.

EXERCISE 5.3

Creating a Blank Database in Microsoft Access

1. Click Start and then Computer.

2. Click Microsoft Office and then Microsoft Access 2010.

   Microsoft Access is now started, and it asks you to select one of the available templates for creating a database.

3. Click Blank Database (Figure 5.4).

FIGURE 5.4 Creating a new database in Microsoft Access

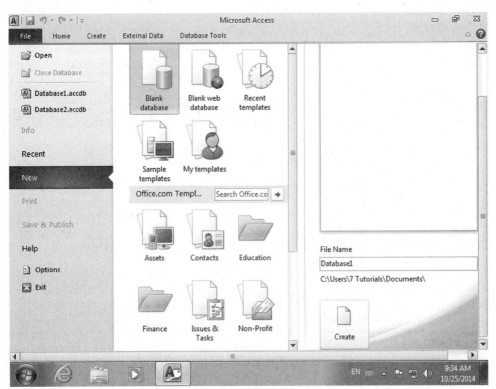

4. Type a name for the file in the File Name text box on the right.

5. Click Create, and an empty database is created.

6. Close Microsoft Access.

Saving Your Microsoft Office Files

When you first create a Microsoft Office file, you need to click the Save button in order to save it and keep your work on your computer. If you don't save it, your work will be lost and you will have to start all over again if your computer crashes. The Save button is found on the top-left corner of any Microsoft Office application window. In Figure 5.5 you can see it in Microsoft Word.

FIGURE 5.5   The Save button in Microsoft Word

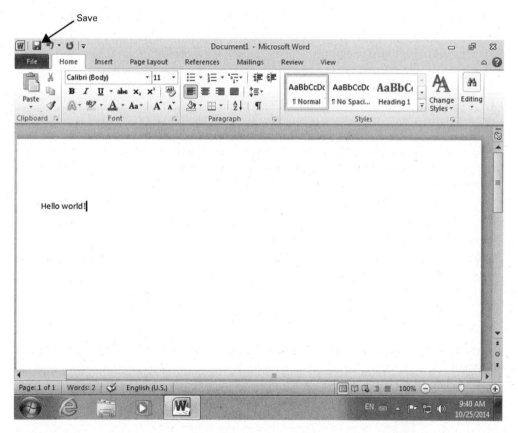

You can also use the Ctrl+S keyboard shortcut in order to save your file. When you press Save or use Ctrl+S, the Save As dialog appears (Figure 5.6). This dialog allows you to choose where you want to save your file and to type a name for it.

FIGURE 5.6 The Save As dialog

Once you click Save, the file is saved where you wanted with the name that you specified, and you can use it at any time and continue your work with it.

After you first save a file, if you make any changes to it, you'll be asked whether you want to save those changes when you close the file (Figure 5.7). You have the following options:

Save Saves your latest changes into the file and closes the file. Your changes will be available the next time you open the file, and you can resume your work where you left off.

Don't Save Doesn't save your latest changes into the file and closes the file. The file will remain as it was when you opened it.

Cancel Doesn't save your latest changes and doesn't close the file. It remains open, and you can continue your editing and save your work later.

FIGURE 5.7 A prompt asking if you want to save changes made to a Microsoft Word document

In the File menu (Figure 5.8), you will also find a Save As option alongside Save. When you first save a file, Save and Save As work the same way. However, after you save a file for the first time and you continue your work on it, the two commands will work as follows:

Save   Will keep your edits and changes and save them to the file you started working on, using its existing location and name.

Frequent saves are a good idea when working on a document because they will prevent losing a good portion of your work if something unpredicted happens and your file is closed without you getting the chance to save your work. To prevent you from losing too much work if something unexpected happens, Microsoft Office also saves your work automatically into a hidden file, at regular intervals.

Save As   Creates a copy of your document that includes your latest edits and changes. You can choose to save this copy in another location, and you can provide a new name for it. The original file will not have the changes that you are saving with Save As. You can also use this option for saving as a different file type.

FIGURE 5.8   The File menu in Microsoft Word

In Exercise 5.4 you will learn how to save a document and then save a copy of it when using Microsoft Word.

EXERCISE 5.4

Saving Your Work When Using Microsoft Word

1. Start Microsoft Word 2010, and a new empty document is created.

2. Type the words **Hello world!** and press Enter.

3. Click the Save button in the top-left corner.

4. Select the Desktop as the folder where you want to save it, accept the default filename, and click Save (Figure 5.9).

FIGURE 5.9   The Save As dialog

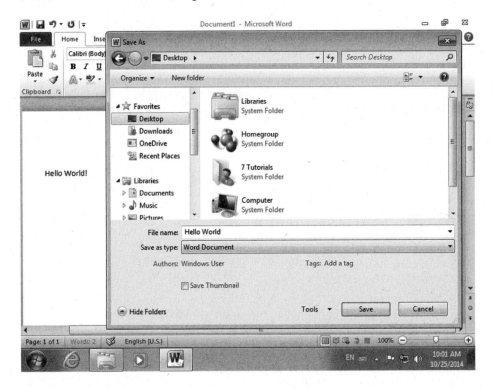

5. Press Enter and then type the word **Hello!**.

6. Click File and then Save As.

7. Keep the Desktop as the folder where you want to save it, and type the name **Hello World2** for the file (Figure 5.10).

FIGURE 5.10 Saving the Hello World2 Word document

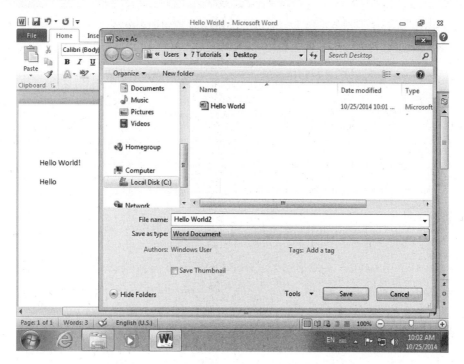

8. Click Save.

   Notice how the new document Hello World2 contains two lines of text.

9. Close Microsoft Word 2010.

10. Double-click the Hello World document on your Desktop to open it.

11. Notice how the first file that you saved contains just one line of text.

12. Close Microsoft Word 2010.

Working with Several Windows at the Same Time

When doing your work, chances are that you will have to use several files at the same time. You might need to take data from multiple documents to create a new one, or you may need to create a PowerPoint presentation that is based on data found in Word documents and Excel worksheets. That's why it is good to know several keyboard shortcuts that will help you navigate through multiple windows as quickly as possible.

In Exercise 5.5 you will learn the necessary keyboard shortcuts that will help you navigate easily through multiple windows.

EXERCISE 5.5

Switching among Multiple Microsoft Office Windows

1.   Start Microsoft PowerPoint.

     A new, blank presentation is created, named Presentation1.

2.   Start Microsoft Word.

     A new, blank document is created, named Document1.

3.   With the Microsoft Word window open on the screen, press Ctrl+N on your keyboard.

     A new blank document is created, named Document2.

4.   To switch to the previous Microsoft Word window, press Ctrl+Shift+F6 on your keyboard.

5.   To switch to the next Microsoft Word window, press Ctrl+F6 on your keyboard. Notice that you are back to Document2.

6.   Press Alt+Tab on your keyboard; then keep Alt pressed and release Tab.

     You will see a list with all the applications that are opened on your computer.

7.   Press the Tab key while keeping Alt pressed until you select Presentation1 – Microsoft PowerPoint and then release both Alt and Tab (Figure 5.11).

FIGURE 5.11   Switching among windows with Alt+Tab

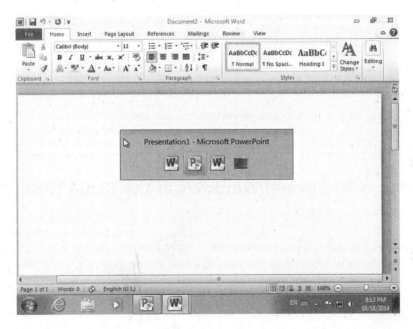

You have switched to Microsoft PowerPoint and the blank presentation that you created.

8. Press Ctrl+W to close the active presentation.

9. Press Alt+F4 to close Microsoft PowerPoint.

10. Press Alt+Tab on your keyboard until you select Document1 – Microsoft Word.

11. Press Ctrl+F10 to maximize or restore the selected Microsoft Word window.

12. Press Ctrl+F4 to close the active document.

13. Press Alt+F4 to close the remaining Microsoft Word window.

The keyboard shortcuts from this exercise apply to all Microsoft Office applications. Go ahead and try them out in other Microsoft Office applications, not just Word and PowerPoint. To help you recap what you have learned, here's the list of all the keyboard shortcuts that we used:

- Create a new document: Ctrl+N

- When more than one window is open, switch to the next window: Ctrl+F6

- When more than one window is open, switch to the previous window: Ctrl+Shift+F6

- Switch to the next opened window: Alt+Tab

- Close the active document: Ctrl+W or Ctrl+F4

- Maximize or restore a selected window: Ctrl+F10

Modern versions of Windows, including Windows 7, have a feature called Snap that allows you to quickly resize and arrange your opened windows. One of the most common ways of using it is to snap two application windows side by side, each taking half of the display, so that you can work with them in parallel.

You can snap a window to the left or right side of the screen using either the mouse or the keyboard. The easiest method is to use the keyboard. When you open an application window, simply press the Windows+left-arrow keys or Windows+right-arrow keys on the keyboard to snap that window to the left or right side of the screen.

In Exercise 5.6 you will learn how to snap two application windows side by side, each taking up half of the screen.

EXERCISE 5.6

Snapping Two Application Windows Side by Side

1. Start Microsoft PowerPoint.

A new, blank presentation is created, named Presentation1.

2. Start Microsoft Word.

A new, blank document is created, named Document1.

3. Move the mouse cursor to the title bar of the Microsoft Word window, click it, and keep the left mouse button pressed.

4. With the left mouse button still pressed, slowly drag the Microsoft Word window to the right side of the screen until you see a shadow of that window taking up the right half of the screen, as shown in Figure 5.12.

FIGURE 5.12   Dragging a window to the right side of the screen

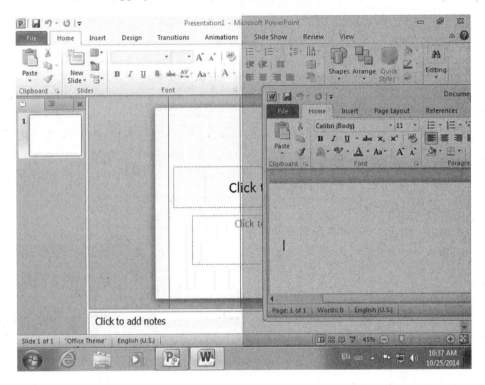

5. Release the left mouse button when the shadow is shown.

    Notice how the Microsoft Word window is moved to the right side of the screen, taking up exactly half of your screen.

6. Click the title bar of the Microsoft PowerPoint window and keep the left mouse button pressed.

7. With the left mouse button still pressed, slowly drag the Microsoft PowerPoint window to the left side of the screen until you see a shadow of that window taking up the left half of the screen, as shown in Figure 5.13.

FIGURE 5.13   Dragging a window to the left side of the screen

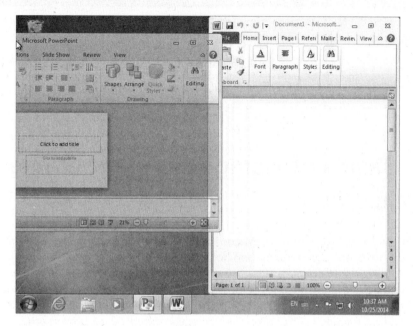

8.   Release the left mouse button when the shadow is shown (Figure 5.14).

FIGURE 5.14   Two windows side by side

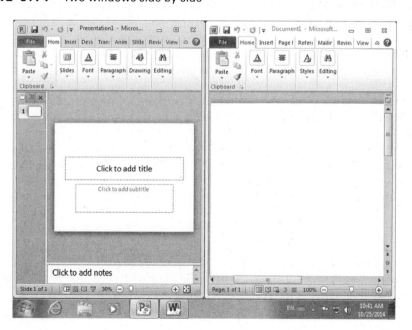

9.   Notice how the Microsoft PowerPoint window is moved to the left side of the screen, taking up exactly half of your screen.

Once the two application windows are snapped side by side, you can easily work with both at the same time. To change the focus from one window to another, all you have to do is click inside the window where you want to work.

The Basics of Using Microsoft Office Applications

Now that you know how to start all Microsoft Office applications, how to create new empty documents and presentations, and how to work with several windows on the screen, it is time to learn the basics of working with documents, worksheets, and presentations. In this section you will learn many useful skills, including how to use keyboard shortcuts in order to be more productive in Microsoft Office, how to check the spelling of your documents, how to undo your changes, how to select and sort data, how to print your work, and more. Let's get started.

Keyboard Shortcuts for Using the Ribbon Productively

When you work with an application from the Microsoft Office suite, it is a good idea to learn, know, and use several keyboard shortcuts that will help you navigate the product and its user interface faster, saving you precious time. While the applications that make up Microsoft Office suite are different and are used for different purposes, they have elements and keyboard shortcuts that are common to all of them. In this section we will focus on those common shortcuts.

The most common user interface element is the ribbon (Figure 5.15). This is a set of large toolbars placed on several tabs, grouped by function. These tabs are filled with graphical buttons and other graphical control elements. In the figure you can see how the ribbon looks in Microsoft Word, Microsoft Excel, Microsoft PowerPoint, and Microsoft Access.

You will notice some common tabs on the ribbon. For example, all applications have a Home tab with commonly used features for copying and pasting text, formatting it, and so on. In Word, Excel, and PowerPoint you will also encounter the Insert, Review, and View tabs, which you use to insert pictures, charts, and other elements, as well as to review your work and view it in different ways.

FIGURE 5.15   The ribbon in various Microsoft Office applications

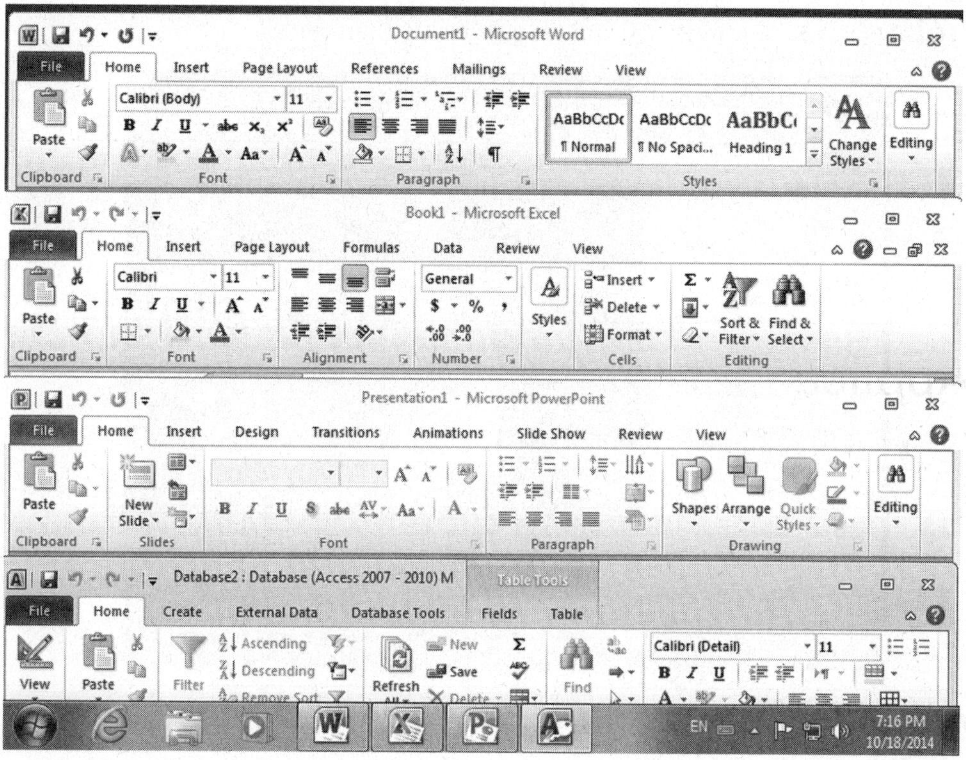

You can navigate the ribbon easily with the mouse by clicking the different tabs and buttons, but you can also navigate by using keyboard shortcuts instead of the mouse. In Exercise 5.7 you will learn how to navigate the ribbon in Microsoft Office using the keyboard.

EXERCISE 5.7

Navigating the Ribbon in Microsoft Office Using the Keyboard

1. Start Microsoft Word by clicking Start ➤ All Programs ➤ Microsoft Office ➤ Microsoft Word 2010 (Figure 5.16).

    A new, blank document is created.

2. Press the Alt key on your keyboard.

    You will see a letter or number displayed over each feature that is available on the ribbon (Figure 5.17). These are called KeyTips.

FIGURE 5.16 The Microsoft Word shortcut in the Start menu

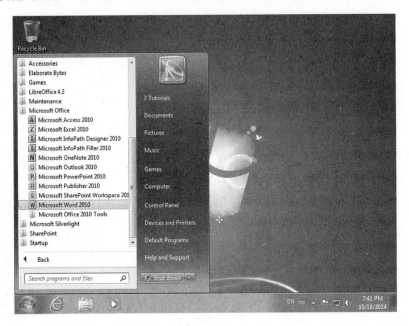

FIGURE 5.17 KeyTips displayed on the Microsoft Word ribbon

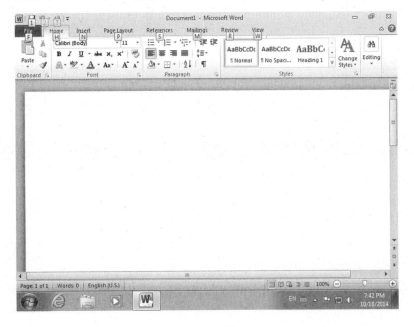

3. Press N on your keyboard to navigate to the Insert tab on the ribbon.

Note the new buttons and options that are available and the KeyTips that are displayed to access them.

4. Press Alt to hide the KeyTips.

5. Press F10 on your keyboard to activate them again.

6. Press W on your keyboard to go to the View tab.

Note the new buttons and options that are available and the KeyTips that are displayed to access them.

7. Press F10 to hide the KeyTips.

8. Press Ctrl+F1 on your keyboard to hide the ribbon.

9. Press Ctrl+F1 to restore the ribbon.

10. Press Alt+F to display the File menu (Figure 5.18). Look at the items that are included in this menu and then press Esc to close it.

FIGURE 5.18 The File menu in Microsoft Word

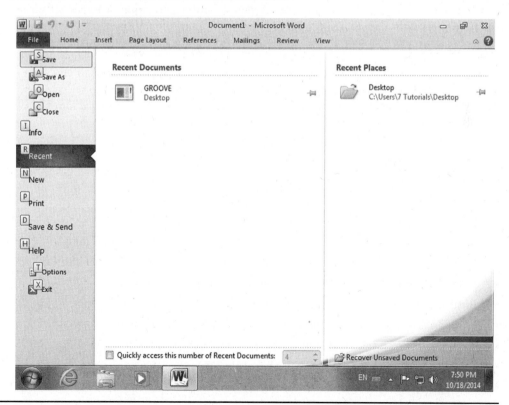

The keyboard shortcuts in this exercise work in all Microsoft Office applications that have a ribbon. Try going through the same steps in Microsoft Excel or Microsoft PowerPoint to see how they work. To help you review what you have learned, here's the list of all the keyboard shortcuts in this exercise:

- Display the KeyTips on the ribbon: Alt or F10
- Press the letter shown in the KeyTip over the feature that you want to use.
- Expand or collapse the Ribbon: Ctrl+F1
- Activate the File menu: Alt+F

Selecting, Copying, and Moving Data When Using Microsoft Office Applications

One of the most basic things that you need to learn when using any kind of application is how to select data so that you can do things with it like copying it to another location, moving it to another location, formatting it, and so on.

Selecting data can be done with the mouse or with the keyboard or with both. When using the mouse, selecting data is easy: move the mouse cursor to the beginning of the data that you want to select, press and hold the left mouse button, and move the mouse cursor till you have selected the data that you want to work with. When the data is selected, release the left mouse button. If you want to quickly select a word, double-click it. When you triple-click a word, its entire paragraph is selected.

You can also combine the use of the mouse and the keyboard. For example, if you want to select a large block of text, first click at the beginning of where you want to select. Then, press and hold the Shift key on your keyboard and click at the end of your selection. The text between your first click and the second is now selected.

There are also some useful keyboard shortcuts that you may want to learn and use:

- Select or unselect one character to the left: Shift+left arrow
- Select or unselect one character to the right: Shift+right arrow
- Select or unselect one word to the left: Ctrl+Shift+left arrow
- Select or unselect one word to the right: Ctrl+Shift+right arrow
- Select from the insertion point to the beginning of the entry/line: Shift+Home
- Select from the insertion point to the end of the entry/line: Shift+End
- Extend a selection one line down: Shift+down arrow
- Extend a selection one line up: Shift+up arrow
- Extend a selection to the end of a paragraph: Ctrl+Shift+down arrow
- Extend a selection to the beginning of a paragraph: Ctrl+Shift+up arrow
- Extend a selection one screen down: Shift+Page Down
- Extend a selection one screen up: Shift+Page Up

- Extend a selection to the beginning of a document: Ctrl+Shift+Home
- Extend a selection to the end of a document: Ctrl+Shift+End
- Extend a selection to include the entire document: Ctrl+A

To help you master the process of selecting data, work through Exercise 5.8, where you will learn how to select data in Microsoft Word. In order to complete this exercise, please download the Sample1.docx practice document to your computer.

EXERCISE 5.8

Selecting Data in Microsoft Word

1. Click Start and then Computer.

2. Browse to the location of the Sample1 Word document and double-click it.

   It will be opened with Microsoft Word.

3. Place the mouse cursor at the beginning of the word *Exercise*.

4. Press and hold the left mouse button and drag it to the right until the word *Exercise* is selected (Figure 5.19).

FIGURE 5.19   A Microsoft Word document

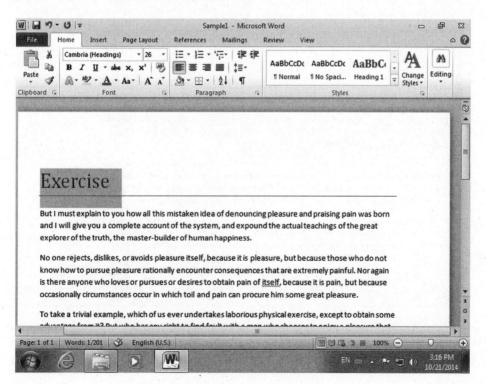

EXERCISE 5.8 *(continued)*

5. Release the left mouse button and notice that the whole word remains selected.

6. Click at the beginning of the word *Exercise* just before the letter *E*. Notice how that word is no longer selected.

   Repeat the same selection by pressing Ctrl+Shift+right arrow on your keyboard.

7. Undo your selection by pressing Shift+Home on your keyboard.

8. Move the mouse to the beginning of the first sentence in the document and click just before the letter *B*.

9. Press and hold the left mouse button and drag it to the right until the first line is selected.

10. Then, drag it down until the first paragraph is selected, as shown in Figure 5.20.

FIGURE 5.20   A paragraph selected in a Microsoft Word document

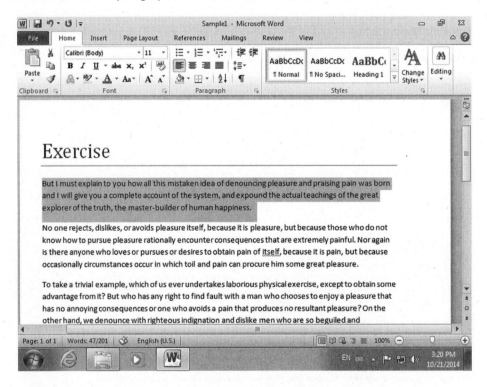

11. Click at the beginning of the selected paragraph, just before the letter *B*.

    Notice how the paragraph is no longer selected.

12. Repeat the same selection by pressing Ctrl+Shift+down arrow on your keyboard.

13. Undo your selection by pressing Ctrl+Shift+up arrow on your keyboard.

14. Click at the beginning of the word *Exercise* just before the letter *E*.

15. Press and hold the left mouse button and drag it to the right until the word *Exercise* is selected.

16. With the left mouse button still pressed, drag the mouse cursor down until you select the entire text in your document (Figure 5.21).

FIGURE 5.21   Selecting the entire text in a Microsoft Word document

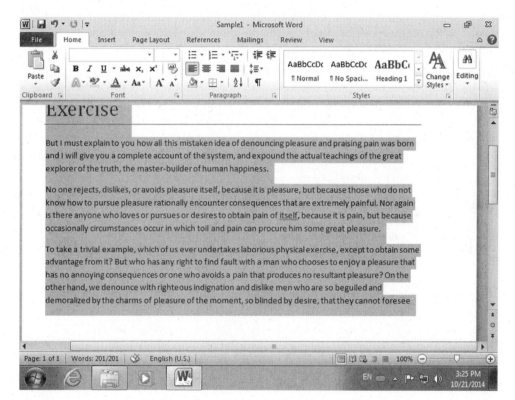

17. To undo your selection, click anywhere in the document.

Now repeat the same selection by pressing Ctrl+A on your keyboard.

18. Press the up-arrow key on your keyboard to undo your selection and go back to the beginning of the document.

19. Close the Sample1 Word document without saving your changes.

Once the data is selected, you can use it. Some of the most common things that you can do with your data are to copy it or move it to another location. These operations can be performed in multiple ways, both by using the mouse and the keyboard. One way is to use the ribbon in Microsoft Office. In the Home tab you can find the Clipboard section on the left side. After you select some data from your document, you see that there are four buttons available (Figure 5.22):

Cut   Removes your selection from the document and holds it in your computer's memory. This command is used when you want to move your selection to another location.

Copy   Creates a copy of your selection and holds it in your computer's memory. The original data will remain where it is.

Paste   Takes the item that is currently stored in your computer's memory and copies it or moves it to the current position depending on the command that you used previously. You cannot use Paste unless you have used Cut or Copy before.

Format Painter   Copies the formatting of your selection and stores it in your computer's memory. To apply the formatting, select the data where you want to copy the formatting from the initial selection, without using the Paste button.

FIGURE 5.22   The Cut, Copy, Paste, and Format Painter buttons in Microsoft Word

You can also use the keyboard for performing these operations:
- Ctrl+C for Copy
- Ctrl+X for Cut
- Ctrl+Shift+C for Format Painter
- Ctrl+V for Paste

Another way of working with these commands is with the help of the context menu:

1. Once you have selected the data that you want to copy or move, right-click your selection (Figure 5.23).
2. In the context menu that appears, select Copy or Cut, depending on what you want to do.
3. Then, go to the place where you want to copy or move your data and right-click again.
4. Use one of the available Paste options:

Keep Source Formatting   Preserves the look of the original selection

Merge Formatting   Changes the formatting so that it matches the text that surrounds it

Keep Text Only   Pastes the data that you have selected without its original formatting

FIGURE 5.23   The context menu in Microsoft Word

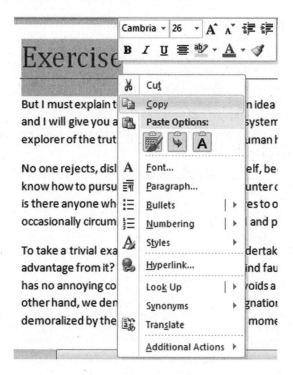

By default, when you use the Paste command without using the context menu and its options, the data will be pasted using the original look of your selection.

In Exercise 5.9 you will learn how to select and then copy and paste data in a Microsoft Office document, using Microsoft Word. In order to complete this exercise, you must have the `Sample1.docx` practice document downloaded to your computer.

EXERCISE 5.9

Copying and Pasting Data in Microsoft Word

1. Click Start and then Computer.

2. Browse to the location of the Sample1 Word document and double-click it.

   It will be opened with Microsoft Word.

3. Select the word *Exercise*.

4. Right-click anywhere on the word *Exercise* and then click Copy in the context menu (Figure 5.24).

FIGURE 5.24 The context menu in Microsoft Word

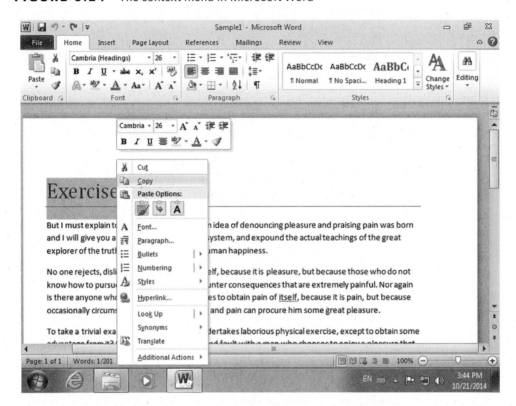

5. Go to the bottom of the document, immediately after the last word, *foresee*, and click where the word ends.

   The mouse cursor will be moved to that position.

6. Press Enter on your keyboard, and a new empty line is added to the document.

7. Right-click anywhere on that empty line and then click the first button in the Paste Options section of the context menu.

   It is named Keep Source Formatting. Notice that the word *Exercise* is now copied on the last line of the document (Figure 5.25).

FIGURE 5.25   The modified Microsoft Word document

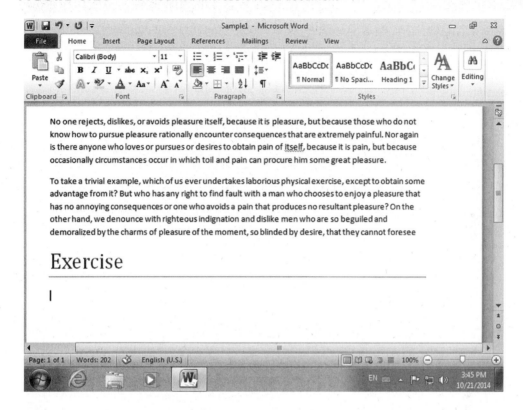

8.   Close the Sample1 Word document without saving your changes.

Copying and pasting data works in a similar way in all applications, including others from the Microsoft Office suite. Now that you know how to do this, you'll learn how to cut data from a place in a document and move it to somewhere else. Exercise 5.10 shows you how this is done in Microsoft Word. In order to complete this exercise, make sure the Sample1.docx practice document has been downloaded to your computer.

EXERCISE 5.10

Moving Data in Microsoft Word

1.   Click Start and then Computer.

2.   Browse to the location of the Sample1 Word document and double-click it.

It will be opened with Microsoft Word.

EXERCISE 5.10 *(continued)*

3. Select the word *Exercise*.

4. In the Home tab of the ribbon, go to the Clipboard section and click the Cut button.

   You will see the word *Exercise* disappear from the document (Figure 5.26).

FIGURE 5.26 The Microsoft Word document with a deletion

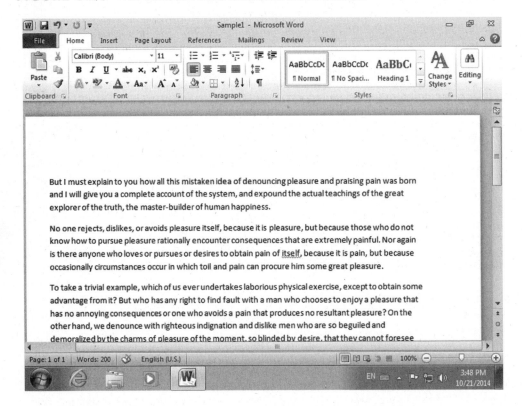

5. Go to the bottom of the document, immediately after the last word, *foresee*, and click where the word ends.

   The mouse cursor will be moved to that position.

6. Press Enter on your keyboard, and a new empty line is added to the document.

7. In the Home tab of the ribbon, go to the Clipboard section and click the Paste button.

   The word *Exercise* is now moved to the bottom of the document.

8. Close the Sample1 Word document without saving your changes.

Dragging and Dropping Data When Using Microsoft Office Applications

Another basic but important concept that you should master when using applications of all kinds, including the Microsoft Office suite, is *drag and drop*—a gesture that you do with the mouse in which you select an object like text or an image and then grab it and drag it to a different location. With the left mouse button still pressed, you drag your selection to the desired location and then release the mouse button. The object you selected is now moved from the initial location to the final one.

To help you get the hang of it, in Exercise 5.11 you will learn how to drag and drop data when using Microsoft PowerPoint. In order to complete this exercise, please download the Presentation1.pptx practice file to your computer.

EXERCISE 5.11

Dragging and Dropping Data When Using Microsoft Office Applications

1. Click Start and then Computer.

2. Browse to the location of the Presentation1 PowerPoint presentation and double-click it.

   It will be opened with Microsoft PowerPoint.

3. In Microsoft PowerPoint, click the image with the left mouse button and keep it pressed.

   The image is selected (Figure 5.27).

FIGURE 5.27　Selecting an image in Microsoft PowerPoint

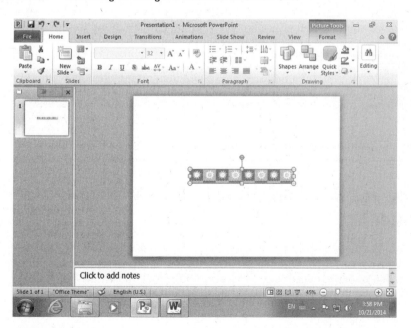

4. With the left mouse button still pressed, slowly drag the image to the bottom of the presentation.

5. Release the mouse button when you reach the bottom (Figure 5.28).

FIGURE 5.28   Moving an image in Microsoft PowerPoint

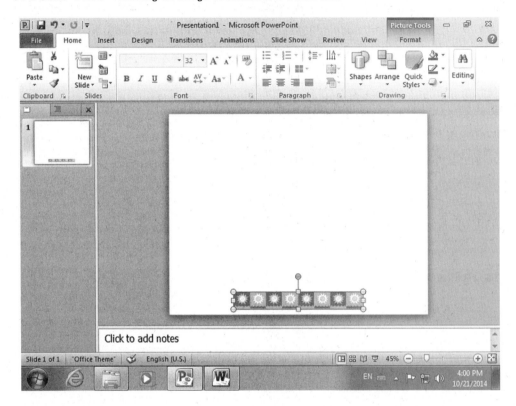

6. Close the Presentation1 PowerPoint presentation without saving your changes.

Finding and Replacing Data in Your Microsoft Office Documents

When working on all kinds of documents, chances are that you want to quickly find a certain word or a certain paragraph. You can do that with the help of the Find feature. You can type one or more keywords and Microsoft Office will find all the occurrences of your keywords in the document that you have opened. You can then navigate through all the matches very quickly until you find the one you need.

You may also need to replace a word or a sequence of words with another to improve the way you communicate in your documents. This can be done with the help of the Find and Replace tool that's available in all Microsoft Office applications.

In Exercise 5.12 you will learn how to find data when using Microsoft Word as well as how to replace data. In order to complete this exercise, you will use the `Sample1.docx` practice document you previously downloaded to your computer.

EXERCISE 5.12

Finding and Replacing Data in Microsoft Word

1. Click Start and then Computer.

2. Browse to the location of the Sample1 Word document and double-click it.

    It will be opened with Microsoft Word.

3. On the ribbon, in the Home tab, go to the Editing section and click the Find button.

    A Navigation pane is shown on the left side of the Microsoft Word window.

4. Type the word **that** in the Navigation pane and press Enter on your keyboard.

    Microsoft Word searches for all the instances of the word *that* and highlights them in yellow.

5. To navigate through all the results it found, click the down arrow in the Navigation pane (Figure 5.29).

FIGURE 5.29   The Navigation pane in Microsoft Word

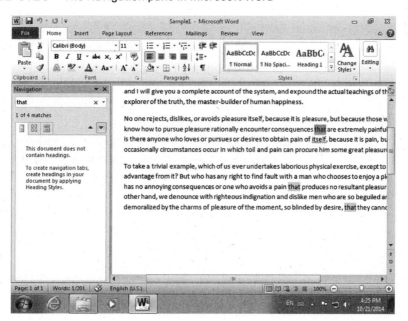

6. Close the Navigation pane by clicking the X button on its top-right corner.

7. On the ribbon, in the Home tab, go to the Editing section and click the Replace button.

8. In the Find And Replace window, type the word **that** in the Find What text field.

9. Type the word **who** in the Replace With text field and click Replace All (Figure 5.30).

FIGURE 5.30   The Find And Replace dialog

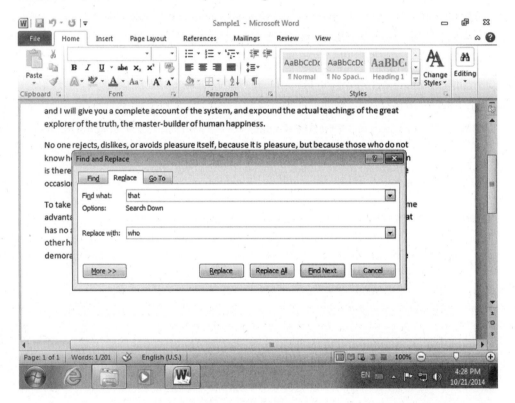

Microsoft Word informs you that it has reached the end of the document and asks if you want to continue searching at the beginning (Figure 5.31).

10. Click Yes.

Microsoft Word informs you that it has completed its search and that it has made a number of replacements (Figure 5.32).

FIGURE 5.31   Making text replacements in a Microsoft Word document

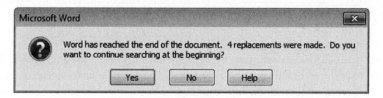

FIGURE 5.32   Microsoft Word completing the requested replacements

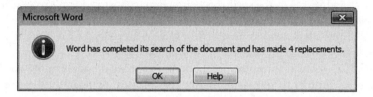

11. Click OK.

12. Notice that the word *that* has been replaced with the word *who* throughout the entire document.

13. Close the Sample1 Word document without saving your changes.

Checking the Spelling of Your Microsoft Office Documents

When writing anything, it is almost impossible not to make a minor mistake or two. You may misspell a couple of words, make some minor grammar errors, and so on. This can happen to anyone at any time, no matter how fine your language skills are.

To help users, many applications have built-in spell checkers, including the Microsoft Office suite. With the help of its spell checker, you can quickly identify all kinds of spelling and grammar mistakes and fix them in seconds. However, you should keep in mind that this feature isn't foolproof and it is no substitute for knowing grammar. In some cases, it does make wrong recommendations.

Also, when you are writing a document, Microsoft Office tends to automatically highlight misspelled words so that you identify them while writing without using its spell checker. In Figure 5.33, notice how the word *Exercse* is highlighted with a red line beneath it, signaling that it is misspelled.

When you use the spell checker in Microsoft Office, each mistake is highlighted, and one or more solutions are suggested for fixing it. You can choose to use any of those suggestions, or you can choose to ignore them, depending on what you think about its recommendations.

FIGURE 5.33   Misspelled text in a Microsoft Word document

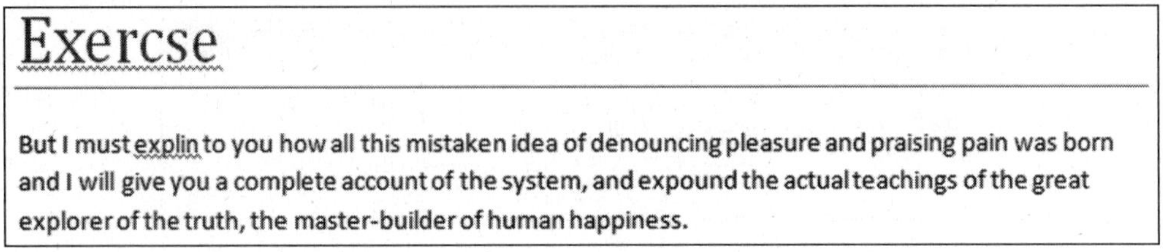

> # Exercse
> ──
> But I must explin to you how all this mistaken idea of denouncing pleasure and praising pain was born and I will give you a complete account of the system, and expound the actual teachings of the great explorer of the truth, the master-builder of human happiness.

You can also add words to the spell checker dictionary that it doesn't recognize and flags as misspelled. This is handy for correctly spelled specialized technical terms, such as *simulant*, and proper nouns and foreign words, such as *Steyn* and *neue*. You can start the spell checker at any time by pressing the F7 key on your keyboard.

In Exercise 5.13 you will learn how to check and improve the spelling of your Microsoft Word documents. In order to complete this exercise, please download the `Sample2.docx` practice document to your computer.

EXERCISE 5.13

Checking Spelling in Microsoft Word

1.   Click Start and then Computer.

2.   Browse to the location of the Sample2 Word document and double-click it.

   It will be opened with Microsoft Word. Notice that some words, including the title of this document, are misspelled.

3.   On the ribbon, click the Review tab (Figure 5.34), go to the Proofing section, and click the Spelling & Grammar button.

   The Spelling and Grammar checker is now displayed.

FIGURE 5.34   The Review tab in Microsoft Word

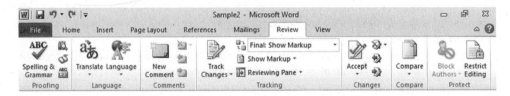

You can see the first word that was written incorrectly and several suggestions of correct words (Figure 5.35).

FIGURE 5.35   The Spelling And Grammar dialog

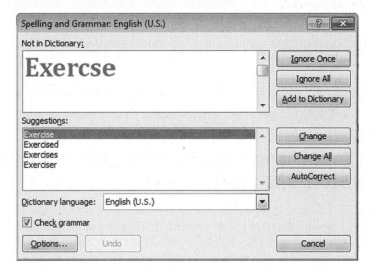

4.   Leave the default suggestion selected and click Change.

5.   Repeat step 4 for the next two words that are highlighted as misspelled.

     The word *itself* is incorrectly highlighted as a grammar error.

6.   Click Ignore Once and the word will not be corrected (Figure 5.36).

FIGURE 5.36   Receiving suggestions for corrections

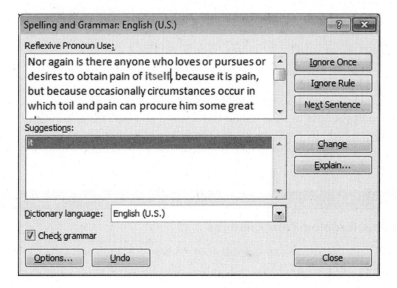

7. Repeat step 4 for the next two words that are highlighted as misspelled.

   You are now informed that the spelling and grammar check is complete.

8. Click OK.

   Notice how all incorrectly spelled words in this document have been corrected.

9. Close the Sample2 Word document without saving your changes.

Undoing Your Changes and Mistakes When Working with Microsoft Office Documents

While working on a document, you might make a mistake, or you might just change your mind and want to rewrite the most recent sentence that you wrote. When that happens, you can easily undo your recent edits by clicking the Undo button on top-left corner of the window, just above the ribbon. If you have clicked Undo too many times, you can redo your changes by clicking the Redo button near it. In Figure 5.37 you can see where these two buttons are placed.

FIGURE 5.37   The Undo and Redo buttons

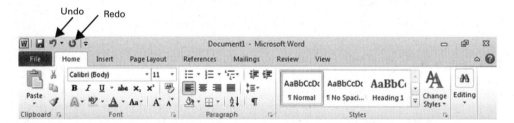

As always, you can also use your keyboard. The shortcut for Undo is Ctrl+Z, while the shortcut for Redo is Ctrl+Y.

The Undo and Redo tools work only as long as your document is open, only for current editing session. If you save it, close it, and then open it at a later time, you won't be able to undo the changes that you made during the previous editing session.

In Exercise 5.14 you will learn how to undo or redo your changes while editing a Microsoft Word document.

Undoing and Redoing Your Changes

1. Start Microsoft Word by clicking Start ➢ All Programs ➢ Microsoft Office ➢ Microsoft Word 2010.

   A new, blank document is created (Figure 5.38).

FIGURE 5.38   A Microsoft Word document

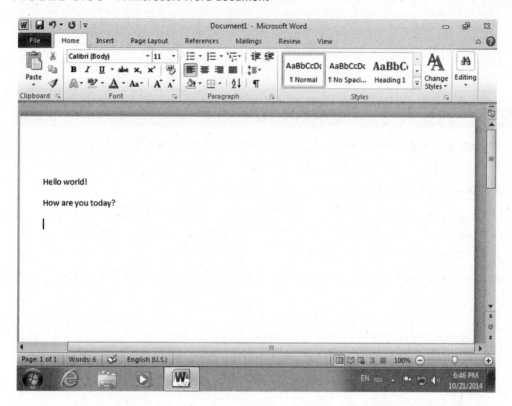

2. Type the words **Hello world**! and then press Enter on your keyboard.

3. Type **How are you today**? and then press Enter on your keyboard.

4. Click the Undo button once, on the top-left corner of the Microsoft Word window.

5. Notice how all the text that you have written disappears.

6. Click the Redo button once, found near the Undo button.

    Notice how your text is restored in the document.

7. Close Microsoft Word.

Hiding Your Data from Tables and Charts

When you work with lots of tables and charts, you may want to hide a portion of your data so that you see only what interests you at the moment. You can do that with ease when using Microsoft Office, and what's great about it is that your hidden data remains stored inside your documents. It is never lost. You can make updates to the rest of your document and, later on, decide to unhide your data and continue using it.

If you are working on a table that has a chart that's taking data from it, when you hide a portion of your data, that data is also hidden from the chart. As a result, both the table and the chart get updated automatically and display only the data that is not hidden.

To help you learn how to hide your data from tables and charts, work through Exercise 5.15, which showcases this feature using Microsoft Excel. In order to complete this exercise, please download the Book1.xslsx practice file to your computer.

EXERCISE 5.15

Hiding or Unhiding Data from Tables and Charts in Microsoft Excel

1. Click Start and then Computer.

2. Browse to the location of the Book1 Excel file and double-click it.

   It will be opened with Microsoft Excel. Notice that this spreadsheet has three columns with data and a chart that displays the same data in a visual format.

3. Click the B column to select it.

4. Right-click the B column and then click Hide in the context menu (Figure 5.39).

FIGURE 5.39   Hiding a column in Microsoft Excel

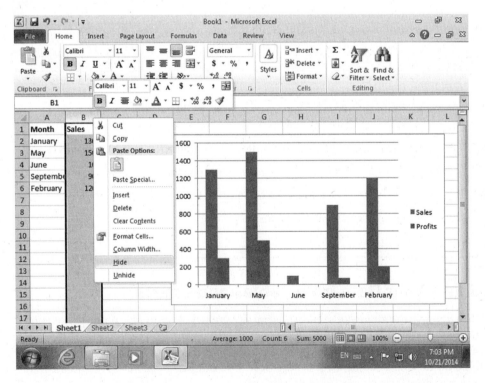

Notice how the B column is now hidden and the chart has been updated so that it no longer displays the data from this column.

5. Click the A column to select it and then press and hold the Shift key on your keyboard. Now click the C column to select it.

6. Right-click the C column and, in the context menu, click Unhide (Figure 5.40).

FIGURE 5.40   Unhiding a hidden column in Microsoft Excel

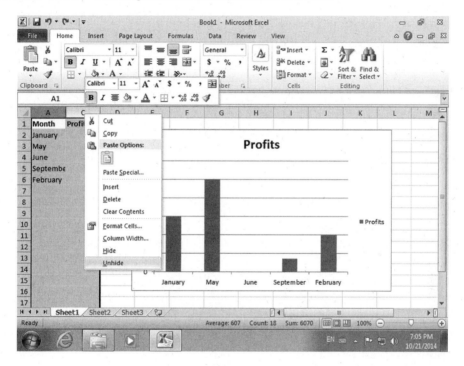

Notice how the B column is visible again and the chart has been updated automatically to include its data.

7. Close Microsoft Excel without saving your changes to the Book1 file.

Selecting Non-adjacent Cells in Microsoft Excel Tables

When you work with tables of all kinds in Microsoft Excel, you may need to select different cells that are not adjacent and format them differently in order to highlight certain aspects that are of interest to you.

This can be done only by using both the mouse and keyboard, and in Exercise 5.16 you will learn how it is done. In order to complete this exercise, make sure you have downloaded the Book1.xslsx practice file to your computer. In this exercise you will select the months with sales above 1000 and highlight them in bold.

EXERCISE 5.16

Selecting Non-adjacent Cells in Microsoft Excel Tables

1. Click Start and then Computer.

2. Browse to the location of the Book1 Excel file and double-click it.

   It will be opened with Microsoft Excel.

3. Click the A2 cell to select it and make it the active cell. Its value is January.

4. Press and hold the Ctrl key on your keyboard.

5. Click the A3 and then the A6 cells without releasing the Ctrl key.

6. Once all the desired cells are selected, release the Ctrl key.

   Notice how the three cells are selected and highlighted (Figure 5.41).

FIGURE 5.41   Selecting cells in Microsoft Excel

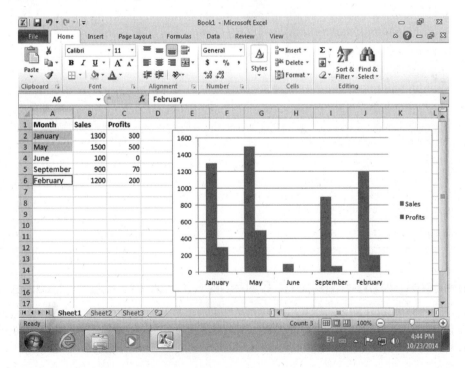

7. On the ribbon, in the Home tab, go to the Font section and click the B (Bold) button.

8. Click somewhere on the empty space in the Book1 Excel file and notice how the selected cells are now formatted differently from the others (Figure 5.42).

FIGURE 5.42   A Microsoft Excel worksheet

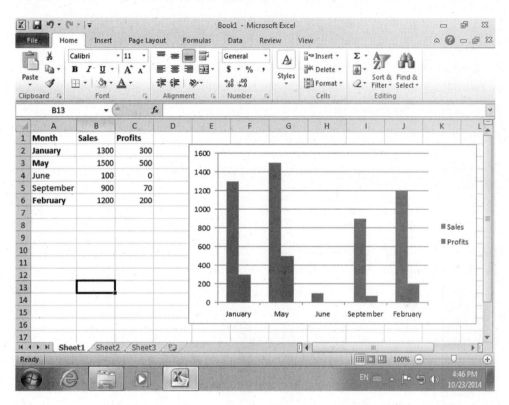

9. Close Microsoft Excel without saving your changes to the Book1 file.

Sorting Data When Working with Microsoft Excel Files

When you work with data, you may need to sort a range or table of data in more than one way. For example, you can sort employees first by department and then by last name or you can sort your financial results by the most profitable months. Whatever the criteria that you want to use for sorting, Microsoft Excel offers you the tools that you need.

In Exercise 5.17 you will learn how to sort the data in your worksheets by simple criteria. In order to complete this exercise, you must have the Book1.xslsx practice file on your computer.

EXERCISE 5.17

Sorting Data When Working with Microsoft Excel Files

1. Click Start and then Computer.

2. Browse to the location of the Book1 Excel file and double-click it.

    It will be opened with Microsoft Excel.

3. Click column A to select it.

4. On the ribbon, in the Home tab, go to the Editing section and click the Sort & Filter button.

5. Click Sort A To Z (Figure 5.43).

FIGURE 5.43   Sorting data in Microsoft Excel

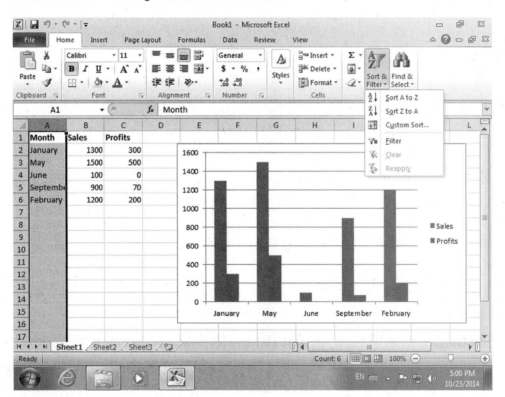

Microsoft Excel warns you that it found data next to your selection.

6. Select Expand The Selection, and click Sort.

    Notice how your table is sorted using the first letter of each month.

7. Click column C to select it.

8. On the ribbon, in the Home tab, go to the Editing section and click the Sort & Filter button.

9. Click Sort Smallest To Largest (Figure 5.44).

FIGURE 5.44   Sorting data in Microsoft Excel

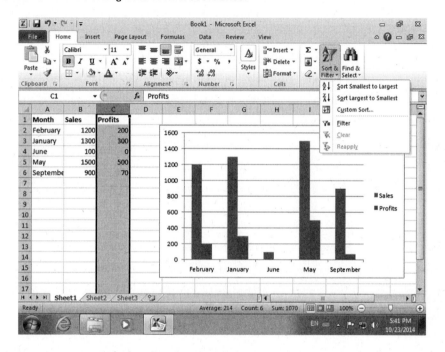

Microsoft Excel warns you that it found data next to your selection.

10. Select Expand The Selection and click Sort.

Notice how the table is sorted by profits, with the least profitable month being placed first and most profitable being placed last.

11. Close Microsoft Excel without saving your changes to the Book1 file.

Adjusting the Way You View Microsoft Office Files

When you are working on a Microsoft Office file, you may want to view it as it will appear in different formats. Depending on its type (Word document, Excel file, and so on), Microsoft Office offers different ways of viewing your work. They are all found in the View tab on the ribbon.

If you are viewing a Microsoft Word document, you have access to the following document views:

Print Layout   View the document as it will appear on the printed page. This is the default view for Word documents.

Full Screen Reading   View the document in full screen in order to maximize the space available for reading.

Web Layout   View the document as it would look on a web page.

Outline   View the document as an outline and show the outlining tools.

Draft   View the document as a draft and allow quick text editing.

If you are viewing a Microsoft Excel file, you have access to the following workbook views:

Normal   View it using the normal Microsoft Excel view.

Page Layout   View the file as it will appear on the printed page.

Page Break Preview   View a preview of where pages will break when the worksheet is printed.

Custom Views   Save a set of display and print settings as a custom view.

Full Screen   View the file in full screen in order to maximize the space available for editing.

If you are viewing a Microsoft PowerPoint presentation, you have access to the following presentation views:

Normal   View the presentation using the normal Microsoft PowerPoint view.

Slide Sorter   View the presentation in a format that allows you to quickly sort slides.

Notes Page   View the notes page for each slide to edit the speaker notes as they will look when you print them out.

Reading View   View the presentation as a slide show that fits within the window.

Another important tool for viewing your Office files as you want is Zoom. You can magnify the file that you are working on by 200 percent or more to see it better. This is especially useful if you have some eyesight problems or when you want to zoom in on a special element in your file. The Zoom tool is available in all Microsoft Office applications, and it offers different orders of magnification, depending on the application that you are using.

As you will see in Exercise 5.18, switching among the different views is very easy. We will demonstrate how to use this feature in Microsoft Word. Keep in mind that it works similarly in other Microsoft Office applications. In order to complete this exercise, you must have the Sample1.docx practice document on your computer.

EXERCISE 5.18

Changing the Way You View Your Microsoft Word Documents

1.   Click Start and then Computer.

2.   Browse to the location of the Sample1 Word document and double-click it.

It will be opened with Microsoft Word.

3. On the ribbon, click the View tab.

4. In the Document Views section, click Full Screen Reading.

Notice how the way you view your document changes (Figure 5.45).

FIGURE 5.45   The Full Screen Reading view in Microsoft Word

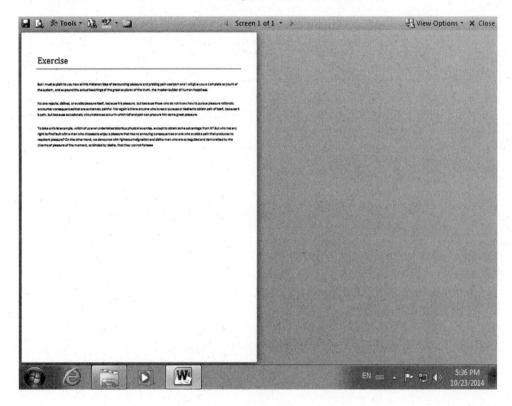

5. Click the Close button in the top-right side of the window.

6. In the Document Views section, click Draft.

Notice how the way you view your document changes (Figure 5.46).

7. To get back to the default way of viewing the document, in the Document Views section, click Print Layout.

8. In the Zoom section of the View tab, click the Zoom button.

The Zoom dialog opens (Figure 5.47).

FIGURE 5.46   The Draft view in Microsoft Word

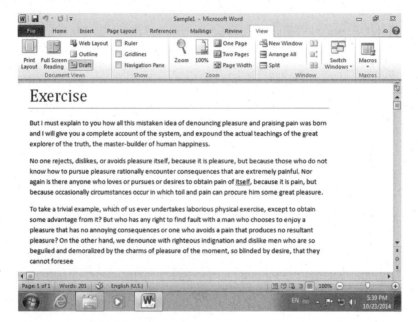

FIGURE 5.47   Setting the zoom in Microsoft Word

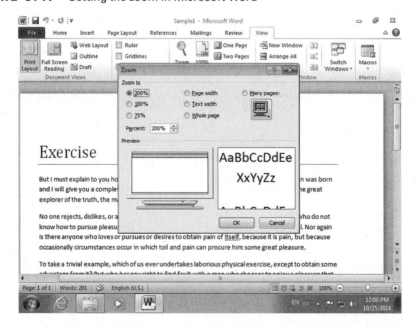

9. Select 200% as the Zoom To value and click OK.

Notice how the size of the document changes and how large the text is displayed.

10. To get back to the normal way of viewing the document, click the 100% button in the Zoom section of the View tab, on the ribbon.

11. Close the Sample1 Word document without saving your changes.

Adjusting the Size and the Orientation of Your Microsoft Office Files

When you create a Microsoft Office file like a document or a worksheet, you can adjust both the orientation that is used when creating it and the size.

Portrait   The default orientation is Portrait, similar to the orientation of a painting of a person hanging in an art gallery and the orientation used by the pages in a standard book.

Landscape   You can turn Portrait orientation 90 degrees to Landscape; as the name implies, it's the orientation of paintings of landscapes, such a countrysides. This is especially handy for files with large tables that need to fit one piece of paper.

The default size differs from country to country. For example, the default paper size that is used in the United States is Letter 8.5″ × 11″. In Europe, the default paper size is A4 (21 cm × 29.7 cm). You can easily switch to another paper size and adjust your Microsoft Office files accordingly.

In Exercise 5.19 you will learn how to adjust the orientation and the size of a Microsoft Word document. In order to complete this exercise, you must have the Sample1.docx practice document on your computer.

EXERCISE 5.19

Changing the Orientation and the Size of Your Microsoft Word Documents

1. Click Start and then Computer.

2. Browse to the location of the Sample1 Word document and double-click it.

It will be opened with Microsoft Word.

3. On the ribbon, click the Page Layout tab.

4. In the Page Setup section, click Orientation and then Landscape (Figure 5.48).

Notice how the orientation of the document has changed.

5. In the Page Setup section (Figure 5.49), click Size and then A4.

Notice how the size of the page has changed.

6. Close the Sample1 Word document without saving your changes.

FIGURE 5.48   Setting the orientation in Microsoft Word

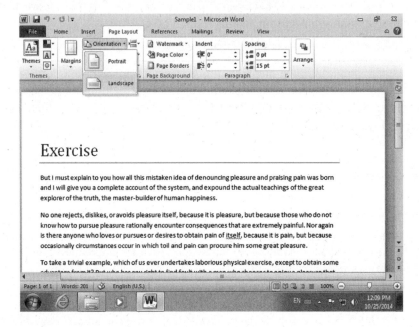

FIGURE 5.49   Setting the page size in Microsoft Word

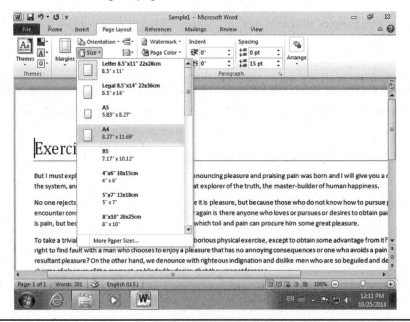

Printing Your Documents from Microsoft Office

All Microsoft Office applications allow you to print your work. The Printing options are accessed from the File menu on the top left. If you click File ➤ Print, you will see the following printing options and settings:

Copies   Choose the number of copies that you want to print.

Printer   Select the printer where you want to print your document.

Pages   Select the pages that you want to print. You can print all pages in your document, the current page or selection, or a custom range.

Sides   Select the sides of the page on which you want to print. You can print either on one side of the page or on both sides.

Collated   You can select whether you want the pages to be printed collated or uncollated.

Orientation   You can choose between Portrait and Landscape orientation.

Paper Size   Select the size of the page that you want to print on.

Margins   Select how you want the margins to be when printing your document.

Pages Per Sheet   Select how many pages you want to print per sheet of paper.

On the right side of the Print section you will see a preview of what will be printed according to your settings. When you have finished setting everything up, click the Print button, and the document will be printed using the printer and settings you selected.

You can also access the printing options by pressing Ctrl+P on your keyboard.

In Exercise 5.20 you will learn how to print documents from Microsoft Word. In order to complete this exercise, you must have the Sample1.docx practice document on your computer.

EXERCISE 5.20

Printing Your Microsoft Word Documents

1.   Click Start and then Computer.

2.   Browse to the location of the Sample1 Word document and double-click it.

  It will be opened with Microsoft Word.

3.   Click File in the top-left corner of the Microsoft Word window.

4.   In the File menu, click Print to access all your printing options (Figure 5.50).

5.   In the Copies box type **2**.

  Two copies of the document will be printed instead of one.

6.   Click Portrait Orientation and change it to Landscape Orientation.

FIGURE 5.50   The Print menu in Microsoft Word

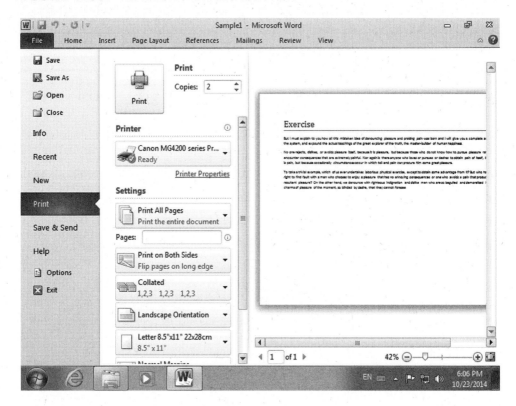

7. Leave all other printing settings unchanged.

    Notice how your document will be printed in the Print Preview on the right.

8. Click Print and wait for your document to be printed twice, on one piece of paper, using Landscape orientation and with a copy on each side of the page.

9. Close the Sample1 Word document without saving your changes.

Where to Get Help with Using Microsoft Office

Microsoft Office is a very complex product with lots of tools and features. Very few people know how to use them all, and most of us need only a small fraction of what this suite is capable of doing. However, chances are that you will eventually need to work on a more complex document or worksheet, which involves using advanced functions or formatting that you have not learned yet. When that happens, there are quite a few resources for documentation and instructions about Microsoft Office and how it works.

The easiest way to learn about each button and feature in the Microsoft Office user interface is to bring your mouse pointer over an option and wait for two seconds. A small balloon will pop up, giving you more details about the option you are hovering over. If there is additional help for that option, then it displays the Press F1 For More Help tip, as shown in Figure 5.51. You can press F1 key to get further help on that option.

FIGURE 5.51   A Help tip for the Shading button in Microsoft Word

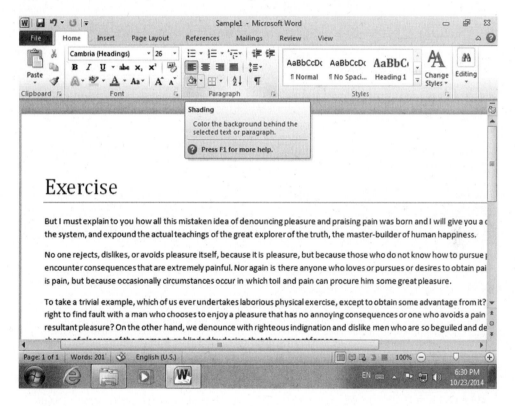

One of the quickest and best ways to learn more about what you want to do is to use the built-in Help documentation. When using a Microsoft Office application like Microsoft Word, press F1 on your keyboard or click the Help button on the top-right corner of the window (Figure 5.52). A Help window opens where you can type one or more keywords that describe what you want to do, and it will show you where to find documentation and tutorials on a wide variety of topics, features, and functions.

FIGURE 5.52 The Help button and window in Microsoft Word

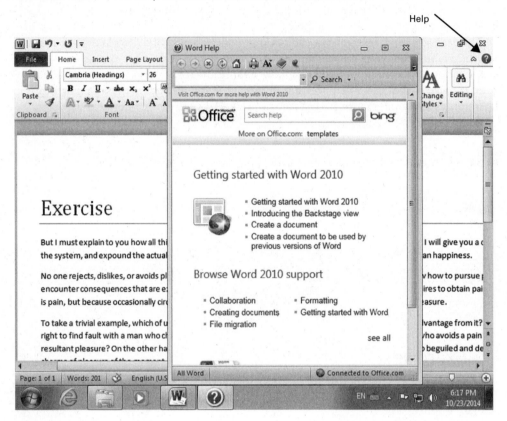

Another good source for finding help when using Microsoft Office is the following website: https://support.office.com.

Here you will find all kinds of guides and tutorials as well as troubleshooting tips for all kinds of errors and problems that may show up when you use Microsoft Office.

If you need to speak with others and ask for help, a great place to start is the Microsoft Answers Community, which can be found at this address: http://answers.microsoft.com/

Here you will be able to speak with Microsoft employees who are actively monitoring this community, technical experts, and other users.

If you are using Microsoft Office at work and you need help with solving a problem, don't hesitate to call the IT support department and ask for their help. Also, if you need to increase your level of knowledge when using Microsoft Office applications, check with the IT department to see whether they have training courses available, books, or other documentation that will help you get the most out of using this product.

The Basics of Formatting Your Microsoft Office Files

When you create documents, worksheets, and presentations, it is very important that you format them. Formatting not only makes your work look good but also helps get your message across to your audience more effectively. Microsoft Office gives you access to all kinds of formatting tools, from basic text formatting attributes like the font used and the size to how your titles and paragraphs are styled. In the following sections you will become familiar with all the basic formatting tools that are available in Microsoft Word and other Microsoft Office applications and learn how to use them.

Formatting the Text in Your Documents

In all Microsoft Office applications where you work with text, you have access to several formatting tools. They are always found on the ribbon, in the Font section of the Home tab. In Figure 5.53 you can see the formatting tools that are available in Microsoft Word. Similar tools are available in Microsoft Excel, Microsoft PowerPoint, and even Microsoft Access. The only difference in Microsoft Access is that the Font section is named Text Formatting.

FIGURE 5.53 Formatting tools in Microsoft Word

At the top of the Font section you will find the name of the font that is currently used for the document or the selection that you have made, as well as its size. You can change the font for the whole document or a portion of it. The list of fonts available is very long, and it includes fonts that look very different from one another. When you click the down arrow near the font name, you can see the list of available fonts as well as a preview of how each font looks. As shown in Figure 5.54, the name of each font is displayed using that font so that you get a preview of how your text will look when using it. You can change the font size by performing the following steps:

1. Select text.
2. Click the down arrow near the font size.
3. Choose another size, or type the size that you wish to use and overwrite the current one.

FIGURE 5.54   Changing the font size in Microsoft Word

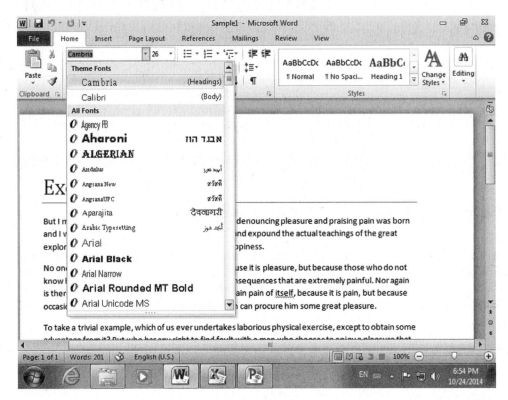

Use Caution in Choosing Fonts

One downside to using more unusual fonts in your documents is that in order for your documents to be viewed correctly by others on other computers, they need to have those fonts installed. That's why it is best that you use popular fonts like Arial, Verdana, Cambria, Calibri, or Times New Roman. They are available in many operating systems, and your documents will look the same no matter which computer you are using.

On the other hand, if you plan to distribute your document in print, such as a leaflet, or convert it to a PDF file, then you can use fonts to your heart's desire.

Beneath the font and the font size you will find important formatting tools like these:

Bold   **Makes the selected text bold.** You can also use the keyboard shortcut Ctrl+B.

Italic   *Italicizes the selected text.* You can also use the keyboard shortcut Ctrl+I.

Underline   <u>Underlines the selected text.</u> You can also use the keyboard shortcut Ctrl+U.

In Exercise 5.21 you will learn how to format the text in your Microsoft Word documents. In order to complete this exercise, you must have the `Sample1.docx` practice document on your computer.

EXERCISE 5.21

Formatting the Text in Microsoft Word Documents

1.   Click Start and then Computer.

2.   Browse to the location of the Sample1 Word document and double-click it.

     It will be opened with Microsoft Word.

3.   Select the word *Exercise* from the title.

4.   On the ribbon, go to the Font section of the Home tab and click the B (Bold) button.

5.   Then, click somewhere else inside your document to deselect the word *Exercise*.

     Notice how the title of the document is now written in Bold.

6.   Select the first paragraph from the document, just beneath the title.

7.   Press Ctrl+I on your keyboard and click somewhere else inside the document to deselect the paragraph.

     Notice how the selected text is now italicized.

8.   Select the second paragraph from the document.

9.   On the ribbon, go to the Font section of the Home tab, click the down arrow near the font name, and then select Arial.

10. Click the down arrow near the font size, and then select 8 as the size.

11. Click the U (Underline) button and then click somewhere else inside the document to deselect the paragraph.

     Notice how the selected text is now underlined, and it uses a different font and font size from the rest of the text. The final result should look similar to Figure 5.55.

12. Close the Sample1 Word document without saving your changes.

EXERCISE 5.21 *(continued)*

FIGURE 5.55 A formatted document in Microsoft Word

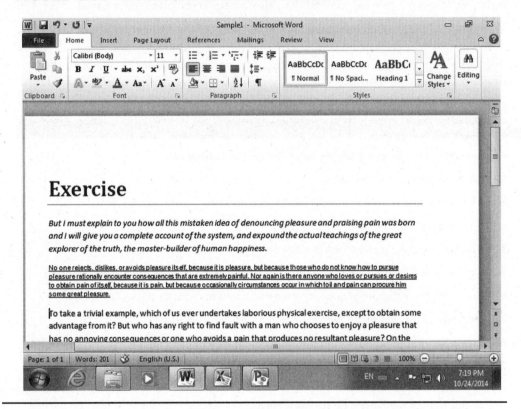

Using Styles to Format Your Documents

You can enhance the look of your documents and their readability by using a feature named Styles. A *style* is a set of formatting characteristics, like the font name and size, color, paragraph alignment and spacing, borders, and shading. The styles are found on the ribbon, in the Styles section of the Home tab. They are available only in Microsoft Word and Microsoft Excel.

A style can be applied to the headings of a document, any of its paragraphs, as well as elements like bulleted lists. Styles are helpful also because they help you reduce the number of steps involved in formatting a document. For example, let's assume that you want to format the heading in a document. Instead of selecting the heading, setting the font and the size as well as setting it to Bold, you can achieve the same results by selecting it and then applying the Heading 1 style.

To access the available styles, first select the text that you want to format and then click the down arrow in the Styles section. In Figure 5.56 you can see the styles that are available by default in Microsoft Word.

FIGURE 5.56   Changing the style in Microsoft Word

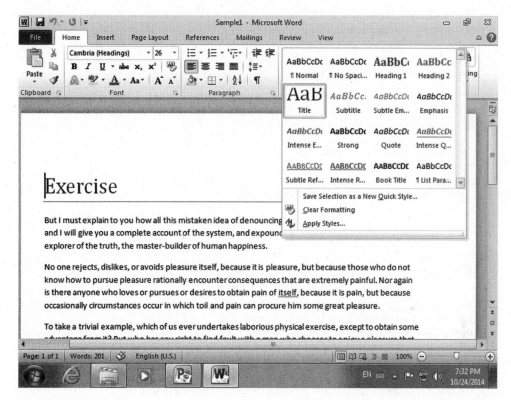

As you can see, there are styles for the title of your document, headings, paragraphs, and lists. In Exercise 5.22 you will learn how to use them when working on Microsoft Word documents. In order to complete this exercise, use the `Sample1.docx` practice document you previously downloaded to your computer.

EXERCISE 5.22

Using Styles in Microsoft Word Documents

1. Click Start and then Computer.

2. Browse to the location of the Sample1 Word document and double-click it.

    It will be opened with Microsoft Word.

EXERCISE 5.22 (continued)

3. Select the word *Exercise* from the title.

4. On the ribbon, go to the Styles section of the Home tab, and click the down arrow to see a list with the available styles for your selection.

5. Click the Book Title style (Figure 5.57), and then click somewhere else inside your document to deselect the word *Exercise*.

FIGURE 5.57   Applying the Book Title style in Microsoft Word

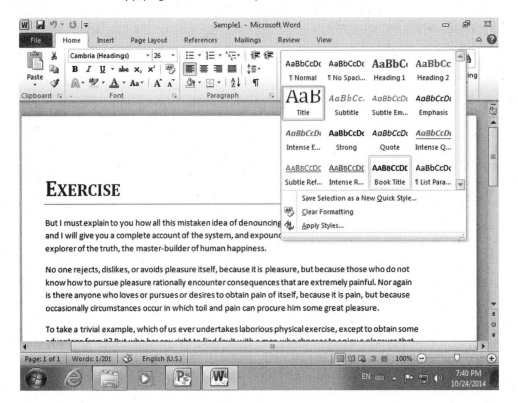

Notice how the title is now formatted differently.

6. Select the first paragraph from the document, just beneath the title.

7. On the ribbon, go to the Styles section of the Home tab, and click the down arrow to see a list with the available styles for your selection.

8. Click the Quote style and then click somewhere else inside your document to deselect the paragraph.

Notice how the paragraph is now formatted differently.

9. Select the second paragraph from the document.

10. On the ribbon, go to the Styles section of the Home tab and click the down arrow to see a list with the available styles for your selection.

11. Click the Strong style and then click somewhere else inside your document to deselect the paragraph.

Notice how the paragraph is now formatted differently. The final result should look similar to Figure 5.58.

FIGURE 5.58   A formatted document in Microsoft Word

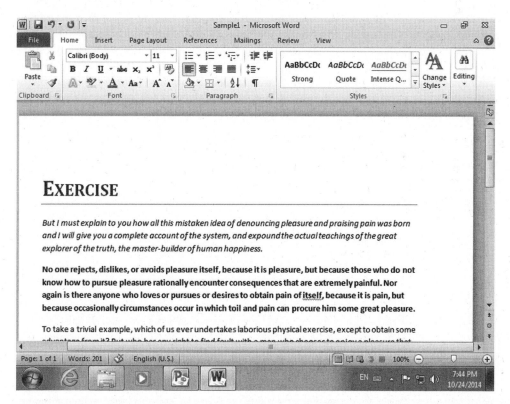

12. Close the Sample1 Word document without saving your changes.

Working with Multimedia Files in Microsoft Office

When you create more complex documents and presentations, you may need to add pictures and all kinds of files that enhance your message and your presentations. In order to be able to do that, you need to master the basics of adding files to your documents and adjusting them.

In this section you will first learn how to add multimedia files to your Microsoft PowerPoint presentations, and then you'll learn how to adjust the pictures that you have added.

Adding Multimedia Files to Your Presentations

In order to make your documents more convincing, you may need to insert pictures, videos, or audio recordings. You may also need to insert shortcuts to other documents that provide more detailed information about a specific subject. This can easily be done with Microsoft Office.

All the options for inserting other files into your documents are found in the Insert tab on the ribbon (Figure 5.59). There you will find buttons for inserting pictures, screenshots, charts, and all kinds of files.

FIGURE 5.59 The Insert tab in Microsoft PowerPoint

In Exercise 5.23 you will learn how to add a picture to a Microsoft PowerPoint presentation as well as how to add a shortcut to a Microsoft Word document. In order to complete this exercise, please make sure you have downloaded the `Presentation1.pptx`, `Picture1.jpg`, and `Sample1.docx` practice files to your computer.

EXERCISE 5.23

Inserting a Picture into a Microsoft PowerPoint Presentation

1. Click Start and then Computer.

2. Browse to the location of the Presentation1 PowerPoint presentation and double-click it.

    It will be opened with Microsoft PowerPoint.

3. Click the Insert tab on the ribbon.

4. Click the Picture button in the Images section.

    The Insert Picture dialog is shown (Figure 5.60).

FIGURE 5.60   The Insert Picture dialog

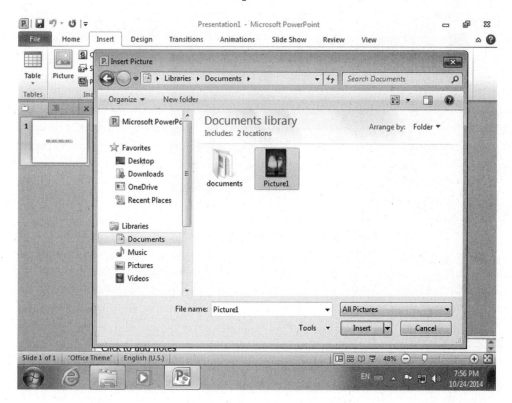

5. Browse to the location where the `Picture1.jpg` file is found, select it, and click Insert.

    The picture you selected is now added to your presentation.

6. Click somewhere else inside the presentation to see how it looks.

7. Click the Insert tab on the ribbon.

8. Go to the Text section of the Insert tab and click the Insert Object button highlighted in Figure 5.61.

    The Insert Object dialog is shown.

FIGURE 5.61   The Insert Object button in Microsoft PowerPoint

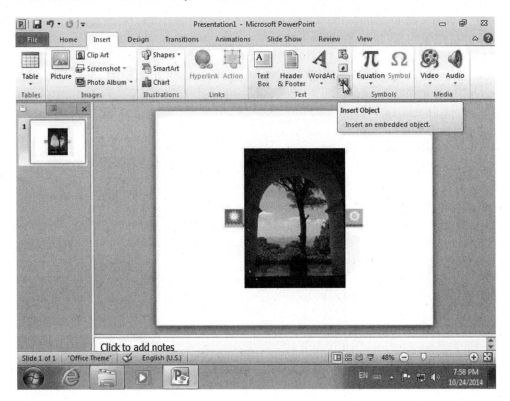

9. Select Create From File and then click Browse.

   The Browse dialog is shown (Figure 5.62).

10. Browse to the location where the Sample1.docx file is found, select it, and click Open.

   You are taken back to the Insert Object dialog (Figure 5.63).

11. Select Link and then Display As Icon. Then, click OK.

   The Sample1.docx file is now linked to your presentation. You are taken back to the Microsoft PowerPoint window where you will see a Microsoft Word icon representing a shortcut to the selected file.

12. Double-click the Microsoft Word Document icon from your presentation.

   The Sample1.docx file is opened in Microsoft Word.

FIGURE 5.62   The Browse dialog

FIGURE 5.63   The Insert Object dialog

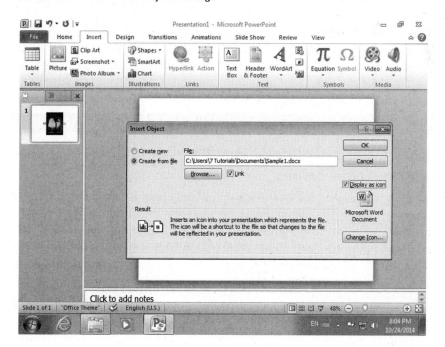

13. Close the Sample1 Word document without saving your changes.

14. Close the Presentation1 PowerPoint presentation without saving your changes.

Adjusting the Pictures Used in Your Presentations

When adding pictures to your documents, you will need to adjust them so that they fit into your document and achieve their desired purpose. Microsoft Office includes several adjusting tools, including the following:

Rotate   The act of changing the position of an image. You can rotate a picture by using several presets offered by Microsoft Office or by using the rotating handle that is displayed when you double-click the image that you want to rotate.

Resize   The act of changing the dimensions of an image to improve the way it fits into your document. To resize an image, you first double-click it and then use the resizing handles that are displayed on its margins. With the help of the mouse you can drag any resizing handle to the desired position and change the size of the image.

Crop   Refers to the removal of the outer parts of an image to improve framing, accentuate subject matter, or change aspect ratio. You can crop an image manually, by using the crop handles displayed when using this tool or by using any of the available cropping presets.

In Exercise 5.24 you will learn how to adjust the display of pictures in your Microsoft PowerPoint presentations. You will first rotate a picture, resize it, and then crop it. In order to complete this exercise, please use the `Presentation1.pptx` practice file you previously downloaded to your computer.

EXERCISE 5.24

Adjusting Pictures in Microsoft PowerPoint Presentations

1. Click Start and then Computer.

2. Browse to the location of the Presentation1 PowerPoint presentation and double-click it.

   It will be opened with Microsoft PowerPoint.

3. Double-click the image found inside the presentation to select it and access the formatting tools that are available for it.

   The Format tab is shown on the ribbon as the active tab.

4. In the Format tab on the ribbon, go to the Arrange section and click the Rotate button.

   A menu is shown with several options, as shown in Figure 5.64.

FIGURE 5.64   Options for rotating a picture

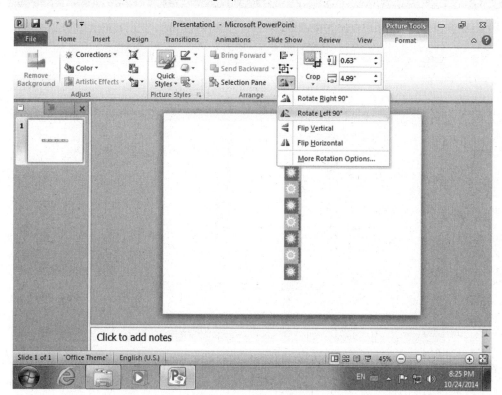

5. Click Rotate Left 90°.

    Notice how the image is now rotated to the left by 90°.

6. With the image still selected, move the mouse cursor to the middle of its right margin, where a sizing rectangle is shown.

    Notice how the mouse cursor changes to a two-headed arrow.

7. Click the resizing rectangle, and with the left mouse button still pressed, drag the image slowly to the right. Release it before reaching the right margin of the presentation (Figure 5.65).

8. Notice how the image has been resized.

9. In the Format tab on the ribbon, go to the Size section and click the Crop button.

    You will see several black crop handles displayed on the margins of the image (Figure 5.66).

FIGURE 5.65   Resizing an image in Microsoft PowerPoint

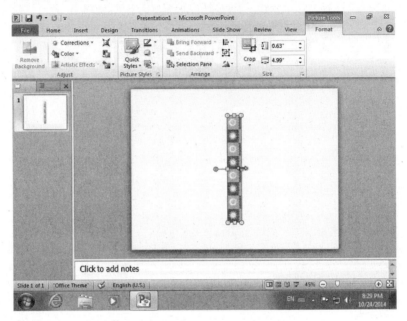

FIGURE 5.66   Cropping an image in Microsoft PowerPoint

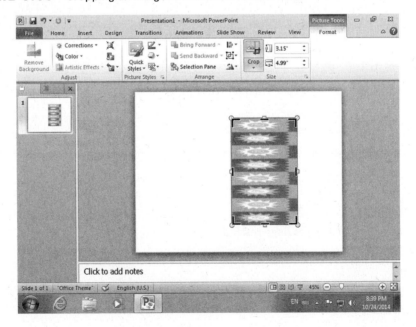

10. Click and hold the middle handle on the right margin of the image.

11. With the left mouse button still pressed, drag the handle slowly to the left.

12. Release the handle after cropping the image a bit and then click somewhere else inside the presentation.

    Notice how portions of the image have been removed.

13. Close the Presentation1 PowerPoint presentation without saving your changes.

Summary

In this chapter we covered a lot of ground, and we tried to give you the basics that you need to master in order to create simple Microsoft Office files like documents, worksheets, or presentations.

You learned how to start the Microsoft Office applications that are available in this suite, how to create your first empty files, and how to save them. We taught you how to work with multiple application windows at the same time so that you can be more productive and quickly copy and paste data from one window to another.

Then we moved on to subjects like how to select data, find data, or replace it with other data. You learned how to check and improve the spelling and grammar used in your Microsoft Office files, how to undo the changes that you do not want to keep, and how to redo your recent modifications. You learned different ways of selecting and sorting data, as well as how to adjust the way you view your documents, including their size and orientation. When you have finished editing your Microsoft Office files, you may want to print them and share them with others. In this chapter we also covered the basics of printing any Microsoft Office file.

When creating a Microsoft Office file, it is a good idea to format it so that you improve the way it looks. Doing that will ensure that it is easier to understand the data that it includes and that your message gets across to your audience more clearly. That's why we demonstrated how to use the basic formatting tools that are available in Microsoft Office. Don't hesitate to experiment with them and master the way they work so that you are more effective in your communication with others.

In some documents, presentations, and worksheets you may need to insert pictures that enhance your message or help you prove your point. We shared the basic things that you need to know about importing other files into your Microsoft Office files: things like how to insert a picture or a shortcut to another Microsoft Office file. We also shared how to adjust the pictures that you add into your Microsoft Office files so that you improve the way they fit into your documents and the end result helps you achieve your objectives.

Exam Essentials

Learn how to open and close Microsoft Office applications and files.   Before you can create any file with Microsoft Office, you need to know how to start the applications from this suite. Also, it is very useful to know how to open Microsoft Office files that were created by you and others, as well as how to close both the Microsoft Office files and the applications that you are using.

Know how to use multiple windows at the same time and switch among them   You may have to work with multiple application windows and files. Knowing how to quickly switch among them and how to snap windows side by side in order to work with two windows at the same time will help you become more productive.

Learn useful keyboard shortcuts for Microsoft Office applications.   Your productivity will be enhanced if you learn the keyboard shortcuts for common tasks like accessing options from the ribbon, saving your work, closing files or applications, and the like.

Know how to select data, copy it, move it, or drag it around your Microsoft Office files.   When you work with multiple Microsoft Office files, you will have to select data, copy it to different documents, move it inside your files, and drag it from one place to another.

Know how to find and replace data in your Microsoft Office files.   When you view a document, you may want to quickly jump to where the data that interests you is found. That's why you should know how to use the Search feature. Also, you may have made a mistake in your document and you want to replace your incorrect data with the correct data. That's why you should know how to use the Replace feature.

Learn how to improve the spelling and grammar for your Microsoft Office files.   Chances are that you will make both spelling and grammar mistakes when creating a Microsoft Office file. It is useful to know how to quickly fix these mistakes using the features that are offered by this suite of applications.

Learn how to undo your mistakes and redo your recent changes.   If you are in a rush, chances are that you will make many small mistakes when creating a Microsoft Office file. Using the Undo tool will help you undo those mistakes as quickly as possible and allow you to fix them. Also, you may change your mind about a recent change that you undid and want to redo it.

Know how to select data, hide it, or sort it.   When working with lots of data sets, you will need to perform many operations with them. Knowing how to select data in all kinds of ways, hide it when you don't need to see it but you want to keep it, or sort it using different criteria will make you more productive in your work.

Learn how to adjust the way you are viewing Microsoft Office files, their size, and orientation.   In most cases, you will be OK with the default way of viewing your Microsoft Office files. However, in some cases, you may need to adjust things like the paper size that is used, the orientation, the magnification, or the way you are viewing these files.

Know how to print your Microsoft Office files.   You may need to share your work with others. One way to do this is to print the files that you have created and share them with your co-workers.

Understand what kind of help you can get or find when using Microsoft Office.   You may need to know more about a certain function or feature of Microsoft Office, or you may need to learn how to do a certain action in this suite. It is very useful to know what kind of documentation is available, how to access it, and how to use it. Also, it is good to know where you can get help if you are having issues with Microsoft Office.

Know how to format your Microsoft Office files.   Your Microsoft Office files will need to look good in order to be easy for others to read and understand. That's why you should know how to use the formatting and styling tools that are available in this suite.

Learn how to add multimedia files into Microsoft Office.   In order to be more effective in your communication with others, you may need to insert multimedia files in your Microsoft Office documents, things like pictures or videos. You should know to adjust the way they are integrated into your Microsoft Office files.

Key Terms

Before you take the exam, be certain you are familiar with the following terms:

Crop	Rotate
Drag and drop	Style
Resize	

Review Questions

1. What is the correct procedure for opening a Microsoft Word document from your computer? (Choose all that apply.)

   A. Click Start ➤ All Programs ➤ Microsoft Office ➤ Microsoft Word 2010.

   B. Click Start ➤ Computer. Browse to the location of the Word document that you want to use and click it.

   C. Click Start ➤ All Programs ➤ Microsoft Office ➤ Microsoft Word 2010. Then, click File ➤ Open. Browse to the location of the Word document that you want to use, select it, and click Open.

   D. Click Start ➤ Computer. Browse to the location of the Word document that you want to use and double-click it.

2. What is the difference between Save and Save As?

   A. Save keeps your edits and changes and saves them to your file, using its existing location and name. Save As keeps your edits and changes and saves them to a copy of your file that can be stored in another location, with a different name.

   B. Save is used to save your latest changes into the file and the file is closed. Save As doesn't save your latest changes by keeps the file open.

   C. Save and Save As behave the same way when saving your file for the first time and there is no difference between them.

   D. Save As asks you to select where you want to save the file and give it a name.

3. Which keyboard shortcut allows you to select all the text found inside a document?

   A. Shift+End

   B. Ctrl+A

   C. Shift+Page Down

   D. Ctrl+V

4. What does the Spelling and Grammar tool do in Microsoft Word? (Choose all that apply.)

   A. Checks the spelling and provides suggestions for improvement

   B. Checks the formatting and provides suggestions for improvement

   C. Counts the number of words, characters, and pages that are found inside your document

   D. Checks the grammar and provides suggestions for improvement

5. What happens when you hide a column from a table? (Choose all that apply.)

   A. The column is no longer visible to users.

   B. The data from the column is stored in your file.

   C. The data from the column is deleted and lost.

   D. The data from the column is no longer used in charts.

6. How do you undo your most recent changes to the document? (Choose all that apply.)

   A. Press Ctrl+V on your keyboard.   V ~ paste

   B. Press Ctrl+Z on your keyboard.

   C. Click the Undo button on top-left corner of the window, just above the ribbon.

   D. Click the File menu and then the Undo option.

7. How do you select non-adjacent cells in an Excel table?

   A. Click the first cell that you want to select. Then click the other non-adjacent cells that you want to select.

   B. Click the first column that you want to select. Press and hold the Ctrl key on your keyboard and, with the mouse, click the column near it.

   C. Click the first cell that you want to select. Press and hold the Alt key on your keyboard and, with the mouse, click the other non-adjacent cells that you want to select.

   D. Click the first cell that you want to select. Press and hold the Ctrl key on your keyboard and, with the mouse, click the other non-adjacent cells that you want to select.

8. How do you print a Microsoft Word document? (Choose all that apply.)

   A. Click File ➤ Print. Configure the printing options, preview how your document will be printed, and click the Print button.

   B. Press Ctrl+Y on your keyboard. Configure the printing options, preview how your document will be printed, and click the Print button.

   C. Press Ctrl+P on your keyboard. Configure the printing options, preview how your document will be printed, and click the Print button.

   D. Click File ➤ Save&Send. Configure the printing option, preview how your document will be printed, and click the Print button.

9. What formatting characteristics can be changed by using styles?

   A. The font name, size, and color

   B. The font name and size, the color, the paragraph alignment and spacing, and the borders and shading

   C. Whether the selected text is bold, italic, or underlined

   D. The headings of a document

10. Which formatting tool can you use to remove the outer parts of an image and improve its framing, or change its aspect ratio, or accentuate the subject matter?

   A. Rotate

   B. Resize

   C. Crop

   D. Print

Chapter

6

Using Microsoft Word

THE FOLLOWING IC3 GS4: KEY APPLICATIONS EXAM OBJECTIVES ARE COVERED IN THIS CHAPTER:

✓ **Organizing Data**

- Demonstrate how to organize text and data into tables within a word processor. Further demonstrate the ability to add columns, rows, merge and split cells within those tables. Demonstrate how to move, copy, and paste user data within an application such as a word processor, spreadsheet, presentation package, database manager, or other software application product.

- Demonstrate how to organize text and data into lists within a word processor. Further demonstrate the ability to order and re-order those lists according to various criteria (alphabetize, lowest-to-highest, by date, etc.).

✓ **Layout**

- Demonstrate how to set line and paragraph spacing within a word processor.

- Demonstrate how to arrange user data and set options within a word processor so as to cause those text and data to display and print in a particular format or layout. Within that context control the attributes and structures listed in the objective to display and print as specified, including ways to save, change, and delete those saved configurations.

- Demonstrate how to indent text within a word processing program.

In this chapter we will take a deeper dive into Microsoft Office applications and cover the details of using Microsoft Word. You will first learn how to configure the layout of your documents so that they look good and help you get your message across. You will learn how to do things like adjusting the spacing of your documents, aligning the text, organizing documents into columns, indenting the text, and setting the margins for your documents or your paragraphs.

Then we will take a look at how to better organize the data in your documents and share things like how to create lists and sort them according to different criteria, how to create tables, and how to better organize them. Finally, you will learn how to add page numbers to your documents so that you can easily keep track of the page location, even after you have printed your document.

Configuring the Layout of Your Documents

It is easy to start typing text into your documents, and it doesn't require any special skills. However, in order to communicate well with others, you will have to improve the default layout of your documents. Luckily, Microsoft Word provides many useful tools that will help you with this. In this section we will cover each of them individually.

Adjusting Line and Paragraph Spacing in Your Documents

When you create a document, Microsoft Word automatically inserts extra spaces between all the lines of text in a paragraph and between paragraphs to improve the document's readability. Spacing can be measured in either lines or points. In Microsoft Word 2010 the default spacing is set to 1.15 points, and 10 points are added after each paragraph. In other versions of Microsoft Word the spacing may be different.

If you are not happy with the default spacing of your document, you can adjust both the line spacing and the paragraph spacing for the entire document or just for specific portions of it. You can increase spacing to improve readability or reduce it to fit more text on the page.

The quickest way to change and improve the spacing of your documents is to use the quick styles that are available in Microsoft Word. We explained them in Chapter 5, and we also demonstrated how to use them.

However, you can also manually change the spacing for specific selections of text, and in Exercise 6.1 we will demonstrate how this is done. In order to complete this exercise, please download the Sample1.docx practice document to your computer.

EXERCISE 6.1

Changing the Line and Paragraph Spacing in Microsoft Word

1. Click Start and then Computer.

2. Browse to the location of the Sample1 Word document and double-click it.

   It will be opened with Microsoft Word.

3. On the ribbon, in the Home tab, go to the Paragraph section and click the Line And Paragraph Spacing button shown in Figure 6.1.

FIGURE 6.1   Spacing options available in Microsoft Word

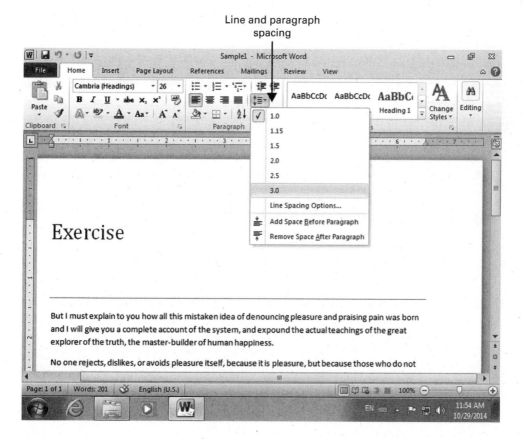

4. Click 3.0 as the value for line spacing.

Notice how the line spacing has been increased after the line where the heading of this document is written, similar to Figure 6.2.

FIGURE 6.2 Using different line spacing in Microsoft Word

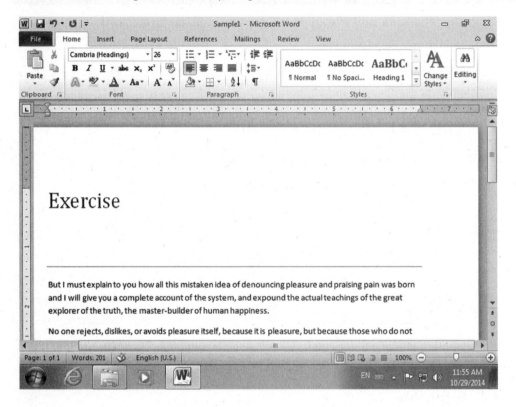

5. Select the second paragraph from the Sample1 document, the one that starts with "No one rejects."

6. On the ribbon, in the Home tab, go to the Paragraph section and click the Line And Paragraph Spacing button.

7. Click Remove Space After Paragraph (Figure 6.3).

FIGURE 6.3   Removing the space after a paragraph in Microsoft Word

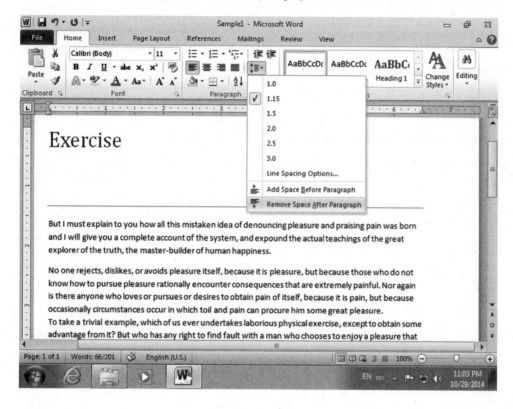

Notice how the space after this paragraph is removed and the third paragraph starts immediately after it.

8. Close the Sample1 Word document without saving your changes.

Aligning the Text in Your Documents

Horizontal alignment determines the appearance and orientation of the edges of the paragraphs in your documents. Your text can be left aligned, right aligned, centered, or justified. When the text is left aligned, it means that the left edge of the text is flush with the left margin, while right aligned means that the right edge of the text is flush with the right margin. When the text is justified, it means that it is aligned evenly along the left and right margins of your selection.

By default, Microsoft Word documents are left aligned, but you can change the alignment to whatever you want, for a single paragraph, a set of paragraphs, a table, or the entire document. In Exercise 6.2 you will learn how to do this. In order to complete this exercise, please download the Sample3.docx practice document to your computer.

EXERCISE 6.2

Changing the Alignment of the Text in Microsoft Word

1. Click Start and then Computer.

2. Browse to the location of the Sample3 Word document and double-click it.

   It will be opened with Microsoft Word.

3. Select the first paragraph of text, just beneath the heading. This paragraph starts with the words "But I must explain."

4. On the Home tab of the ribbon, go to the Paragraph section and click the Align Text Right button (Figure 6.4).

FIGURE 6.4   Align Text Right in Microsoft Word

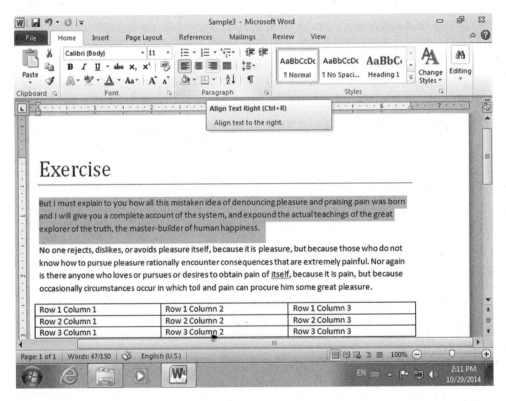

Notice how the selected paragraph is now aligned to the right margin of the page.

5. Select the second paragraph of text, which starts with the words "No one rejects."

6. On the Home tab of the ribbon, go to the Paragraph section and click the Justify button (Figure 6.5).

FIGURE 6.5   The Justify button in Microsoft Word

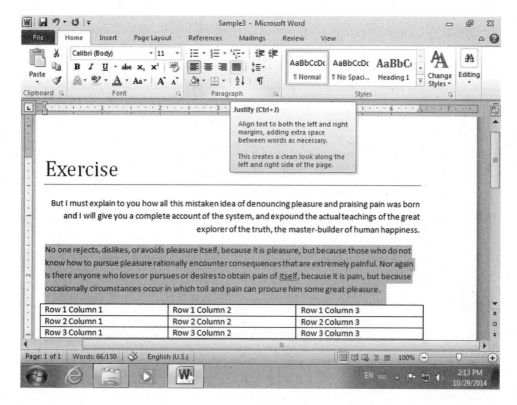

Notice how the selected paragraph is now aligned along the left and right margins of the page.

7. Select the table with three rows and columns at the end of the Sample3 document.

8. On the Home tab of the ribbon, go to the Paragraph section and click the Center button (Figure 6.6).

FIGURE 6.6   The Center button in Microsoft Word

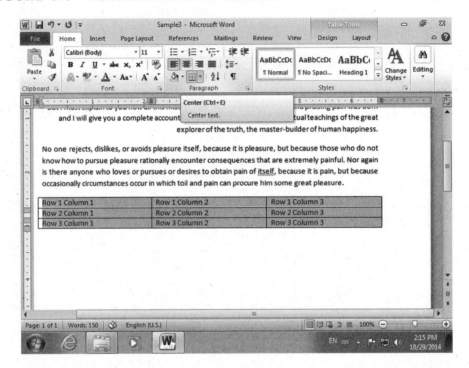

Notice how the text inside the table is now aligned to the center of each column.

9. Close the Sample3 Word document without saving your changes.

. You can also use keyboard shortcuts to align the text in your selection:

- Align Text Left: Ctrl+L
- Center: Ctrl+E
- Align Text Right: Ctrl+R
- Justify: Ctrl+J

In order to learn them, don't hesitate to go through the previous exercise and, instead of using the mouse, use these keyboard shortcuts to align each text selection.

Organizing Your Documents into Columns

You can organize your Microsoft Word documents into columns in order to increase their readability. This works especially well with documents that are not very long and that need to use a format similar to that of a newspaper or magazine.

Microsoft Word includes the necessary tools to quickly split your documents into columns. You can easily create documents that are organized into one, two, or three columns. Exercise 6.3 demonstrates how this is done. In order to complete this exercise, please download the Sample4.docx practice document to your computer.

EXERCISE 6.3

Organizing a Microsoft Word Document into Columns

1. Click Start and then Computer.

2. Browse to the location of the Sample4 Word document and double-click it.

   It will be opened with Microsoft Word.

3. Select all the text in the document by pressing Ctrl+A on your keyboard.

4. On the ribbon, click the Page Layout tab and go to the Page Setup section.

5. Click the Columns button and then click Two, as shown in Figure 6.7.

FIGURE 6.7 Setting the number of columns in Microsoft Word

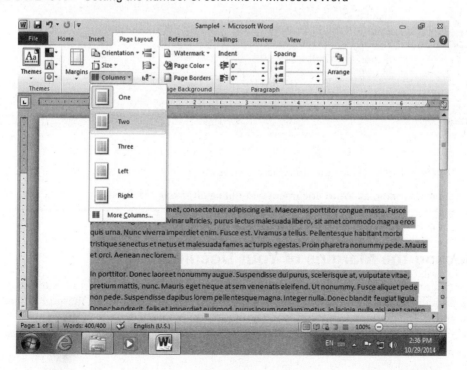

Notice how the text in your document is now organized in two columns.

6. Click the Columns button again and then click Three, like in Figure 6.8.

FIGURE 6.8 Setting a different number of columns in Microsoft Word

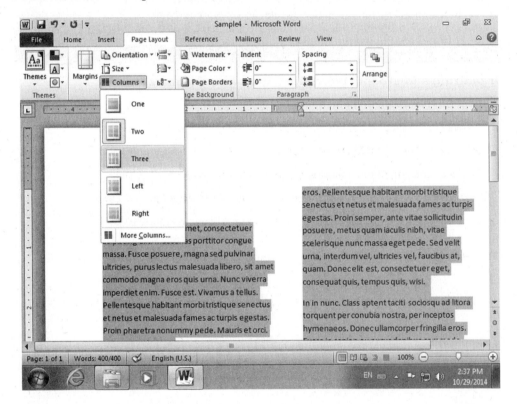

Notice how the text in your document is now organized in three columns.

7. Close the Sample4 Word document without saving your changes.

Setting the Margins of Your Documents

Margins are blank spaces around the edges of a page. You insert the text and graphics in the printable area between the margins. You can increase or decrease the margins of your documents at any time, for all kinds of reasons. For example, let's assume that you are writing a research paper or a book. You may want to add margins for binding the pages that are part of it, using the Mirrored margins preset. The margins on the left page become a mirror of those on the right page.

You can change the page margins either by choosing from one of Microsoft Word's predefined settings like Mirrored margins or by creating custom margins. In Exercise 6.4 you will learn how to change the margins of a document using Microsoft Word's predefined settings. In order to complete this exercise, please download the Sample4.docx practice document to your computer.

EXERCISE 6.4

Changing the Margins of a Microsoft Word Document

1. Click Start and then Computer.

2. Browse to the location of the Sample4 Word document and double-click it.

   It will be opened with Microsoft Word.

3. On the ribbon, click the Page Layout section and then go to the Page Setup section.

4. Click the Margins button and then click Mirrored (Figure 6.9).

FIGURE 6.9   Setting mirrored margins in Microsoft Word

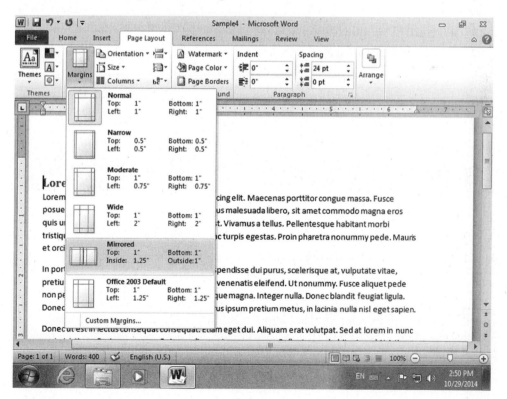

The Mirrored preset is now applied for the margins of your document. You will notice some small differences when compared to the Normal preset.

5.   Click the Margins button again and then click Narrow (Figure 6.10).

FIGURE 6.10   Setting narrow margins in Microsoft Word

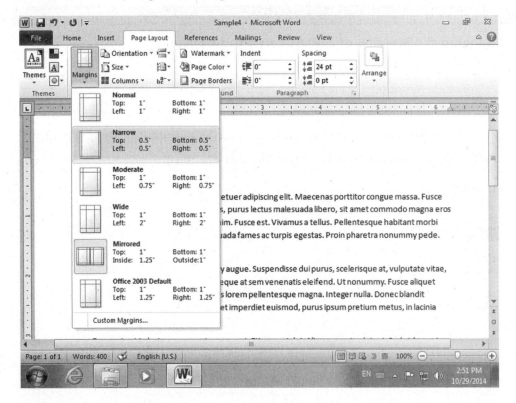

Notice how the margins of the document have been changed.

6.   Close the Sample4 Word document without saving your changes.

You may have noticed while going through this exercise that the margins are not that visible when you edit a document. They mostly affect the way you print the document and how much text fits on a page. If you print the Sample4 document using the Normal, Mirrored, and Narrow presets, you will be able to see just how different the margins of your documents are.

Displaying the Ruler When Editing Documents

The *ruler* is a measurement tool that allows you to align text, graphics, tables, and other elements in your documents. By default, the ruler is disabled in Microsoft Word 2010. When you enable it, you see both a horizontal ruler at the top of the document and a vertical ruler on the left side of the document (Figure 6.11). The ruler measures the width of the document from the left margin to the right. With it, you can move the margins of your document, change the indentation, and so on.

FIGURE 6.11 The ruler in Microsoft Word

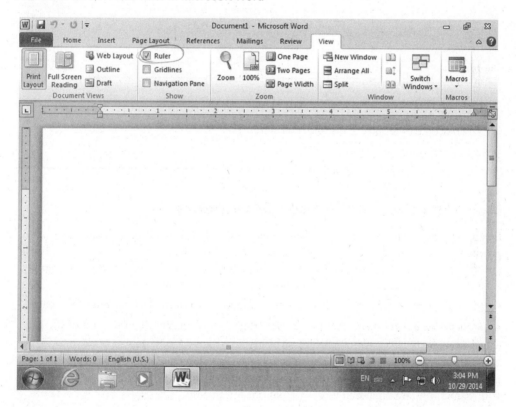

After you enable the ruler, it will remain enabled each time you open Microsoft Word until you disable it manually. The same is true when disabling it: it will remain disabled until you enable it manually.

In Exercise 6.5 you will learn how to enable and disable the ruler in Microsoft Word.

EXERCISE 6.5

Enabling or Disabling the Ruler in Microsoft Word

1. Start Microsoft Word 2010.

2. Click the View tab on the ribbon and go to the Show section.

3. Check the Ruler box to enable the ruler (Figure 6.12).

FIGURE 6.12   The View tab in Microsoft Word

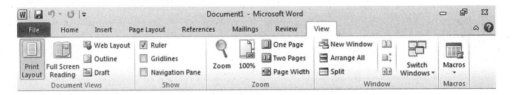

4. Uncheck the Ruler box to disable the ruler.

5. Close Microsoft Word 2010.

Indenting the Text in Your Documents

Indenting paragraphs is useful because it makes text easier to read. In the context of word processing software like Microsoft Word, an *indent* is the distance or the number of blank spaces that are used to move a line of text or a paragraph farther away from the margin than the rest of the text. Indents can be both positive and negative:

- A positive indent moves the line or paragraph away from the left margin of the page.

- A negative indent moves the line or paragraph away from the right margin of the page. A negative indent is also called an *outdent*.

Indenting text adds structure to your documents by allowing them to separate information. Generally, it is best that you indent only the first line of each paragraph so that your paragraphs are separated visually from one another.

An alternative to indenting is the *full-block style*: putting extra space between the paragraphs in lieu of indenting the first line. This is commonly used for business letters and other business documents. An easy way to increase the space between the paragraphs is to tap the Enter key twice when making a new paragraph. A better way, especially for long documents, is to set a space of 10 points after the paragraphs.

There are many ways to indent your text, and the quickest is by using the Tab key on your keyboard. When starting a new document, press Tab once on your keyboard and Microsoft Word will create a first-line indent. In Figure 6.13 you can see an example of such an indent.

FIGURE 6.13   Pressing Tab once to indent your text

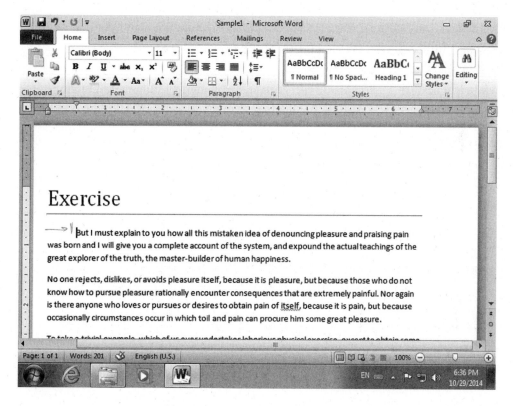

You can also use the indent commands on the ribbon. They are found on the Home tab, in the Paragraph section, and they are highlighted in Figure 6.14.

FIGURE 6.14   The Increase and Decrease Indent buttons

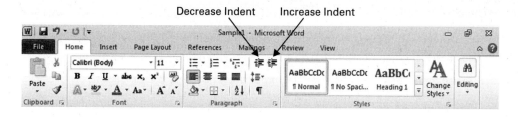

The Increase Indent command increases the indent by increments of ½ inch, whereas the Decrease Indent command decreases the indent by increments of ½ inch. The main difference between using these commands and the Tab key is that the Tab key creates a first-line indent, whereas the Increase Indent command applies to all lines in a paragraph.

If you enable the ruler, you can also use it to indent the text in your documents. There you will find three types of indent markers:

First Line Indent Marker   The marker that formats the first line indent in a paragraph *TAB*

Hanging Indent Marker   The marker that formats all lines but the first line in a paragraph *MLA formatting*

Left Indent Marker   The marker that separates the paragraph from the left margin

You can see all the indent markers on the ruler, highlighted in Figure 6.15.

FIGURE 6.15   The indent markers that are available in Microsoft Word

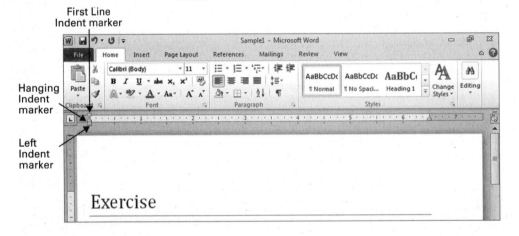

In Exercise 6.6 you will learn how to use indents in your Microsoft Word documents. In order to complete this exercise, please use the Sample1.docx practice document you previously downloaded to your computer. Also, you should enable the ruler in Microsoft Word before starting this exercise.

EXERCISE 6.6

Indenting the Text in Your Microsoft Word Documents

1. Click Start and then Computer.

2. Browse to the location of the Sample1 Word document and double-click it.

    It will be opened with Microsoft Word.

3. Using the mouse cursor, click at the beginning of the first paragraph, just before the word *But*.

4. Press Tab on your keyboard.

   Notice how a first-line indent is added to the first paragraph.

5. Click at the beginning of the second paragraph, just before the word *No*.

6. In the Home tab of the ribbon, go to the Paragraph section and click the Increase Indent button.

   Notice how all the lines of text in the second paragraph are indented.

7. Click at the beginning of the third paragraph, just before the word *To*.

8. On the ruler, select the Hanging Indent marker with the mouse and drag it to the right until you reach 1 inch.

9. Release the mouse button when your reach 1 inch, as shown in Figure 6.16.

FIGURE 6.16   Using the ruler to set the Hanging Indent marker

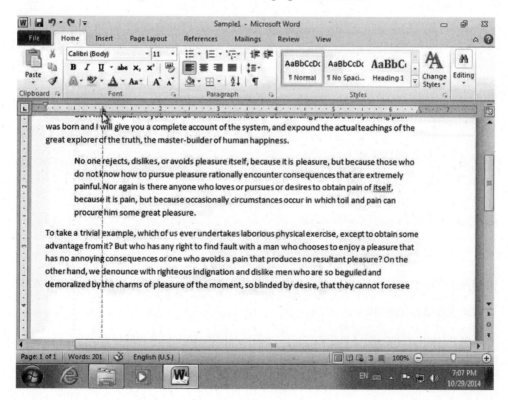

10. Notice how all the lines of text except the first one are indented. The end result should like similar to Figure 6.17.

FIGURE 6.17 Indented text in Microsoft Word

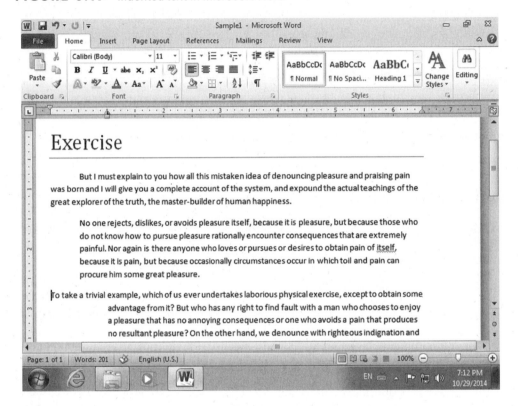

11. Close the Sample1 Word document without saving your changes.

Using Tabs to Control Where the Text Is Placed in Your Documents

Tabs or tab characters are a good way to control where the text is placed in your documents. When you press the Tab key on your keyboard, the insertion point for the text is moved ½ inch to the right. Pressing this key can either add a tab or create a first-line indent, depending on where the insertion point is. As you saw in the previous section, if the insertion is at the beginning of a paragraph, it will create a first-line indent. If it is anywhere else, it will create a tab.

On the left side of the ruler, you can also find a tab selector. If you click that, you can browse through the following tab stops and select the one that you want to use:

Left Tab   Sets the start position of the text that will then run to the right as you type.

Center Tab   Sets the position to the middle of the text. The text centers on this position as you type.

Right Tab   Sets the right end of the text, and the text moves to the left as you type.

Decimal Tab   Aligns numbers around a decimal point, regardless of the number of digits. You can align numbers only around a decimal point.

Bar Tab   Inserts a vertical bar at the tab position.

You can see the tab selector highlighted in Figure 6.18. By default, it is set to use the Left Tab. If you click it, it changes to the Center Tab and so on.

FIGURE 6.18   The tab selector in Microsoft Word

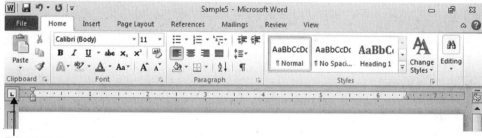

Tab selector

In Exercise 6.7 you will learn how to use tabs in your Microsoft Word documents. In order to complete this exercise, please download the Sample5.docx practice document to your computer. Also, you should enable the ruler in Microsoft Word before starting this exercise.

EXERCISE 6.7

Using Tabs to Control Where the Text Is Placed in Your Microsoft Word Documents

1.   Click Start and then Computer.

2.   Browse to the location of the Sample5 Word document and double-click it.

    It will be opened with Microsoft Word.

EXERCISE 6.7 *(continued)*

3. Select all the text in the document by pressing Ctrl+A on your keyboard.

4. Make sure that the Left Tab is selected. Then, click the ruler at the number 4 to set the Left Tab at 4 inches (Figure 6.19).

FIGURE 6.19   Setting the Left Tab in Microsoft Word

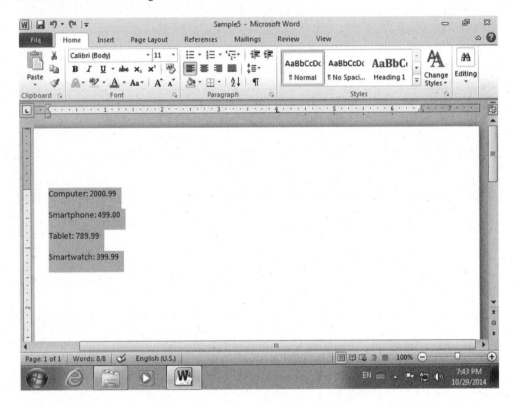

5. Click between the word *Computer:* and *2000.99* and press the Tab key.

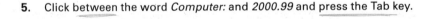

Notice how the number 2000.99 is moved to the right exactly where you positioned the Left Tab, similar to Figure 6.20.

FIGURE 6.20   Using tabs in Microsoft Word

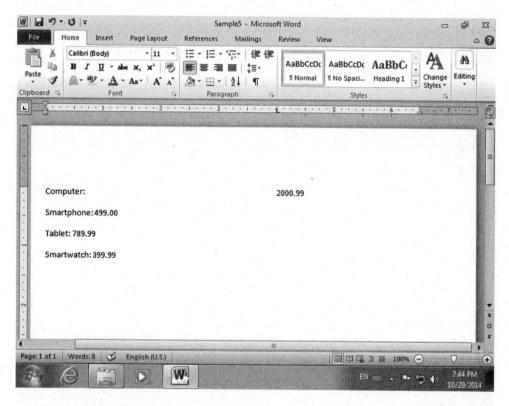

6. Click between the word *Smartphone:* and the number after it and press the Tab key.

7. Repeat step 6 for the words *Tablet* and *Smartwatch*.

EXERCISE 6.7 *(continued)*

Notice how the numbers are now aligned exactly where you positioned the Left Tab, as shown in Figure 6.21.

FIGURE 6.21   Text aligned to the Left Tab

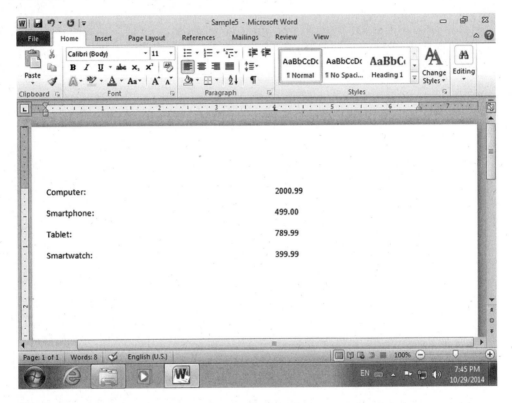

8.   Close the Sample5 Word document without saving your changes.

Organizing the Data in Your Documents

Now that you know how to improve the layout of your documents and how to make everything look dandy, it is good to also learn how to better organize the data in your documents. For example, some data is best put into lists or into tables and not into a typical text paragraph. For example, numerical data is best placed in tables, while enumerations of different elements are best placed into lists. Tables are useful when presenting data with two or more dimensions of information, while lists are useful when presenting data with a single dimension of information.

Microsoft Word makes it easy for you to organize data into these types of elements, and in this section we will demonstrate how to create lists and tables as well as how to use some tools for organizing them better.

Lastly, we will show you how to add page numbers to your document so that you can keep track of where you are inside a document, even when you read it in printed form.

Creating Bulleted and Numbered Lists

Arranging information in lists can make it easier to understand and to edit. In Microsoft Word, you can create simple bulleted and numbered lists as well as multilevel lists. In order to create lists, you need to use the ribbon and navigate to the Home tab. There you will find a section named Paragraph and three buttons that are about creating lists:

Bullets   Starts a simple one-level bulleted list

Numbering   Starts a simple one-level numbered list

Multilevel List   Starts a more complex multilevel list that can include bullets, numbers, and/or letters

In Figure 6.22 you can see these three buttons and where they are located.

FIGURE 6.22   The buttons for Bullets, Numbering, and Multilevel List

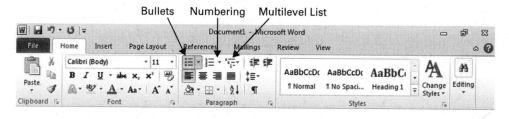

In Exercise 6.8 you will learn how to create bulleted and numbered lists in Microsoft Word.

EXERCISE 6.8

Creating Lists in Microsoft Word

1. Start Microsoft Word 2010 if it isn't already open.

2. On the Home tab of the ribbon, go to the Paragraph section and click the Bullets button.

   A bulleted list is created.

3. Type **Adrian** and press Enter.

4. Type **Mary** and press Enter.

5. Press Enter to finish the bulleted list.

6. Press Enter one more time to add a new line after the bulleted list.

EXERCISE 6.8 *(continued)*

7.   On the Home tab of the ribbon, go to the Paragraph section and click the Numbering button.

     A numbered list is created.

8.   Type **Car** and press Enter.

9.   Type **Plane** and press Enter.

10. Press Enter again to finish the numbered list.

     The end result should look similar to Figure 6.23.

FIGURE 6.23   Two lists in Microsoft Word

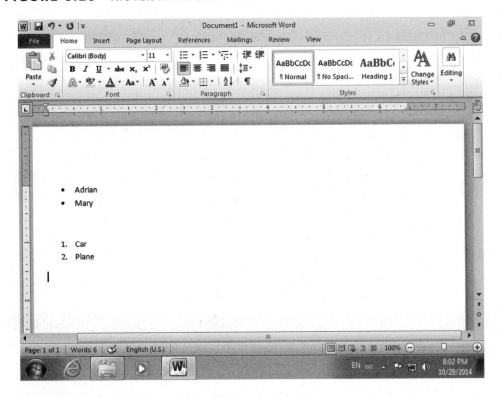

11. Close Microsoft Word 2010 without saving your work.

Sorting Single-Level Lists

Many users don't know that they can easily sort their single-level lists in Microsoft Word documents using simple criteria. For example, if you have a list with text, you can sort it in alphabetical order. If you have a list with numbers, you can sort it from the lowest to the highest number.

All this is done with the help of the Sort button that's found on the Home tab on the ribbon, in the Paragraph section.

In Exercise 6.9 you will learn how to sort your single-level lists in Microsoft Word documents. In order to complete this exercise, please download the Sample6.docx practice document to your computer.

EXERCISE 6.9

Sorting Lists in Microsoft Word Documents

1. Click Start and then Computer.

2. Browse to the location of the Sample6 Word document and double-click it.

   It will be opened with Microsoft Word.

3. Select the bulleted list with names.

4. On the Home tab on the ribbon, go to the Paragraph section and click the Sort button.

   The Sort button is shown in Figure 6.24.

FIGURE 6.24   Sorting a list in Microsoft Word

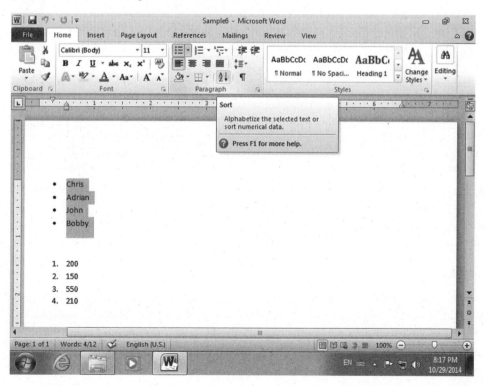

EXERCISE 6.9 *(continued)*

5. Leave the default settings unchanged and click OK.

    Notice how the bulleted list is now sorted in alphabetical order.

6. Select the second list with numbers.

7. On the Home tab on the ribbon, go to the Paragraph section and click the Sort button.

    The Sort Text window is shown in Figure 6.25.

FIGURE 6.25   The Sort Text window

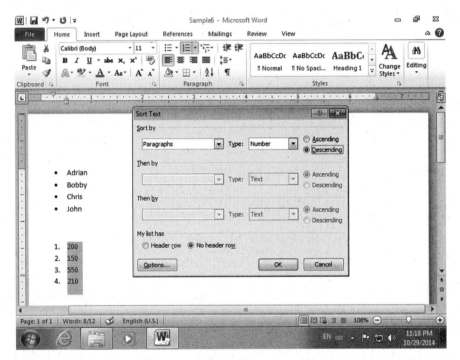

8. Select Descending to sort the list in descending order and click OK. Notice how the numbered list is now sorted in descending order.

9. Close the Sample6 Word document without saving your changes.

Creating Tables

A *table* is a collection of related data in a structured format that consists of columns and rows. In Microsoft Word you can create all kinds of tables with different dimensions by following these steps:

1. On the ribbon, select the Insert tab and look for the Tables section.

    There you will find the Table button.

2. Click it, and you have access to a grid with a maximum of 10 rows and 8 columns.

3. On the grid, highlight the number of rows and columns that you want in your table, and click it.

    The table will be inserted into your document and you can start filling it with data.

In Exercise 6.10 you will learn how to create a simple table in Microsoft Word.

EXERCISE 6.10

Creating Tables in Microsoft Word

1. Start Microsoft Word 2010 if it isn't already open.

2. Click the Insert tab of the ribbon and go to the Tables section.

3. Click the Table button and hover your mouse over the grid with columns and rows.

4. Select a 2 × 2 table (Figure 6.26) and click the grid.

FIGURE 6.26   Adding a 2x2 table in Microsoft Word

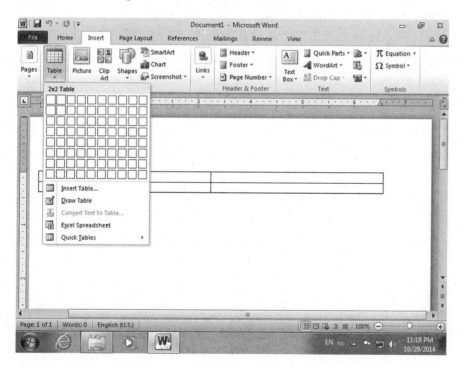

A table with two rows and columns is inserted into the document.

5. In the first row and the first column of the tablet type the letter **A**.

6. Press Tab on your keyboard to move to the second column on the first row.

7. Type the letter **B**.

8. Press Tab to move to the first column and the second row.

9. Type the letter **C**.

10. Press Tab again to move to the second column and the second row.

11. Type the letter **D**.

    The end result should look similar to Figure 6.27.

FIGURE 6.27   Filling a table with data in Microsoft Word

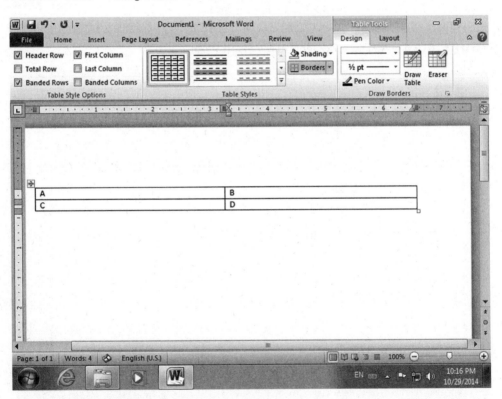

12. Close Microsoft Word 2010 without saving your work.

Adding or Removing Rows and Columns in Your Tables

When you have selected a table or a cell in a table, the Layout tab is shown on the ribbon. In this tab you will find lots of tools for aligning data plus tools for adding or removing columns and for merging and splitting cells. They are found in the Rows & Columns section (Figure 6.28). Here are the options that you can use for adding rows or columns near the cell that you have selected:

Insert Above   Adds a new row directly above the selected row

Insert Below   Adds a new row directly below the selected row

Insert Left   Adds a new column directly to the left of the selected column

Insert Right   Adds a new column directly to the right of the selected column

FIGURE 6.28 The buttons for inserting columns and rows in Microsoft Word

In the Rows & Columns section you will also find a Delete button. If you click it (Figure 6.29), you will get access to the following options:

Delete Cells   Deletes rows, columns, or cells, depending on what you select in the Delete Cells dialog

Delete Columns   Deletes the selected column

Delete Rows   Deletes the selected row

Delete Table   Deletes the selected table

FIGURE 6.29 The options for deleting cells, columns, rows, and tables in Microsoft Word

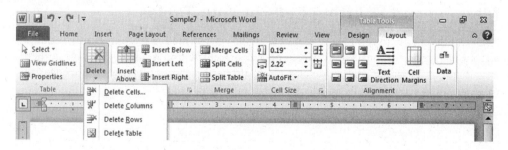

In Exercise 6.11 you will learn how to add new rows and columns to a table in Microsoft Word and then delete them. In order to complete this exercise, please download the Sample7.docx practice document to your computer.

EXERCISE 6.11

Adding or Deleting Rows and Columns When Working with Tables

1. Click Start and then Computer.

2. Browse to the location of the Sample7 Word document and double-click it.

    It will be opened with Microsoft Word.

3. Click inside the Computer B cell (third row, first column) to select it.

4. On the ribbon, click the Layout tab and go to the Rows & Columns section.

5. Click Insert Below, and a fourth row is added beneath the third.

6. Click inside the cell from the first column of the fourth row.

7. Click Insert Left in the Rows & Columns section of the Layout tab.

    An empty column is added to the left.

8. With the new column still selected, click the Delete button in the Rows & Columns section of the Layout tab.

9. Click Delete Columns, and the newly added column is removed.

10. Click anywhere inside the fourth row of the table.

11. With the new column still selected, click the Delete button in the Rows & Columns section of the Layout tab.

12. Click Delete Rows, and the fourth row is removed.

13. Close the Sample7 Word document without saving your changes.

Merging and Splitting Cells in Your Tables

You can also choose to combine two or more table cells located in the same row or column into a single cell. This is called *merging*. The Merge Cells button becomes available in the Layout tab of the ribbon, in the Merge section, after you select at least two table cells. You can also split a cell into multiple cells, using the Split Cells button.

In Exercise 6.12 you will learn how to merge cells and split cells in a table when using Microsoft Word. In order to complete this exercise, you will use the Sample7.docx practice document that you previously downloaded to your computer.

EXERCISE 6.12

Merging and Splitting Cells When Working with Tables

1. Click Start and then Computer.

2. Browse to the location of the Sample7 Word document and double-click it.

   It will be opened with Microsoft Word.

3. Select cells 2 and 3 on the third column, as shown in Figure 6.30.

FIGURE 6.30   Selecting cells in a table

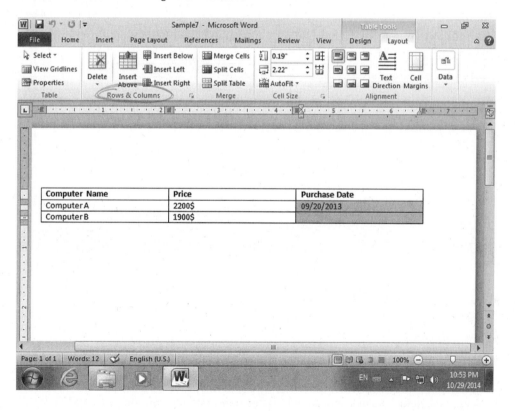

4. On the ribbon, click the Layout tab and go to the Merge section.

5. Click Merge Cells and notice how the two cells are now merged into one cell, similar to Figure 6.31.

FIGURE 6.31   Merging cells in a table

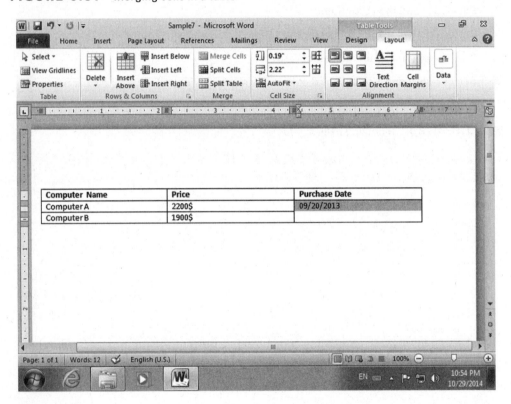

6. With the merged cell still selected, on the ribbon click the Layout tab and go to the Merge section.

7. Click Split Cells.

    You are asked to select the number of columns and rows into which you want to split the selected cell.

8. Leave the default values unchanged (two columns and one row) and click OK.

The cell is now split in two columns and one row, as shown in Figure 6.32.

FIGURE 6.32   Splitting cells in a table

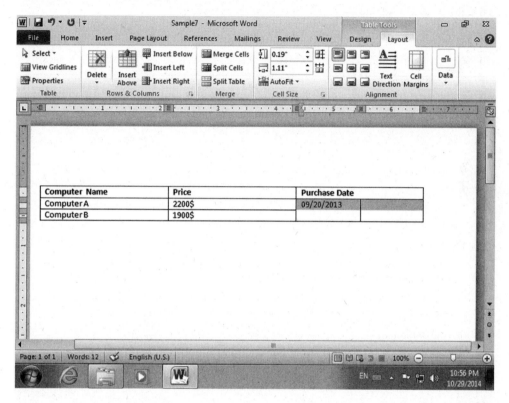

9.   Close the Sample7 Word document without saving your changes.

Adding Page Numbers to Your Documents

When you create large documents with many pages, you may want to add page numbers to keep them in order. Adding page numbers in Microsoft Word is very easy, and it takes only a few clicks:

1.   On the ribbon, select the Insert tab and click the Page Number button in the Header & Footer section.

A menu is displayed with several options for the placement of the page numbers, shown in Figure 6.33.

FIGURE 6.33   Adding page numbers in Microsoft Word

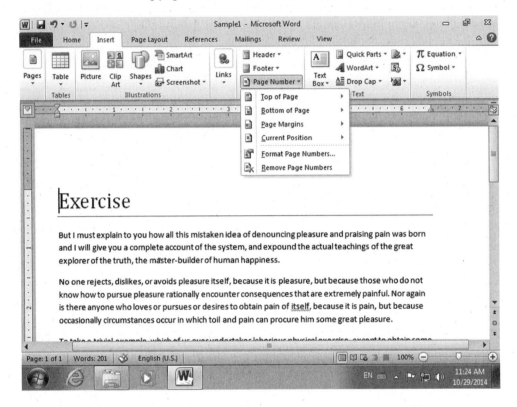

2.   Choose one of the following:

- On the top of each page
- On the bottom of each page
- On the margins of each page
- At your cursor's current position

For each of these options you can then choose from several presets for the page numbers. For example, if you want to add the page numbers to the bottom of each page, you can add them to the lower-left corner, the middle, or the lower-right corner of each page.

In Exercise 6.13 you will learn how to add page numbers to your Microsoft Word documents. In order to complete this exercise, please use the Sample1.docx practice document you downloaded previously.

EXERCISE 6.13

Adding Page Numbers to Your Microsoft Word Documents

1. Click Start and then Computer.

2. Browse to the location of the Sample1 Word document and double-click it.

    It will be opened with Microsoft Word.

3. Click the Insert tab on the ribbon.

4. In the Header & Footer section, click Page Number and then Bottom Of Page.

5. Select the second option: Plain Number 2, shown in Figure 6.34.

FIGURE 6.34   Adding page numbers in Microsoft Word

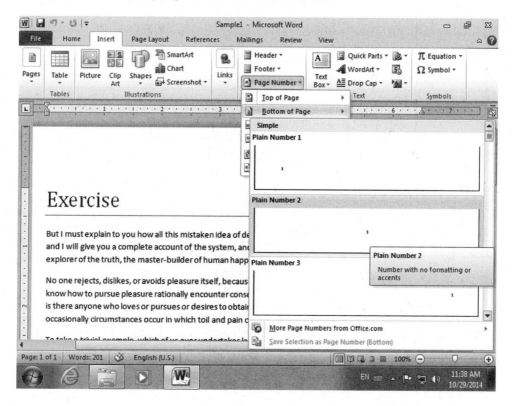

Notice how the page numbers are added to the bottom of each page, exactly in the middle.

EXERCISE 6.13 *(continued)*

6. On the ribbon, in the Design tab, click the Close Header And Footer button (Figure 6.35).

FIGURE 6.35   Page numbers added to the bottom of each page

7. Close the Sample1 Word document without saving your changes.

Summary

In this chapter we focused on using Microsoft Word for creating all kinds of documents. First, you learned how to configure the layout of your documents so that they look good and that they fit onto the printed page as you need them.

Then we showed you how to better organize your data using lists and tables. That's because certain types of data are better organized and shared this way and not in traditional text paragraphs.

At the end of this chapter we showed you how to add page numbers to your documents—a feature very useful for printing and reading large documents.

Exam Essentials

Know how to adjust the spacing and the alignment of your text.   In order to make a document easier to read, it is good to adjust the spacing between paragraphs and lines of text. Another good idea is to improve the alignment of your text.

Learn how to set the margins for your printed documents.   Knowing how to set the margins for your documents will help you improve how much text can fit into a printed page.

Know how to use the ruler.   The ruler can help you improve the alignment of all kinds of text elements and have your document look the way you want it to, as quickly as possible.

Understand how to create and sort lists.   Some types of data are best shared using lists: bulleted or numbered. You should know how to create lists and how to sort those using different criteria.

Learn how to create tables and manage cells.   In your work you may need to create all kinds of tables, including some that are more complex and include merged or split cells.

Key Terms

Before you take the exam, be certain you are familiar with the following terms:

indent	outdent
margins	ruler
merging	table

Review Questions

1. Which tool on the ribbon can you use to change spacing of the lines of text or that of a paragraph in Microsoft Word? (Choose all that apply.)

   A. Paragraph

   B. Styles

   C. Line and Paragraph Spacing

   D. Increase Indent

2. What is the keyboard shortcut for aligning the text in a selection to the right margin, in Microsoft Word?

   A. Ctrl+Copy

   B. Ctrl+Left

   C. Ctrl+All

   D. Ctrl+R ight

3. In up to how many columns can you organize a Microsoft Word document?

   A. Three columns

   B. Two columns

   C. One column

   D. Infinite number of columns

4. What happens when you change the margins of a Microsoft Word document? (Choose all that apply.)

   A. You change how much text and graphics fit on a page.

   B. You set where the document starts and ends.

   C. You set how many pages you can have in a document.

   D. You change how much blank space there is around the edges of a page.

5. What can you do with the ruler in Microsoft Word? (Choose all that apply.)

   A. Align text

   B. Set the number of pages

   C. Align graphics

   D. Align tables

6. What is an indent in a Microsoft Word document? (Choose all that apply.)

   A. The number of lines in a paragraph

   B. The number of blank spaces that are used to move a line of text or a paragraph away from the left or right margin of a page

   C. The distance that is used to move a line of text or a paragraph away from the left or right margin of a page

   D. The number of tabs pressed on your keyboard

7. Where do you find the Increase Indent and Decrease Indent tools on the Microsoft Word ribbon?

  A. In the Page Setup section of the Page Layout tab

  B. In the Text section of the Insert tab

  C. In the Paragraph section of the Home tab ✓

  D. In the Styles section of the Home tab

8. What happens when you press the Tab key while creating a Microsoft Word document?

  A. The insertion point for the text is moved ½ inch to the right. *by default*

  B. The insertion point for the text is moved ½ inch to the left.

  C. The insertion point for the text is moved ¼ inch to the right.

  D. The insertion point for the text is moved ¼ inch to the left.

9. In which order can you sort the text in a bulleted, non-numerical list, using the Sort tool from Microsoft Word? (Choose all that apply.)

  A. In ascending alphabetical order ✓

  B. From the lowest to the highest number ✓

  C. In descending alphabetical order ✓

  D. In a random alphabetical order ✗

10. What is a merged cell in a Microsoft Word table?

  A. Two non-adjacent cells that are combined into one cell ✗ *impossible*   *ab cannot merge*

p 266 **B.** Two or more cells that are combined into one cell ✓

  C. Two or more cells located in the same row or column that are combined into one cell ✓

  D. Once cell that is split into two or more cells ✗ *it's split, not merge*

Chapter

7

Using Microsoft Excel

THE FOLLOWING IC3 GS4: COMPUTER FUNDAMENTALS EXAM OBJECTIVES ARE COVERED IN THIS CHAPTER:

✓ **Spreadsheet Layout**

- Insert/delete

- Demonstrate how to add, insert, remove, delete rows and columns in a spreadsheet environment.

- Demonstrate how to adjust the size of cells and the amount of data displayed in a cell within a spreadsheet.

- Demonstrate how to adjust the alignment and positioning of cells and the positioning and orientation of data as displayed in cells within a spreadsheet.

- Navigation

- Demonstrate how and when to merge or un-merge cells within a spreadsheet, including how to preserve, manage, and arrange data within the merged or un-merged cells.

✓ **Data Management**

- Filter and sort

- Formulas and Functions

- Number format

- Cell format

- Charts, graphs

Microsoft Excel is a spreadsheet application that allows you to organize, sort, calculate, manipulate, and visualize data.

Microsoft Excel worksheets are organized into columns and rows but can also include other features, such as graphs and charts, which we'll discuss in this chapter.

We will start by explaining the basic concepts like worksheets and workbooks, show how to navigate between the cells in your tables, and demonstrate how to change their alignment and positioning as well as their formatting. Then, we will explain how to add or remove columns and rows of data, how to merge and unmerge cells, and how to set the number format used for a cell or a group of cells.

Toward the end of this chapter we will focus on more advanced topics like sorting and filtering your data, using formulas and functions to make all kinds of simple or advanced calculations, and adding charts and graphs so that you can visualize your data.

There's a lot of ground to cover, so let's get started.

Navigating among Worksheets, Workbooks, and Cells

When you open Microsoft Excel and create a new file, that file is called a *workbook*. A workbook contains one or more *worksheets*, which consist of cells organized into columns and rows. By default, Microsoft Excel creates three empty worksheets for each new workbook, as shown in Figure 7.1. They are always named Sheet1, Sheet2, and Sheet3.

They can be easily renamed or removed, depending on your needs, by right-clicking any of them and choosing the action you want to perform.

Worksheets are often incorrectly referred to as spreadsheets. This is wrong because a *spreadsheet* is an application that is used for organization, analysis, and storage of data in tabular form. It is not a file that results from using that application. Therefore, when you use the word *spreadsheet*, you are not referring to the file created using Microsoft Excel but to the Microsoft Excel application that you are using to create workbooks.

FIGURE 7.1   The difference between workbooks and worksheets

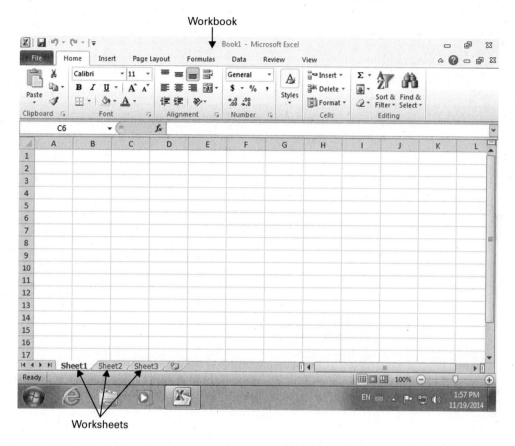

Navigating between Worksheets
==============================

To navigate between worksheets, simply click the name of the worksheet you want to use, on the bottom of the Microsoft Excel file window. You can also use the keys Ctrl+PgUp on your keyboard to switch between worksheets, from left to right. Ctrl+PgDn switches between worksheets, from right to left.

If you have more than one workbook opened in Microsoft Excel, then you can easily switch between them using the mouse.

1. Click the Microsoft Excel icon on the taskbar (Figure 7.2).

2. In the preview window, click the workbook that you want to switch to.

3. Do the same to get back to the previous workbook.

You can also use Ctrl+F6 on your keyboard to switch to the next workbook window. This shortcut works only when more than one workbook window is open.

FIGURE 7.2   Switching between workbooks

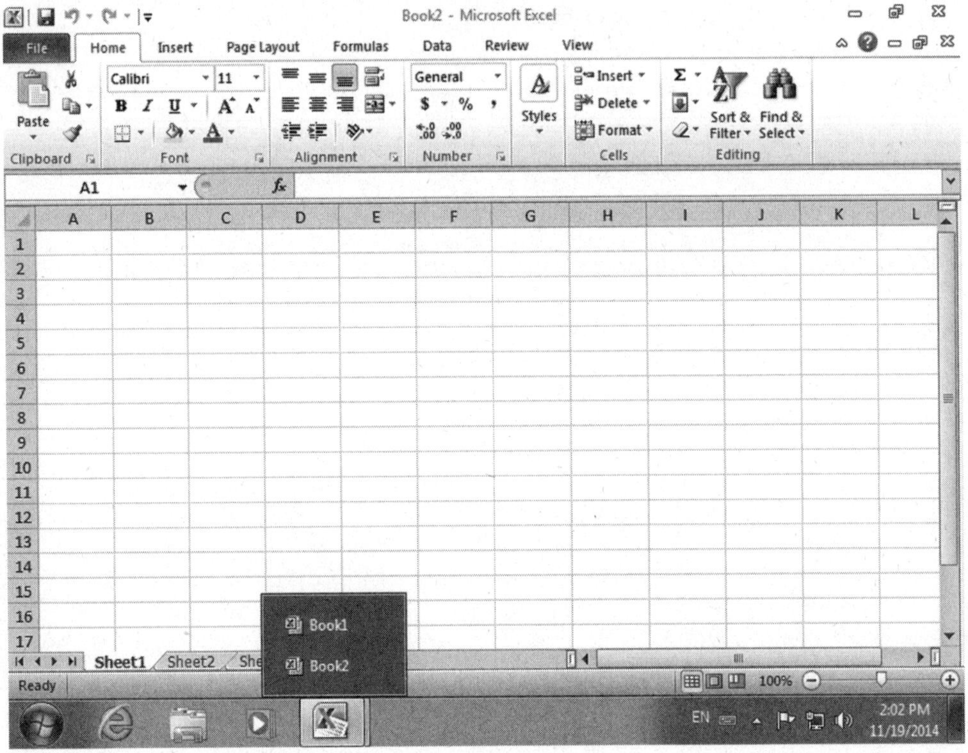

Navigating between Cells

When working with Microsoft Excel files or workbooks, you will need to know how to go from cell to cell so that you can edit them. To do that, you can either use the mouse and click the cell that you want to activate or use keyboard shortcuts like Tab, which takes you to the next cell, or Shift+Tab, which takes you to the previous cell. In Exercise 7.1 we will demonstrate how this is done. In order to complete this exercise, please download the Book1.xlsx practice file to your computer.

EXERCISE 7.1

Navigating between Cells in a Worksheet

1. Click Start and then Computer.

2. Browse to the location of the Book1.xlsx Excel file and double-click it.

   It will be opened with Microsoft Excel.

3. Click in the A1 cell (column A, row 1) to activate it.

    Notice that the cell is selected and now you can work with it.

4. To navigate to the cell next to it, B1 (column B, row 1), press Tab on your keyboard.

5. To get back to the previous cell, A1, press Shift+Tab on your keyboard.

6. Close Microsoft Excel without saving your changes.

If you want to quickly jump to a cell in a worksheet, you can use the *Name box* that is found in the top-left box above the worksheet and just below the ribbon. You can see it highlighted in Figure 7.3.

FIGURE 7.3   The Name box in Microsoft Excel

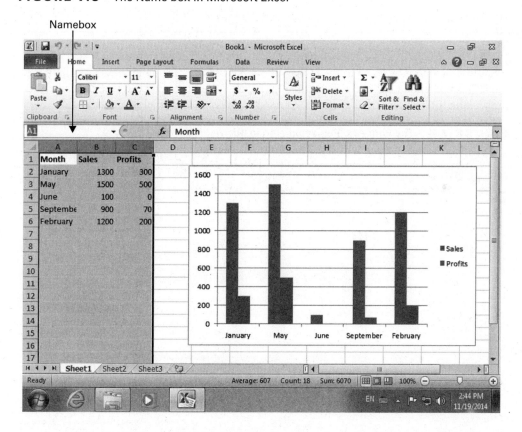

To use it, simply type the location of the cell that you want to jump to, starting with the column letter and then with the row number. For example, if you want to jump to row 5 on the first column, you need to type **A5** in the Name box and then press Enter on your keyboard. In Exercise 7.2 you will learn how to use the Name box in Microsoft Excel. In order to complete this exercise, please use the Book1.xlsx practice file you downloaded to your computer.

EXERCISE 7.2

Jumping to a Specific Cell in a Worksheet

1. Click Start and then Computer.

2. Browse to the location of the Book1.xlsx Excel file and double-click it.

   It will be opened with Microsoft Excel.

3. Click inside the Name box, type **A5**, and press Enter.

   Notice how the A5 cell is now selected, with the value September.

4. Click inside the Name box, type **C6**, and press Enter.

   Notice how the C6 cell is now selected, with the value 200.

5. Close Microsoft Excel without saving your changes.

You can also jump to a cell based on its value, using the Search feature in Microsoft Excel. You can find Search by going to the Home tab on the ribbon, clicking Find & Select, and then Find. This opens the Find And Replace dialog (Figure 7.4), where you can type the value you are looking for. The same dialog can be accessed by pressing Ctrl+F on your keyboard.

FIGURE 7.4 The Find And Replace dialog in Microsoft Excel

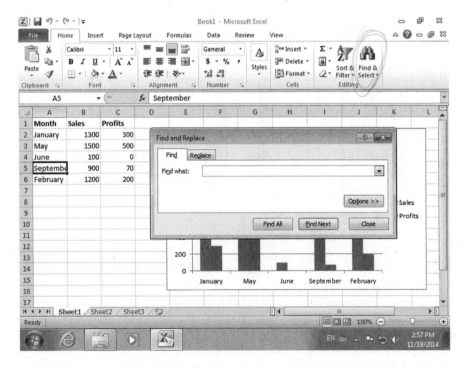

In Exercise 7.3 you will learn how to use Search in Microsoft Excel. In order to complete this exercise, please download the Book2.xlsx practice file to your computer.

EXERCISE 7.3

Searching for a Specific Value in a Worksheet

1. Click Start and then Computer.

2. Browse to the location of the Book2.xlsx Excel file and double-click it.

   It will be opened with Microsoft Excel.

3. On the Home tab on the ribbon, click Find & Select in the Editing section (Figure 7.5).

FIGURE 7.5 The Find & Select menu in Microsoft Excel

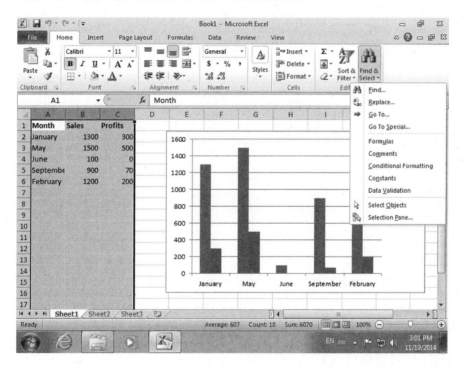

EXERCISE 7.3 *(continued)*

4. Now click Find.

5. In the Find And Replace dialog (Figure 7.6), type **70** and then click Find Next.

   Notice how column C5 is selected, with the value 70.

FIGURE 7.6   The Find And Replace dialog in Microsoft Excel

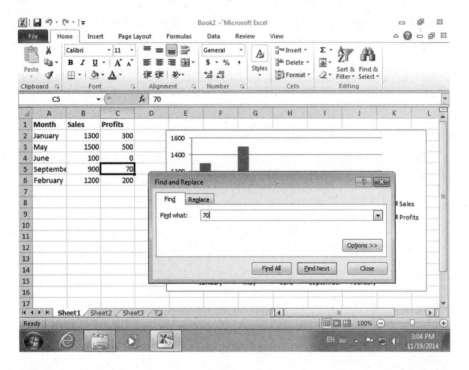

6. Click Close.

7. Close Microsoft Excel without saving your work.

Changing the Alignment and the Positioning of Cells

As in any other Microsoft Office application, you can easily change the alignment and the positioning of your data in Microsoft Excel, using several tools that are available on the Home tab on the ribbon. You can find them in the Alignment section. There are six buttons for aligning your data and one for accessing all the available orientation options. They are highlighted in Figure 7.7.

FIGURE 7.7   The ribbon in Microsoft Excel

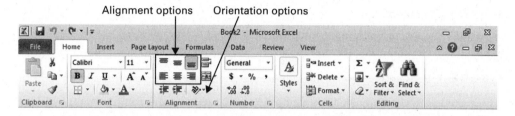

You can align your data to the top of the cell, centered between the top and the bottom of the cell, or aligned to the bottom of the cell, to the left of the cell, to the center, or to the right of the cell.

As shown in Figure 7.8, you can orient the data in your cells with the following options: Angle Counterclockwise, Angle Clockwise, Vertical Text, Rotate Text Up, and Rotate Text Down.

FIGURE 7.8   The orientation options in Microsoft Excel

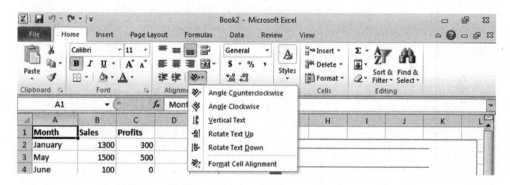

In Exercise 7.4 you will learn how to change the alignment and orientation of cells in Microsoft Excel. In order to complete this exercise, please use the Book2.xlsx practice file you previously downloaded to your computer.

EXERCISE 7.4

Changing the Alignment and Orientation of Cells in a Worksheet

1. Click Start and then Computer.

2. Browse to the location of the Book2.xlsx Excel file and double-click it.

   It will be opened with Microsoft Excel.

EXERCISE 7.4 *(continued)*

3. Select the A column by clicking its name.

4. On the ribbon, navigate to the Alignment section of the Home tab.

5. Click the Center button.

   Notice how the text is centered in all the rows of column A, like in Figure 7.9.

FIGURE 7.9   Centered text in column A

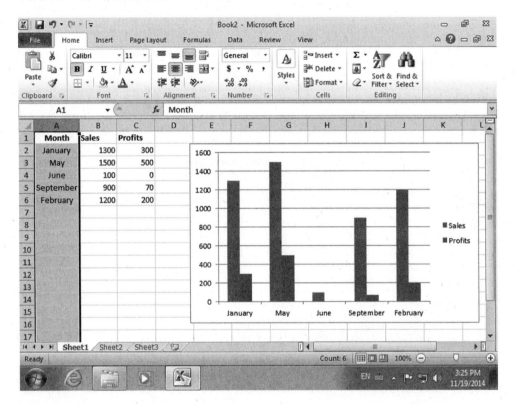

6. Select column C by clicking its name.

7. Click the Orientation button in the Alignment section and then click Angle Clockwise.

   Notice how the text in this column has changed its orientation, as shown in Figure 7.10.

FIGURE 7.10 Data that is oriented at an angle, clockwise

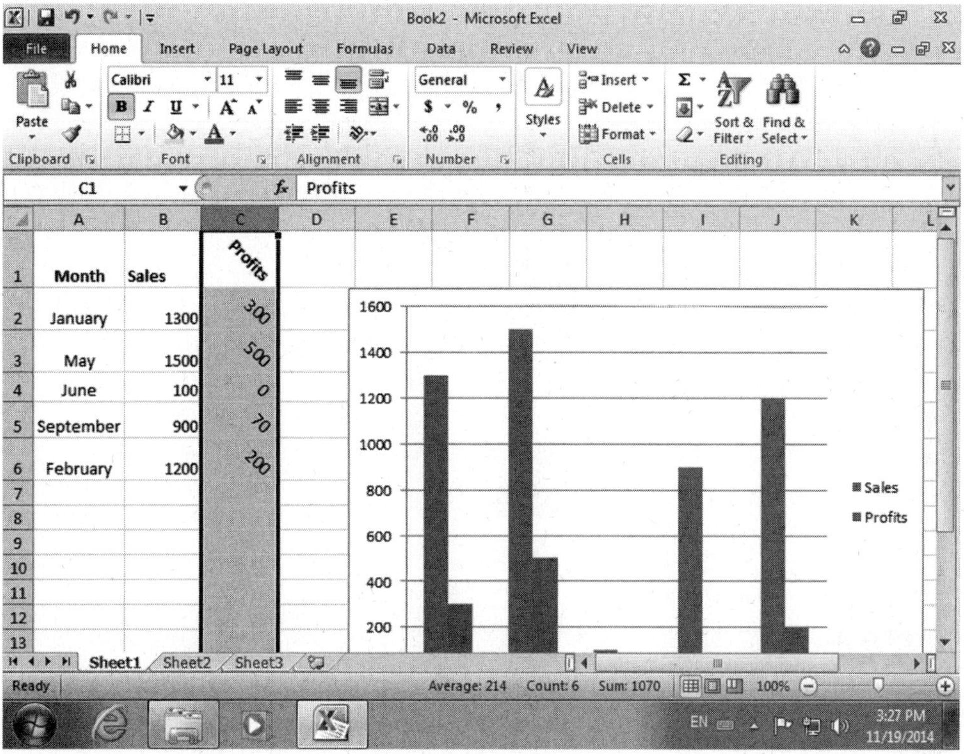

8. Close Microsoft Excel without saving your work.

Changing the Size of Cells

By default, each cell in Microsoft Excel is the same size. However, you usually won't enter the same type and amount of data in each. For some data the default size of a cell might be enough, while for others it might not be. That's why you should know how to adjust the size of a cell so that it can display more or less data, depending on your needs.

When the data no longer fits into a cell, Microsoft Excel starts to substitute characters for data that is too long, and it shows characters like ####, depending on how many characters can be displayed in that cell. The data itself is not truncated, though. It is only displayed in a truncated fashion, as shown in Figure 7.11.

FIGURE 7.11   Truncated data displayed by Microsoft Excel

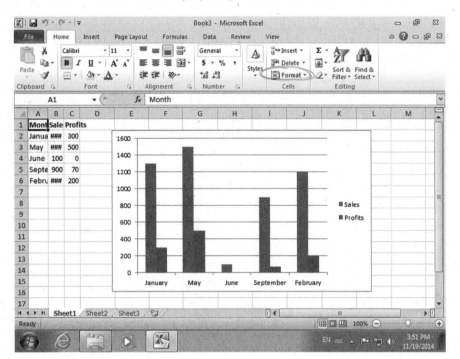

The size of cells in an entire row or column can be changed using the boundaries that are available in Excel or by using the Format menu, in the Cells section of the Home tab on the ribbon.

In Exercise 7.5 you will learn how to change the height of a row and the width of a column, using the options available on the ribbon. In order to complete this exercise, please download the Book3.xlsx practice file to your computer.

EXERCISE 7.5

Changing the Width of a Column and the Height of a Row

1. Click Start and then Computer.

2. Browse to the location of the Book3.xlsx Excel file and double-click it.

    It will be opened with Microsoft Excel.

3. Select column B by clicking it.

4. On the ribbon, go to the Cells section in the Home tab. There, click the Format button (Figure 7.12) and then Column Width.

FIGURE 7.12   The Format menu in Microsoft Excel

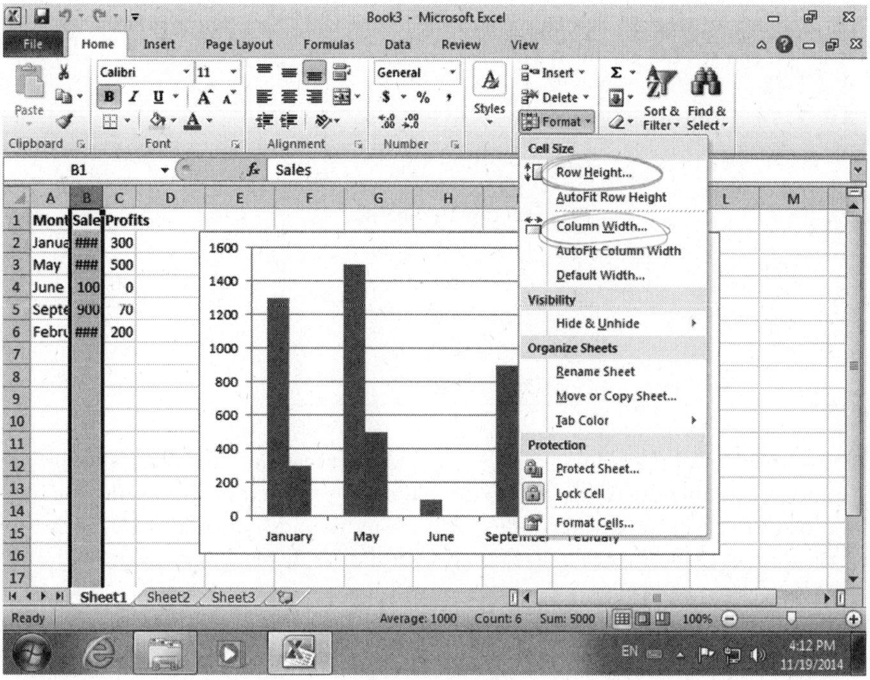

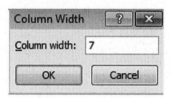

5. In the Column Width window, type **7** and click OK (Figure 7.13).

FIGURE 7.13   Setting the column width

Column Width

Column width: 7

OK   Cancel

Notice how the width of column C has changed and now you can view all its data correctly.

6. Select row 1 by clicking it.

7. On the ribbon, go to the Cells section in the Home tab. There, click the Format button and then Row Height.

8. In the Row Height window, type **45** and click OK.

    Notice how the height of the row has changed.

9. Close Microsoft Excel without saving your work.

Another way of changing the width of a column and the height of a row is to use the mouse pointer and place it above the boundaries of a row or column. Then, it will turn into a double-sided arrow, which you can drag to the left or right (for columns) and up or down (for rows). You can see the arrow in Figure 7.14.

FIGURE 7.14   The double-sided arrow in Microsoft Excel

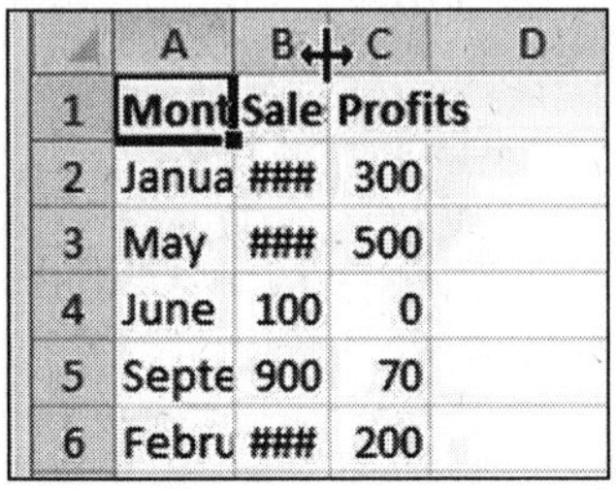

	A	B	C	D
1	Mont	Sale	Profits	
2	Janua	###	300	
3	May	###	500	
4	June	100	0	
5	Septe	900	70	
6	Febru	###	200	

Drag this arrow until the column width or row height is what you want. Another useful way of using this double-sided arrow is to double-click it when it is displayed. This will make Microsoft Excel automatically adjust that column's width or that row's height so that it fits all the data in each of its cells so that all your data is displayed correctly, with no wasted space or truncated cells.

Formatting How Cells Are Displayed

In order to make a worksheet look good and communicate more effectively, it is advisable to format it a bit and use basic tools like fonts, size, bolding, colors, and more. All these basic tools are found on the ribbon. Click the Home tab (Figure 7.15) and look for the Font section. There you will find the following options: the font and the font size, bold, italic, underline, increase font size, decrease font size, borders, fill color, and font color. You can use them to format both individual cells and a range of cells.

FIGURE 7.15   The Home tab on the Microsoft Excel ribbon

In Exercise 7.6 you will learn how to use the formatting tools available to change how a cell or range of cells is displayed. In order to complete this exercise, please use the Book2. xlsx practice file you downloaded earlier.

EXERCISE 7.6

Changing the Formatting of Cells

1. Click Start and then Computer.

2. Browse to the location of the Book2.xlsx Excel file and double-click it.

   It will be opened with Microsoft Excel.

3. Select the C4 cell with the value 0.

4. In the Home tab on the ribbon, go to the Font section and click the Font Color button.

   Notice how the cell is now formatted and displayed in red.

5. Select row 1 by clicking it.

6. In the Home tab on the ribbon, go to the Font section, click the Font drop-down list (Figure 7.16), and select Arial.

FIGURE 7.16   The Font drop-down menu in Microsoft Excel

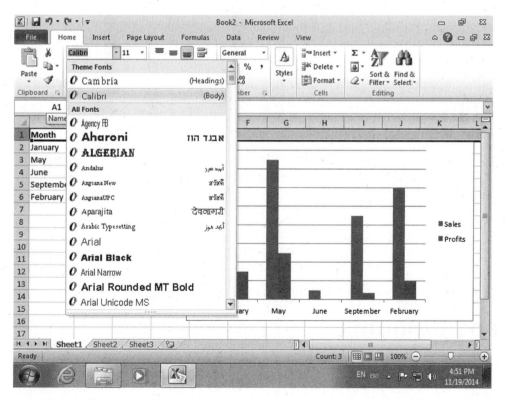

EXERCISE 7.6 *(continued)*

7. Select cell B2 by clicking it.

8. In the Home tab on the ribbon, go to the Font section and click the Fill Color button. Notice how the cell now has yellow as a background color, like in Figure 7.17.

FIGURE 7.17   A formatted table in Microsoft Excel

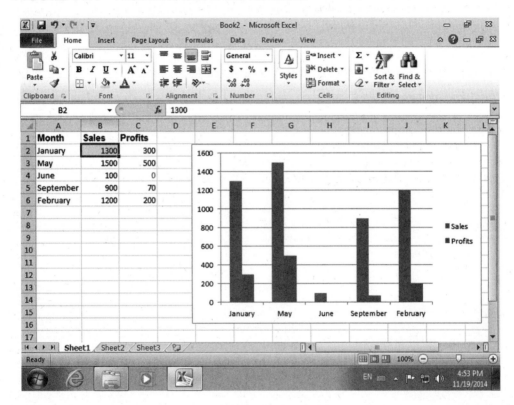

9. Close Microsoft Excel without saving your work.

Adding and Removing Rows and Columns

When creating worksheets, you will sometimes need to add and remove rows and columns of data. Luckily, this is very easy to do, and it takes only a bit of practice in order to do it correctly every time. The tools that you can use for these operations are found on the ribbon, in the Cells section of the Home tab. Click the Insert button in that section, and you will find the necessary tools for inserting rows and columns (Figure 7.18).

FIGURE 7.18   The menu for inserting rows and columns

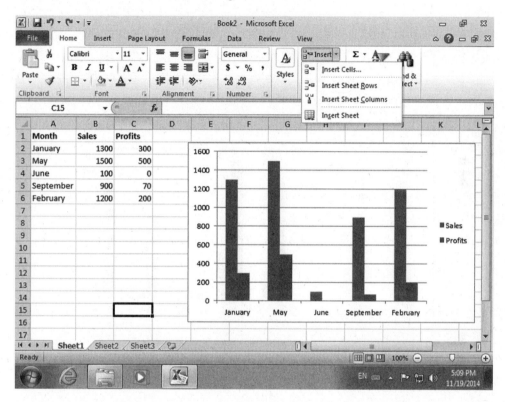

The Delete button can be used to delete any row or column that you select.

In Exercise 7.7 you will learn how to add and remove both rows and columns in your Microsoft Excel workbooks. In order to complete this exercise, please use the Book2.xlsx practice file you downloaded earlier.

EXERCISE 7.7

Adding and Removing Rows and Columns in Your Workbooks

1. Click Start and then Computer.

2. Browse to the location of the Book2.xlsx Excel file and double-click it.

   It will be opened with Microsoft Excel.

3. Select column A.

EXERCISE 7.7 *(continued)*

4.   On the ribbon, go to the Cells section of the Home tab and click Insert (Figure 7.19).

FIGURE 7.19   The menu for inserting columns and rows

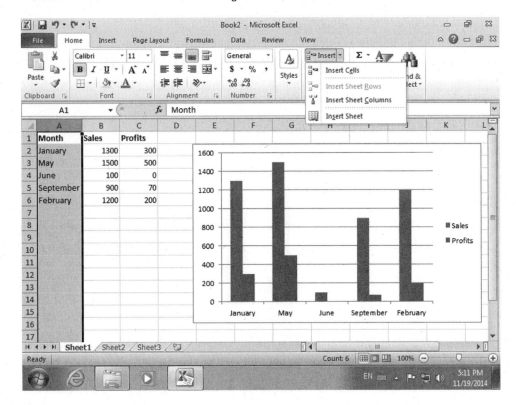

5.   Click Insert Sheet Columns, and an empty column is added to the left.

6.   With the newly added column still selected, click the Delete button in the Cells section on the ribbon.

   Notice that the newly added column is removed.

7.   Select row 6.

8.   On the ribbon, go to the Cells section of the Home tab and click Insert.

9.   Click Insert Sheet Rows, and an empty row is added above what was previously row 6.

10. With the newly added row still selected, click the Delete button in the Cells section on the ribbon.

11. Close Microsoft Excel without saving your work.

Merging or Unmerging Cells

Merging is the process of creating one cell out of two or more selected cells. When you merge more than one cell that contains data, only the data in the upper-left or upper-right cell is kept, depending on your current view direction. The remaining data is deleted. Microsoft Excel offers several merging tools:

Merge & Center   Joins the selected cells into one larger cell and centers the content in the new cell

Merge Across   Merges each row of the selected cells into a larger cell

Merge Cells   Merges the selected cells into one cell

These tools can be accessed using the Merge menu. On the ribbon, go to the Home tab and look for the Alignment section. There you will see the Merge & Center button and a small arrow pointing downward near it, as shown in Figure 7.20. Click it and you will be able to access all these merging options.

FIGURE 7.20   The Merge options that are available in Microsoft Excel

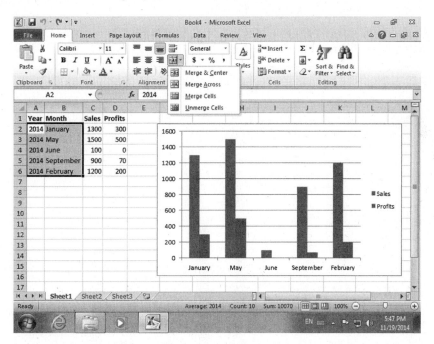

You can unmerge merged cells or split them into multiple new cells. However, when you do this, the data from the previous cells, before they were merged, is lost, and only the data from the existing merged cell is kept and used.

In Exercise 7.8 you will learn how to merge and unmerge cells in your Microsoft Excel workbooks. In order to complete this exercise, please download the Book4.xlsx practice file to your computer.

EXERCISE 7.8

Merging and Unmerging Cells in Your Workbooks

1. Click Start and then Computer.

2. Browse to the location of the Book4.xlsx Excel file and double-click it.

   It will be opened with Microsoft Excel.

3. Select cells A2 and B2.

4. Go to the Alignment section on the Home tab of the ribbon and click the arrow near the Merge & Center button.

5. Then click Merge Cells.

6. A warning is displayed that the selection contains multiple data values and only the upper-leftmost data will be kept. Click OK.

   Notice that the two cells have been merged.

7. With the newly merged cell still selected, click again the arrow near the Merge & Center button (Figure 7.21).

FIGURE 7.21   The Merge options that are available in Microsoft Excel

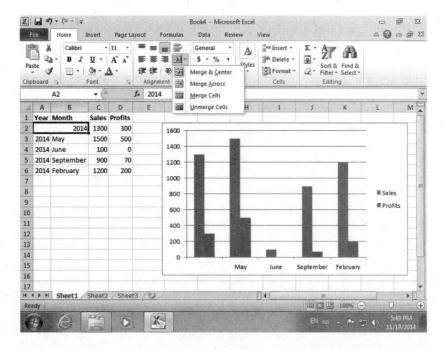

8.   Now click Unmerge Cells.

Notice that the cells are now unmerged and only the data from the A2 cell has been kept. The initial value of the B2 cell is now lost.

9.   Close Microsoft Excel without saving your work.

Using Number Formats in Microsoft Excel Workbooks

Microsoft Excel allows you to improve the way values are displayed in your cells by changing the number formats (Figure 7.22). You can choose any of the following formats:

General   The general format that is used by Microsoft Excel, in which cells have no specific number format

Number   Used for the general display of numbers and can include decimals

Currency   Used for general monetary values

Accounting   Used for accounting formats that line up currency symbols and decimal points in a column

Date   Optimized for displaying the date and time in different ways

Time   Optimized for displaying the time in different ways

Percentage   Displays the value of a cell with a percent symbol

Fraction   Optimized for displaying fractions

Scientific   Optimized for displaying scientific data, formulas, and calculations

Text   Treats cells as text even when a number is in the cell

Special   Useful for tracking lists and database values

Custom   Allows you to create your own custom formats based on the default ones that are available

FIGURE 7.22   The number formats that are available in Microsoft Excel

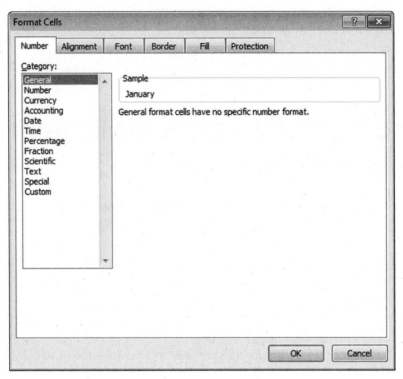

In Exercise 7.9 you will learn how to set the number format for a selection of cells. In order to complete this exercise, please use the Book2.xlsx practice file you downloaded earlier.

EXERCISE 7.9

Setting the Number Format for a Selection of Cells

1. Click Start and then Computer.

2. Browse to the location of the Book2.xlsx Excel file and double-click it.

   It will be opened with Microsoft Excel.

3. Select column C and then right-click it (Figure 7.23).

FIGURE 7.23   The context menu

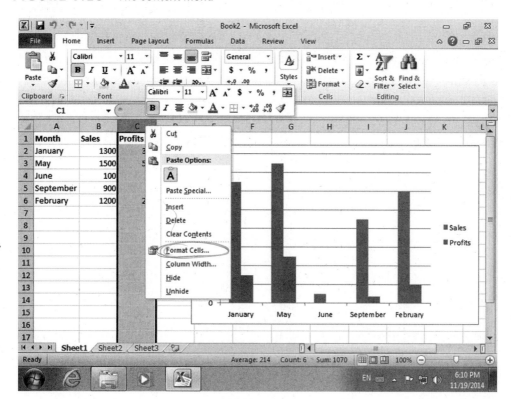

4. Click Format Cells, and the window with the same name opens.

5. Click Currency and then OK.

   Notice how the formatting of the cells in the C column changes according to the format that you have selected.

6. Close Microsoft Excel without saving your work.

Sorting and Filtering Data

As you add more content to a worksheet, organizing the information becomes especially important. You can quickly reorganize a worksheet by sorting your data using the specialized tools that are available in Microsoft Excel (Figure 7.24). They can be found in the Data tab on the ribbon. Look for the Sort & Filter section, where you will first find three sorting options:

Sort A to Z   Sorts the selection so that the lowest values are at the top of the column

Sort Z to A   Sorts the selection so that the highest values are at the top of the column

Sort   Shows the Sort dialog box to sort data on several criteria at once, from their values to their coloring and so on

FIGURE 7.24   The Sort dialog box

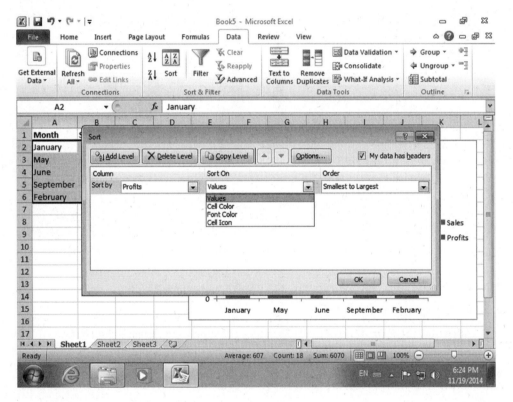

You can also find sorting and filtering options on the Home tab on the ribbon. Look for the Editing section and click the Sort & Filter button. There you will find all the available options.

Sorting Data

You can sort an entire table or only a column, depending on your needs. Using the first two sorting options is very easy: you select the data set that you want to sort and then click the appropriate button. Creating your own sorting criteria is more complicated though. We will demonstrate how it is done in Exercise 7.10. In order to complete this exercise, please download the Book5.xlsx practice file to your computer.

EXERCISE 7.10

Sorting Data

1. Click Start and then Computer.

2. Browse to the location of the Book5.xlsx Excel file and double-click it.

   It will be opened with Microsoft Excel.

3. Select the entire table, from cell A1 to cell C6, as shown in Figure 7.25.

FIGURE 7.25 A Microsoft Excel workbook with a table selected

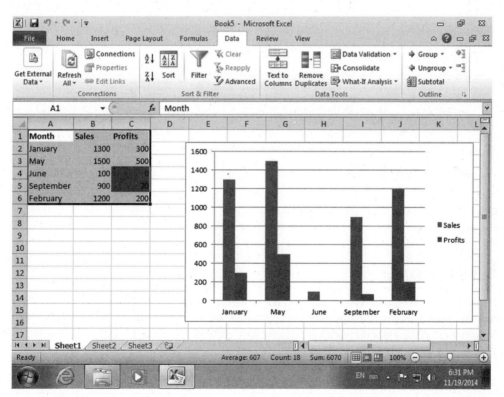

4. On the ribbon, click the Data tab and then the Sort button in the Sort & Filter section.

5. In the Sort dialog box (Figure 7.26), click Sort By and select Profits.

6. Click Sort On and select Cell Color.

7. Click No Cell Color and select the color red.

FIGURE 7.26 The Sort dialog box

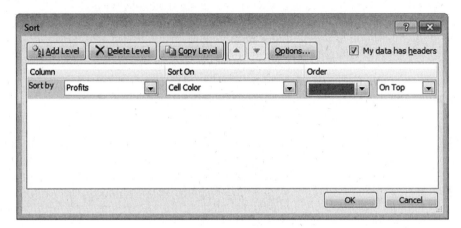

8. Leave On Top selected and click OK.

   Notice how the table is sorted by Profits, and the months with the lowest profits, colored in red, are listed first.

9. Close Microsoft Excel without saving your work.

Filtering Data

If your worksheet contains a lot of data, it can be difficult to find information quickly. You can use filters to narrow down the data in your worksheet, allowing you to view only the information you need. Filtered data displays only the rows that meet the criteria that you specify and hides the rows that you do not want displayed. After you filter data, you can copy, find, edit, format, chart, and print the subset of filtered data without rearranging or moving it.

You can filter by more than one column due to the fact that filters are additive. Each additional filter is based on the current filter and further reduces the subset of data. In order for filtering to work correctly, your worksheet should include a header row where you type the name of each column. You cannot filter columns that do not have their name written in their first row.

In Exercise 7.11 you will learn how to use filters in Microsoft Excel. In order to complete this exercise, please use the Book5.xlsx practice file you downloaded to your computer.

EXERCISE 7.11

Filtering the Data in Your Workbooks

1. Click Start and then Computer.

2. Browse to the location of the Book5.xlsx Excel file and double-click it.

   It will be opened with Microsoft Excel.

3. Select the entire table, from cell A1 to cell C6.

4. On the ribbon, click the Data tab and then the Filter button in the Sort & Filter section.

5. Click the Profits filter, deselect the value 0, and click OK (Figure 7.27).

FIGURE 7.27   Filtering data by profit in Microsoft Excel

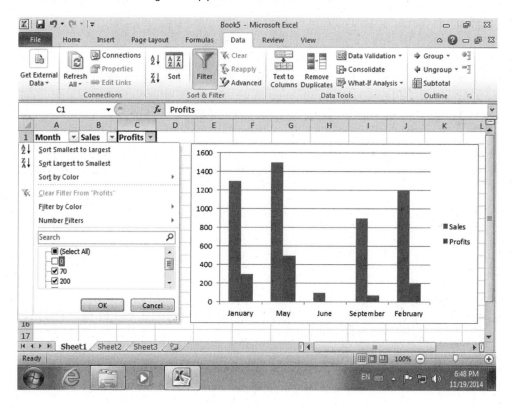

You are now viewing all the months with a profit that is different from 0.

6. Click the Sales filter, deselect the value 900, and click OK (Figure 7.28).

FIGURE 7.28 Filtering data by sales in Microsoft Excel

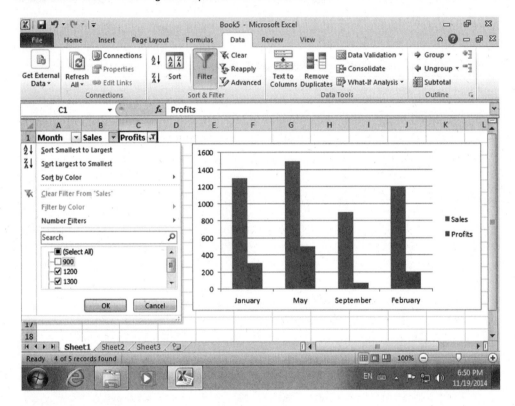

You are now viewing all the months with sales that are different from 900 and the profit that is different from 0.

7. Close Microsoft Excel without saving your work.

Using Common Formulas and Functions

Above the work area in Microsoft Excel and just beneath the ribbon you can find the *formula bar*, highlighted in Figure 7.29. It is labeled with the function symbol (*fx*). If you click it, you can see the formula applied for the selected cell. This formula can be a mathematical operation like 1+3; a mathematical operation using references to other cells; or statistical averages, conversion formulas, and so on. You begin entering your formula with an equal sign and then by using the correct language, including numbers (or constants), math operators, cell references, and functions. The formula bar can be used to enter or edit a formula, a function, or data in a cell.

FIGURE 7.29   The formula bar in Microsoft Excel

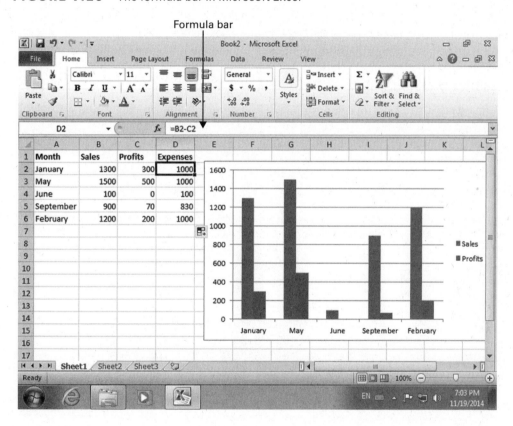

When you click the formula bar or when you type an equal (=) sign in a cell, you will activate the formula bar, and you can start using it.

Using Mathematical Operators

In Exercise 7.12 you will learn how to use common mathematical operators together with relative cell references in Microsoft Excel. In order to complete this exercise, please use the Book2.xlsx practice file.

EXERCISE 7.12

Using Mathematical Operators

1. Click Start and then Computer.

2. Browse to the location of the Book2.xlsx Excel file and double-click it.

   It will be opened with Microsoft Excel.

3. Click cell D1, type **Expenses**, and then press Enter on your keyboard.

4. In cell D2 type **=B2-C2** and press Enter (Figure 7.30).

FIGURE 7.30   Using mathematical operators in formulas

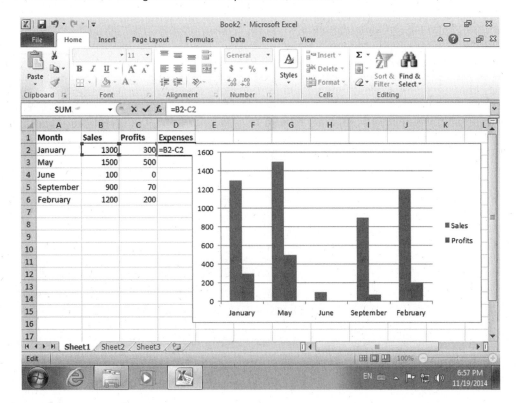

5. Select cell D2 and then move the mouse cursor to the square displayed on its bottom-right corner.

6. Click that square and drag the mouse cursor down to cell D6.

7. Release the mouse button and notice how the D column has been automatically populated with the expenses of each month in the table.

8. Click cell D6 and notice how the formula applied for it is =B6-C6, in the formula bar, similar to what you have written as the formula for cell D2.

9. Close Microsoft Excel without saving your work.

Using Relative and Absolute References

When you create formulas and calculations, you can use references to other cells, like the ones used in the previous exercise. By default, these references are relative, meaning that they change when a formula is copied to another cell. They can also be absolute, meaning that they remain constant, no matter where they are copied.

When copied across multiple cells, relative references change based on the relative position of rows and columns. For example, if you copy the formula =A1+B1 from row 1 to row 2, the formula will become =A2+B2. Relative references are especially convenient whenever you need to repeat the same calculation across multiple rows or columns.

If you want to maintain the original cell reference in this example when you copy it, you make the cell reference absolute by preceding the columns (A and B) and row (1) with a dollar sign ($). Then, when you copy the formula (=$A$1+$B$1) from row 1 to row 2, the formula stays exactly the same.

To help you learn the difference between relative references and absolute references, let's work together through Exercise 7.13, which demonstrates it in a practical manner. In order to complete this exercise, please download the Book6.xlsx practice file to your computer.

EXERCISE 7.13

Using Relative and Absolute References

1. Click Start and then Computer.

2. Browse to the location of the Book6.xlsx Excel file and double-click it.

   It will be opened with Microsoft Excel.

3. In cell D2 type **=B2-C2** and press Enter (Figure 7.31).

FIGURE 7.31 Using a relative reference in your calculations

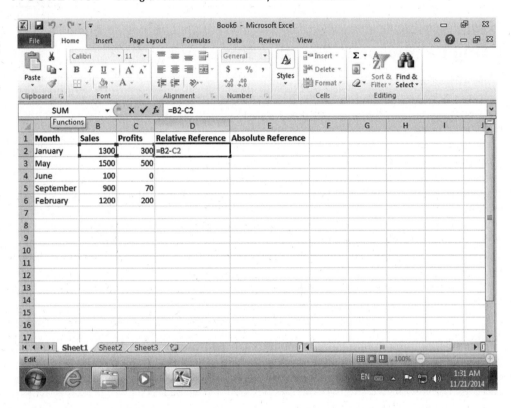

4. Select cell D2 and then move the mouse cursor to the square displayed on its bottom-right corner.

5. Click that square and drag the mouse cursor down to cell D6.

6. Release the mouse, and notice how the D column has been automatically populated with the expenses of each month in the table.

7. In cell E2 type **=$B$2-$C$2** and press Enter (Figure 7.32).

FIGURE 7.32   Using an absolute reference into your calculations

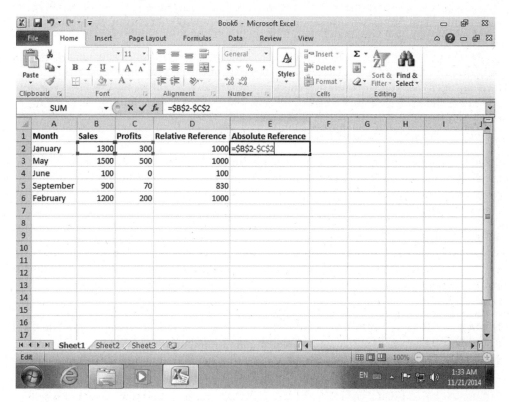

8. Select cell E2 and then move the mouse cursor to the square displayed on its bottom-right corner.

9. Click that square and drag the mouse cursor down to cell E6.

10. Release the mouse button and notice how the E column has been automatically populated with the expenses of the month of January.

   Notice the differences in values between columns D and E.

11. Close Microsoft Excel without saving your work.

Using Functions

A lot of computational power is at your disposal with functions, which are prepackaged formulas built into Microsoft Excel that perform specific calculations. All functions are followed by a set of parentheses, and most require specific arguments to be entered between those parentheses. When you use functions, range references are perfectly acceptable to use as arguments, when appropriate.

With most functions, you can combine different types of arguments, including single-cell references, cell ranges (C6:C8), static values (12), and even other formulas. It is recommended that you enter cell references into formulas rather than static values because you can see and change values entered into cells, but they are hidden in formulas; only the result of the formula is displayed.

Some of the most commonly used functions are as follows:

COUNT()   Counts the number of cells that contain numbers, and counts numbers within the list of arguments. Use it to get the number of entries in a number field that is in a range or array of numbers. For example, you can enter the following formula to count the numbers in the range A1:A7: =COUNT(A1:A7).

SUM()   Adds all the numbers that you specify as arguments. Each argument can be a range, a cell reference, an array, a constant, a formula, or the result from another function. For example, =SUM(A1:A7) adds all the numbers that are contained in cells A1 through A7. For another example, =SUM(A1, A3, A5, A7) adds the numbers that are contained in cells A1, A3, A5, and A7.

AVERAGE()   Returns the average (arithmetic mean) of the arguments that are provided. For example, if the range A1:A7 contains numbers, the formula =AVERAGE(A1:A7) returns the average of those numbers.

We mentioned earlier that you can use other formulas as arguments. For example, you can use =SUM(AVERAGE(A1:A7), AVERAGE(B1:B7)) as the sum of the averages for cells A1 to A7 and B1 to B7.

In Exercise 7.14 you will learn how to use common functions like SUM(), AVERAGE(), and COUNT() in Microsoft Excel. In order to complete this exercise, please use the Book2.xlsx practice file you have on your computer.

EXERCISE 7.14

Using Common Functions

1. Click Start and then Computer.

2. Browse to the location of the Book2.xlsx Excel file and double-click it.

   It will be opened with Microsoft Excel.

3. In cell A7 type =**COUNT(A2:A6)** and press Enter (Figure 7.33).

FIGURE 7.33   Using the COUNT function

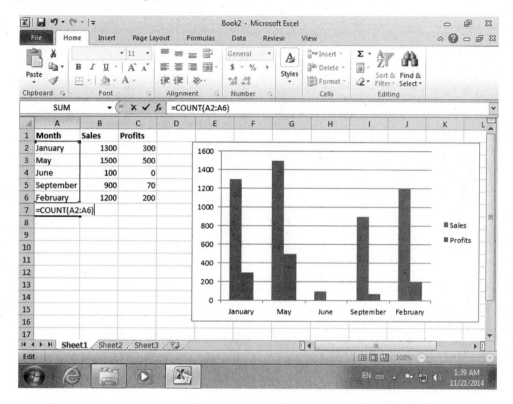

Notice that the end result is 0, meaning that there are no cells that contain numbers in column A.

4. In cell B7 type =**SUM(B2:B6)** and press Enter (Figure 7.34).

The end result is 5000, meaning the sum of all the sales in the table. If you double-check on your own, you will notice that this is the correct result.

5. In cell C7 type =**AVERAGE(C2:C6)** and press Enter (Figure 7.35).

Notice that the end result is 214, meaning the average profit for all the months in the table. If you double-check on your own, you will notice that this is the correct result.

6. Close Microsoft Excel without saving your work.

FIGURE 7.34 Using the SUM function

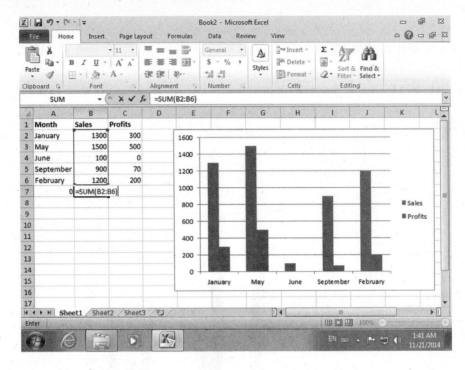

FIGURE 7.35 Using the AVERAGE function

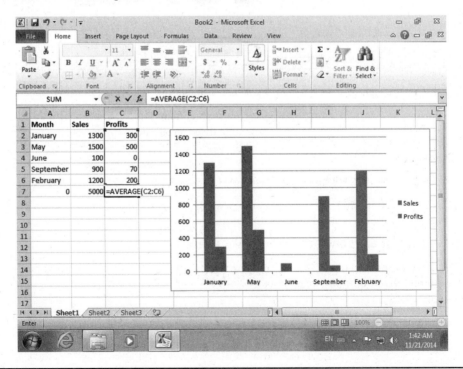

When you select a range of cells in Microsoft Excel, it automatically performs three calculations—Average, Count, and Sum—and it displays them in the status bar. This tiny little bar is the last bar found on the bottom of the Microsoft Excel window, and it is highlighted in Figure 7.36. If you don't need to create a formula, this is a real timesaver.

FIGURE 7.36   The Status bar in Microsoft Excel

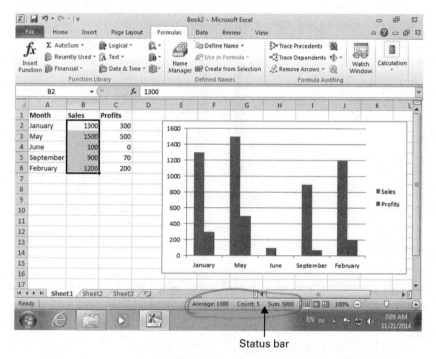

Status bar

Microsoft Excel offers many types of formulas, including logical, financial, mathematical, and so on. If you would like to spend some time discovering the many formulas that are available, go to the Formulas tab on the ribbon (Figure 7.37). There you will find a section named Function Library with all the different functions organized by type.

Click each type of function to discover a list of the most frequently used functions in every category. When you click a function, you will get to a window where you can create that function using specific arguments and learn more about what it does and how it works.

You can find a complete list of functions for Microsoft Excel at http://bit.ly/11kux0c.

Adding Charts and Graphs

Charts and graphs are the most used graphics available in Microsoft Excel, complementing its number-crunching prowess. They are very useful because they help you visualize dry numeric data, revealing underlying trends and unanticipated fluctuations that might otherwise be difficult to discern.

FIGURE 7.37   The Formulas tab in Microsoft Excel

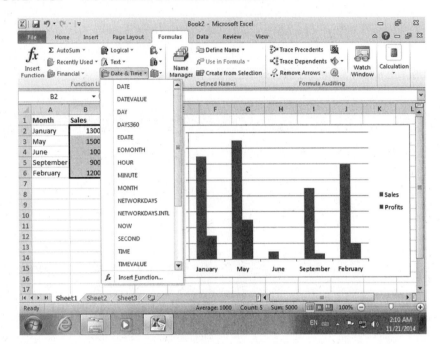

In order to create a chart or graph, you must first select the data that you want to include in it. Then click the Insert tab on the ribbon (Figure 7.38). There you will find the Charts section with several buttons for inserting all kinds of graphs and charts:

Column   Inserts a column chart that is used to compare values across categories

Line   Inserts a line chart that is used to spot trends over time

Pie   Inserts a pie chart that is used to display the contribution of each value to the total

Bar   Inserts a bar chart that is used for comparing multiple values

Area   Inserts an area chart that is used to emphasize differences between several sets of data over time

Scatter   Inserts a scatter chart that is used to compare pairs of values

Other Charts   Allows you to insert other kinds of charts like stock, surface, doughnut, bubble, and radar

FIGURE 7.38   The Insert tab in Microsoft Excel

Inserting a Line Chart

You can easily change the way a chart or graph looks using chart styles, by adding labels, moving them around, resizing them, and more.

In Exercise 7.15 you will learn how to insert a line chart in Microsoft Excel, add labels to it, and change its position. In order to complete this exercise, please download the Book7.xlsx practice file to your computer.

EXERCISE 7.15

Inserting a Line Chart into Your Worksheet

1. Click Start and then Computer.

2. Browse to the location of the Book7.xlsx Excel file and double-click it.

   It will be opened with Microsoft Excel.

3. Select cells A1 to B6.

4. Click the Insert tab on the ribbon and then the Line button (Figure 7.39) in the Charts section.

FIGURE 7.39 Inserting a line chart in your worksheet

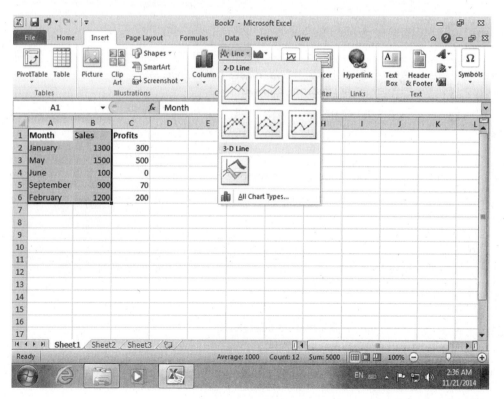

5. From the list of line charts, click the first 2-D Line, the one on the top-left side of the list.

    A line chart is added, sharing the sales trend over time.

6. Select the chart and drag it to the right side of the worksheet, near the table.

7. Click somewhere outside the chart to deselect it.

8. Right-click the line showing the trend inside the line chart, and in the context menu click Add Data Labels (Figure 7.40).

FIGURE 7.40   The context menu for a Line chart

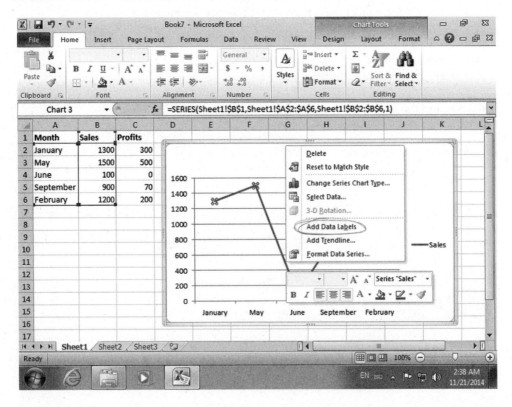

9. Click somewhere outside the chart to deselect it.

    Notice how the sales numbers have been added as labels for each month.

10. Close Microsoft Excel without saving your work.

Inserting a Pie Chart

The charts that you are creating can also be moved to a different worksheet than the one you are using for your data. This makes it easier to work with your workbook, especially when it includes lots of data. Keeping your data and your charts separate is a good idea in this scenario.

In Exercise 7.16 you will learn how to insert a pie chart in Microsoft Excel and how to move it to another worksheet than the one you are using for working with your data. In order to complete this exercise, please use the Book7.xlsx practice file you downloaded to your computer.

EXERCISE 7.16

Inserting a Pie Chart into Your Worksheet

1. Click Start and then Computer.

2. Browse to the location of the Book7.xlsx Excel file and double-click it.

   It will be opened with Microsoft Excel.

3. Select cells A1 to B6.

4. Click the Insert tab on the ribbon and then the Pie button in the Charts section.

5. From the list of pie charts, click the first 2-D Pie, the one on the top-left side of the list (Figure 7.41).

FIGURE 7.41   Inserting a pie chart into your worksheet

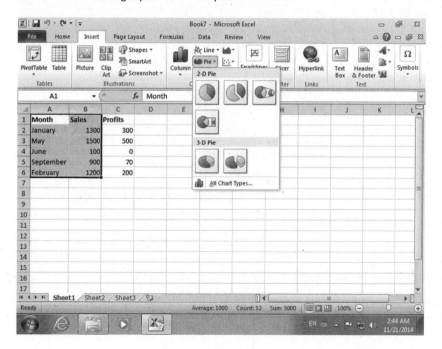

A pie chart is added, showing the share of sales of each month from the total.

6. Right-click the margin of the chart and select Move Chart (Figure 7.42).

FIGURE 7.42 The context menu for a pie chart

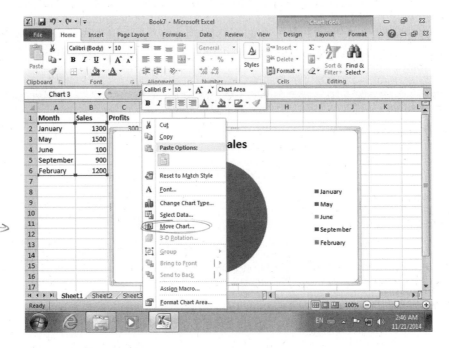

7. In the Move Chart dialog, select Object In and then Sheet2 (Figure 7.43).

FIGURE 7.43 The Move Chart dialog

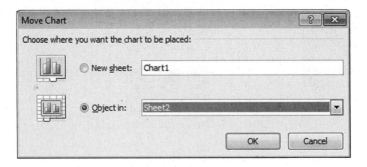

8. Click OK, and the pie chart is moved to Sheet2.

9. Close Microsoft Excel without saving your work.

Inserting a Bar Graph

A great thing about charts and graphs is that they are always connected to their data source. This means that while you are working on your data and you make changes to it, the charts and graphs associated with it update themselves automatically.

In Exercise 7.17 we will demonstrate how to add a bar graph and how it gets updated when you update the data from its source. In order to complete this exercise, please use the Book7.xlsx practice file on your computer.

EXERCISE 7.17

Inserting a Bar Graph into Your Worksheet

1. Click Start and then Computer.

2. Browse to the location of the Book7.xlsx Excel file and double-click it.

   It will be opened with Microsoft Excel.

3. Select cells A1 to C6.

4. Click the Insert tab on the ribbon and then the Bar button in the Charts section.

5. From the list of bar graphs, click the first 2-D Bar, the one on the top-left side of the list (Figure 7.44).

FIGURE 7.44   Adding a bar graph to your workbook

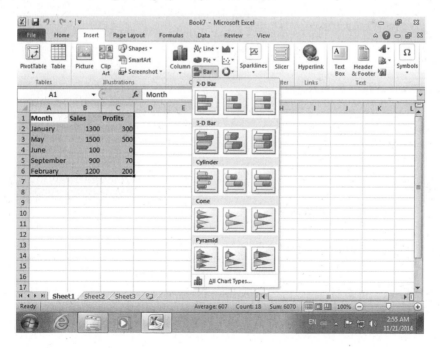

A bar graph is created, comparing sales and profits month by month.

6. Select the graph and drag it to the right side of the worksheet, near the table.

7. Click cell C4 in the table and then enter **1000** as its value. Press Enter when finished.

Notice how the bar graph is automatically updated for the month of June and is automatically displaying 1000 as the profit for that month, like in Figure 7.45.

FIGURE 7.45   The updated bar graph

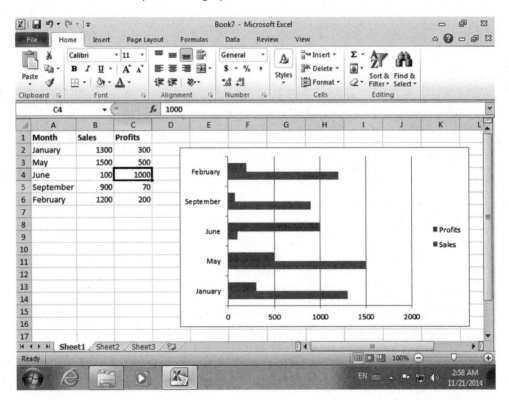

8. Close Microsoft Excel without saving your work.

Summary

When you are working with large data sets, it is best to use Microsoft Excel. This powerful tool can help you add data as quickly as possible, format it, and organize it as best as possible. You can easily change the size of your cells so that they are large enough to display your data, format how the data is displayed in each cell, and add or remove as many columns and rows as you need.

When working with larger data sets, you may also want to merge certain cells, based on different criteria. Microsoft Excel offers you the tools that you need for doing so. You can also specify which types of data you are entering in a cell or group of cells so that Microsoft Excel knows how to best display it and use it in your calculations. And speaking of calculations, Microsoft Excel offers the most advanced features for making mathematical, statistical, or financial calculations, using many different formulas and functions.

In order to spot different data sets or trends in your tables, you can use sorting and filtering so that you get the job done as quickly as possible.

Finally, Microsoft Excel offers everything you need in order to visualize your data, using all kinds of graphs and charts.

Now that you know the most important basics about using Microsoft Excel, we will move on to Microsoft PowerPoint and demonstrate how to use it to make presentations.

Exam Essentials

Know how to navigate Microsoft Excel. You cannot be productive when using Microsoft Excel without knowing how to navigate through its user interface, switch between worksheets and workbooks, or jump from one cell to another.

Know how to change the size of cells and how to format them. In order to correctly fit your data into worksheets, you may need to change the size of your cells as well as their formatting so that you can easily read the data and edit it.

Learn how to use number formats. Microsoft Excel allows you to improve the way values are displayed in your cells by changing the number formats. The number formats are applied not only to the way data is displayed by Microsoft Excel but also to the calculations and formulas you are using with the cells that are formatted.

Know how to sort and filter your data. When working with large data sets, it is very important that you know how to sort your data and filter it, using all kinds of criteria.

Understand how to use formulas and functions. In order to truly unlock the computing prowess of Microsoft Excel, it is essential that you understand how to make calculations using all kinds of formulas and functions.

Learn how to insert charts and graphs.   Visualizing data is mandatory in order for it to be truly useful to you. This will help you reveal underlying trends and unanticipated fluctuations that might otherwise be difficult to discern.

Key Terms

Before you take the exam, be certain you are familiar with the following terms:

formula bar   workbook

Name box   worksheets

spreadsheet

Review Questions

1. What are the characteristics of a workbook? (Choose all that apply.)

   A. A Microsoft Excel file

   B. A collection of spreadsheets ⅹ p 279

   C. A table of data ⅹ worksheet, not table

   D. A collection of worksheets

2. What is a spreadsheet?

   A. A Microsoft Excel file

   B. An application that is used for organizing, analyzing, and storing data in tabular form

   C. A worksheet

   D. A collection of worksheets

3. How do you change a row's height in Microsoft Excel?

   A. Select the row, click the Home tab, go to the Cells section, and click Format, followed by Row Height.

   B. Select the row, click the Format tab, go to the Cells section, and click Format, followed by Row Height.

   C. Select the row, click the Page Layout tab, go to the Cells section, and click Row Height.

   D. Select the row, click the Home tab, go to the Cells section, and click Insert, followed by Insert Sheet Rows.

4. How do you increase the font size of a cell? (Choose all that apply.)

   A. Click the cell to select it, click the Page Layout tab, go to the Font section, and click the Increase Font Size button. ⅹ

   B. Click the cell to select it, click the Home tab, go to the Font section, and click the Increase Font Size button.

   C. Click the cell to select it, click the Home tab, go to the Font section, click the Font Size drop-down list, and select a larger font size.

   D. Click the cell to select it, click the Page Layout tab, go to the Page Setup section, click Size, and select a larger size. ⅹ

5. How does Microsoft Excel use number formats?   p 297

   A. The number formats are applied to the way data is displayed.

   B. The number formats are applied to the way data is numbered.

   C. The number formats are applied to the way data is displayed as well as to the calculations and formulas you are using with the cells that are formatted.

   D. The number formats are applied to the way data is displayed as well as to the way it is added into graphs.

6. How do you change the format of a cell to Number?

    A. Right-click the cell, click Format Cells, select Scientific, and click OK.

    B. Click the cell, click Format Cells, select Scientific, and click OK.

    C. Click the cell, click Format Cells, select Number, and click OK.

    D. Right-click the cell, click Format Cells, select Number, and click OK. *p. 269*

7. What kind of data can you filter in Microsoft Excel?

    A. A cell

    B. A row

    C. One or more columns

    D. Multiple cells that are not placed one near the other

8. Where will you find the tools for sorting and filtering data in Microsoft Excel? (Choose all that apply.)

    A. On the Data tab on the ribbon, in the Sort & Filter section

    B. On the Home tab on the ribbon, by clicking the Sort & Filter button in the Editing section

    C. On the Data tab on the ribbon, by clicking the Sort & Filter button in the Editing section

    D. On the Home tab on the ribbon, in the Sort & Filter section

9. How do you enter a formula into a cell?

    A. Click the cell and type = and then the numbers that make up your formula.

    B. Click the cell and then type the numbers that make up your formula.

    C. Click the cell and type = and then the numbers (or constants), math operators, cell references, and functions that make up your formula.

    D. Right-click the cell and type = and then the numbers (or constants), math operators, cell references, and functions that make up your formula.

10. Where are the tools for inserting charts and graphs into a worksheet?

    A. On the Insert tab on the ribbon, in the Illustrations section

    B. On the Insert tab on the ribbon, in the Charts section

    C. On the Formulas tab on the ribbon, in the Charts section

    D. On the Review tab on the ribbon, in the Illustrations section

Chapter

8

Using Microsoft PowerPoint

THE FOLLOWING IC3 GS4: KEY APPLICATIONS EXAM OBJECTIVES ARE COVERED IN THIS CHAPTER:

✓ **Presentation Activities**

✓ **Inserting Content**

- Demonstrate how to insert text into a presentation application so as to display properly and effectively in the desired font face, size and style in a slide show.

- Demonstrate how to insert a table into or create a table and insert text into it in a presentation application so as to display properly and effectively in the desired font face, size and style in a slide show.

- Demonstrate how to insert an audio, video, animations, and other media clips into a presentation application so as to display properly and effectively with the desired timing and control in a slide show presentation.

- Demonstrate how to insert a chart into or create a chart and insert text, numbers, and shapes into it in a presentation application so as to display properly and effectively in the desired colors, layout, and format in a slide show presentation.

- Demonstrate how to insert shapes, graphics, and pictures of various formats, file formats, sizes, palettes, etc. into or create shapes and graphics and insert content into them in a presentation application so as to display properly and effectively in the desired colors, layout, and format in a slide show presentation.

✓ **Slide Management**

- Demonstrate how to add slides into or create slides within a presentation application.

- Demonstrate how to delete slides from or remove slides from within a presentation application.

- Describe how to alter the presentation order of slides or move them around within a presentation application.

✓ **Slide Design**

- Layout

- Animations

- Transitions

Microsoft PowerPoint is another important tool in the Microsoft Office suite; it allows you to create all kinds of presentations. It is easy to use, and what you see is really what you get. With each new version, Microsoft adds more features, making it one of the most powerful presentation tools available to date.

In this chapter we will cover the basics that you need to know in order to use Microsoft PowerPoint: how to add and remove slides, how to arrange them in the order you want, how to change their design and layout, and how to add content to them and format it. Finally, we will also cover how to add animations and transitions, if you feel the need to make your presentations more dynamic.

Adding and Removing Slides When Creating Presentations

Presentations are made of slides. A *slide* is a single page of a presentation that is created with presentation software like Microsoft PowerPoint or Impress (the presentation application from the LibreOffice suite).

When you start Microsoft PowerPoint, a presentation with a blank slide is created, where you can add the title and the subtitle of your presentation. You will see this slide twice: once in a thumbnail preview, in a column on the left side of the Microsoft PowerPoint window, and then, fully, on the right side of the window, where you edit each slide.

The column on the left is named the *slides pane*, while the big area on the right is the area where you edit your slides and add text, graphics, multimedia files, and more. In Figure 8.1 the slides pane and the editing area are highlighted.

In order to create a presentation you need to have more than just one slide, and knowing how to add and remove slides is the first basic skill that you need to master when using Microsoft PowerPoint. Such additions and abstractions can be done by using buttons on the ribbon, keyboard shortcuts, or the menu that is shown when you right-click a slide.

In Exercise 8.1 you will learn how to add and remove slides in your presentations.

FIGURE 8.1 The Microsoft PowerPoint user interface

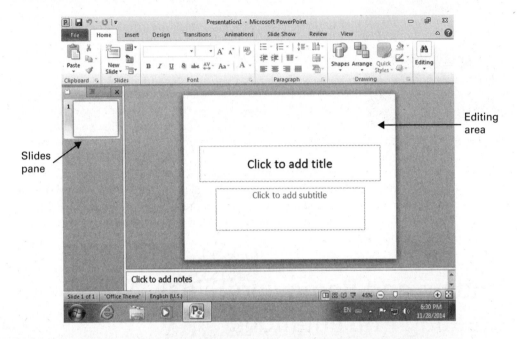

Slides pane

Editing area

EXERCISE 8.1

Adding and Removing Slides when Creating Presentations

1. Click Start ➤ All Programs ➤ Microsoft Office ➤ Microsoft PowerPoint 2010 (Figure 8.2).

    A new blank presentation is created, with an empty slide.

2. On the Home tab on the ribbon, look for the Slides section and click New Slide.

    Notice how a new empty slide is added to the presentation.

3. Right-click the second slide, and in the menu that is shown (Figure 8.3), click New Slide.

    Notice how a third empty slide is added to the presentation.

4. Press Ctrl+M on your keyboard, and notice how a fourth empty slide is added to the presentation.

5. Select the second slide and press Del (Delete) on your keyboard.

    Notice how the second slide is removed, and now you have only three slides in your presentation.

6. Right-click the third slide, and in the menu that is shown, click Delete Slide.

    Notice how the third slide is removed.

7. Close Microsoft PowerPoint without saving your changes.

FIGURE 8.2 The Microsoft PowerPoint shortcut in the Start menu

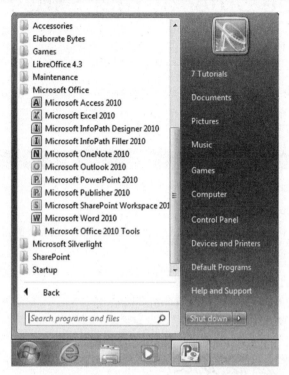

FIGURE 8.3 The context menu in Microsoft PowerPoint

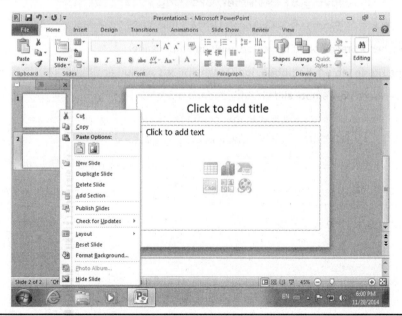

Changing the Order of Your Slides

When creating a presentation, you will almost certainly need to rearrange the order of your slides. This can be done very easily by simply dragging and dropping the slides into their new position, in the slides pane. You can also use Cut and Paste to move them around.

In Exercise 8.2 you will learn how to change the order of your slides in Microsoft PowerPoint. In order to complete this exercise, please download the Presentation2.pptx practice file to your computer.

EXERCISE 8.2

Changing the Order of Your Slides

1.   Click Start and then Computer.

2.   Browse to the location of the Presentation2.pptx PowerPoint file and double-click it.

      It will be opened with Microsoft PowerPoint.

3.   Go to the slides pane and click each slide one by one.

      Notice their title: the first slide contains the title of the presentation (Sample Presentation) and then each slide is numbered, starting with Slide 2 and ending with Slide 5.

4.   Click the second slide to select it and then drag it at the end of the presentation, after Slide 5 (Figure 8.4).

FIGURE 8.4   Dragging a slide to a new position

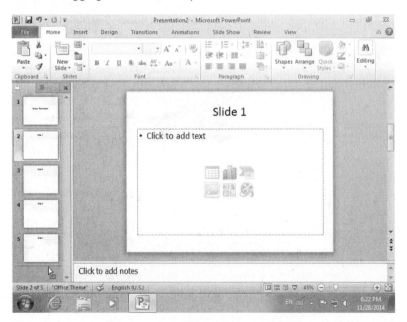

Notice how the fifth slide is now named Slide 2 because you have moved Slide 2 to the end of the presentation.

5. Click the second slide, which is named Slide 3, to select it.

6. On the Home tab on the ribbon, go to the Clipboard section and click the Cut button.

7. Now select slide number 4, which is titled Slide 2.

8. On the Home tab on the ribbon, go to the Clipboard section and click the Paste button.

Notice how the slide titled Slide 3 is now moved to the end of the presentation.

9. Select each slide one by one and notice their titles and their new order: Sample Presentation, Slide 4, Slide 5, Slide 2, Slide 3.

10. Close Microsoft PowerPoint without saving your changes.

Changing the Design and the Background of Your Presentations

When creating a new presentation in Microsoft PowerPoint, you will find that the default slides are white. This is not necessarily the best design for communicating effectively, and you may want to apply a visual theme for your slides and a specific background style.

Luckily, Microsoft PowerPoint includes plenty of built-in themes that you can choose from. You will find them in the Design tab on the ribbon, in the Themes section, shown in Figure 8.5.

FIGURE 8.5　The Design tab in Microsoft PowerPoint

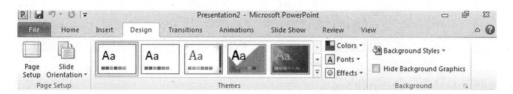

Applying a new theme changes major visual design details like the effects applied to titles and text, the way tables and charts are displayed, and the layouts and backgrounds of your slides. You can apply a new theme to your presentation with just one click.

Each theme applies a different background to your presentation. However, each theme has more than one background style that you can choose from. In the Design tab on the ribbon, you'll see the Background section, where you'll find the Background Styles button, shown in Figure 8.6. If you click it, you will see a list with all the available styles that can be applied to the background for the current theme. These styles differ from theme to theme.

FIGURE 8.6 Background styles available in Microsoft PowerPoint

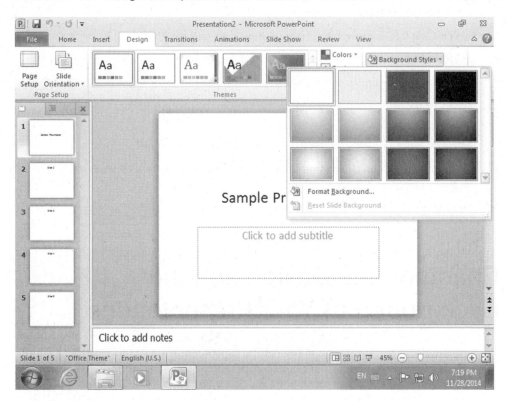

In Exercise 8.3 you will learn how to change the theme applied to your presentations, as well as the background style. In order to complete this exercise, please use the Presentation2.pptx practice file you previously downloaded to your computer.

EXERCISE 8.3

Changing the Theme and the Background Style Applied to Your Presentation

1. Click Start and then Computer.

2. Browse to the location of the Presentation2.pptx PowerPoint file and double-click it.

   It will be opened with Microsoft PowerPoint.

3. Click the Design tab on the ribbon and then the arrow pointing downward, in the Themes section.

   A list of themes is displayed.

4. In the Built-In section of themes, click the one named Aspect (the first in the second row of themes, shown in Figure 8.7).

    The new theme is now applied. Notice how different it is from the previous blank slides.

FIGURE 8.7   The themes that are built into Microsoft PowerPoint

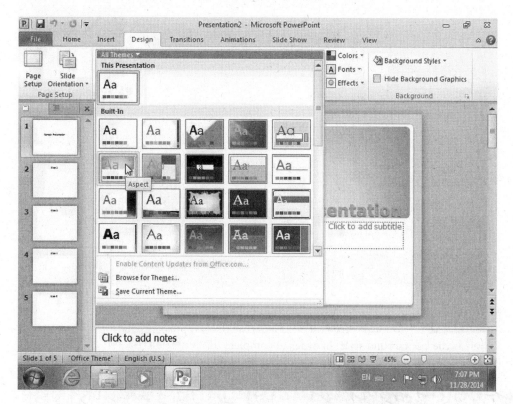

5. Click the second slide to select it and notice the background.

6. In the Design tab on the ribbon, go to the Background section and click Background Styles.

    A list with different background styles is shown.

7. Click the first style in the third row, named Style 9, to apply it (Figure 8.8).

    Notice how the style of the background has changed.

FIGURE 8.8   A list of background styles in Microsoft PowerPoint

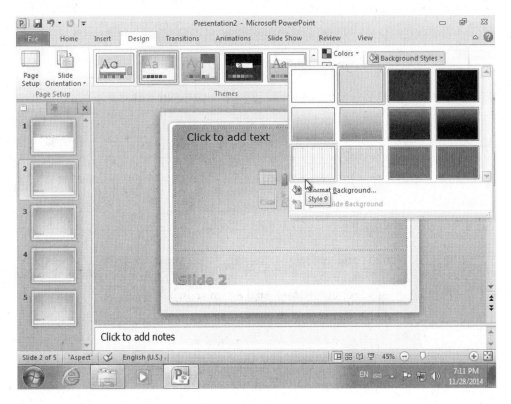

8.   Close Microsoft PowerPoint without saving your changes.

Adding and Formatting the Text in Your Presentations

Now that you know how to add or remove slides and change their order and design, it is time to learn how to populate your presentations with text. After all, you have a message to send to your audience and you have to write it.

Adding text into Microsoft PowerPoint presentations is done the same as in Microsoft Word. You click where you want to add the text and start typing. When finished, you can also format the text and make it look as you wish.

The tools for formatting the text are again similar to those found in Microsoft Word. You can find them on the Home tab on the ribbon. Look for the Font section, and there you will find the options for changing the font and the size and making the text bold, italic, underlined, and so on. You can view them in Figure 8.9.

FIGURE 8.9   The Home tab on the Microsoft PowerPoint ribbon

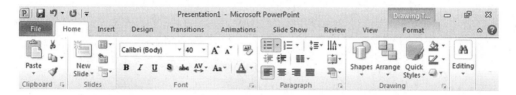

In Exercise 8.4 you will learn how to add text to your presentations and how to format it using the tools available on the Home tab of the Microsoft PowerPoint ribbon.

EXERCISE 8.4

Adding Text to Your Presentations and Formatting It

1. Click Start ➢ All Programs ➢ Microsoft Office ➢ Microsoft PowerPoint 2010.

    A new blank presentation is created, with an empty slide.

2. Click where it says "Click to add title" and type **My Presentation**.

3. Click somewhere else outside the first slide.

4. Select the text you just typed.

5. In the Home tab on the ribbon, go to the Font section and click the B (Bold) button.

6. Add a new slide.

7. Click where it says "Click to add title" and type **My slide**.

8. Click somewhere else outside the first slide.

9. Select the text you just typed.

10. In the Home tab on the ribbon, go to the Font section and click the Fonts list (Figure 8.10).

11. Select Arial from the list of fonts.

12. Click where it says "Click to add text" and type **Sample text**.

13. Select the text you just typed.

14. In the Home tab on the ribbon, go to the Font section and click the Increase Font Size button twice (Figure 8.11).

    Notice how the text in your slides has changed.

FIGURE 8.10   The fonts that are available in Microsoft PowerPoint

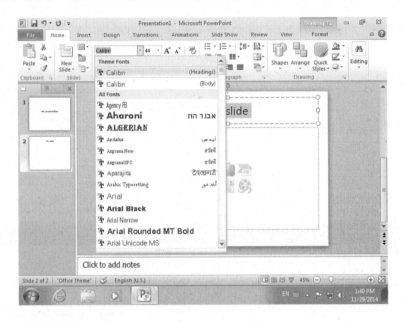

FIGURE 8.11   The Increase Font Size button in Microsoft PowerPoint

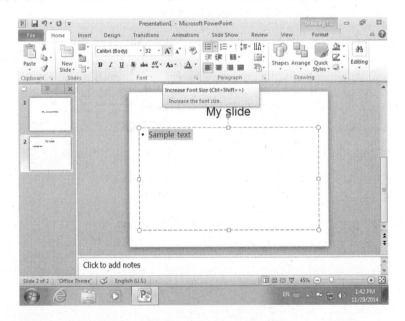

15. Close Microsoft PowerPoint without saving your changes.

Changing the Layout of Your Slides

Even though it is not apparent at first, Microsoft PowerPoint has several types of layouts for your slides, and you can easily switch between them. By default, each presentation starts with a Title slide, which has fields for adding the title and the subtitle of your presentations. Then, each new slide that is added uses the Title and Content layout, which has a field on the top for adding the title of the slide; the rest of the slide is for adding text. Microsoft PowerPoint also includes the following layouts that can be used for any slide in your presentation:

Section Header   Includes a field for adding the tile of a section in your presentation and another for adding text.   *title + text*

Two Content   Includes a field for the title of the slide and two columns for adding text and other elements.   *1 title / 2 columns*

Comparison   Includes a field for the title of the slide and two columns, each with its own title and field for adding text and other elements.   *+ columns have titles*

Title Only   Includes only a field for the title of the slide.

Blank   A completely empty slide where you can add anything you wish.

Content with Caption   Has two columns of different size. The one on the left has a field for the title and one for adding text. The one on the right has only a field for adding text.

Picture with Caption   Has a field for adding a picture, one for adding the title, and one for adding text.   *only*

The layouts that are available can be found in the Home tab on the ribbon by clicking the Layout button in the Slides section, shown in Figure 8.12.

FIGURE 8.12   The slide layouts that are available in Microsoft PowerPoint

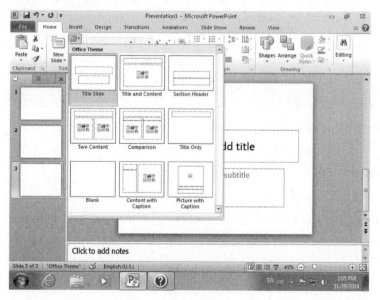

You can also right-click a slide, click Layouts, and then click one of the available layouts to apply it. You can view some of the layouts that are available in Figure 8.13.

FIGURE 8.13 Changing the slide layouts using the right-click menu

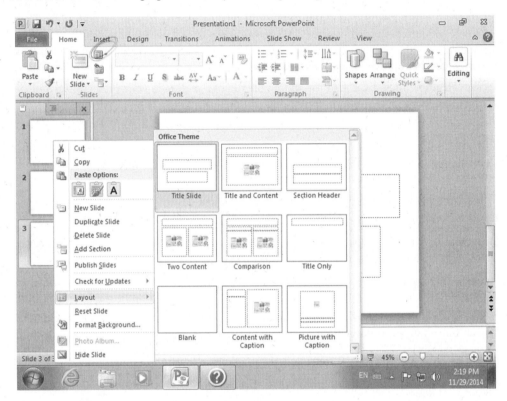

In Exercise 8.5 you will learn how to change the layout of your slides in Microsoft PowerPoint.

EXERCISE 8.5

Changing the Layout of Your Slides

1. Click Start ➢ All Programs ➢ Microsoft Office ➢ Microsoft PowerPoint 2010.

    A new blank presentation is created, with an empty slide.

2. On the Home tab on the ribbon, in the Slides section, click New Slide.

3. In the same section, click the Slide Layout button and select Two Content from the list of layouts.

    Notice how the layout of the second slide has changed.

4. On the Home tab on the ribbon, in the Slides section, click New Slide.

5. Right-click the newly added slide, and click Layout followed by Picture With Caption.

    Notice how the layout of the third slide has changed.

6. Close Microsoft PowerPoint without saving your changes.

Adding Shapes and Pictures to Your Slides

In Microsoft PowerPoint you can also add visual elements to your slides, like shapes and pictures. The list of shapes that are available is very long, and it includes lines, rectangles, basic shapes (circles, triangles, hearts, clouds, stop signs, and the like), block arrows, equation shapes, flowcharts, stars and banners, callouts, and action buttons (play, stop, fast forward, and so on).

Inserting shapes is done from the Insert tab on the ribbon. Look for the Shapes button in the Illustrations section. When you click it, you can view the complete list of shapes that are available and select the shape that you want to add. You can see some of the shapes that are available in Figure 8.14.

FIGURE 8.14   Shapes that are available in Microsoft PowerPoint

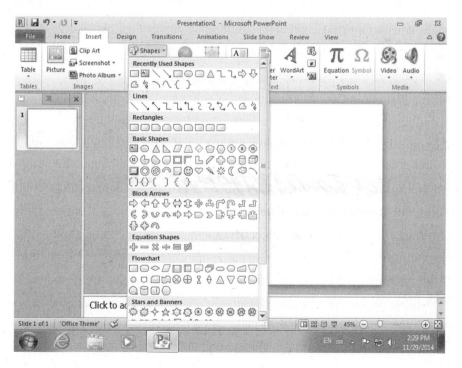

Once you add a shape into your presentation, several controls are displayed for resizing it, rotating it, changing its position, and so on. You can use them to make that shape as big or as small as you need it to be and position it where you want it. If you double-click a shape, the Format tab is opened on the ribbon, as shown in Figure 8.15. You can use the options available in this tab to change the shape's style, colors, effects, size, and so on.

FIGURE 8.15   The Format tab on the ribbon and the options for formatting a shape

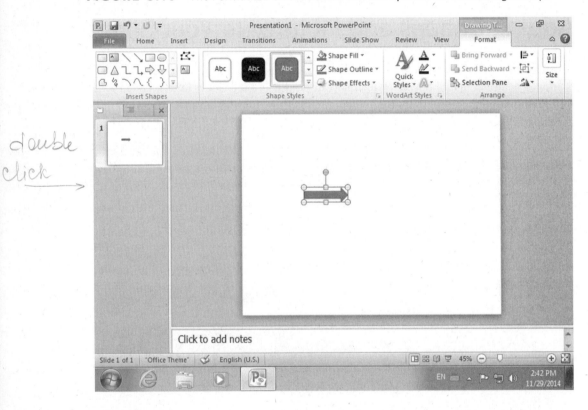

In Exercise 8.6 you will learn how to add a shape to your slides in Microsoft PowerPoint and change the way it looks.

EXERCISE 8.6

Adding Shapes to Your Presentations

1.   Click Start ➢ All Programs ➢ Microsoft Office ➢ Microsoft PowerPoint 2010.

   A new blank presentation is created, with an empty slide.

2.   Click the Insert tab on the ribbon and the click the Shapes button in the Illustrations section.

The list of available shapes is opened.

3.   Click the first the rectangle in the Rectangles section (Figure 8.16).

FIGURE 8.16   The list of shapes that are available in Microsoft PowerPoint

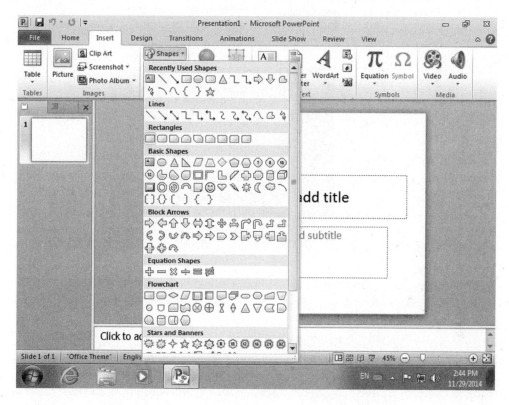

4.   Click in the top-left corner of the slide to add the rectangle.

5.   With it still selected, drag its bottom-right corner to the bottom-right corner of the slide, until it occupies almost the entire slide.

6.   Double-click inside the rectangle to view the Format tab on the ribbon and its formatting options.

7.   In the Shape Styles section, click the second available style: Colored Fill- Black Dark 1 (Figure 8.17).

Notice how the style of the shape has changed.

8.   Close Microsoft PowerPoint without saving your changes.

EXERCISE 8.6 *(continued)*

FIGURE 8.17   The formatting options that are available for a shape

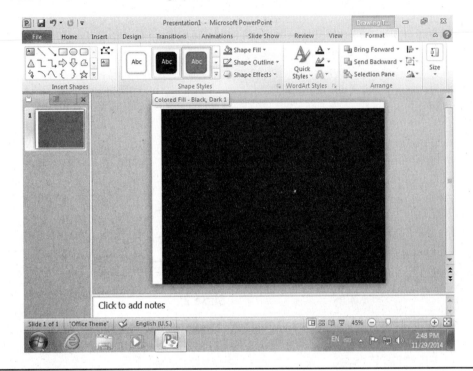

Adding pictures to your presentations can also be done using the Insert tab on the ribbon. We covered this topic in detail in Chapter 5, in the section about working with multimedia files in Microsoft Office, so we won't go into detail about it here. There we demonstrated how to insert pictures and how to adjust their size and position in your presentation. Don't hesitate to read it again and experiment with all the options that are available for adding pictures to your slides.

Adding Tables to Your Presentations

When you create a Microsoft PowerPoint presentation, there are two ways to add tables to your slides:

- You can insert a table from the Insert tab, using the Table button in the Tables section, and populate it manually with text.

- You can copy and paste a table you created previously in Microsoft Excel and change only the way it is displayed in your slides.

Note that tables are not dynamically linked. When you paste a table from Excel into PowerPoint, you paste its current content. If you make updates to it later on in the Microsoft Excel file, they won't be reflected in your Microsoft PowerPoint presentation.

Limit in PowerPoint

(!)

Need bigger table
Excel

When you use the Insert tab from the Microsoft PowerPoint ribbon, you can manually add a table containing up to 10 rows and 8 columns, as shown in Figure 8.18. When you copy a table from Microsoft Excel, you don't have this limitation.

FIGURE 8.18   The Insert tab on the ribbon and the options for formatting a shape

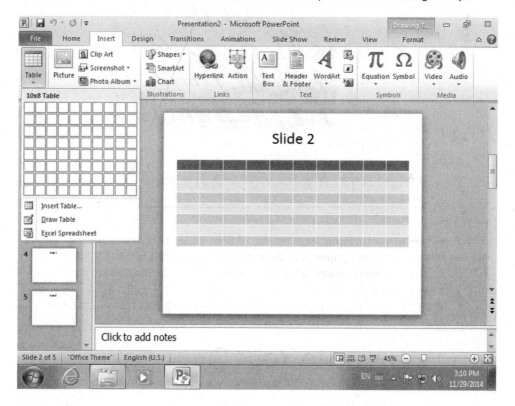

In Exercise 8.7 you will learn how to add tables to your presentations in Microsoft PowerPoint. In order to complete this exercise, please download the Presentation2.pptx and the Book7.xlsx practice files to your computer, if you haven't done so already.

EXERCISE 8.7

Adding Tables to Your Presentations

1. Click Start and then Computer.

2. Browse to the location of the Book7.xslx Excel file and double-click it.

   It will be opened with Microsoft Excel.

3. Go back to the Windows Explorer window, browse to the location of the Presentation2.pptx PowerPoint file, and double-click it.

   It will be opened with Microsoft PowerPoint.

4. Select the second slide and click the Insert tab on the ribbon.

5. Click inside the area on the slide where it says "Click to add text."

6. Click the Table button in the Tables section of the Insert tab.

7. Select a 3 × 3 table (Figure 8.19).

FIGURE 8.19 Adding a table into a presentation

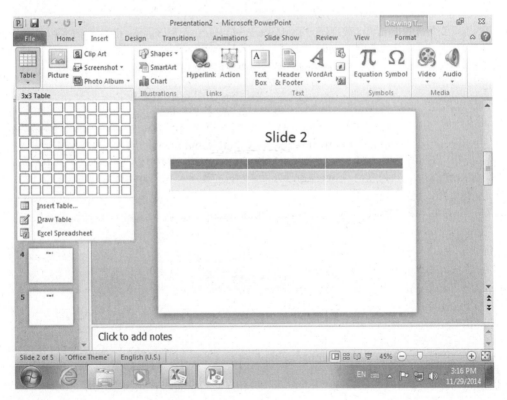

Notice that a table with three rows and columns is added to the slide.

8. Switch to the Microsoft Excel window where the `Book7.xslx` file is open.

9. Select the table found inside the file and click the Copy button in the Clipboard section of the Home tab on the ribbon.

10. Switch to the Microsoft PowerPoint window, where the `Presentation2.pptx` file is open.

11. Click the third slide and then click the Paste button in the Clipboard section of the Home tab on the ribbon.

    Notice how the table from Microsoft Excel has been added to the third slide of your presentation.

12. Close Microsoft PowerPoint and Microsoft Excel without saving your changes.

Formatting the Tables in Your Presentations

You can format the text inside tables just like any other text in Microsoft PowerPoint. All the formatting tools are available on the Home tab on the ribbon, in the Font section. There you will be able to change things like the font and its size; set the text to bold, italic, or underline; and more.

Microsoft PowerPoint also offers table styles that can be used to quickly change the looks of your tables. *Table styles* are a combination of different formatting options, including color combinations that are derived from the theme colors of the presentation you are working on.

You can find the table styles by first selecting a table and then going to the Design tab on the ribbon. There you will find the Table Styles section with all the available styles, alongside other options and tools for formatting your tables, as shown in Figure 8.20.

FIGURE 8.20   The Design tab on the ribbon and the options for formatting a table

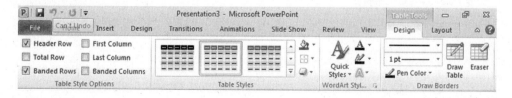

In Exercise 8.8 you will learn how to format the tables in your Microsoft PowerPoint presentations. In order to complete this exercise, please download the `Presentation3.pptx` practice file to your computer.

EXERCISE 8.8

Formatting the Tables in Your Presentations

1. Click Start and then Computer.

2. Browse to the location of the `Presentation3.pptx` PowerPoint file and double-click it. It will be opened with Microsoft PowerPoint.

3. Go to Slide 2 and select the first row in the table.

4. On the Home tab on the ribbon, go to the Font section and click the Font drop-down list.

5. Select Arial as the font and then set the size to 20 by clicking the Size drop-down list and selecting 20 (Figure 8.21).

FIGURE 8.21   Changing the font size

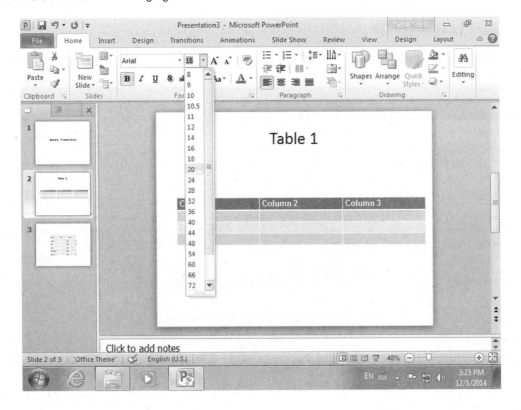

6. Click the Italic button in the Font section.

Notice how the text in the first row of the table has changed according to your settings.

7. Go to Slide 3 and double-click one of the margins of the table to select it.

8. Click the Design tab on the ribbon and go to the Table Styles section.

9. Click the down arrow on the bottom-right corner of the Table Styles area, and a list with styles is opened.

10. Scroll to the section named Best Match For Document and select the style named Theme Style 2 - Accent 6. It is the last style in the bottom-right corner of the list, shown in Figure 8.22.

Notice how the look of the entire table has changed.

FIGURE 8.22   Changing the table style

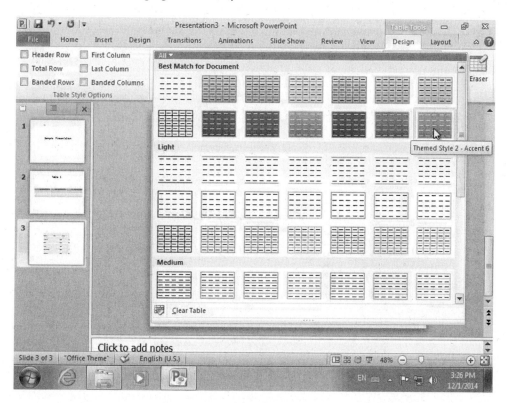

11. Close Microsoft PowerPoint without saving your changes.

Adding Charts to Your Presentations

A great way of communicating data is through the use of charts. Just like when using tables, there are two ways of adding charts to your presentations:

- You can create the chart directly using the tools that are available in Microsoft PowerPoint.

- You can copy a chart made in a Microsoft Excel file and paste it into your presentation. The data in the chart becomes linked to that Excel file, and any changes you make in the Excel file are refreshed in the chart added to your PowerPoint presentation.

When you create a chart in Microsoft PowerPoint, you can choose from many types of charts, just like you would in Microsoft Excel: columns, lines, pie charts, bar charts, and so on. You can see the types of charts that are available in Figure 8.23.

FIGURE 8.23 The Insert Chart dialog in Microsoft PowerPoint

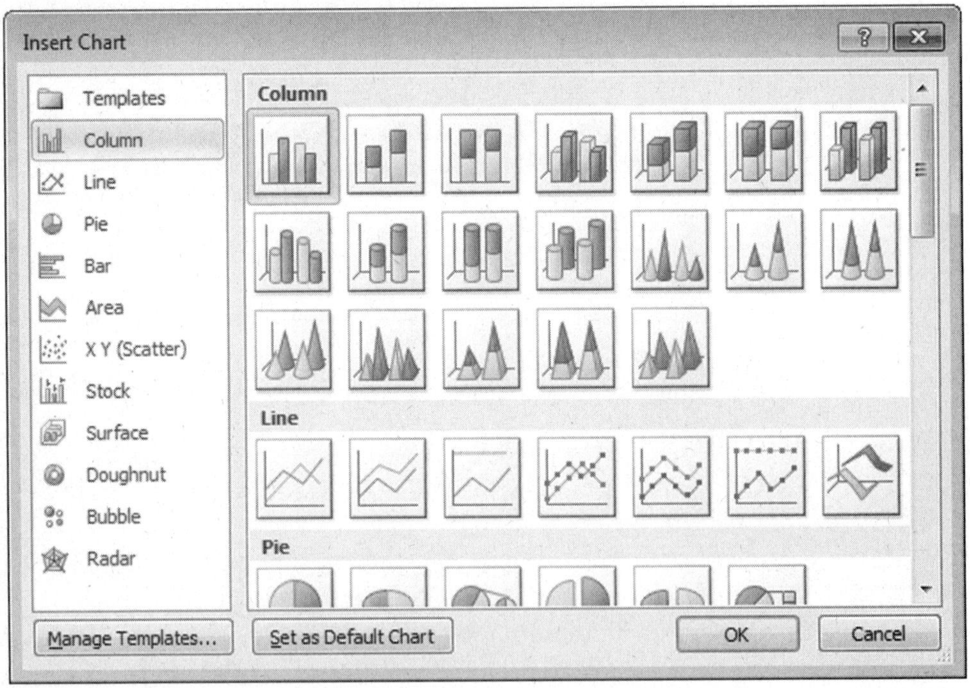

Since you know by now how to copy and paste data from Microsoft Excel to Microsoft PowerPoint, in Exercise 8.9 we will share how to create a chart in Microsoft PowerPoint using the tools available in this application.

EXERCISE 8.9

Inserting Charts into Your Presentations

1. Click Start ➤ All Programs ➤ Microsoft Office ➤ Microsoft PowerPoint 2010.

    A new blank presentation is created, with an empty slide.

2. Create a new slide, where you will add your first chart.

3. Click the Insert tab on the ribbon, and in the Illustrations section click Chart.

4. Select Pie in the Insert Chart window and then click OK.

    A Microsoft Excel window is opened alongside Microsoft PowerPoint with prepopulated data for your pie chart (Figure 8.24).

FIGURE 8.24   Adding a pie chart into a Microsoft PowerPoint presentation

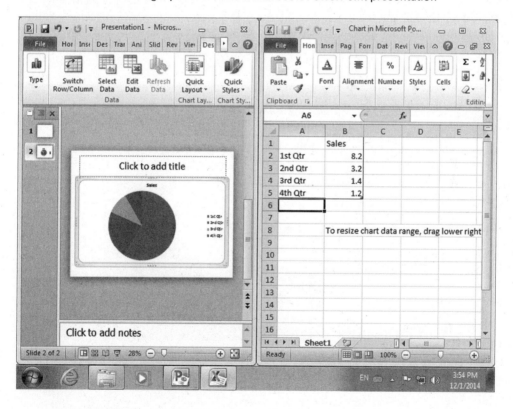

5. In the Microsoft Excel window, select cell B2 and type **10**.

6. Select cell B3 and type **20**. Select cell B4 and type **30**. Select cell B5 and type **40**.

EXERCISE 8.9 *(continued)*

7. Close the Microsoft Excel window and go to back to your presentation.

    Notice how the pie chart has been updated to reflect the numbers you entered.

8. Close Microsoft PowerPoint without saving your changes.

Adding Video and Other Multimedia Files to Your Presentations

Microsoft PowerPoint is also capable of inserting video and audio files into you presentations. When you insert them, a link is added into your slide that points to the original multimedia file you are adding. Also, a media player is automatically added, with controls for playing the file that you have added. This player can be resized or moved to another area in your slide, just like any other element. You can view it in Figure 8.25.

FIGURE 8.25   The video player available in Microsoft PowerPoint

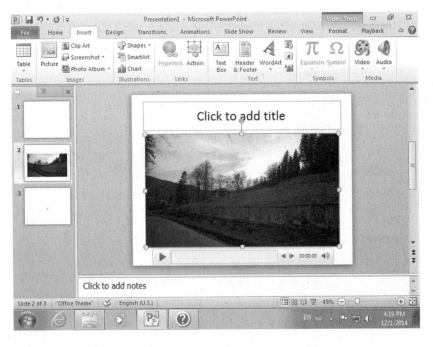

Microsoft PowerPoint is capable of adding and playing the following types of multimedia files.

Audio files	Video files
.aiff	.asf
.au	.avi
.mp3	.mp4
.mp4	.mov
.wav	.mpg
.wma	.wmv

In Exercise 8.10 we will demonstrate how to add a video file in a Microsoft PowerPoint presentation. In order to complete this exercise, please download the `Movie1.wmv` practice file to your computer.

EXERCISE 8.10

Adding Video to Your Presentations

1. Click Start ➤ All Programs ➤ Microsoft Office ➤ Microsoft PowerPoint 2010.

   A new blank presentation is created, with an empty slide.

2. Click the Insert tab on the ribbon and then click the Video button in the Media section.

3. In the Insert Video dialog, browse to the location of the `Movie1.wmv` practice file, select it, and click Insert (Figure 8.26).

FIGURE 8.26   The Insert Video dialog

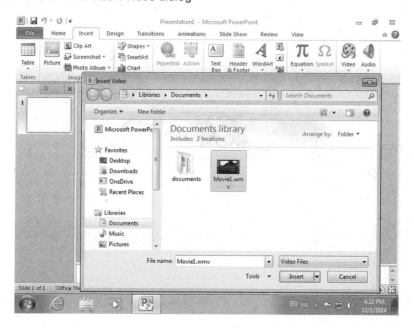

A movie player is added to your presentation for the video file that you have added.

4. Click the Play button in this player and watch the video being played automatically.

5. Close Microsoft PowerPoint without saving your changes.

Adding Animations to Your Presentation

If you need to make your presentation more dynamic, you may want to consider adding animations to it. For example, you can set an entrance or exit effect for the text in your slides or for visual elements like charts. However, you should not overuse animations because they tend to distract the audience from the message of your presentation. Use them sparingly and only if they serve your purpose and do not distract from it.

Before adding an animation, you need to select the element to which you will add it: the title of the slide, a line of text, a table, a chart, a picture, and so on. The tools for setting animations are found in the Animations tab on the ribbon. You can choose from all kinds of animation styles (entrance, emphasis, or exit). You can set the motion paths, set when the animation is triggered, and so on. You can see examples of available animations in Figure 8.27.

FIGURE 8.27 Adding animations in Microsoft PowerPoint

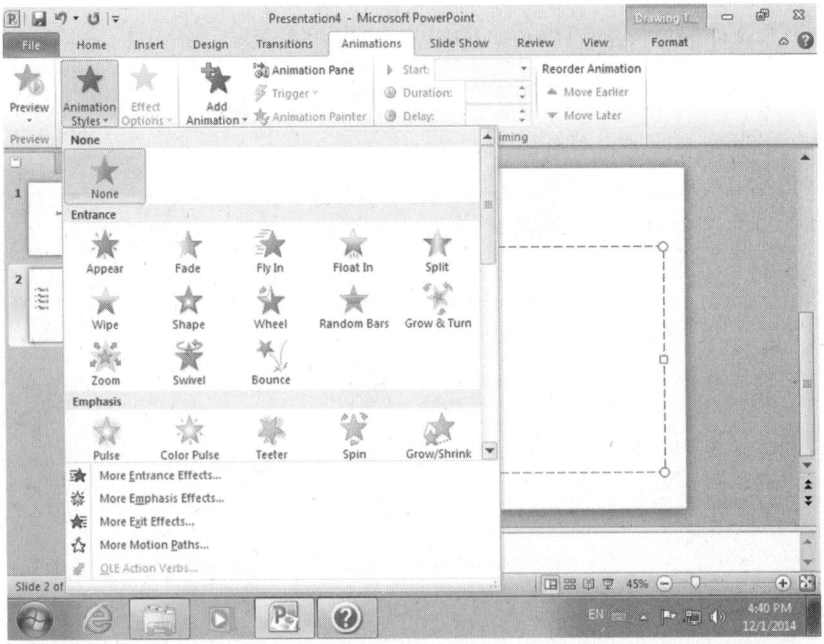

By default, the animations are triggered when the user clicks the mouse. You can set other triggers too, but in order to keep things simple and manageable, it is best that you keep this trigger and do not set it to something else.

When setting an animation for an element, you can see a preview of it in the Microsoft PowerPoint editing window. There's also a Preview button in the Animations tab on the ribbon that you can use. However, the completed animation is best viewed as a slide show, by pressing F5 on your keyboard and then using the left mouse button to move from slide to slide and from animation to animation.

When an element in a slide has an animation set for it, Microsoft PowerPoint signals it by adding a numbered label near it, like in Figure 8.28. This label is shown while editing your presentation until you remove the animation set for that element.

FIGURE 8.28   The Microsoft PowerPoint user interface

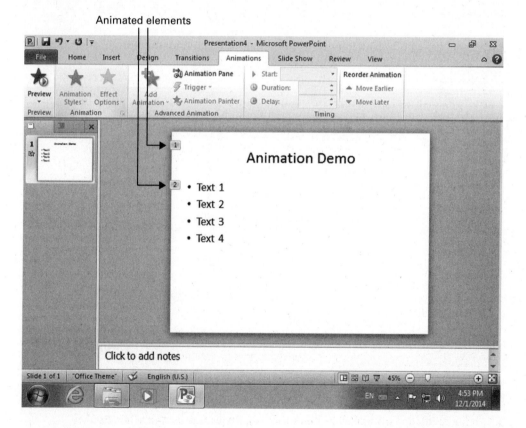

In Exercise 8.11 we will demonstrate how to add animations to different text elements in your presentations. To complete this exercise, please download the `Presentation4.pptx` practice file to your computer.

EXERCISE 8.11

Adding Animations to Your Presentations

1. Click Start and then Computer.

2. Browse to the location of the `Presentation4.pptx` PowerPoint file and double-click it.

    It will be opened with Microsoft PowerPoint.

3. Select the tile of the slide, Animation Demo, and click the Animations tab on the ribbon.

4. In the Animation section, click the Animation Styles button and select Fly In (Figure 8.29).

FIGURE 8.29   Adding animations to a presentation

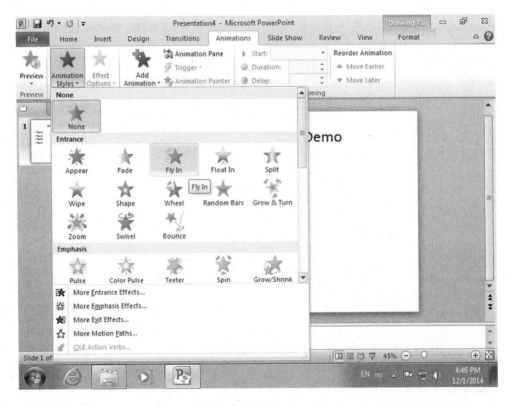

5. Select the first line of text that says "Text 1."

6. In the Animation section, click the Animation Styles button and select Bounce.

7. Press F5 on your keyboard to start the slide show you just created and view the animations that you added.

8. Click the left mouse button once to trigger the first animation.

9. Click the left mouse button again to trigger the second animation.

10. Click the left mouse button twice to exit the slide show and get back to Microsoft PowerPoint.

11. Close Microsoft PowerPoint without saving your changes.

Setting Transitions between Slides and Viewing Your Presentations

Another way of making your presentations more dynamic is to use transitions between slides. After creating your presentation, you will present it to others as a *slide show*—a series of images, graphics, text, and other multimedia content—on a projection screen or computer display. Moving between slides is done using the left mouse button or the spacebar on your keyboard. When slides are changed, there is no animation between them. They are simply displayed one after the other. You can set transitions, which are similar to animations, but they affect only what happens when moving from one slide to the next, not how the elements on your slides are displayed.

You can select one or more slides in a presentation and go to the Transitions tab on the ribbon. There you will find a long list of transitions, in the Transition To This Slide section. Click the arrow pointing downward, found on the bottom-right corner of this section, to access this list. You can see some of the available transitions in Figure 8.30.

When a transition is set for a slide, a star-like icon is displayed near its number, in the slides pane. If you want to stop using transitions for one or more slides, follow these steps:

1. Select the slides you are interested in.

2. Select None in the Transition To This Slide section of the Transitions tab on the ribbon.

NOTE When you've finished creating your presentations and setting the transitions between slides, don't forget to save them using the Save button.

FIGURE 8.30 The transitions that are available in Microsoft PowerPoint

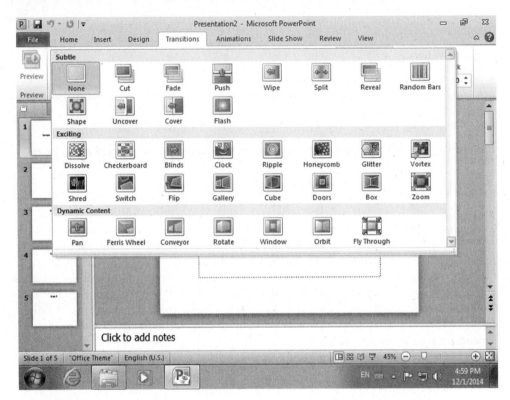

To view your presentations, you can use both the mouse and the keyboard. The fastest way of starting the slide show of your presentation is to press F5 on your keyboard. However, you can also go to the Slide Show tab on the ribbon (Figure 8.31) and click the From Beginning button in the Start Slide Show section.

FIGURE 8.31 The Slide Show tab on the ribbon in Microsoft PowerPoint

In Exercise 8.12 we will demonstrate how to add transitions between slides and how to view your presentations in Microsoft PowerPoint as a slide show. In order to complete this exercise, please use the Presentation2.pptx practice file you downloaded previously to your computer.

EXERCISE 8.12

Adding Transitions between Slides and Viewing Your Presentations

1. Click Start and then Computer.

2. Browse to the location of the `Presentation2.pptx` PowerPoint file and double-click it.

    It will be opened with Microsoft PowerPoint.

3. Select slide 2 and click the Transitions tab on the ribbon.

4. In the Transitions To This Slide section, click Cut.

5. Select slide 3, and in the Transitions To This Slide section, click Fade.

6. Select slides 4 and 5, and in the Transitions To This Slide section, click Push.

7. Click the Slide Show tab on the ribbon, and then click the From Beginning button in the Start Slide Show section.

    The presentation is started.

8. Press the spacebar on your keyboard to move to the next slide.

9. Left-click slowly and navigate from slide to slide, while paying attention to the transitions between slides.

10. When you arrive at the end of the slide show, left-click again to return to Microsoft PowerPoint.

11. Close Microsoft PowerPoint without saving your changes.

Summary

When working in business environments, chances are that you will have to make presentations and deliver them in front of your co-workers. While Microsoft PowerPoint won't be able to help you with your public-speaking skills, it will help you create effective presentations that help you deliver your message.

Microsoft PowerPoint is a very visual work environment and creating presentations is relatively easy. You add data to your slides, format it to look as you want it to, and add charts that help you make your point, and you are set. If you want to create more visually complex presentations, you can also invest some time into inserting animations or setting special transitions between slides. You can even insert multimedia files like video clips or audio tracks. In this chapter we covered all the basic tools that help you do all these things. If you go through everything and do all the exercises, you will master the basics required for creating effective presentations in Microsoft PowerPoint.

In the next chapter we will cover Microsoft Access and share how to create and use small databases to get meaningful data and information from them.

Exam Essentials

Know how to add or remove slides in your presentations. Information in Microsoft PowerPoint should be bite sized. It is better to create more slides with small amounts of information than to add all the information in as few slides as possible.

Learn how to change the design of your presentations. Microsoft PowerPoint offers plenty of tools for changing the theme of your presentation, the layout of your slides, the background, and so on. You should master all these tools in order to create good-looking presentations.

Know how to add tables and charts. Effective presentations are supported by data. Sharing data is best done through the use of tables and charts. Knowing how to add them will make your presentations more effective.

Learn how to add pictures, video, and other multimedia files. If you fill your presentations only with text, you won't be a very effective communicator. Adding pictures or video clips to them will help increase your effectiveness in delivering the presentation.

Understand how to use animations and transitions. If you want to create presentations that are more dynamic and complex from a visual perspective, you may want to use animations and transitions.

Key Terms

Before you take the exam, be certain you are familiar with the following terms:

slide	slides pane
slide show	table styles

Review Questions

1. What is a slide?

    A. A Microsoft PowerPoint file

    B. A single page of a presentation that is created with presentation software

    C. A presentation

    D. A multimedia file

2. What is a slide show? (Choose all that apply.)

    A. A collection of slides that are projected one after the other

    B. A single page of a presentation that is created with presentation software

    C. A file created with Microsoft PowerPoint

    D. A series of images, graphics, text and other multimedia content on a projection screen or computer display

3. What is the name of the place where you can rearrange slides in the order you wish?

    A. The ribbon

    B. The slide show

    C. The slide pane

    D. The editing area

4. How do you remove a slide from your Microsoft PowerPoint presentation? (Choose all that apply.)

    A. Select the slide in the slide pane and press Delete on your keyboard.

    B. On the ribbon, click Cut in the Slides section of the Home tab.

    C. On the ribbon, click Editing followed by Delete in the Slides section of the Home tab.

    D. Right-click the slide in the slide pane, and in the menu that is shown, click Delete Slide.

5. From where can you change visual design details like colors, the layouts for slides, and their background with a single choice in Microsoft PowerPoint?

    A. On the ribbon, click Design, go to the Themes section, and click Fonts.

    B. On the ribbon, click Design, go to the Themes section, and click Background Styles.

    C. On the ribbon, click Slide Show, go to the Themes section, and click Custom Slide Show.

    D. On the ribbon, click Design, go to the Themes section, and click the theme that you want to apply.

6. How do you change the layout of a slide in Microsoft PowerPoint? (Choose all that apply.)

   A. In the slides pane, right-click the slide and click Add Section.

   B. In the slides pane, right-click the slide, click Layout, and then click the new layout.

   C. Select the slide in the slides pane and go to the Home tab on the ribbon. In the Slides section, click the Slide Layout button and then the layout that you want to apply.

   D. Select the slide in the slides pane and go to the Design tab on the ribbon. In the Themes section, click the Background Styles button and then the layout that you want to apply.

7. How do you add a shape in a Microsoft PowerPoint presentation?

   A. Click the Insert tab on the ribbon, look for the Illustrations section, and click Shapes.

   B. Click the Insert tab on the ribbon, look for the Illustrations section, click Chart, and then click the desired shape.

   C. Click the Insert tab on the ribbon, look for the Illustrations section, click Shapes, and then click the desired shape.

   D. Click the Insert tab on the ribbon, look for the Illustrations section, click Shapes, and then click the desired shape. Then, click inside the slide where you want to add the shape.

8. What are the two ways of adding a chart to a Microsoft PowerPoint presentation? (Choose all that apply.)

   A. Go to the Insert tab, look for the Illustrations section, click Chart, select the Chart that you want to add, and click OK.

   B. Go to the Insert tab, look for the Illustrations section, and click Chart.

   C. Open the Microsoft Excel file containing the chart that you want to add, copy it, and then paste it into your Microsoft PowerPoint presentation.

   D. Insert the chart into Microsoft Excel, and then import the Microsoft Excel file into Microsoft PowerPoint.

9. Animations in a Microsoft PowerPoint presentation can be applied to the following. (Choose all that apply.)

   A. The title of a slide

   B. The text from a slide

   C. The pictures added into your slides

   D. The transitions between slides

10. How do you view your presentation as a slide show? (Choose all that apply.)

   A. Press F1 on your keyboard.

   B. Press F5 on your keyboard.

   C. Go to the Slide Show tab on the ribbon and click the From Beginning button, in the Start Slide Show section.

   D. Go to the View tab on the ribbon and click the Normal button, in the Presentation Views section.

Chapter

9

Using Microsoft Access

THE FOLLOWING IC3 GS4: KEY APPLICATIONS EXAM OBJECTIVES ARE COVERED IN THIS CHAPTER:

✓ **Basic Database Interactions**

✓ **Record Managements**

- Run reports

- Search and use stored queries

- Input data (records)

Microsoft Access allows you to structure and store your information in a set of database tables and efficiently manage and share large amounts of data, much more than would be possible in a Microsoft Excel file.

In addition to offering a way to quickly locate information, the database ensures consistency in the information by linking together the data in different tables. And while storing and maintaining data is the main strength of Microsoft Access, this application also gives you the tools to present your data to others using attractive forms and reports.

In this chapter we will focus on the basics of using Microsoft Access so that you know how to add data to the tables that make up a database, how to search for data, how to use the queries stored in a database, how to run reports, and how to create your own simple reports. Let's get started.

Adding, Modifying, and Removing Data in a Microsoft Access Database

We mentioned earlier in this book that *databases* are organized collections of data. Databases are organized in *tables*, which are a means of arranging data in rows and columns. Each column in a table represents a field, which has a name, a type, and other optional properties like a description. To give you an example, you can have a table with the columns First name, Last name, and Age. The first two columns have their type set as text (because text is what you enter in them) while the last has the type set as number because age is a number. In any table you have a specified number of columns that is set when the database is created and any number of rows. Each row in a table is a record with data entered by users.

Databases are optimized to store large amounts of information, for example, the data that's used to run a business: clients, daily sales, suppliers, profits, and so on.

There are many ways to add data to a database in Microsoft Access, from importing it from sources like Microsoft Excel files and other databases to entering it manually. Since this subject is very complex and varied, we will try to keep things simple and show you the easiest way of adding data manually to an existing database. When you open a Microsoft Access database, you will see on the left side of the window an area named All Access Objects, also known as the Navigation Pane (Figure 9.1). This area contains a list of tables that are used for storing data. You may also find things like reports, queries, forms, macros, and other types of objects, some of which we will cover in this chapter.

FIGURE 9.1   All Access Objects in Microsoft Access

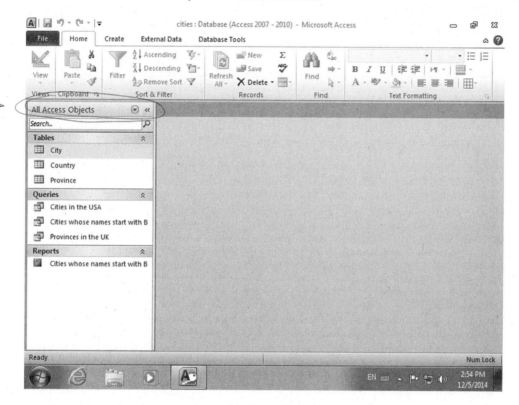

If the All Access Objects column is minimized, you will see only the text Navigation Pane (Figure 9.2) and an arrow for maximizing it. Click it and you will see a list of all the objects that are found in the database.

To access a table and the data that is stored inside, double-click it. You will find it in the Tables section of the Navigation Pane. You will now see all the data that exists in that table. You can edit and change anything you wish from the existing records, or you can scroll down to the end of the table and add new rows of data.

One important difference in Microsoft Access versus other Microsoft Office applications is that your changes and edits are saved and stored automatically. Even if you don't click the Save button, your edits are stored in the database and available for others.

FIGURE 9.2   The Navigation Pane in Microsoft Access

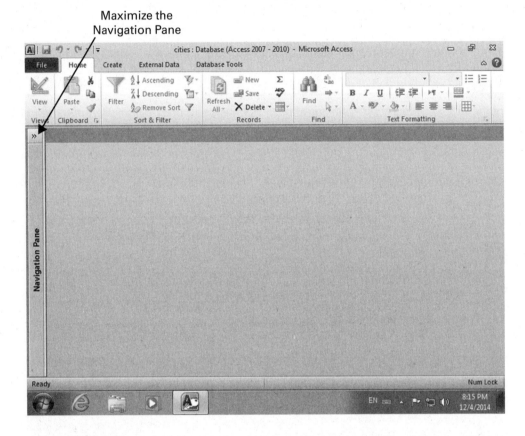

In Exercise 9.1 you will learn how to add a new record with data in a table, as well as modify and remove existing data. In order to complete this exercise, please download the cities.accdb practice file to your computer.

EXERCISE 9.1

Adding, Modifying, and Removing Data in a Microsoft Access Database

1. Click Start and then Computer.

2. Browse to the location of the cities.accdb file and double-click it.

    It will be opened with Microsoft Access.

3. In the Navigation Pane, double-click the City table.

    You will see a list with the cities that were added to the database.

4. Scroll down to the end of the table until you see an empty row that starts with (New), as shown in Figure 9.3.

FIGURE 9.3   Rows of data in a Microsoft Access table

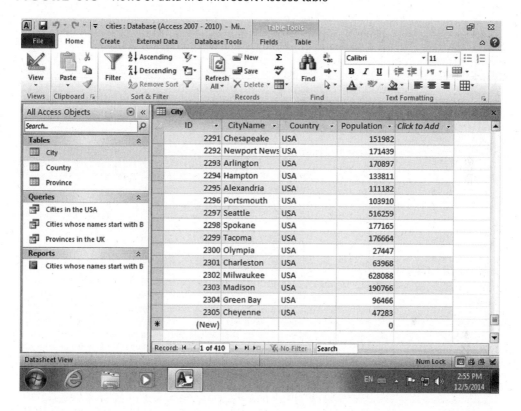

5. Click the CityName column of the row that starts with (New) and type **Lost Springs**.

6. Click in the Country column of that same row and type **USA**. Then, click in the Population column of that row and type **4**.

Notice how the new row of data has been added to the table and the ID has been prepopulated by the database according to the rules that have been set by the administrator who created it.

7. In the newly added row, click the CityName column, select Lost Springs, and type **Barrow** instead.

8. Click the Population column on the same row, delete the value 4, and type **4212** instead.

Notice how the values of the last row are modified according to your edits.

9. To select the last row, move the mouse cursor to the left side of the first column, ID. You should see an arrow pointing left, as shown in Figure 9.4.

FIGURE 9.4   Selecting a record in a Microsoft Access table

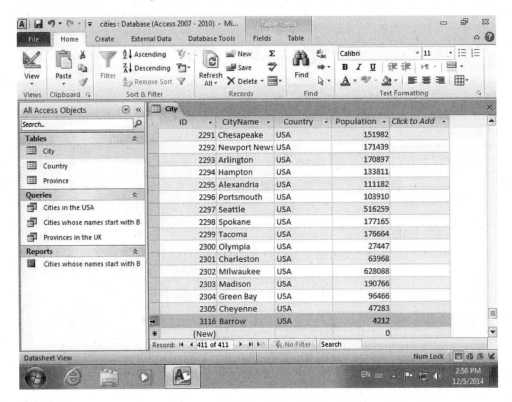

10. Click the left mouse button when the arrow is displayed to select the entire row.

11. Then, in the Home tab on the ribbon, look for the Records section, and click Delete.

    You are informed that you are about to delete 1 record and asked to confirm if you are OK with this (Figure 9.5).

FIGURE 9.5   Deleting a record in a Microsoft Access table

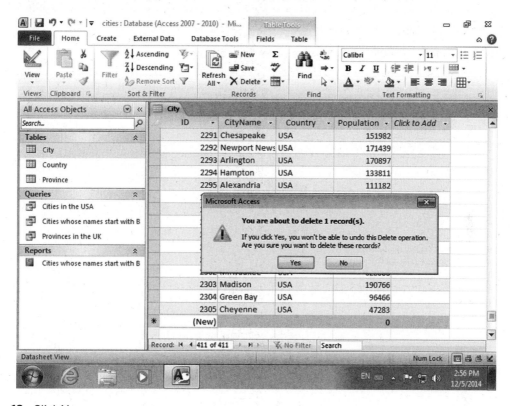

12. Click Yes.

Notice how the record that you added is removed from the table.

13. Close Microsoft Access.

Adding, modifying, and removing data is done using the same steps in all the tables in your database. However, you should keep in mind that each table has its own structure and data and each table will look different.

Using Search in a Microsoft Access Database

Finding data in a Microsoft Access database can be done in many ways, depending on how the database was set up. You can use specialized forms, reports, and stored queries. However, one of the simplest ways of finding anything is to use the traditional Find feature that's available in any Microsoft Office application. On the Home tab on the ribbon are the Find section and the Find button. If you click the Find button, the Find And Replace dialog will appear (Figure 9.6). You can also activate it by pressing Ctrl+F on your keyboard.

FIGURE 9.6 The Find And Replace dialog in Microsoft Access

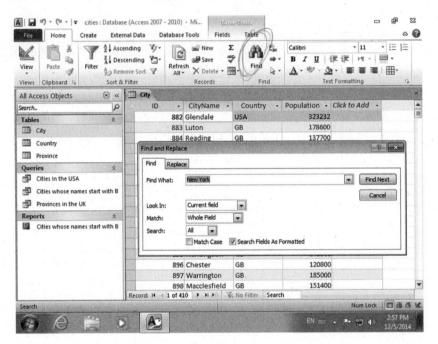

In the Find And Replace dialog, you can type what you are looking for and then select where to look. By default, Microsoft Access performs searches in the current field of the current table. That's why it is very important that before you make a search you select the correct table where you want to make your search and the field that you are interested in. Another option is to click the down arrow in the Look In field and select Current Document (meaning the current table) instead of Current Field, which is the default value for where Microsoft Access performs the search (Figure 9.7).

FIGURE 9.7 The values for the Look In field, in the Find And Replace dialog

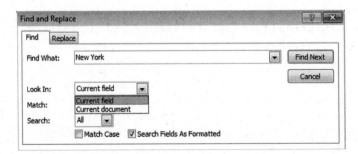

When you select Current Document, the search is made throughout the document rather than in just a selected field, and it will be easier to find what you are looking for.

In Exercise 9.2 you will learn how to find data in a table using the Find feature in Microsoft Access. In order to complete this exercise, please use the `cities.accdb` practice file you downloaded earlier to your computer.

EXERCISE 9.2

Using Search in a Microsoft Access Database

1. Click Start and then Computer.

2. Browse to the location of the `cities.accdb` file and double-click it.

   It will be opened with Microsoft Access.

3. In the Navigation Pane, double-click the City table.

   You will see a list of the cities that were added to the database.

4. Press Ctrl+F on your keyboard.

5. In the Find And Replace dialog, type **Cincinnati** in the Find What field.

6. Click the down arrow in the Look In drop-down list and select Current Document (Figure 9.8).

FIGURE 9.8   Finding a record in a Microsoft Access table

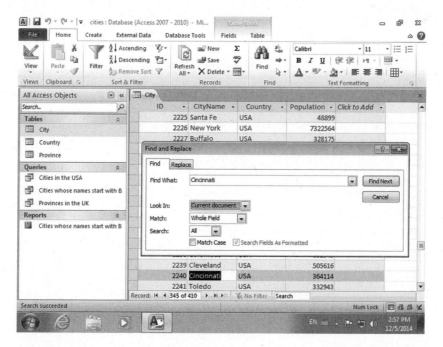

EXERCISE 9.2 *(continued)*

7. Click Find Next.

8. In the Find And Replace dialog, click Cancel, look at the entry that was found and note the population recorded in the database for Cincinnati.

9. Close Microsoft Access.

Using Stored Queries in a Microsoft Access Database

definition

When working with databases, an important concept to understand is that of queries. A *query* is a request for data results, for action on data, or for both. Queries can be used to answer simple questions, find data from multiple tables and present it in one place, perform calculations, combine data from different tables, and even modify your data.

In this section we will focus on the simplest and most common use for queries: finding data from different tables in a database. When working with a Microsoft Access database, the administrator can create queries and store them in the database, hence the term *stored query*. When such queries are available, you will see them listed in the Queries section of the Navigation Pane (Figure 9.9). In order to run them, all you have to do is double-click them and you'll see the appropriate search results automatically.

FIGURE 9.9 Queries stored in a Microsoft Access database

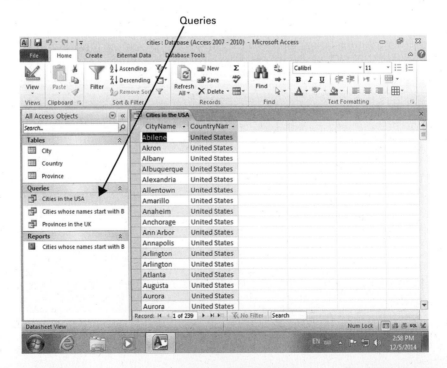

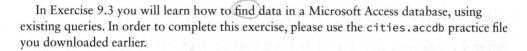

In Exercise 9.3 you will learn how to find data in a Microsoft Access database, using existing queries. In order to complete this exercise, please use the `cities.accdb` practice file you downloaded earlier.

EXERCISE 9.3

Using Stored Queries to Find Data in a Microsoft Access Database

1. Click Start and then Computer.

2. Browse to the location of the `cities.accdb` file and double-click it.

   It will be opened with Microsoft Access.

3. In the Navigation Pane, look for the Queries section and double-click the Cities In The USA query.

   You will see a list of all the cities in the United States that were added to the database.

4. Double-click the query named Cities Whose Names Start With B.

   You will see a list of all the cities from the database whose names start with the letter *B*.

5. Lastly, double-click the query named Provinces In The UK.

   You will see a list of all the provinces from the UK that were added to the database (Figure 9.10).

FIGURE 9.10   Running queries in a Microsoft Access database

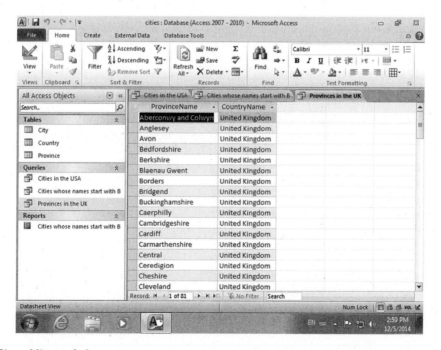

6. Close Microsoft Access.

Running Predefined Reports in a Microsoft Access Database

Reports are a way of viewing, formatting, and summarizing information from a Microsoft Access database. You can create both simple reports that share data from a single table and more complex ones that show data from multiple tables, formatted in a manner that makes it easy to view and understand what is presented.

A report comes in handy when you want to present the information in your database for any of the following uses:

- Display or distribute a summary of your data.

- Archive snapshots of data.

- Provide details about individual records in the database.

- Create labels for any kinds of databases. The most common use of labels is for mailing, but any Access data can be printed in a label format for a variety of purposes.

Well-administered databases generally include built-in reports that can be used whenever necessary. When reports are available, you will see them listed in the Reports section of the Navigation Pane (Figure 9.11). In order to run them, all you have to do is double-click them and they will automatically display the data you requested.

FIGURE 9.11   Reports stored in a Microsoft Access database

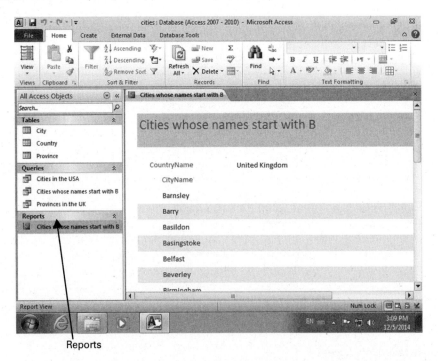

Reports

In Exercise 9.4 you will learn how to run a predefined report in a Microsoft Access database. In order to complete this exercise, please use the cities.accdb practice file you downloaded to your computer.

EXERCISE 9.4

Running a Predefined Report in a Microsoft Access Database

1. Click Start and then Computer.

2. Browse to the location of the cities.accdb file and double-click it.

    It will be opened with Microsoft Access.

3. In the Navigation Pane, look for the Reports section and double-click the report named Cities Whose Names Start With B.

    Notice the report that is loaded with the cities whose names start with *B* listed by country and sorted in ascending order.

4. Scroll down the report until you view it in its entirety.

5. Close Microsoft Access.

Creating Simple Reports in a Microsoft Access Database

Users can also create their own reports, if the administrator of the Microsoft Access database gave them permission to do so. Microsoft Access offers many tools for creating reports, and they are all found in the Reports section on the Create tab of the ribbon, shown in Figure 9.12.

FIGURE 9.12   Options for creating reports in a Microsoft Access database

There you will find the following options:

Report   Creates a simple, tabular report containing all of the fields in the table or query you selected in the Navigation Pane.

advanced **Report Design**   Creates a blank report in Design view. You can then make advanced changes to it, add custom control types, write code, and so on. Only advanced users tend to use this option.

blank **Blank Report**   Creates a blank report so that you can insert fields and controls and design the report the way you want.

simple **Report Wizard**   Helps users create simple, customized reports in a very visual way. This option is well suited for beginners and less-advanced users who are working with Microsoft Access databases.

(?) **Labels**   Starts the Label Wizard that allows you to create labels for the data found in your database, as well as which fields you want to display and how you want them sorted.

In this chapter we will focus on the simplest way of creating reports: using the Report Wizard. When you start it, you need to select the source for your report. Sources for your reports can be either tables or queries but not both. For each source, you need to select the fields that you want to include in the report. The wizard will then help you set how you want to view the data, including how to sort it, group it, and so on. Before you can create a report and view it, you have to give it a name, which must be different from that of other reports. The reports you create are automatically stored in the database and can be used at a later time to view data according to how you have set up the report.

In Exercise 9.5 you will learn how to create a simple report in a Microsoft Access database, using the Report Wizard. In order to complete this exercise, please use the cities.accdb practice file you downloaded earlier.

EXERCISE 9.5

Creating Simple Reports in a Microsoft Access Database

1. Click Start and then Computer.

2. Browse to the location of the cities.accdb file and double-click it.

   It will be opened with Microsoft Access.

3. Click the Create tab on the ribbon and look for the Reports section. There, click the Report Wizard button (Figure 9.13).

   The Report Wizard is started.

4. Click the Tables/Queries drop-down list and select as the source of your report the query named Provinces In The UK (Figure 9.14).

FIGURE 9.13   The Report Wizard button

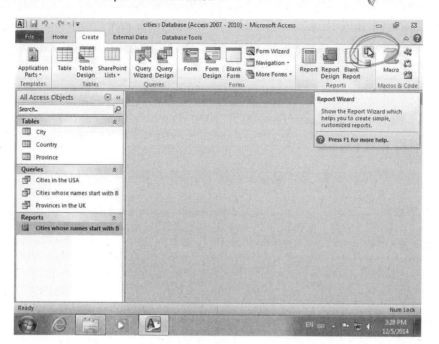

FIGURE 9.14   Selecting tables or queries in the Report Wizard

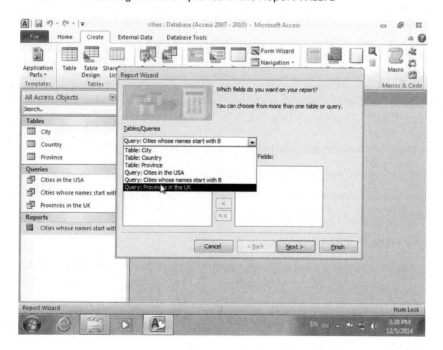

EXERCISE 9.5 *(continued)*

Two fields are shown as available in the Available Fields section.

5. Click the >> button to select them both and move them to the Selected Fields section (Figure 9.15).

FIGURE 9.15   Selecting fields in the Report Wizard

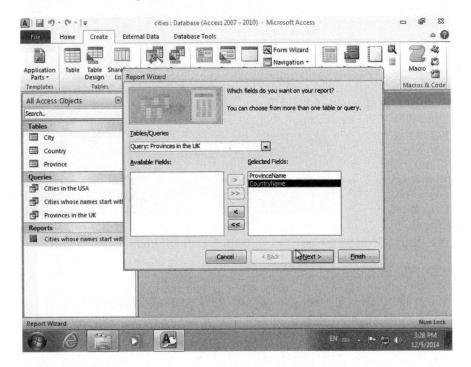

6. Click Next, and you are asked to select how you want to view your data.

7. Select By Province and click Next (Figure 9.16).

    You are now asked whether you want to add any grouping levels.

8. Select ProvinceName to group everything by province, and click Next (Figure 9.17).

    You are asked what sort order you want for your records.

9. Click the first drop-down list and select ProvinceName (Figure 9.18). Then, click Next.

    You are asked to select how to lay out your report (Figure 9.19).

FIGURE 9.16   Selecting how to view data in the Report Wizard

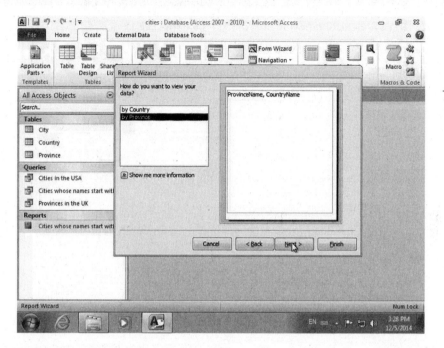

FIGURE 9.17   Adding grouping levels in the Report Wizard

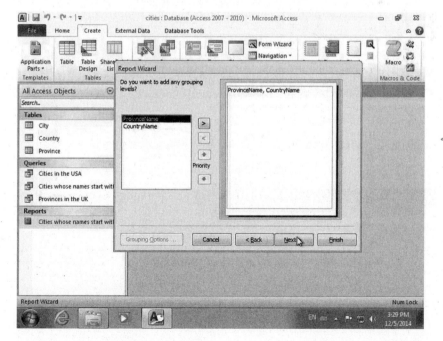

EXERCISE 9.5 *(continued)*

FIGURE 9.18   Selecting how to sort data in the Report Wizard

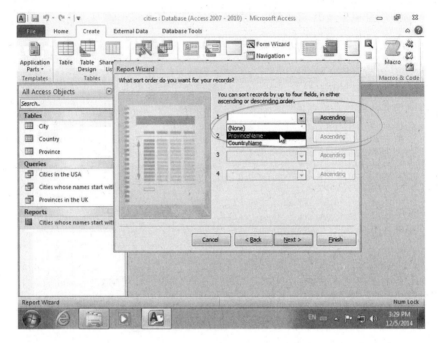

FIGURE 9.19   Selecting how to lay out the report in the Report Wizard

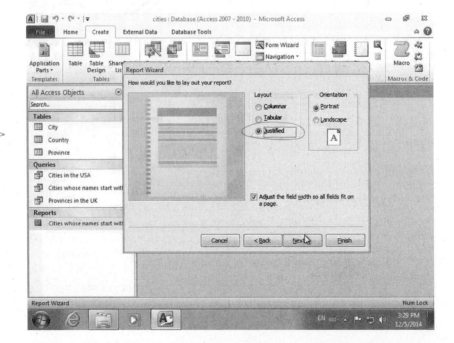

10. Select Justified and click Next.

You are asked to give a title for the report.

11. Type **Provinces in the UK** and click Finish (Figure 9.20).

FIGURE 9.20   Naming the report in the Report Wizard

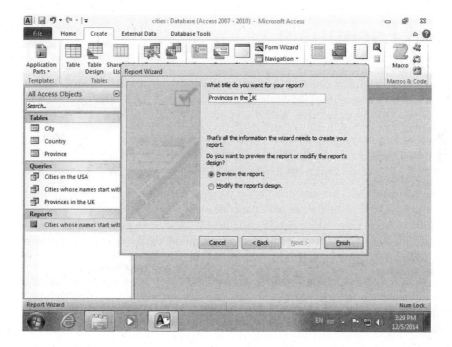

The report is now generated and stored in your database, and you can view it at any time.

12. Scroll up and down the report and see how it looks, and notice how the data is grouped and sorted.

13. Close Microsoft Access.

Summary

As you have seen in this chapter, working with Microsoft Access databases is different from working with Microsoft Excel files. This application is built and optimized to store large amounts of data, and it gives you more advanced tools for maintaining and using it.

In this chapter you learned one way of adding data to the tables that make up a Microsoft Access database, how to search for data in a table, how to use stored queries to find the data you are looking for, how to run reports created by you or other users including the database administrator, and how to create your own basic reports that present data in a simple and readable manner.

In the next chapter we will focus on the collaboration features that are included in Microsoft Office: how to work on the same document with others and how to share your work with other users.

Exam Essentials

Know how to add, modify, or remove data from a database.   When you use a database, you have to know how to add, modify, or remove data from it. A database that is not actively maintained by its users stops being useful very fast.

Learn how to find data in a database.   A database is useful because it stores plenty of information. Learning how to find the data that interests you will help you become more productive when you use Microsoft Access databases.

Understand what queries are and how to use them.   Queries can be used to answer simple questions, to find data from multiple tables and present it in one place, to perform calculations, to combine data from different tables, and even to modify the data. Understanding what queries are, how they work, and how to use them are important parts of using Microsoft Access productively.

Know how to use and create reports   Reports are a way of viewing, formatting, and summarizing information from a Microsoft Access database. You should know how to run a report and how to create a simple report that shares the data you are looking for in a readable format.

Key Terms

Before you take the exam, be certain you are familiar with the following terms:

databases	reports
query	tables

Review Questions

1. What is a database? (Choose all that apply.)

   A. A spreadsheet ✗

   B. An organized collection of data

   C. A way of presenting data to others ✗

   D. A collection of tables that are used to store and arrange data

2. What is a table when referring to databases? (Choose all that apply.)

   A. A means of arranging data in rows and columns

   B. A data set with a set number of columns and any number of rows

   C. A collection of fields and records

   D. A way of presenting data to others

3. What is a query in the context of a database? (Choose all that apply.)

   A. A question

   B. A request for printing data

   C. A request for action on data

   D. A request for data results

4. What is a report in the context of a database? (Choose all that apply.)

   A. A way of viewing information from a database

   B. A way of printing information from a database

   C. A way of summarizing information from a database

   D. A way of formatting information from a database

5. How do you access the Find tool in Microsoft Access? (Choose all that apply.)

   A. Press Ctrl+F on your keyboard.

   B. Press Ctrl+S on your keyboard.

   C. Click the Home tab on the ribbon and then the Find button in the Find section.

   D. Click the Home tab on the ribbon and then the Go To button in the Find section.

6. How do you run a query stored in a Microsoft Access database?

   A. Click Create on the ribbon, go to the Queries section, and click Query Design.

   B. Double-click the query name in the Navigation Pane.

   C. Click the query name in the Navigation Pane.

   D. Click Database Tools on the ribbon, go to the Queries section, and click Queries.

7. How do you run a report stored in a Microsoft Access database?

    A. Click Create on the ribbon, go to the Forms section, and click Form Design.

    B. Click the report name in the Navigation Pane.

    C. Double-click the report name in the Navigation Pane.

    D. Click Database Tools on the ribbon, go to the Reports section, and click Reports.

8. What can you use as a source for a report in a Microsoft Access database? (Choose all that apply.)

    A. A database

    B. Tables

    C. Queries

    D. A table and a query

9. How do you view the data stored in a Microsoft Access table?

    A. Click the table name in the Navigation Pane.

    B. Right-click the table name in the Navigation Pane.

    C. Double-click the table name in the Navigation Pane.

    D. Right-click the table name in the Navigation Pane and select Design View.

10. What can you do with the Report Wizard in Microsoft Access?

    A. Create simple, customized reports in a visual way

    B. Create blank reports in Design view

    C. Create labels for the data found in your database

    D. Print data from a report

Chapter

10

Collaborating with Others When Working in Microsoft Office

THE FOLLOWING IC3 GS4: KEY APPLICATIONS EXAM OBJECTIVES ARE COVERED IN THIS CHAPTER:

✓ **Collaboration**

✓ **Comments**

  ▪ Review comments

  ▪ Accept or Reject

  ▪ Add comments

✓ **Sharing Files**

  ▪ Share using e-mail

  ▪ Network storage

  ▪ Cloud

Sometimes you will have to collaborate with others on a project. For example, you may need to create a presentation and share it with your boss so that they can give you feedback and approve it. Or you may need to share it with a few co-workers and get different data from each of them so that you can finalize the presentation. In this process you will exchange comments, data, and suggestions for improvements.

Microsoft Office offers several features that help make collaboration easy. For example, you can add comments to Microsoft Word documents, Microsoft Excel files, or Microsoft PowerPoint presentations. You can also review the comments that you have received from others and enable a feature called Track Changes, which automatically tracks the changes that are made to a Microsoft Word document.

Finally, there are also several ways to share your work with others. The most common way of doing this is through email: you send a message to your co-workers and attach the files that you are working on. Other methods include using network storage solutions or modern cloud storage solutions. In this chapter we will cover all of them and help you understand the basics of how they work and what you should pay attention to when using them.

Adding Comments to Your Microsoft Office Files

When working on Microsoft Office files with others, you can communicate with your collaborators by using the Comments feature. This feature is found in Microsoft Word, Microsoft Excel, and Microsoft PowerPoint. You can easily leave comments for others to review. In your comments you can provide useful feedback for others that can help them improve the files you are working on.

The features related to using comments are always found in the Review tab on the ribbon. There you will find a New Comment button that you can use to add a comment to an element in your file. That element can be a word, a sentence, a table, an image, and so on. When you save the file that you are working on, the comments are saved with it. The people who open your file can view your comments and take action based on them. The keyboard shortcut for adding a new comment is Ctrl+Alt+M.

In Exercise 10.1 you will learn how to add new comments to your Microsoft Office files. In order to complete this exercise, please download the Sample1.docx and Presentation3.pptx practice files to your computer.

EXERCISE 10.1

Adding Comments to Your Microsoft Office Files

1. Click Start and then Computer.

2. Browse to the location of the `Sample1.docx` file and double-click it.

   It will be opened with Microsoft Word.

3. Select the title of the document—Exercise—and click the Review tab on the ribbon.

4. In the Comments section, click the New Comment button.

   A special field is displayed on the right side of the document, where you can add your comment.

5. Type **This exercise is incomplete** and click somewhere outside the comment field to save it (Figure 10.1).

FIGURE 10.1   Adding a comment to a Microsoft Word document

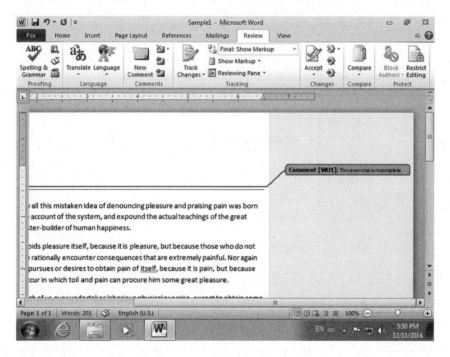

Notice how the comment is added to the document.

6. Click the Windows Explorer icon on the taskbar, browse to the location of the `Presentation3.pptx` file, and double-click it.

   It will be opened with Microsoft PowerPoint.

EXERCISE 10.1 *(continued)*

7. In the Slides pane, select the second slide.

8. Click the table found in the middle of the slide to select it, and click the Review tab on the ribbon.

9. In the Comments section, click the New Comment button.

    A special field is displayed, where you can add your comment.

10. Type **This table is empty** and click somewhere outside the comment field to save it.

11. Click the symbol that is shown for your newly added comment to view it (Figure 10.2).

FIGURE 10.2   Adding a comment to a Microsoft PowerPoint presentation

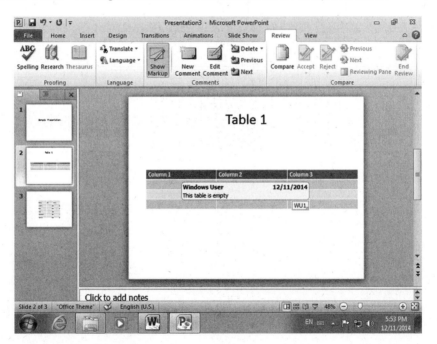

12. Close Microsoft PowerPoint and then Microsoft Word, without saving your work.

   The procedure for adding comments is very similar in Microsoft Excel.

Reviewing the Comments That Were Added to a Document

When you work with others on your Microsoft Office files, most probably you will exchange many comments with suggestions for improvements. Before you finish your work, you may want to review them all. Luckily, on the Review tab on the ribbon, in the Comments section, you will find the buttons you need for navigating to the next or the previous comment.

In Exercise 10.2 you will learn how to review the comments that are found in a Microsoft Word document. In order to complete this exercise, please download the `Sample8.docx` practice file to your computer.

Reviewing Comments in Microsoft Word

1. Click Start and then Computer.

2. Browse to the location of the `Sample8.docx` file and double-click it.

    It will be opened with Microsoft Word.

3. Click the Review tab on the ribbon and look for the Comments section.

4. Click the Next Comment button.

    The first comment in the document is highlighted (Figure 10.3).

FIGURE 10.3 Viewing the next comment in Microsoft Word

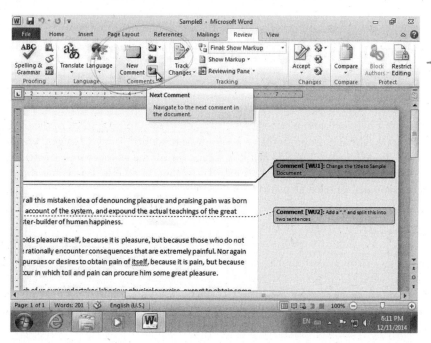

EXERCISE 10.2 *(continued)*

5. Read the comment and click the Next Comment button again.

6. Click the Next Comment button again and read the next comment.

7. Now click the Previous Comment (Figure 10.4) button found just above Next Comment.

FIGURE 10.4 Viewing the previous comment in Microsoft Word

Notice that you are back to the previous comment.

8. Click the Previous Comment button again to go to the comment prior to the current one.

9. Close Microsoft Word without saving your work.

Tracking Changes in a Microsoft Word Document

When you work with others on a document, it is a good idea to keep track of the changes each of you make. Microsoft has implemented a feature named *Track Changes*, which is available only in Microsoft Word. When it is turned on, all the changes that are made to the document are kept and can be viewed at any time, as long as no one deactivates this feature. When someone turns off change tracking, you will be able to revise the document without marking what has changed.

I recommend that you always use Track Changes when working with others on the same document because it stores and highlights all changes that are made to the document in a visual manner. This way you can immediately identify changes that are incorrect, review what others have modified, and accept their changes or reject them. Together with the Comments feature, Track Changes creates a great environment for working collaboratively on the same document.

In Exercise 10.3 you will learn how to enable Track Changes in a Microsoft Word document. In order to complete this exercise, please use the Sample8.docx practice file you downloaded previously to your computer.

EXERCISE 10.3

Enabling Track Changes in Microsoft Word

1. Click Start and then Computer.

2. Browse to the location of the Sample8.docx file and double-click it.

    It will be opened with Microsoft Word.

3. Click the Review tab on the ribbon and look for the Tracking section.

4. Click the Track Changes button to activate this feature (Figure 10.5).

FIGURE 10.5   Activating Track Changes in Microsoft Word

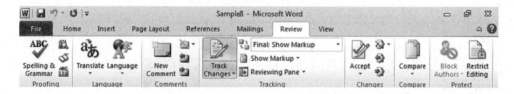

5. Select the title of the document—Exercise—and replace it with **Sample Document**.

    Notice how the old tile is kept but it is struck-through (Figure 10.6). The new title is displayed just to its right. Microsoft Word keeps both the old and the new titles due to you activating the Track Changes feature.

EXERCISE 10.3 *(continued)*

FIGURE 10.6   Changes tracked by Microsoft Word

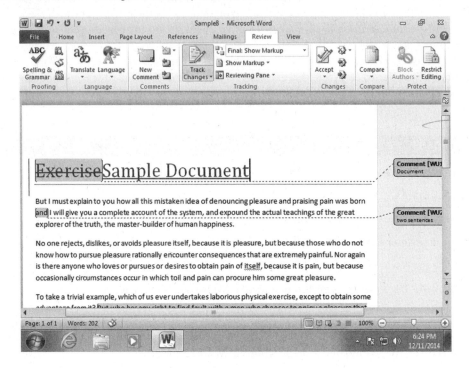

6.   Close Microsoft Word without saving your work.

Reviewing Changes in a Microsoft Word Document

When you're getting close to finalizing your Microsoft Word document, you may want to review all the changes that were made, accept the ones that make sense, and reject the ones that don't. Microsoft Word offers all the tools you need for doing that in the Review tab on the ribbon. Go to the Changes section and you will find the several buttons (Figure 10.7). Hover with the mouse over them, without clicking them; and this is what you will learn about these buttons:

Accept And Move To Next   Accepts the current change and moves the next change tracked by Microsoft Word

Reject And Move To Next   Rejects the current change and moves the next change tracked by Microsoft Word

Previous Change   Navigates to the previous revision in the document so that you can accept it or reject it

Next Change   Navigates to the next revision in the document so that you can accept it or reject it

FIGURE 10.7   The Changes section in the Review tab on the ribbon

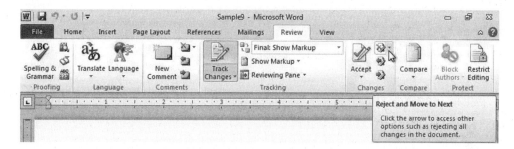

If you click the Accept and Reject buttons, you will also get access to additional review options, but we won't cover them in this chapter.

In Exercise 10.4 you will learn the basics of how to review and accept or reject changes in a Microsoft Word document. In order to complete this exercise, please download the Sample9.docx practice file to your computer.

EXERCISE 10.4

Reviewing Changes in Microsoft Word

1. Click Start and then Computer.

2. Browse to the location of the Sample9.docx file and double-click it.

   It will be opened with Microsoft Word.

3. Click the Review tab on the ribbon and look for the Changes section.

4. Click the Next Change button (Figure 10.8) to highlight the first change in the document.

FIGURE 10.8   The Next Change button in Microsoft Word

EXERCISE 10.4 *(continued)*

5. Click Reject And Move To Next to move to the next change.

6. Click Reject And Move To Next again.

   Notice how the original title is restored.

7. Click the Next Change button to highlight the next change.

8. Click Accept.

   The change is accepted, and you are moved to the next change.

9. Click Accept again.

   You are taken to the last change available for review.

10. Click Accept.

    You are asked whether you want to continue searching from the beginning of the document (Figure 10.9).

FIGURE 10.9 Tracking changes in Microsoft Word

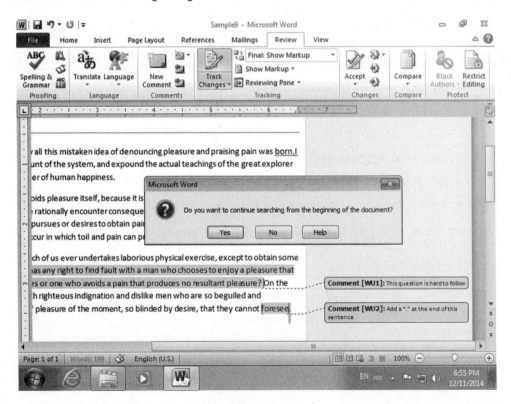

11. Click No and notice how the document has changed.

12. Close Microsoft Word without saving your work.

Sharing Your Work Files Using Email

In a business environment, chances are that if you are using Microsoft Office to do your work, you are also using Microsoft Outlook to send and receive emails. Or, you may use a web-based email client that is specifically made for the employees in your company. No matter which kind of email client you are using, you will surely have to share files with your co-workers. Luckily, attaching files to your emails is very easy, and anyone can do it. The only thing you have to watch for is that you don't attach files that are very large or attach too many files to the same email. That's because corporate email services generally have limitations when it comes to attachments. For example, in some companies there is a rule that you can't attach files that are larger than 10 MB to your emails. These rules vary from company to company, and they are set by the network administrator(s).

Another important rule when sending work files to others is to be mindful to whom you are sending those files. Avoid sending work files to large email lists because chances are that those files will end up with people who shouldn't be receiving them, and they may then have access to confidential information that may be misused. Most companies have policies related to how work documents and confidential information should be shared with others. Be sure that you know them and apply them in your day-to-day work.

One downside to sharing your work with others via email is that you don't have easy access to the edits they make to the documents that you have shared. If someone else makes changes to a document, they have to send the document back to you so that you can view the new version. When you collaborate with others via email on a document like the company's travel policy, it is best to use versioning as a way of keeping track of the different versions of the document and its evolution. For example, if you create a Microsoft Word document and share it with a co-worker, you should name it something meaningful like `Travel Policy v1.docx` and share it with them. Then, they will make some edits, save it as `Travel Policy v2.docx`, and share it again with you. With each new round of edits and sharing, you should increase the version number of the document. This way, when you receive a new version, you can easily save it on your computer alongside previous versions and look for what's new. Using Track Changes is also a great idea because it makes it easy to identify what has changed from version to version.

In Exercise 10.5 you will learn how to attach files to an email message in Microsoft Outlook. In order to complete this exercise, please download the `Presentation3.pptx` and `Sample9.docx` practice files to your computer.

EXERCISE 10.5

Attaching Files to an Email in Microsoft Outlook

1. Click Start and then All Programs.

2. Click Microsoft Office and then Microsoft Outlook 2010.

3. In Microsoft Outlook, click the Home tab on the ribbon and then New E-mail
    (Figure 10.10).

FIGURE 10.10   The New E-mail button in Microsoft Outlook

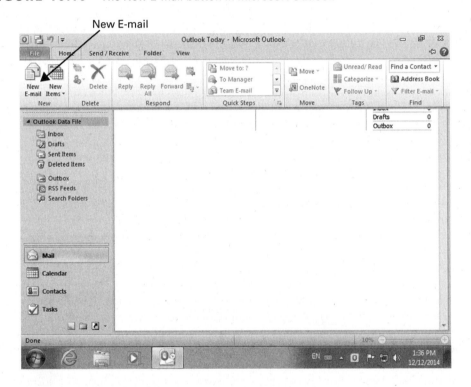

4. In the Untitled – Message window, click the Insert tab on the ribbon (Figure 10.11).

5. Click Attach File, and the Insert File window opens.

6. Browse your computer to the location where you have saved files Presentation3.pptx
    and Sample9.docx.

7. Click the first file of the two and then press and hold the Ctrl key on your keyboard.

8. With the Ctrl key still pressed, click the second file and then release the Ctrl key.

9. Click Insert to add the two files as attachments to your email (Figure 10.12).

FIGURE 10.11   The Insert tab in the email message window

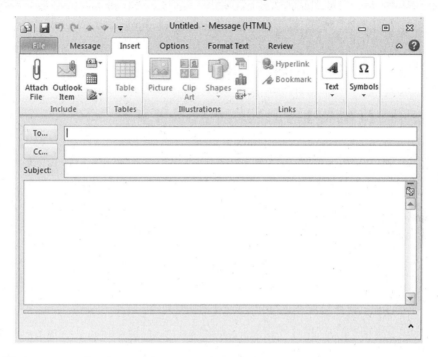

FIGURE 10.12   The Insert File window

10. In the email message window, type the email address of the person you want to send it to, in the To field.

11. In the Subject field type a subject for the email.

12. In the body of the email type a message for that person (Figure 10.13).

FIGURE 10.13   Writing an email in Microsoft Outlook

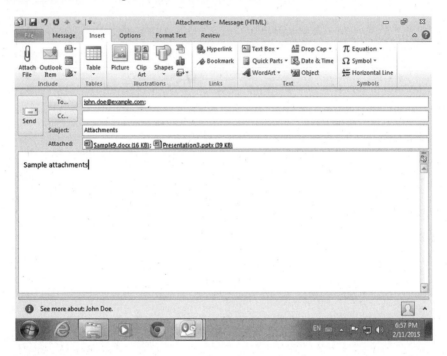

13. Click the Send button to send the email and wait for it to be sent.

14. Close Microsoft Outlook.

Storing Documents Using Network Attached Storage Solutions

Some companies use so-called *network attached storage (NAS)* solutions for storing files for all or a group of users in that company. These are specialized devices that are connected to the network and are used for storing files and sharing them among employees.

These devices are file servers (both small and large, depending on the needs of the company), and they can be accessed from Windows Explorer, just like any other computer on the network (Figure 10.14). In Windows Explorer, click the Network section and then double-click the server or network device where files are stored.

FIGURE 10.14   Accessing computers and devices on the network in Windows Explorer

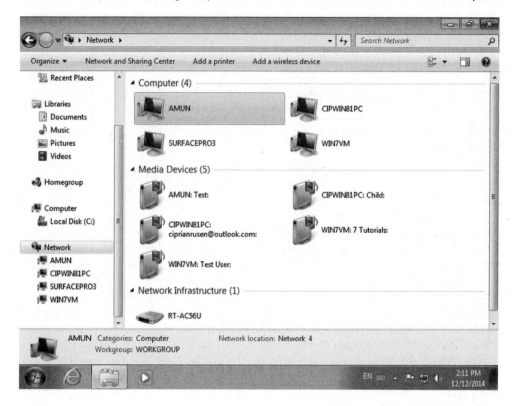

Depending on how your network is configured, you may or may not have to authenticate using a username and password before accessing the files stored on the file server. Once you are in, you can browse files as you would normally do in Windows Explorer. You can copy and paste files, move them around, or create new ones.

One downside with network storage solutions is that you don't know when others have accessed the same file and whether they are working on that file at the same time as you are. That's why some kind of document versioning is highly advised when you use such solutions. You can name each new version of a document with Document v1.docx or Document v2.docx, or you can use the date as a versioning method. For example, each time you create a new version of a document you can add the date when you made your changes to its name: Document 121214.docx, meaning Document created on December 12, 2014.

Storing Documents Using Cloud Storage Solutions

When people refer to computers and networks, you will often hear the term *cloud* or *cloud computing*. This is a form of computing in which large groups of remote servers are networked to allow centralized data storage and online access to computer services or resources. Clouds can be public, private, or hybrid:

Public They are accessible from the Internet and managed by a specialized company like Microsoft, Amazon, Google, and others.

Private They are accessible only inside a company's network and managed by the company owning them.

Hybrid A hybrid is a composite of two or more clouds that are both private and public that are bound together.

Cloud computing focuses on maximizing the effectiveness of the shared resources. They are shared by multiple users and dynamically reallocated according to the demand coming from users. This has multiple advantages, including lowering costs, reducing environmental damage, reducing the power consumption, and so on.

Cloud storage is a way of storing data across multiple servers in public, private, or hybrid clouds. Even though cloud storage is made up of many distributed resources, it acts as one entity and offers advantages like data redundancy and durability (the same data is stored across multiple servers and is never lost), as well as lower costs.

There are many providers of cloud storage solutions that are suited to companies of all sizes, as well as individual users. The most popular cloud storage solutions are OneDrive, Dropbox, Box, Google Drive, Amazon Cloud Drive, and Apple iCloud.

When you use a cloud storage solution, you need to install a client on your computer. With the help of this client you can synchronize your files with the cloud storage service as well as all other devices where you have the client installed. Cloud storage offers several advantages:

Accessing Your Files on Mobile Devices One major advantage is that cloud storage services have clients for mobile devices like tablets and smartphones, and you can use them to access your files from anywhere.

Securing Your Files Another advantage is that your files are safe and they never get lost even if your computer gets stolen, breaks down, or is destroyed in a fire or natural disaster. Those files always have a copy in the cloud, and if you install the cloud storage client on another computer and authenticate with your user account, you can access your files and work from there.

Accessing Your Files Anywhere Also, cloud storage solutions offer a way to access your files online, from a web browser. You log into a specific website and you can view your files, download them, and work on them.

Sharing Your Files   You can set up share folders and give access to other people who can use the files you place in the folder, as well as add files for sharing. For example, you might set up a folder for sharing recipes, and then when shopping for groceries, each user can pull up recipes on a mobile device.

Collaborating   Another advantage of cloud storage solutions is that they allow you to collaborate with others on your files. For example, with the help of *OneDrive* and Microsoft Office, you can have two people work at the same time on the same document. OneDrive automatically stores each edit and allows you to see the area from your document that is changed by the other person. Cloud storage solutions also automatically store revisions of the same document so that you can revert easily to an older version if the newest one is not what you want. Google Drive also offers similar collaboration features.

Even though cloud storage services look and work differently, some principles are generally the same. For example, in order to store your files in the cloud and access them from anywhere, you must install a client that's specific to the service you are using. If you install OneDrive from Microsoft, then you will see a OneDrive shortcut in Windows Explorer (Figure 10.15). Look for it in the Favorites section, in the pane on the left side of the window.

FIGURE 10.15   The OneDrive shortcut in Windows Explorer

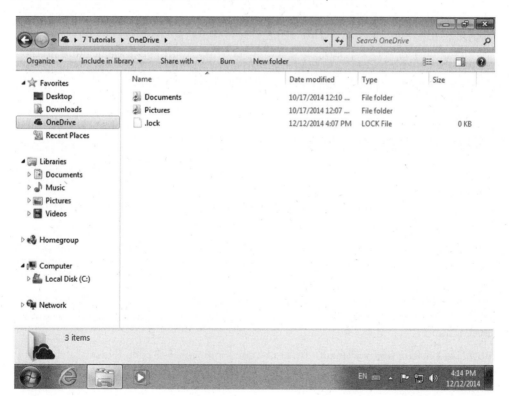

When you click the shortcut, you can access your files like you always do in Windows. You can copy and paste new files, remove the ones you don't need, open existing files, work on them, and so on. Every change you make is then automatically synchronized to the cloud storage service by the client that you have installed. The same is true if you are using Dropbox, Google Drive, and other services.

Summary

In this chapter you learned a lot about what it means to collaborate with others when doing your work in Microsoft Office:

First, you learned how to leave comments for others so that you can give them useful feedback that will help them improve their work. You also learned how to review the comments that you receive from others.

Then, we moved on to how to track changes when working on Microsoft Word documents and have them stored and displayed automatically. When you get close to finalizing a document, it is good to review all those changes, accept those that make sense, and reject those that don't, so we shared how this is done as well.

Then, we moved on to sharing your work with others through different media: email, network storage, and cloud storage. We covered the advantages and limitations of all three methods.

With this chapter we have finished our coverage of Microsoft Office applications. In the next chapter we will start discussing the Internet: what it is, what it does, what it means to browse the Web, how to download files from the Internet, and so on.

Exam Essentials

Know how to add and review comments.   When working with others on the same documents, you need to know how to add and review comments so that you can work together effectively.

Learn how to track changes in a document.   When working collaboratively on a document, it is a great idea to track the changes each person makes so that they are easily identified and seen by all the people involved in that work.

Understand how to review the changes in a document.   When finalizing a document, you should review all the changes that were made, accept those that make sense, and reject those that don't.

Know how to share files via email.   The most common way of sharing files with others is through email. It is mandatory that you know the basics of sharing files with others through this medium.

Understand how network storage and cloud storage solutions work.   Some companies use network storage solutions or cloud storage solutions in order to store the files of their employees. Knowing the basics about how these services work will help you learn faster the specifics of the service that is used by your company.

Key Terms

Before you take the exam, be certain you are familiar with the following terms:

cloud or cloud computing	network attached storage (NAS)
cloud storage	Track Changes

Review Questions

1. Where do you find the New Comment button in Microsoft Office?

   A. On the Design tab of the ribbon, in the Page Setup section

   B. On the View tab of the ribbon, in the Comments section

   C. On the Review tab of the ribbon, in the Comments section

   D. On the Insert tab of the ribbon, in the Text section

2. Where are comments displayed in Microsoft Word?

   A. On the right side of the document, in a separate column

   B. In the middle of the document

   C. On the left side of the document, in a separate column

   D. On the bottom of the document

3. How do you quickly navigate to the previous comment in a Microsoft Word document?

   A. Click the View tab on the ribbon and then the Previous Comment button found in the Comments section.

   B. Click the Review tab on the ribbon and then the Previous Comment button found in the Comments section.

   C. Click the Review tab on the ribbon and then the Next Comment button found in the Comments section.

   D. Click the Home tab on the ribbon and then the Decrease Indent button found in the Paragraph section.

4. How do you start tracking the changes made in a Microsoft Word document?

   A. Click the View tab on the ribbon and then the Track Changes button in the Tracking section.

   B. Click the Review tab on the ribbon and then the Track Changes button in the Tracking section.

   C. Click the Insert tab on the ribbon and then the Pages button in the Pages section.

   D. Click the Review tab on the ribbon and then the Next Change button in the Tracking section.

5. How do you accept the current change and move to the next change that is tracked in a Microsoft Word document?

   A. Click the View tab on the ribbon and then the Accept And Move To Next button in the Tracking section.

   B. Click the View tab on the ribbon and then the Accept And Move To Next button in the Changes section.

   C. Click the Review tab on the ribbon and then the Accept And Move To Next button in the Tracking section.

   D. Click the Review tab on the ribbon and then the Accept And Move To Next button in the Changes section.

6. Which of the following are good practices when sending an email with attachments from your work email account? (Choose all that apply.)

   A. Do not send the email to a large email list.

   B. Do not send emails with large files or many files attached.

   C. Attach as many files as you wish.

   D. Respect your company's policies for sharing work documents with others.

7. What is cloud computing? (Choose all that apply.)

   A. A way of maximizing the effectiveness of shared computing resources

   B. A network found in clouds

   C. A typical computer network with lots of servers and users

   D. A form of computing in which large groups of remote servers are networked to allow centralized data storage and online access to computer services and resources

8. What are the advantages of cloud storage? (Choose all that apply.)

   A. Lower costs

   B. More control

   C. Reduced environmental damage

   D. Reduced power consumptions

9. What are network attached storage solutions? (Choose all that apply.)

   A. External hard disks that are connected to a computer

   B. Specialized storage devices that are connected to the network

   C. Linux servers that are connected to the network

   D. Solutions for storing files for all or a group of the users in a company

10. Which are examples of cloud storage solutions? (Choose all that apply.)

   A. Microsoft Office

   B. OneDrive

   C. Google Drive

   D. Adobe Photoshop

Living Online

PART

III

Chapter

11

Using the Internet

THE FOLLOWING IC3 GS4: LIVING ONLINE EXAM OBJECTIVES ARE COVERED IN THIS CHAPTER:

✓ **Browsers**

✓ **Internet vs. Browsers vs. WWW**

- Explain the concepts of: Internet, Browsers, WWW.

- Explain the differences between: Internet, Browsers, WWW.

- Demonstrate how to use each: Internet, Browsers, WWW.

✓ **Navigation**

- Domains

- Explain how hyperlinks function in a web browser environment.

- Demonstrate how and why you would want to set a homepage.

- Demonstrate how to move back, forward and refresh in a variety of browsers. Identify universal symbols used for each term.

- Explain why favorites/bookmarks are helpful. Describe how to establish, save, invoke, and delete a bookmark.

- Explain what a plugin is and its function. Describe how to find, install, configure, use, disable, enable, and delete a plugin.

- Explain how the History function of a browser works and how to use it. Describe how to clear history.

- Demonstrate how to search using an internet browser, including the use of advanced features such as using basic Boolean logic including, Or, And, plus sign +, quotation marks ", etc.

- Tabs

- Downloading/Uploading

In the third part, "Living Online," we start by talking about the Internet and the World Wide Web. You will learn what they are, what their names mean, and the mandatory terminology that will help you make sense of everything.

The Web is such an important part of our lives that everyone should know the basics of browsing the Web. That's why we will share things like how to use web browsers, the basics of navigating the Web, downloading and uploading files, and setting a homepage in your web browser.

Toward the end of this chapter we will take a deeper dive and cover more complex subjects like how to use and clear your browsing history, how to use favorites or bookmarks, how to search for text inside a web page from your web browser, and how to use plug-ins and add-ons to enhance your web-browsing experience.

There is a lot of ground to cover, so let's get started.

Understanding the Terminology about the Internet and the WWW

Everyone has heard the term *Internet*, but even though we use it on a daily basis, not that many of us know what this word means. The *Internet* is a global network of interconnected networks that use standardized communication protocols—a set of rules that specify how data is transmitted—to exchange data. It operates without being governed by any entity, and each network that is part of the Internet joins it voluntarily while remaining autonomous from other networks. To put it more simply, the Internet is the physical network of computers and devices (smartphones, tablets, and the like) all over the world.

The origins of the Internet date back to research commissioned by the United States government in the 1960s to build robust communication using computer networks known as the Advanced Research Projects Agency Network (ARPANET). The term *Internet* was first used in December 1974, and the Internet, as a global network of networks, was fully commercialized in the United States by 1995. It started a rapid expansion to Europe and Australia in the mid- to late 1980s and to Asia in the late 1980s and early 1990s. There is no consensus on the exact date when the modern Internet came into being, but most specialists agree that it started to exist in the early to mid-1980s. ARPANET

According to the UN's International Telecommunication Union, in 2014 the world's Internet users surpassed 3 billion or 43.6 percent of the world's population. By region, 42 percent of the world's Internet users were based in Asia, 24 percent in Europe, 14 percent in North America, 10 percent in Latin America and the Caribbean taken together, 6 percent in Africa, 3 percent in the Middle East, and 1 percent in Australia/Oceania.

One of the most frequent mistakes we all make is that when we think of the Internet, the first thing we think about is the World Wide Web (WWW). The terms *Internet* and *World Wide Web* are often used interchangeably, but they're actually not the same thing. The *World Wide Web* (abbreviated as *WWW*, commonly known as the Web) is a system of websites connected by links. Websites are stored on servers on the Internet, and the WWW is a part of the Internet but not the whole of Internet.

> **NOTE** The World Wide Web was invented by the British computer scientist Tim Berners-Lee in 1989. Before the Web, the Internet transmitted only text and was used primarily by military officials and scientists. By utilizing the Hypertext Transfer Protocol (HTTP), web pages can include text, images, videos, and other types of media files.

Websites are locations connected to the Internet that maintain one or more web pages. A *website* is a set of related web pages typically served from a single web domain and hosted on at least one server that is accessible via the Internet. All publicly accessible websites collectively constitute the World Wide Web. web page = document

A *web page* is a document, typically written in text, that can incorporate multimedia content like pictures, audio, and video that is suitable for the World Wide Web and web browsers. web browser app.

A *web browser* is the application that you use to display a web page on a computer or mobile device. It coordinates the various resources and elements that are found on each web page so that they are displayed correctly in a form that is humanly readable. The major web browsers are Internet Explorer, Google Chrome, Mozilla Firefox, Opera, and Safari. The first web browser was invented in 1990, and it was called WorldWideWeb, to suggest that is was the only software needed to navigate websites and web pages found on the real World Wide Web.

Getting back to the Internet, the most common use for the Internet is to browse the World Wide Web using web browsers. However, since the Internet is a global network of interconnected networks, the Internet is capable of doing much more than providing access to websites. With the help of the Internet, we can send email messages to other people, use programs that take real-time data from the Internet and share it with us (for example, traffic data, weather data, stock market data, and so on), transfer files to other people across the globe, chat with others, access other computers across the globe, and much more. The ways the Internet can be used are practically unlimited, whereas the WWW is just one way to use the Internet.

Understanding the World Wide Web

Every website and web page on the World Wide Web has an address that can be used to find it with the help of a web browser. That address is called its *URL* (Uniform Resource Locator), and it consists of the following elements:

Protocol   The specific data-transmission rules for accessing the resource on the Web. For websites and web pages, it can be `http://` (Hypertext Transfer Protocol) or `https://` (the s at the end stands for Secure). It used to be that you had to type the protocol to reach a website, but today's web browsers supply it automatically.

Prefix   www is the prefix used for visiting websites on the Web. Most websites do not require it, and they can be accessed without typing www as the prefix. For example, typing `www.example.com` or `example.com` leads you to the same web page. The www prefix must always be followed by a dot.

Domain Name   This consists of one or more parts or labels, delimited by dots, like example.com. The right label (`com`) is called the top-level domain. Each label to the left of the top-level domain is a subdomain of the domain on its right. In `example.com`, `example` is a subdomain of the `com` domain. Some websites may have multiple subdomains, like `example1.example2.com`. In this scenario, `example 1` is a subdomain of `example 2`, and `example2` is a subdomain of the `com` top-level domain.

Path   This element is optional and is generally used to access a very specific resource on a website, like a certain web page, file, and so on. The path is always preceded by a / and then followed by the address of the resource you are trying to access, such as `example .com/example`.

   The complete URL for `example.com` is the following: `http://www.example.com`. The `http://` protocol is automatically completed by your browser, and you don't have to type it. Also, you can access the same website by using `http://example.com`, without the www prefix. However, some websites may require you to type www and cannot be accessed without this prefix. This behavior varies from website to website and depends on how its administrator has configured it.

Standard Domain Names

As you have seen in earlier examples, the top-level domain is always the last label of the domain name, and it follows the final dot in an address. The list of top-level domains that can be used on the Internet is managed by the Internet Corporation for Assigned Names and Numbers (ICANN). In October 2014, there were 735 active top-level domains, and the list is growing each year. In the early days of the Internet, there were only seven generic top-level domains:

.com   Commercial: a generic top-level domain that is accessible to any person or entity.

.org   Organization: it was originally intended for use by nonprofit organizations. Today, it is open to any person or entity.

.net   Network: it was originally intended for use by domains pointing to networks. It is now open to any person or entity.

.int   International organizations: strictly limited to organizations, offices, and programs that are endorsed by a treaty between two or more nations.

.edu   U.S. higher education: it is used almost exclusively by American colleges and universities.

.gov   U.S. national and state government agencies: it is limited to only such entities.

.mil   U.S. military: it is used only by the United States military.

In the modern era of the Internet, each country has its own top-level domain. For example, UK has .uk, Canada has .ca, Germany has .de, Romania has .ro, Vietnam has .vn, and so on.

Special Domain Names

There are many other types of top-level domains, and new ones are made available each year. ICANN has created a long list of generic domains like .academy (which can be used by academic institutions all over the world), .biz (open to commercial entities all over the world), or .pro, which is reserved for licensed or certified professionals worldwide. A new practice is for famous brands and companies to register their own branded top-level domains. To give you a few examples, Google has .android as the top-level domain for websites that are related to its Android mobile operating system, IBM has its .ibm top-level domain, while the German car manufacturer BMW has its own .bmw top-level domain.

Understanding Hyperlinks

When visiting websites and web pages in your browser, you will encounter many links to other web pages and websites. These links are called *hyperlinks*, and a hyperlink is only a reference to data that can be accessed by clicking it. A hyperlink has an anchor on the page, which can be a selection of text, an image, or another kind of element.

Web browsers usually display hyperlinks in some distinguishing way, like using a different color (usually blue), font, or style. When you move your mouse pointer over a hyperlink, it turns into a hand, signaling that the element you are over is a hyperlink that can take you to another resource. You can see an example in Figure 11.1.

FIGURE 11.1   A hyperlink with a mouse pointer hovering above it

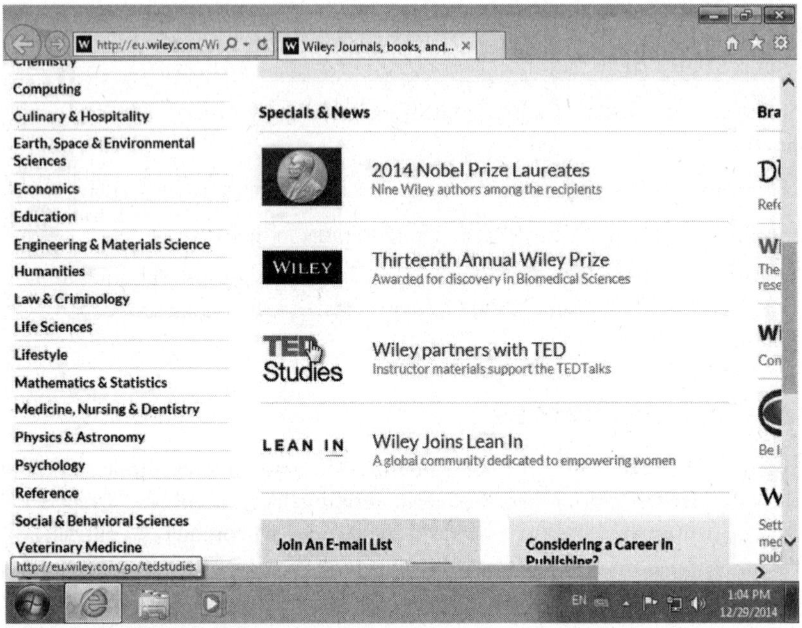

Browsing the Web with a Web Browser

Now that you know the theory behind the Internet and the World Wide Web, as well as their most important concepts, you'll start to put your newfound knowledge to good use and learn how to browse the Web.

There are many web browsers to choose from, depending on the device and the operating system that you are using. For example, on Windows you can find Internet Explorer, Google Chrome, Mozilla Firefox, and Opera. On Mac OS X Safari is the most popular browser, while on mobile platforms like Android you can choose from browsers like Dolphin, Opera Mini, Google Chrome, UC Browser, Maxthon, and many others.

Each web browser looks different from the others, but most of them offer the same capabilities and features. In order to get you acquainted with the concept of a web browser, we will go through a few exercises. First, we will be using Internet Explorer, the browser with the biggest market share on Windows. You open this browser by clicking its icon on the taskbar—the big blue *E*. You can also find it by going to Start menu and clicking All Programs ➢ Internet Explorer, as shown in Figure 11.2.

When you open the Internet Explorer window, the website that is set as your homepage is automatically opened. By default, it is the MSN website. On the top side of the window are several buttons and interface elements, highlighted in Figure 11.3:

Back   An arrow pointing to the left side of the screen. It becomes active after you visit a second web page or website. When you click it, it takes you back to the previous page.

FIGURE 11.2   The shortcuts for Internet Explorer

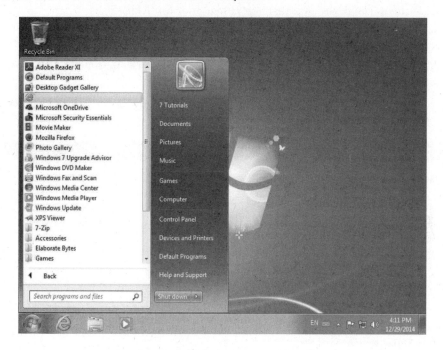

FIGURE 11.3   Buttons in Internet Explorer

Forward   An arrow pointing to the right side of the screen. It becomes active after clicking Back, and it takes you to the page that you visited prior to clicking Back.

Address Bar   A text field next to the Back and Forward buttons where you can type the address of the website that you want to visit.

Refresh   On the right side of the Address bar you will find the Refresh button. Clicking it reloads the current web page.

In Exercise 11.1 you will learn how to open Internet Explorer, use it to browse different websites, and go back and forth between them.

EXERCISE 11.1

Browsing the Web with Internet Explorer

1. Click Start ➢ All Programs ➢ Internet Explorer.

2. Click inside the Address bar, type **microsoft.com**, and then press Enter.

   Notice how Internet Explorer autocompletes the address and takes you to `http://www.microsoft.com`.

3. Click inside the Address bar, type **wikipedia.org**, and then press Enter.

   Notice how the Wikipedia website is now opened instead of Microsoft.com (Figure 11.4). Also, notice how Internet Explorer autocompleted the full URL and took you to `http://www.wikipedia.org`.

FIGURE 11.4   The Wikipedia website loaded in Internet Explorer

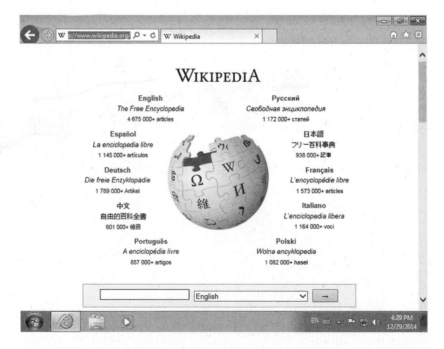

4. Click the Back button and notice how the Microsoft website is loaded instead of Wikipedia.

5. Click the Forward button and notice how the Wikipedia website is loaded.

6. Click the Refresh button to reload the Wikipedia website.

7. Close Internet Explorer.

As mentioned earlier, many web browsers are available, and while they all look different, they are used for the same purpose and have mostly the same features. One of the most popular open-source browsers for Windows is Mozilla Firefox. You open this browser by clicking its icon, which looks like a fox surrounding Earth, on the taskbar. You can also find it by going to the Start menu and clicking All Programs and then Mozilla Firefox, as shown in Figure 11.5.

FIGURE 11.5   The shortcuts for Mozilla Firefox

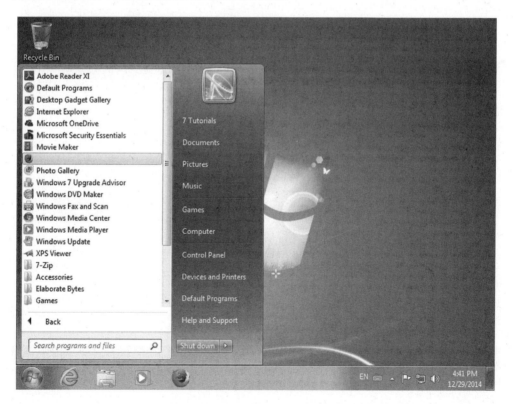

When you open the Mozilla Firefox window, the website that is set as the homepage is automatically opened. At the top of the window are the same buttons as in Internet Explorer. But they look different and, their positioning is not exactly the same, as you can see in Figure 11.6.

FIGURE 11.6   Buttons in Mozilla Firefox

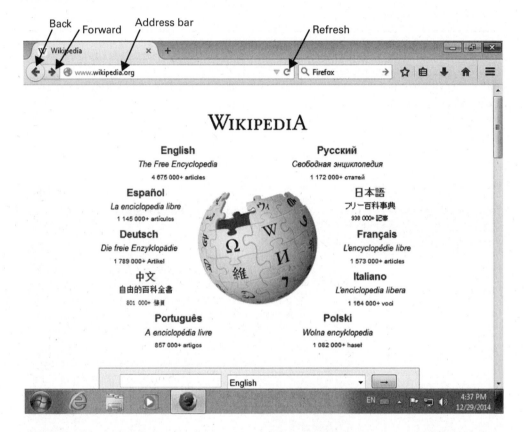

One difference between Internet Explorer and Mozilla Firefox is that in Mozilla Firefox, the Forward button is hidden until you click the Back button, in order to make more room for the Address bar.

In Exercise 11.2 you will learn how open Mozilla Firefox and use it to browse different websites and go back and forth between them.

EXERCISE 11.2

Browsing the Web with Mozilla Firefox

1. Click Start ➢ All Programs ➢ Mozilla Firefox.

2. Click inside the Address bar, type **microsoft.com**, and then press Enter.

Notice how Mozilla Firefox autocompletes the address and takes you to `http://www.microsoft.com`.

3. Click inside the Address bar, type **wikipedia.org**, and then press Enter.

Notice how the Wikipedia website is now opened instead of Microsoft.com. Also, notice how Mozilla Firefox autocompleted the full URL and took you to `http://www.wikipedia.org`.

4. Click the Back button and notice how the Microsoft website is loaded instead of Wikipedia.

5. Click the Forward button and notice how the Wikipedia website is loaded.

6. Click the Refresh button to reload the Wikipedia website.

7. Close Mozilla Firefox.

ctr T = new tab

Using Multiple Tabs While Browsing the Web

When you browse the Web, you will access many websites and web pages. Even though using the Back and Forward buttons is useful, it can become counterproductive to keep using them in order to flip through the websites that you visit during a web-browsing session. To help you out, all modern web browsers use tabs as a tool for switching between web pages.

When you open a web browser, one tab is opened and the website set as the homepage is loaded automatically. You can open a new tab and navigate to another website in the same web browser window by clicking the button for creating a new tab or by pressing Ctrl+T on your keyboard. When the new tab opens, type the address of the website that you want to visit and press Enter. To close a tab, you simply click the small X button on the right side of that tab. To switch between tabs, simply click them.

As shown in Figure 11.7, in Internet Explorer the New Tab button is placed on the right side of the list with tabs. Each tab has its own little X button on its right, which you can use to close it.

In Mozilla Firefox, these buttons look slightly different and they have different names, as shown in Figure 11.8:

- The tabs are placed above the Address bar and not to its right, like in Internet Explorer.

- The button for opening new tabs is found on the right side of the tabs, and it is in the form of a + sign.

Just like in other browsers, you close a tab by clicking the X button on its right. To switch between tabs, simply click them.

FIGURE 11.7 The Close Tab and New Tab buttons in Internet Explorer

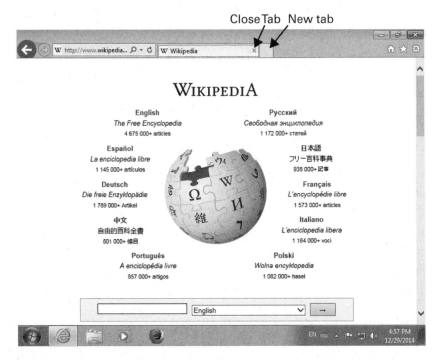

FIGURE 11.8 The Close Tab and Open A New Tab buttons in Mozilla Firefox

Downloading and Uploading Files on the Web

We use the Web not only to find information but also to download files and use them on our computers. Many of us also upload our own files to the Web and post them online for others to view or use.

The term *download* means receiving data on your computer or device from another remote system. This remote system can be a web server, email server, or another similar system. *Download* can mean either any file that is offered for downloading or that has been downloaded or the process of receiving such a file. We download all kinds of files from the Web, ranging from pictures to music, software, books, and other items.

Depending on the type of the file that you download from the Web, you are asked where to save it on your computer and whether you want to run it (this happens only when downloading executable files), like in Figure 11.9. After selecting where you want to save it, the download starts.

FIGURE 11.9   Downloading a file in Internet Explorer

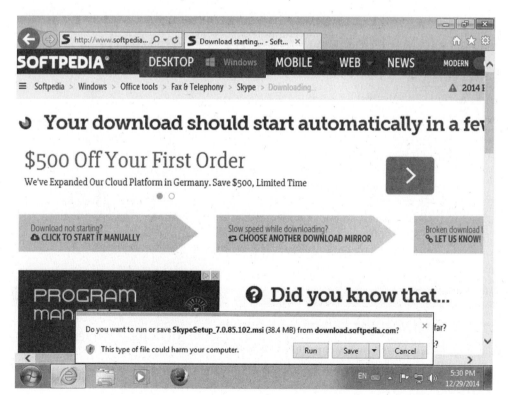

The term *upload* refers to the sending of data from your computer or device to a remote system, like a web server, email server, or another similar system. *Upload* can mean either any file that is uploaded or that has been uploaded or the process of sending such a file. Some common examples of uploads include posting your pictures on Facebook, creating a gallery with your photos on Flickr, or posting a video you have made on YouTube.

Download Speed vs. Upload Speed

After downloading and uploading several files, you will notice that the download is generally faster than the upload. Since most users spend much more time downloading files than they do uploading, Internet service providers have designed their systems to give priority to downloading, and Internet packages are typically asynchronous, meaning that the service provider offers more bandwidth for downloads than for uploads. If you are a person who uploads a lot of content online or you have a company that needs to send lots of data to its clients, it is very important to examine the Internet packages offered by your local provider and take a close look at the speed they advertise for uploads.

Setting a Homepage in Your Web Browser

Most web browsers have a default homepage. This page is loaded each time you start the browser, and you can change it to something else. For example, if you check your email a lot, you may want to set the homepage to be your email service. Or, if you spend a lot of time on Facebook, you may want to set this social network as your homepage.

Each browser has a different user interface with different menus and options, but all of them allow you to set your homepage. However, since we can't cover all web browsers, we will show how this is done in the most popular web browser for Windows, Internet Explorer.

In Exercise 11.3 you will learn how set the homepage in Internet Explorer.

EXERCISE 11.3

Setting the Homepage in Internet Explorer

1. Click Start ➤ All Programs ➤ Internet Explorer.

2. Click the Tools button on the upper-right corner of the Internet Explorer window, or press Alt+X on your keyboard to open the Tools menu (Figure 11.10).

FIGURE 11.10   The Tools button in Internet Explorer

3.   In the Tools menu, click Internet Options (Figure 11.11).

FIGURE 11.11   The Tools menu in Internet Explorer

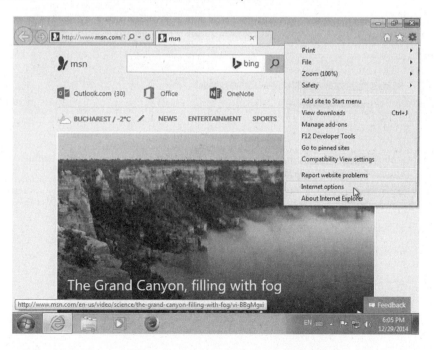

4. In the Internet Options window, go to the Home Page section in the General tab.

    There you will see the homepage that is currently set in Internet Explorer (Figure 11.12).

FIGURE 11.12   The Internet Options window

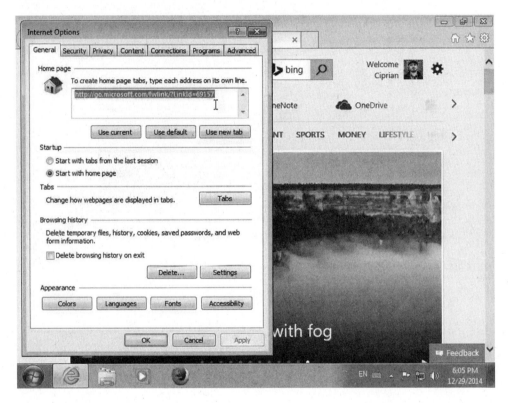

5. Double-click the current homepage and start typing the new one, for example, http://www.facebook.com (Figure 11.13).

FIGURE 11.13   Setting the homepage

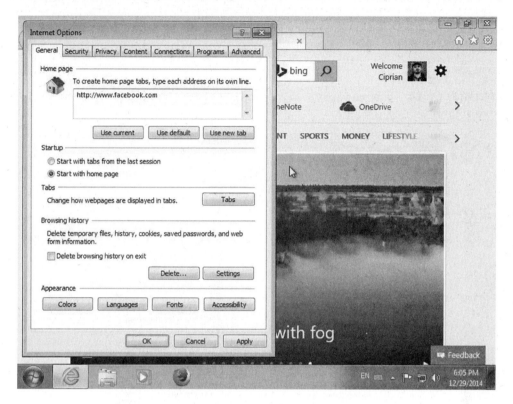

6.   Click OK and then close Internet Explorer.

7.   Open Internet Explorer again, and notice how the homepage that you set is opened automatically when you start the browser.

8.   Close Internet Explorer.

Using and Clearing Your Browsing History

All web browsers store a complete log of the websites and web pages that you have visited. This is useful because you can easily access your history and find the web pages that you have visited in the past. Also, each browser uses your history to autocomplete URLs in the Address bar. This makes navigation faster because you don't have to fully type each URL after you visit it once. As you can see in Figure 11.14, you type only a few letters, the browser suggests the full URL from your history, you press Enter, and the web page is immediately loaded.

FIGURE 11.14 Internet Explorer suggesting URLs based on what you type and your history

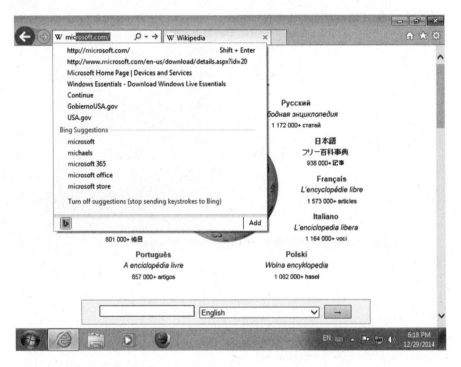

Accessing your browsing history is different from browser to browser, and in Exercise 11.4 we share how it is done in Internet Explorer.

EXERCISE 11.4

Accessing Your Browsing History in Internet Explorer

1. Click Start ➤ All Programs ➤ Internet Explorer.

2. Click the View Favorites, Feeds, And History button (the one in the shape of a star), on the top-right side of the window. You can also press Alt+C on your keyboard (Figure 11.15).

3. Click the History tab to access your browsing history, split by date (Figure 11.16).

FIGURE 11.15   The View Favorites, Feeds, And History button

FIGURE 11.16   The browsing history shown by date

4. Click Today, and then click one of the web pages that you have visited during the day (Figure 11.17).

FIGURE 11.17 Today's browsing history

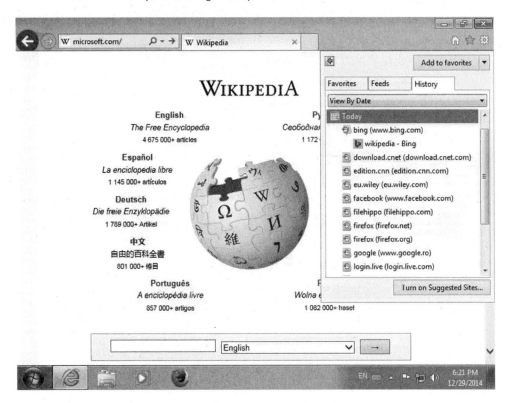

5. Wait for the page to load, and then close Internet Explorer.

One downside to the fact that a browser stores your browsing history is that this history is available to anyone using that browser on the same user account. If you share your computer with others using the same user account, you may want to clear your browsing history regularly.

Another issue is that web browsers tend to become slower after being used for a long time, and clearing your history may help them run faster. Whatever the reasons for clearing your browsing history, this can be done in any web browser.

In Exercise 11.5 we share how to clear your browsing history in Internet Explorer.

Clearing Your Browsing History in Internet Explorer

1. Click Start ➤ All Programs ➤ Internet Explorer.

2. Click the Tools button on the upper-right corner of the Internet Explorer window, or press Alt+X on your keyboard to open the Tools menu.

3. Click Safety and then Delete Browsing History (Figure 11.18). You can also press Ctrl+Shift+Del on your keyboard.

FIGURE 11.18   The Tools menu in Internet Explorer

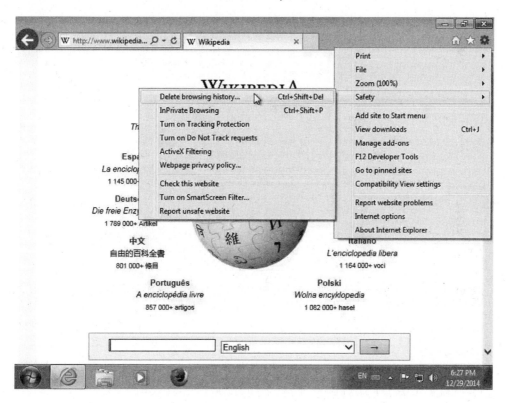

EXERCISE 11.5 *(continued)*

4.   In the Delete Browsing History window, select History and other things that you want
     to delete, and then click Delete (Figure 11.19).

FIGURE 11.19   The Delete Browsing History window

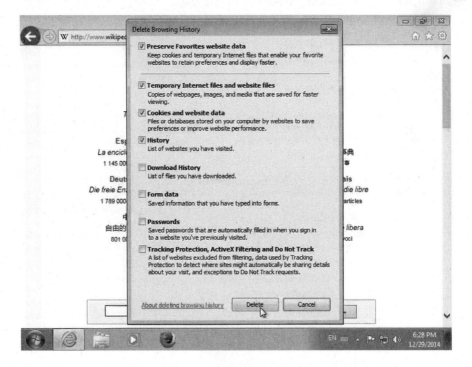

5.   Wait a couple of seconds until Internet Explorer deletes everything that you have
     selected. No prompts or confirmations will be displayed.

6.   Close Internet Explorer.

Using Favorites or Bookmarks in Your Web Browser

Bookmarks or *favorites* are links to websites that make it easy to get back to your favorite
places. The term *bookmarks* is used by most browsers with the exceptions of Internet
Explorer. In this web browser, bookmarks are known as favorites.

The easiest way to find a site that you've bookmarked is to start typing its name in the Address bar. As you type, a list of websites that you've bookmarked, tagged, and visited is shown. Bookmarked sites are generally prioritized in the list of suggestions shown in the Address bar, above your browsing history. All you have to do is click one of the sites, and you'll be taken there instantly.

Bookmarked sites are also displayed in their own menus and toolbars, depending on the web browser. To make a comparison, look at Figure 11.20 to see how favorites are shown in Internet Explorer. To access them, click the View Favorites, Feeds, And History button (the one in the shape of a star), on the top-right side of the window, or press Alt+C on your keyboard.

FIGURE 11.20   Favorites in Internet Explorer

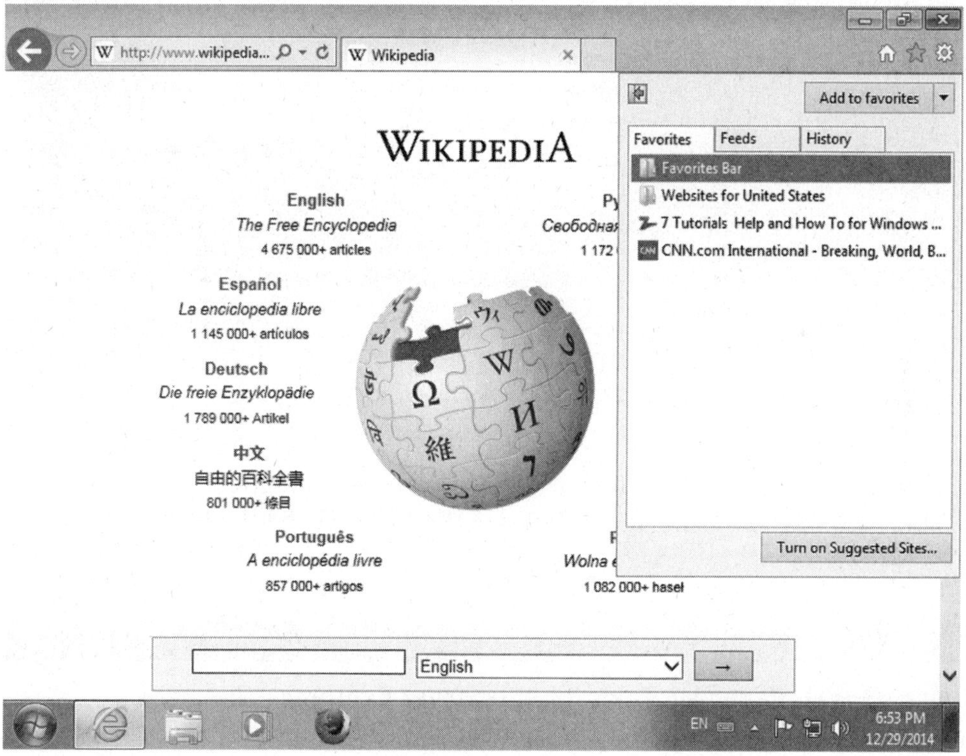

To access a favorite web page, click it and it is immediately loaded in the current tab.

Now look at Figure 11.21 to see how bookmarks are shown in Mozilla Firefox. As you can see, the Bookmarks menu looks different. To access it, click the Show Your Bookmarks button or press Ctrl+Shift+B on your keyboard.

FIGURE 11.21   Bookmarks in Mozilla Firefox

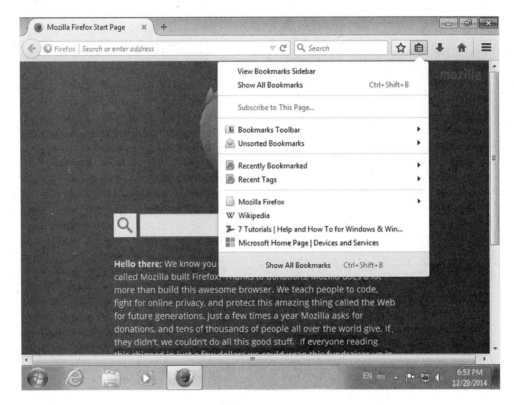

The process for saving a web page as a favorite or bookmark varies from browser to browser. In Exercise 11.6 we share how to save a web page as a favorite in Internet Explorer.

EXERCISE 11.6

Saving a Web Page as a Favorite in Internet Explorer

1. Click Start ➢ All Programs ➢ Internet Explorer.

2. In the Address bar, type **facebook.com** and press Enter on your keyboard.

    Wait for Facebook to load.

3. Click the View Favorites, Feeds, And History button (the one in the shape of a star), on the top-right side of the window (Figure 11.22). You can also press Alt+C on your keyboard.

FIGURE 11.22   The list of favorites in Internet Explorer

4.   Click Add To Favorites.

You can type a name for this web page, or you can leave the default name provided by Internet Explorer.

5.   Click Add, and the website is saved as a favorite (Figure 11.23).

FIGURE 11.23   The Add A Favorite dialog

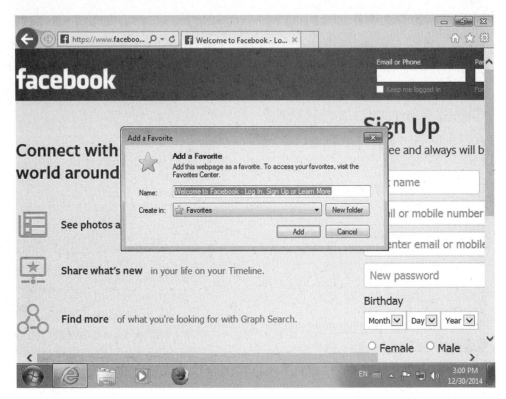

6. To double-check whether the web page was added to your favorites, click View Favorites, Feeds, And History. You can also press Alt+C on your keyboard.

   Notice that Facebook was added to your list of favorites.

7. Close Internet Explorer.

You can manage your list of favorites by dragging and dropping them into the appropriate folders, just as you would do with a file in Windows Explorer. To delete a favorite web page, access the list of favorites, right-click it, and then click Delete. The entry is deleted without any confirmation prompts. The context menu is shown in Figure 11.24.

The process is very similar in other browsers, even though their user interface looks different.

FIGURE 11.24 Deleting a favorite in Internet Explorer

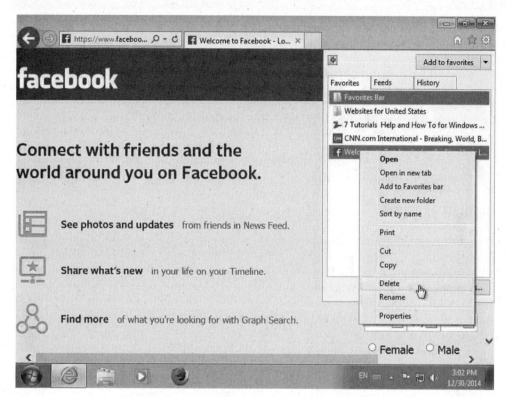

Searching for Text in a Web Page from Your Web Browser

When reading a web page, you may want to quickly search for the portion of text that covers a subject of interest, instead of reading the whole thing and scrolling through the page. All modern web browsers have a Find tool that allows you to make quick searches based on one or more keywords on the page that is currently loaded. The Find dialog is accessed in most browsers by pressing Ctrl+F on your keyboard. We tested it in Internet Explorer, Mozilla Firefox, and Google Chrome, and the shortcut works in all three browsers.

In Exercise 11.7 we share how to quickly search for text on a web page in Internet Explorer.

EXERCISE 11.7

Quickly Searching for Text on a Web Page in Internet Explorer

1.   Click Start ➤ All Programs ➤ Internet Explorer.

2.   In the Address bar, type **Wikipedia.org** and press Enter on your keyboard.

     Wait for Wikipedia to load.

3.   Press Ctrl+F on your keyboard to open the Find dialog at the top of the Internet Explorer window.

4.   In the Find box type **Italiano**. Notice that Internet Explorer says that it has found two matches (Figure 11.25).

FIGURE 11.25   The Find dialog in Internet Explorer

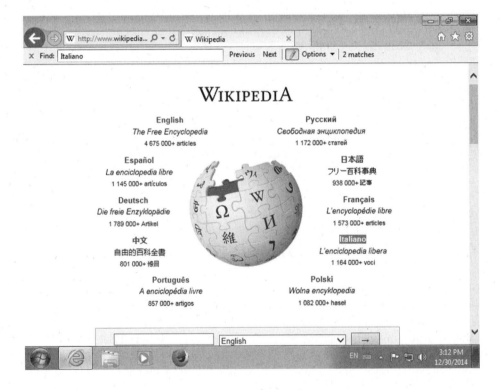

5.   Click Next to move through all the matches that it found.

6.   Close Internet Explorer.

Using Plug-ins, Add-ons, and Extensions in Your Web Browser

When dealing with web browsers you will encounter terms like *plug-ins*, *add-ons*, and *extensions*. They are all software components that add specific features to a browser and enable it to do more. The most popular plug-in for web browsers is Adobe Flash Player, which allows you to view multimedia content that was created with Adobe Flash and posted online. You can download and install Adobe Flash Player online by visiting `http://get.adobe.com/flashplayer/`. You download it and install it on your computer just like any other piece of software.

Modern web browsers also have customized collections of add-ons, plug-ins, and extensions that are maintained by their developers and their community of users. You can find add-ons for Internet Explorer by going to `http://www.iegallery.com`, add-ons for Mozilla Firefox by going to `https://addons.mozilla.org`, and add-ons for Google Chrome by going to `https://chrome.google.com/webstore/category/extensions`.

These add-ons can be installed only from the browsers they are created for. For example, you can't install Internet Explorer add-ons from Mozilla Firefox or the other way around. For each add-on you will find a description of what it does, a couple of pictures, and a button for installing it. When you click the button, the add-on is downloaded, and the web browser handles the installation process (Figure 11.26).

FIGURE 11.26   An add-on for Internet Explorer

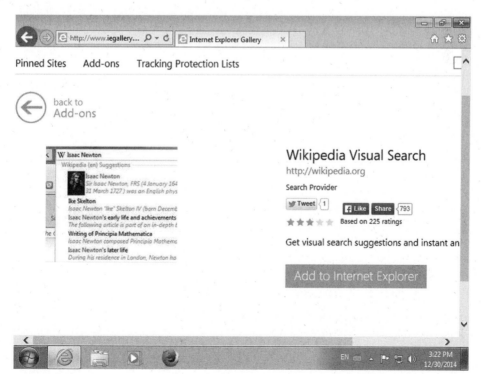

With the help of add-ons, you can extend what you can do with your web browser. For example, you can install multiple search engines, ad blockers, add-ons that block the tracking of your online activities, and so on.

> There's a caveat to using add-ons: installing too many of them will slow down your web browser and decrease the quality of your web-browsing experience. That's why it is recommended to install only plug-ins and add-ons that are useful to you.

Add-ons and plug-ins are managed from the web browser where you are using them. The browser provides the features necessary to access the list of installed add-ons, configure them, disable them, or remove them if you no longer wish to use certain add-ons. The process of accessing and managing add-ons is different from browser to browser, so we won't get into detail in this chapter.

Summary

In this chapter you learned about the Internet and the World Wide Web, what they have in common, and what's different about them. You also learned important concepts like websites, web pages, web browsers, and more.

In order to browse the Web and access information and services online, you need a web browser. We demonstrated how to navigate web pages in a browser, use multiple tabs at the same time, and set your homepage, and we shared a few details about downloading and uploading files and why speeds differ between the two activities.

Then we moved into more advanced subjects like using your browsing history, clearing it, saving web pages as favorites or bookmarks, searching for text in a web page, and using plug-ins to extend what your web browser can do.

In the next chapter we will discuss networking, security, and troubleshooting network problems. It's a very technical chapter, so reserve some quality time for it in order to go through it and understand everything that we will cover.

Exam Essentials

Understand the difference between the Internet and the WWW.   Many people confuse the Internet with the World Wide Web. Knowing what each of them is and what's different between these concepts is a key aspect of living online.

Know what a web browser is and how to use it.   You cannot browse the Web without a web browser. Knowing how to use a web browser is mandatory for being productive when online.

Know how to use the basic features of a web browser.   In order to be productive when browsing the Web, you should know how to navigate among the websites that you have visited, open multiple tabs at the same time, set the homepage, bookmark favorite websites, and more.

Learn how to access and clear your browsing history.   Your browsing history can help you to access web pages that you have visited in the past. You should learn how to access it and how to clear it when appropriate.

Understand what plug-ins are and why they are useful.   Plug-ins, add-ons, and extensions can extend what you can do with a web browser. You should learn what plug-ins are and where you can find them for your web browser.

Key Terms

Before you take the exam, be certain you are familiar with the following terms:

bookmarks	URL
download	web browser
favorites	web page
hyperlink	website
Internet	World Wide Web
upload	WWW

Review Questions

1. What is the Internet? (Choose all that apply.)

   A. A network with many computers and devices

   B. The physical network of computers and devices (smartphones, tablets, and so on) all over the world

   C. Every website and web page in the world

   D. The global network of interconnected networks that use standardized communication protocols to exchange data and information between them

2. In the context of the Internet, what does WWW stand for?

   A. World Wide War

   B. Wild Wild West

   C. World Wide Web

   D. Who What Where

3. What is the World Wide Web? (Choose all that apply.)

   A. A part of the Internet

   B. The physical network of computers and devices (smartphones, tablets, etc.) all over the world

   C. Your company's websites

   D. A system of websites connected by links

4. What is a URL? (Choose all that apply.)

   A. The address of a website or a web page on the WWW

   B. Uniform Resource Locator

   C. The network location of a computer

   D. The address of a webserver

5. What is a web browser? (Choose all that apply.)

   A. An application that you can use to access the Internet

   B. Software that is used to navigate websites and web pages that are found on the World Wide Web

   C. An application that you can use to send email messages

   D. An application that displays a web page on a computer or mobile device

6. What is a hyperlink?

   A. The network address of a website

   B. The address of a website or a web page on the WWW

   C. A reference to data that can be accessed by clicking it

   D. Text displayed in a different color by the web browser

7. Which of the following are examples of uploads? (Choose all that apply.)

  A. Posting your pictures on Facebook

  B. Posting a video on YouTube

  C. Copying a file on your computer

  D. Receiving an email message

8. What is a homepage for a web browser?

  A. A page that is set as a favorite in the web browser

  B. A page that is set as a bookmark in the web browser

  C. A web page that is loaded each time you close a web browser

  D. A web page that is loaded each time you open a web browser

9. What is the browsing history in a web browser?

  A. A complete log of the websites and web pages that you have not visited on the Web

  B. A complete log of the websites and web pages that you have visited

  C. The websites that you have logged in to

  D. A complete log of the emails that you have received

10. In the context of a web browser, what is a plug-in or add-on?

  A. Something that you install to replace your web browser

  B. A piece of software that you install on your computer

  C. A software component that adds a specific feature to a browser and enables it to do more

  D. A way of changing your web browser from Internet Explorer to something else

Chapter

12

Understanding Networking and Its Most Important Concepts

THE FOLLOWING IC3: LIVING ONLINE EXAM OBJECTIVES ARE COVERED IN THIS CHAPTER:

✓ **Internet Connection**

- Speed

- Explain the differences between Dial up and broadband connections and the process each uses to establish a connection.

- Wireless

- Security

✓ **Network Types and Features, Capabilities**

- Explain the concepts associated with the Publicly switched networks.

- Explain the concepts associated with DNS (Domain Name Server).

- Explain the concepts associated with Addressing.

- Explain the concepts associated with and the difference between LAN vs. WAN.

- Explain the concepts associated with VPN.

✓ **Network Troubleshooting**

- Demonstrate the ability to solve simple networking connectivity problems in various settings.

- Explain methods of identifying common network problems.

- Explain the concepts associated with Define IP Addressing.

This chapter is a lot more technical than others, so arm yourself with some patience. You will need a bit more time to digest and understand everything. First, we are going to talk about networks and the different types that are available. Then, we will share the basics about how computers and devices get an address on a network so that they can communicate with other devices and exchange data.

Next, we will move on to security and discuss how to secure wireless networks in your home. We will also talk about important security products like firewalls and gateways. You surely have heard about them, but you may not understand what they are and why they are important. This chapter will clear up all that for you.

Then, we will talk about speed, factors that limit the speed of Internet connections, and how fast wireless networks are. And since almost everyone nowadays is connected to the Internet, we will share more details about the most important types of Internet connections that are available.

Finally, we will explore the basics that you need to know in order to troubleshoot network and Internet-related problems. Don't be afraid; things are not as scary as they sound, and you can understand everything that's shared in this chapter. Without further ado, let's get started.

Understanding Networks: LAN vs. WAN

The networking industry is huge, encompassing hundreds of companies and a massive range of technologies. Practically every company in the world has a network, and almost all need a skilled individual to manage that network. Even if they cannot justify having a full-time administrator of their own, they are likely to have an arrangement with a computer company that does. For the past few years, computer networking has been, is now, and is forecasted to remain one of the primary growth areas of the IT industry.

When computer networking is discussed, it refers primarily to the process of connecting two or more computers together. The true meaning of a network is defined by answering a question: Why would you want to join two computers together in the first place?

In the early days of networking, the two main uses of a computer network were the sharing of data and the shared use of expensive peripherals, such as printers or other devices. Today, these two tasks still form a solid reason to use most networks. But networks are now used in many other and often elaborate ways. The explosive popularity of services such as email, cloud computing, centralized data storage, and much more means that a network infrastructure now underpins modern business.

Without a doubt, a defining point in the history of networking was the creation of the Internet. Although it is difficult to convey in just a few lines, the Internet is basically a massive collection of connected networks. In fact, the term *Internet* (with a capital *I*) is derived from the term *internetwork* (with a lowercase *i*), meaning a group of connected networks. Although it is obvious that the scale of the Internet makes for differences in the technology used, the basis for the Internet is the same as that of many of the networks used in businesses around the world.

Essentially, networking is a concept or principle that requires two kinds of products: hardware and software. There is a computer networking hardware industry (cables, devices for attaching PCs to a network, and the like), and there is a networking software industry (software for sharing files, email, and other data).

At the core, networks share resources among computer systems and centrally manage resources and data. The next question becomes what type of network is required to accomplish this. This is where acronyms like LAN, WAN, and VPN come into play. And then we need to dig a little deeper into the underlying technologies that make the magic happen: TCP/IP and DNS.

Not all networks are created equal. They vary in size, shape, and complexity. Networks are often distinguished by their location; for example, a network confined to a single geographical area is known as a *local area network (LAN)*. A single geographical location may be an apartment, a single building, an office, a school, or a library. LANs are created with network cables as well as wireless technologies. The advantages of a LAN include speed, ease of use, and low cost. In a local network you can find all kinds of devices ranging from desktop computers to laptops, tablets, printers, and so on. The downside is that it is confined to that single geographical location. Figure 12.1 shows an example of a LAN.

FIGURE 12.1   Example of a LAN

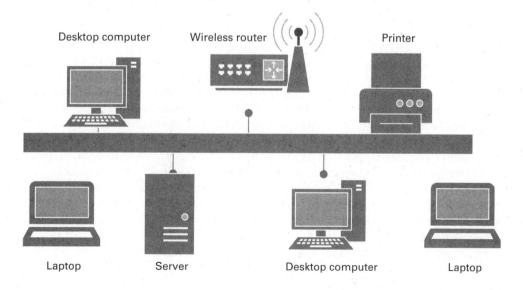

Networks that span multiple geographical locations are known as *wide area networks (WANs)*. They are generally used by businesses and government entities to relay data to employees, clients, suppliers, and business partners from various geographical locations. WANs may connect LANs together to create an internetwork, and the Internet can also be considered a WAN. They are considerably more expensive to support and maintain than LANs. Figure 12.2 shows an example of a WAN.

FIGURE 12.2   Example of a WAN

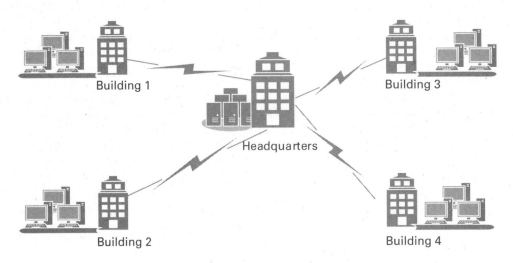

Other Types of Area Networks

In your travels you may encounter the terms PAN, MAN, CAN, and even more. These terms each loosely describe the size of different networks. Personal area networks (PANs) are small networks typically associated with one person. A PAN may be a network used to connect a smartphone using Bluetooth wireless in your car and other personal devices in close proximity. Campus area networks (CANs) are essentially LANs that encompass a larger area but not large enough to be considered a WAN. This may be a large single-location government agency or a large university campus. Finally, a metropolitan area network (MAN) is somewhat larger than a CAN but smaller than a WAN, perhaps a citywide network. So it is possible to configure a PAN, connected to a LAN, while transmitting to a WAN.

Understanding Network Addressing

In order to communicate in a network using the computers and devices that are part of it, you need to use a communication protocol that is understood by all devices. A *communication protocol* is collection of rules that establish how data is transmitted on a computer network. On the Internet and in many networks, everyone uses *TCP/IP*. It is a set of two protocols: the *Transmission Control Protocol (TCP)* and the *Internet Protocol (IP)*. Each of these protocols provides a different function, and together they provide the complete TCP/IP package. TCP provides reliable transmission between systems, and IP is responsible for addressing and route selection. TCP/IP has been with us since the early 1980s, and today it is the default protocol used in most modern networks and for the Internet.

There can be no argument that TCP/IP is a flexible and durable communication protocol. On the other hand, it can be very complex, specifically when it comes to IP addressing. Discussions of IP addressing have left more than one administrator scratching their head, and entire books have been dedicated to the topic. In this section we take a whirlwind tour through TCP/IP addressing with the intention of providing the basics of a complicated topic. For the IC3 exam, an in-depth knowledge of TCP/IP addressing is not required, but a general knowledge of addressing and how it works is certainly important.

IP Addresses

When a computer or device connects to a network, it receives an address, named *IP address* or Internet Protocol address. This is a numerical label assigned to each device participating in the network that uses the Internet Protocol for communication. The IP address actually tells us two things: the IP number of the network it is attached to and the address of the node (device) on that network.

IP addressing comes in two variations: IPv4 (Internet Protocol version 4) and IPv6 (Internet Protocol version 6). IPv4 has been in use for many years, but because more and more devices require addressing, IPv4 addresses are now in short supply. IPv6 was developed in response to IPv4's impending demise. However, IPv4 is still the dominant protocol in use at the time of writing this book.

In an IPv4 network, the IP address consists of four numbers called octets (8 bits), each separated by dots. If you do the math, this means that each IP address is 32 bits in length. An example of an IP address is 192.168.2.1.

The IP address alone is not enough to connect to the network. A subnet mask is also needed, which, like the IP address, is a four-octet number expressed in dotted-numerical format. With the subnet mask, each bit in the address that forms part of the network address is assigned a 1, and each bit that represents part of the node address is assigned a 0. Then, through a process called ANDing, the system is able to determine the necessary information.

To simplify things, let's use an example. Imagine you have an IP address of 167.54.122.12 and a subnet mask of 255.255.0.0. This means that the system would look at the first two octets to determine the network number and the last two octets to determine the node number. In this case, the device would be on network 167.54 and have a node address of 122.12. Add a third octet's worth of bits to the subnet mask to make it 255.255.255.0, and the network address would become 167.54.122, and the node address would become 12.

The Domain Name Service

To gain network access, a client system needs only two key pieces of information:

- A unique IP address
- The corresponding subnet mask

While a system can gain access to the network with just an IP address and a subnet mask, other key information is necessary. This includes the DNS server address and the default gateway.

The *Domain Name Service (DNS)* server performs a relatively basic but vital role for network access: name resolution from hostnames to IP addresses. The *hostname* is the label that is assigned to a device connected to a network. In a LAN, the hostname can be the name of a computer connected to that network. On the Web, the hostname can be the domain name of a website. Rather than rely on flawed human memory to remember these addresses, we can use www.sybex.com or www.disney.com instead of their IP address. When we type www.sybex.com into a web browser, our configured DNS server takes the request and searches through a system of servers to find out the correct TCP/IP address that correlates to www.sybex.com.

After the DNS server has ascertained the correct TCP/IP address, that address is returned to the client, which then contacts the IP address directly. To speed up subsequent requests for the same address, the DNS server adds the address to its cache. For a workstation to send requests to the DNS server, the TCP/IP address of the DNS server must be provided to the workstations. This can be done manually, or the address can be included in the information supplied by a *Dynamic Host Configuration Protocol (DHCP)* server. DHCP does the job of assigning IP addresses, eliminating the need to individually assign IP addresses and in the process making the job of network administrators considerably easier.

When a DHCP server is running on a network, the workstation starts and requests an IP address from the server. The server responds to the request and automatically assigns an IP address to the computer. The workstation acknowledges the reception of the IP number, and the workstation has all the information it needs to become part of the network. This communication between the server and workstation happens automatically and is invisible to the computer user. When a workstation is logged off the network, the IP address is returned and made available to other machines wanting to log onto the network. Figure 12.3 shows the TCP/IP configuration screen of a Windows 7 computer.

For a system to be able to communicate with another system on a different network, it must be able to find a way off the current network and onto the other one. This is the function of a default *gateway*, which routes data to other networks. It does not guarantee to know how to get to other networks (that is a function of routing tables and routing protocols), but it is where the journey starts. For a workstation to send information to the default gateway, it must have its IP address, and the address must be on the same network as it is.

FIGURE 12.3   Internet Protocol Version 4 (TCP/IPv4) Properties

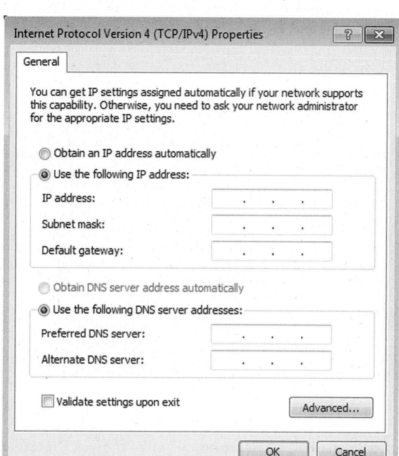

So to recap, there are four key elements to IP addressing:

IP Address   Each client system must have a unique IP address to log onto a network. Commonly the IP address is assigned via DHCP.

Subnet Mask   All systems require a valid subnet mask that identifies the network and the node.

Default Gateway   The default gateway allows the client system to communicate with systems on a remote network without the need to manually add routes to the client system.

DNS Server Address   The DNS server resolves hostnames to IP addresses.

To review the current TCP/IP settings on a client system, you can issue the `ipconfig /all` command from the command prompt. The output from the command shown in Figure 12.4 shows the IP configuration from a Windows computer.

FIGURE 12.4   The TCP/IP configuration from a Windows computer

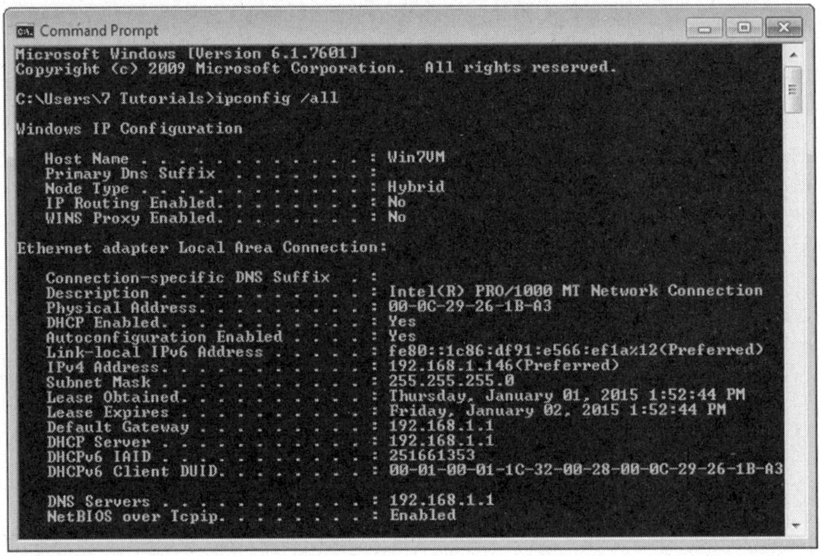

Private IPv4 Address Ranges

After years of loyal service, IPv4 addresses are running out. In the future, IPv6 is destined to overtake version 4 and bring with it enough IP addresses to last a lifetime (this was predicted with IPv4 as well). Until it is widely adopted, you need a method to stretch the IP addresses you currently have available.

The solution has come in the form of classes of nonroutable or private IP addresses. These nonroutable addresses are designed to be used within an organization, and because they are nonroutable, they can be used over and over and be unique to that organization. The caveat is that they cannot be used on the Internet.

The three ranges of nonroutable IP addresses and default subnet masks include the following:

- IP range 10.0.0.0 to 10.255.255.255, subnet mask 255.0.0.0
- IP range 172.16.0.0 to 172.31.255.255, subnet mask 255.255.0.0
- IP range 192.168.0.0 to 192.168.255.255, subnet mask 255.255.0.0

Many organizations use two sets of IP addresses: the private ones used on the internal network and external IP addresses obtained from an ISP that will allow traffic out to the Internet. In your own home network, you will have an external (public) IP address used to access the Internet on your router and private addresses for all of the devices used in the home that are connected to the router.

Using and Securing Wireless Networks

A *wireless network* is any type of computer network that uses wireless data connections for connecting network devices. Wireless networking is a method by which homes, telecommunications networks, and businesses avoid the costly process of introducing cables into a building or as a connection between various equipment locations. Wireless telecommunications networks are generally implemented and administered using radio communication; examples of wireless networks include cellphone networks as well as Wi-Fi local networks that are found in many public places.

If you have a broadband Internet connection at home, you likely have been provided a router that has a wireless access point built in. If not, many people buy an access point from a local retailer and connect it to the router. Either way, this device provides wireless Internet access to everyone in the home (and unfortunately also to the neighbors if it is not secured).

The wireless access point is both a transmitter and receiver of wireless signals and provides the connection point between the wireless device and the Internet. Out of the box the access point will typically work, but to secure and optimize its use, some configuration is typically required. The best place to start with this is the *Service Set Identifier (SSID)* or the network name. This is needed to connect to a wireless access point, and all client systems must choose the correct SSID to connect to the wireless network. Figure 12.5 shows the wireless network configuration parameters that are available on wireless routers manufactured by ASUS.

SSID configuration parameters include the following:

SSID　Perhaps you have been on vacation or in a coffee shop and have seen a list of wireless networks. Or perhaps at home you see all of the other wireless networks in the neighborhood. These are all SSIDs. Client devices must choose the correct SSID to log onto the network. In Figure 12.5, the SSID is Th3G33ks24. All devices in that area need to select Th3G33ks24 in order to get onto that wireless network.

SSID Broadcast　When you see lists of other wireless networks available, it is because SSID broadcast is enabled on the wireless access point. *Broadcast* simply means to display the SSID publicly. If the broadcast is not enabled, the name of the wireless network will not be displayed or shown as a wireless access point option on your device. However, you can disable the SSID broadcast and still connect wireless devices to it because you know the name, but this practice is not recommended because it lowers the security of your wireless network.

FIGURE 12.5   Wireless configuration parameters on an ASUS router

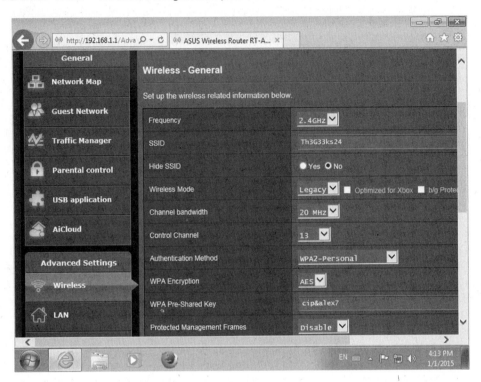

Configuring the security on a wireless network is an important task. An unsecured network may allow anyone to use your Internet connection. At best, they would then get Internet access for free; at worst, they could use your Internet connection for some unscrupulous activity, and you would be stuck with the consequences. Skilled hackers can also break into other computers and devices on your network and steal precious data. Even secured wireless networks are not immune to attacks. If a network is secured with poor encryption or a poor password, a skilled hacker can listen to the signals sent between a wireless network and its devices, analyze them, and steal the data that is being transferred.

Changing How You Authenticate to Wireless Access Points

The first way to secure your network is to configure the *authentication* for the wireless access point. Every access point is secured with a username and password, and every wireless router ships with a generic username and password like admin/admin. Changing this is critical for security. All generic usernames and passwords are readily available online for anyone to see, so when you first get a wireless device like a router, take the time to change these settings.

Most people do not access their router settings on a regular basis and therefore forget the username or password. If this happens, the access points have a reset button typically located on the side or bottom of the device. Press this to restore the device to its default factory settings.

WARNING Don't try this at home! Right now there are several wireless routers in my neighborhood using the manufacturer's original username and password. To access them I need only to type in the IP address of the wireless router in an Internet browser and search out the manufacturer's generic username and password online. Within minutes it is possible to have complete control of the neighbor's wireless router. If anyone in my neighborhood reads this book, this example is theoretical.

Setting the Encryption for Your Wireless Network

Encryption is a key part of wireless security and fortunately not difficult to configure on residential access points (APs). Essentially, encryption is the process of encoding messages or information in such a way that data is difficult or impossible to read should the wrong person get hold of it. Decrypting is the process of returning the data to its original form so it can be understood. There are plenty of protocols in the networking world to encrypt data, and in the wireless world the two primary encryption systems are Wired Equivalent Privacy (WEP) and Wi-Fi Protected Access (WPA).

WEP is the original wireless security standard, and it was designed to provide wireless networks with an equivalent level of security available with wired networking. With WEP a data packet that's sent is encrypted from the sending device all the way to the receiving device. In this way, if someone were to eavesdrop or capture the data in transmission, it could not be easily read. In a short time, WEP proved to be inadequate for complete wireless security. WEP security could be cracked, that is, read, with freely available online utilities.

WPA and *WPA2* were developed as enhancements to WEP security. WPA provided enhanced data encryption using something called the *Temporal Key Integrity Protocol (TKIP)*. A detailed discussion of TKIP is not required for the IC3 exam; however, it is important to know that TKIP is the protocol used to increase WPA security for wireless transmissions. It does this by creating a new 128-bit encryption key for each data packet. Like many other security technologies, WPA and TKIP have a few shortcomings. As a result WPA2 was developed. WPA2 uses a protocol known as Counter Mode with Cipher Block Chaining Message Authentication Code Protocol (CCMP) to replace TKIP. Further, WPA2 can use the Advanced Encryption Standard (AES) for additional security. This all may sound confusing when looking at configuring your wireless network security. The following summarizes the security options in order of most to least effective:

- WPA2 and AES
- WPA and AES
- WPA and TKIP/AES
- WPA and TKIP
- WEP
- No security

Security Networks with Firewalls and Gateways

Security is an essential consideration for today's networks, and when it comes to network security, *firewalls* and *gateways* play an integral role as part of a security plan for any network.

The function of a firewall is easy to understand but often complex to configure and maintain. A firewall can be either a hardware or software device that controls and protects data coming into and out of a network. To do this, firewalls are typically placed on the perimeter of the network to prevent intrusion from the outside. Figure 12.6 shows where a firewall would be located in a network.

FIGURE 12.6   The location of a firewall in a network

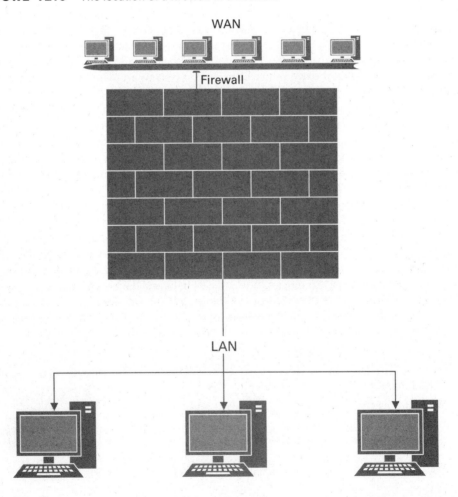

A *gateway* in a network can be used for many different roles and functions. We will describe this concept later on in this chapter, after you become familiar with the firewall concept.

Using a Firewall

The firewall is a method used to control and monitor incoming and outgoing network access. It is the job of the firewall to prevent unauthorized network traffic, both from outside users and from inside network users. All data packets sent to and from the network pass through the firewall, and all of this data is checked to see whether it is allowed for transfer.

A firewall can even look inside a packet of data to determine if the contents are what they say they are. Although the most common use of a firewall is that of protecting the boundary of an organization's network, some companies use firewalls internally as well. This approach is commonly used to protect areas of the network that may contain sensitive data, such as research or accounting data. In this way, security perimeters can be set up inside a network to protect sensitive areas.

Modern operating systems include a software firewall that has some limited capability and wireless routers with firewall capabilities. Figure 12.7 shows the firewall settings that are available on a wireless router manufactured by ASUS.

FIGURE 12.7   Firewall settings available on an ASUS wireless router

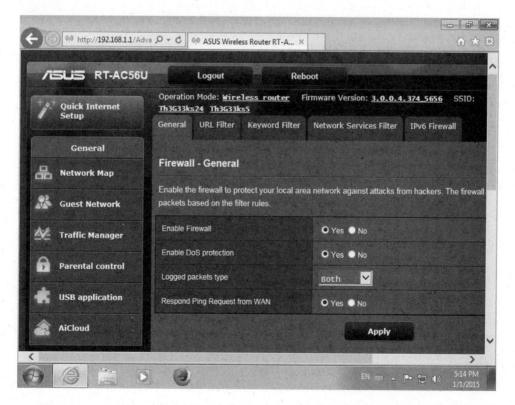

> If you go to your workplace and want to "like" something on Facebook, update Twitter, or spend some time on Tumblr, you may be out of luck. These and other websites may not be part of your company's work environment. How does the company restrict access to these and other sites? This is another function of the firewall. By using the firewall, the company can restrict access to the entire Web or just portions of it.

When you configure a firewall, you need to know which ports are assigned to the various protocols. The networking protocol we use, TCP/IP, is actually a protocol suite with numerous individual protocols combining to create the entire TCP/IP suite. Each of these services within TCP/IP has a port association. As an example, HTTP is a TCP/IP protocol and uses port 80. When a web browser requests a web page, the request is sent through port 80 on the target system and returned to the requester using the same port. During communication, the target port is checked to see which protocol or service is the intended destination. The request is then forwarded to that protocol or service.

A *port* is essentially a doorway that one of the protocols uses. If we block the port, the associated service will be unavailable. Therefore, if we block port 80, all web-browsing traffic is blocked because it goes through that port; 65,535 ports are available. These are broken down into three distinct designations:

Well-known ports: 1–1023

Registered ports: 1024–49151

Dynamic ports: 49152–65535

Fortunately, on the exam you will not need to know how all these ports are assigned, but you may need to know commonly used TCP/IP port assignments and the service associated with those ports.

Table 12.1 shows some common TCP/IP services and their associated port and purpose.

TABLE 12.1   Common port numbers and their purpose

Protocol	Port	Purpose
File Transfer Protocol (FTP)	21	Large file transfers
Hypertext Transfer Protocol (HTTP)	80	Web browsing
Hypertext Transfer Protocol Secure (HTTPS)	443	Used for secure browsing, such as banking sites
Post Office Protocol version 3 (POP3)	110	Downloading email from a server
Domain Name System (DNS)	53	Hostname resolution
Simple Mail Transfer Protocol (SMTP)	25	Sending email

Understanding the Gateway Concept

Defining exactly what the function of a *gateway* is can be difficult, not because of the complexity of the topic but because a gateway can be used for different roles. It is one of the terms that can be used to describe several functions. For the most part, however, the function of the network gateway is to convert one thing into another or provide access from one system to another. If that sounds a little vague, it's supposed to. *Gateway* is a term that can apply to a number of scenarios.

For example, a gateway server can act in the conversion of a protocol, allowing dissimilar networks to communicate. One practical application for such a gateway is allowing information to be passed between Macintosh-based and PC-based networks. The gateway translates protocols—from AppleTalk to TCP/IP.

Translating protocols is only one possible application for a gateway. A network gateway is also a doorway to another network. When you log onto the Internet from home or work, you will be using a gateway to make the transition from one network to the other. For example, at work it is likely that a server acting as a gateway, often a function of a firewall server, will be forwarding your client requests for retrieving web pages to the appropriate websites.

Measuring the Speed of Your Internet Connection

It's hard to imagine life without the Internet. In the workplace it is used for everything from videoconferencing to email, connecting remote users, marketing, research, and more. At home we rely on the Internet to stay in touch with family and friends using social media, pay bills online, plan trips, and shop from the comfort of an armchair.

In any business environment, it is important to be able to access data and applications quickly. As more businesses move services and data into the *cloud*, the speed at which this information can be accessed becomes very critical.

Similarly at home, watching movies, streaming video, and more all require a certain amount of consistent and reliable Internet access. So how does the Internet provide adequate and timely access to the increasing demand for more and more applications? The first thing you need to understand is how Internet capacity is measured.

When you see Internet capacity advertised by an *Internet service provider (ISP)*, you may see it measured in kilobits per second (Kbps), megabits per second (Mbps), and even gigabits per second (Gbps). A *bit* refers to a single unit of information sent in a communication stream, which is represented in binary as a 1 or a 0. Kilo means 1,000; mega 1,000,000; and giga 1,000,000,000. Therefore, Kbps represents 1,000 bits per second transfer rate; mega refers to 1,000,000 bits per second, and so on.

You also see transfer rates listed as kilobytes per second (KBps), megabytes per second (MBps), and gigabytes per second (GBps). A byte is equivalent to 8 bits, and 1 KBps is the equivalent of 1,000 bytes per second. This may sound incredibly fast, and that much data moving at that speed really is amazing. However, depending on what you are doing on the Internet or any other network, it may not be fast enough. Table 12.2 compares transfer speeds.

TABLE 12.2   Comparing transfer rates

Measurement	Also Known As	Transfer Rate
1 Kbps	kbps, kbit/s, kb/s	1,000 bits per second
1 Mbps	mbps, mbit/s, mb/s	1,000,000 bits per second
1 Gbps	gbps, gbit/s, gb/s	1,000,000,000 bits per second
1 KBps	kBps, kB/s	1000 bytes per second
1 MB/s	MBps	1,000,000 bytes per second
1 GB/s	GBps	1,000,000,000 bytes per second

So how do these transfer rates affect what you do at home and work? Let's suppose you have an ISP offering 10 Mbps download for $30 per month, 25 Mbps download for $40, 50 Mbps for $55, and 100 Mbps for $100. How much do you need to spend to get the right access level? It all depends on how many users are connected, what the Internet is used for, and how many devices are on at the same time.

In general, more bandwidth is better, but paying for unused capacity is not good practice, especially in the workplace. Table 12.3 approximates how differing speeds will impact the wait times for what you do on the Internet.

TABLE 12.3   Transmission speeds and approximate Internet response times

Download	56 KBps	2 MBps	10 MBps	25 MBps
Website (300 KB)	42s	1s	<1s	<1s
Download PowerPoint presentation (2 MB)	4m 42s	7s	1s	<1s
Image from digital camera (6 MB)	14m 17s	23s	4s	1s
Complete music CD (650 MB)	25h 47m 37s	42m 17s	8m 40s	3m 23s
Movie (1.5 GB)	59h 31m 25s	1h 37m 39s	20m	7m 48s

Bandwidth vs. Data Throughput

Imagine buying a car that advertised an amazing 60 miles per gallon. Now imagine driving this car from Spokane to Seattle. Would you expect to get 60 MPG for the entire trip? Probably not. More likely, your actual gas mileage would be much less due to idling in the city, going up hills, and extra weight in the vehicle. In fact, unless you were going downhill with a tail wind, you may not hit 60 MPG even once.

This is a little like bandwidth. Bandwidth represents the maximum capacity of a medium and correlates to the total amount of data that is possible to traverse that medium in theoretical ideal conditions. So your Internet service provider may advertise an 8 MBps upload capacity and a 40 MBps download capacity for your Internet connection, but other factors prevent this from happening. So if you send data from Spokane to Seattle, don't expect the advertised speed from start to finish. Data throughput, on the other hand, is defined as the successful movement of data from one location to another in a specified period of time. So you may have 8 MBps capacity but an actual data throughput of 5–7 MBps for your Internet.

Factors Limiting the Speed of Your Internet Connection

Even with a 10 MBps or 20 MBps Internet connection, you may find that your response times are too slow or slower than normal at certain times. There are many factors that can decrease Internet access times and have you wondering if your Internet service is adequate.

The following is a list of five things you can do if your Internet is lagging:

Talk to your ISP.   It may be that your Internet usage is too high for the Internet connection package you have purchased. If you stream video, download significant data, or more, your current package may not suffice. If you are a heavy user at work or at home, your monthly costs can be quite high.

Check your applications.   Many applications that run in the background may be using valuable bandwidth. Windows updates, Skype, and the like may be working in the background limiting resources. You can always turn them off when not in use. Also, the number of Internet browsers or tabs you have open may also affect the resources.

Many applications such as Skype may start up automatically when the computer boots up. For some applications it is a good practice to turn the autostart feature off. However, for background applications such virus scanners, it's best to leave those set to autostart but schedule their updates for a time when they are unlikely to interfere with Internet use. Remember to close down unneeded browser tabs. It is a good practice to streamline this by adjusting the browser to open only a couple of tabs at the same time.

Share your bandwidth.   Many households have tablets, smartphones, laptops, desktops, and gaming consoles all operating at the same time. Your Internet is a shared resource, and this type of heavy use can slow down the connection. In this case you may need to increase available bandwidth with a different package from the Internet service provider.

Check for viruses and malware.   If you notice a sudden drop in Internet and overall computer response times, you may have a virus or malware problem. These programs can work in the background accessing the Internet and generally tie up system resources. Keep your antivirus software up to date and ensure it autoscans your system.

Maintain your system.   Poor performance, not enough memory, a full hard disk, and other general system state issues can certainly reduce your computer's ability to process online requests. General system maintenance is required to keep your system efficient and functioning.

When you look at the properties of your Internet connection in Windows, it tells you the maximum speed that is supported by your connection. However, it won't tell you how fast your actual data transfers are right now. This can be measured using all kinds of applications and online services. One of the most popular websites for measuring the speed of your Internet connection is http://www.speedtest.net. This website automatically tracks your location, chooses a test server that's close to you, and then downloads and uploads data to it. At the end, you are shown the actual speed of those data transfers, and you can compare them with what your ISP promised you in terms of speed.

Wireless Networking Standards and Speeds

An organization known as the Institute of Electrical and Electronics Engineers (IEEE) is responsible for the development of networking standards. These standards determine the speed of a network, the type of media used, and more. In the wireless networking world, the IEEE 802.11 wireless standards are the ones commonly used.

Under the 802.11 standards a number of wireless specifications are identified. These include 802.11a, 802.11b, 802.11g, 802.11n, and 802.11ac. Each of these has its own speeds and characteristics. When configuring your wireless router, you may need to choose one. Table 12.4 shows the characteristics of the 802.11 specifications.

TABLE 12.4   802.11 wireless standards

802.11 Standard	Speed	Transmission Range
802.11a	1 to 2 Mbps	20 feet indoors
802.11b	Up to 11 Mbps	Up to 150 feet indoors
802.11g	Up to 54 Mbps	Up to 150 feet indoors
802.11n	Up to 600 Mbps	175+ feet indoors
802.11ac	Up to 2600 Mbps	175+ feet indoors

Not all of these standards are compatible with each other. To access a wireless network, the client system must use the same wireless standard as the access point. If a wireless device was not designed to work with wireless networks using a certain standard, that device won't be able to identify and connect to wireless networks using that standard.

Even if a wireless standard advertises 54 Mbps or 2600 Mbps, it is a difficult benchmark to reach. Wireless signals are susceptible to a range of interferences. In the home there are plenty of potential wireless interference causes and even more in a work environment. The following is a list of some of the common wireless interference trouble spots:

Radio Frequency Interference   Certain 802.11 wireless standards use a radio frequency of 2.4 GHz. Normally this is not a problem, but many other devices around the house including cordless phones and microwave ovens can also use the range of 2.4 GHz. This can cause significant interference with the wireless signal.

Physical Objects   Physical objects can cause a real problem with wireless signals. Trees, concrete walls, buildings, mirrors, and so on, can prevent wireless signals from traveling through them. Troubleshooting wireless signals will often require checking the location of the wireless access point to verify that physical objects are not causing the wireless signal problems.

Environmental Conditions   Wireless signals that have to travel outside the house can experience integrity loss due to lightning, heavy fog, rain, wind, and so on.

Understanding the Different Types of Internet Connections

While most of us use the Internet daily, the way we access it may vary. Not many years ago, dial-up access was king. Dial-up was a reliable method of Internet access, but as web pages became more complex and communication needs increased, dial-up access was just too slow.

However, there are people today who are still using dial-up either because their Internet needs are very basic (checking the occasional email, for example) or because they live in an area where higher-speed Internet options are not available.

Today, many homes and business use broadband Internet access, which is often provided by an ISP. In this section we look at the various Internet access methods starting with a closer look at dial-up service.

Dial-up Internet Access

Dial-up, also known as *plain old telephone service (POTS)*, is the oldest and slowest form of Internet access. While it is too slow for most applications today, it may be used where no other option is available and sometimes as a backup Internet access option should another method fail. Even so, dial-up has a maximum speed of either 56 Kbps or 128 Kbps, which is far too slow for day-to-day Internet use.

Internet access using a dial-up connection needs a few things to make the connection happen. Key components include the following:

Hardware   In order to access the remote dial-up server, the client system must have the correct hardware installed to make the connection. Most dial-up remote connections require a modem on the client and a server to connect to. The modem is responsible for converting digital signals to analog that can travel over traditional phone lines. The dial-up server is at one end of the connection and authenticates the client request to establish the dial-up link.

Phone Line/Number   To connect to a remote access server over a dial-up connection, you need to have the phone number of the remote server, the IP address or the hostname, and of course a phone line. When the Internet is connected, the phone is not available for regular voice communication.

Transmission Protocols   You will have to choose the transmission protocol (TCP/IP) and security protocols used by the remote server. This configuration falls outside of the scope of IC3, but it's enough to know that properly configured protocols are required. The transmissions protocols are used to ensure that the systems communicate with each other, and the security protocols ensure that communication is protected. The provider provides settings for both, which are configured on the client system.

Security   On the client system, you may need to establish security information so it can be authenticated by the server. The security information includes a username and password combination to be verified by the remote server and data-encryption options.

If anyone has ever used a dial-up connection or continues to do so, you will certainly know that it doesn't always connect. Fortunately there are only a few areas to check to find where the problem lies. These include the following:

- Verify that you have correct authentication information. To access the remote access server, you require a valid username and password for the remote network and permissions to access the server.

- Confirm that you are calling the correct number or trying to connect to the correct server. Oftentimes, connection issues are traced to something simple, and in the case of dial-up, they can be caused by using the wrong phone number. If you are expecting beeps and other sounds and you hear "hello," check the number.

- Check all physical connections. Is the phone jack plugged into the modem?
- Check for a dial tone. This is as easy as picking up the phone and listening.

If all else fails, keep the number to your provider handy. They have trained technicians who can resolve most issues quickly.

Broadband Internet Access

As far as Internet connectivity goes, broadband is a very popular choice. *Broadband* refers to high-speed Internet access that includes cable, digital subscriber line (DSL), wireless broadband, and satellite Internet. Broadband technologies allow businesses and home users access to bandwidth-intensive applications such as videoconferencing, online gaming, streaming audio, and much more. Unlike dial-up connections where dialing into an ISP is required every time you want Internet access, broadband is largely an always-on service.

For example, DSL Internet access uses a standard phone line to provide high-speed access. In fact, DSL technologies offer phone and data transmissions over a standard phone line, but unlike dial-up you can make a phone call while using the Internet. To connect to home DSL broadband, a standard phone cable is plugged into the phone wall jack and to the DSL router provided by the ISP. A modern DSL router has multiple physical ports that devices can be plugged into, but more importantly for today's users, it has wireless capability.

Whether wired or wireless, the DSL router can automatically assign IP addresses and allow multiple devices in the home access to the Internet. Depending on your area, you can buy Internet access plans from 1.5 Mbps to 50 Mbps and up.

Cable Internet access is a robust access method available from most cable TV providers. Cable Internet access is an attractive option to home users and businesses because it is both reliable and cost effective. Internet access requires a router provided by the cable provider and uses a coaxial cable connection. Like DSL, cable Internet is an always-on connection. That means that as long as your computer is on, it's connected to the Internet. Both cable and DSL offer a range of packages for both home and business use, and both have far slower upload speeds than download speeds.

DSL and cable are attractive Internet access technologies but unfortunately are not available everywhere. Satellite offers an access alternative that is a bit more costly but can be accessed from virtually anywhere. With satellite Internet, download speeds are considerably faster than upload speeds, and the packages get expensive quickly. For example, for a 300 Kbps upload and a 2 Mbps download, depending on the provider, you may have to pay between $130 and $160 per month. Satellite access requires a special dish that mounts on the outside of the building to communicate with a satellite, and the information is transmitted between devices. Satellite broadband has some special communication considerations that DSL and cable do not, including the following:

Line of Sight Satellite access is a line-of-sight technology, meaning that the satellite dish you have must have some degree of sight between the sending and receiving devices. Heavy cloud cover and other weather can cause Internet interruption.

Rain Fade   Rain fade refers to signal interference caused by moisture in the atmosphere. It generally takes a significant amount of moisture and the interruption is over quickly, but it can happen.

Latency   As you can imagine, it is a long way from a dish on the side of a house to a satellite in space. Latency refers to the time it takes a signal to travel. If the latency is too high, requests may time out and the communication may fail. As with rain fade, high latency can be an issue from time to time, but it is just part of using satellite Internet.

Satellite is more costly and slower than both cable and DSL, but it does provide access where the others do not.

Broadband Warning

Broadband Internet access is often an always-on service. Unlike dial-up, where a connection must be made every time to connect to the service, broadband such as DSL and cable is just waiting for us to use it. This means that when you are away from the computer, your system could be accessing the Internet for updates or other reasons. Unfortunately, today's operating systems and applications may have security holes that can be exploited. Combine this with an always-on technology and problems may arise.

To help combat this, it is important to use a firewall between you and the Internet to help protect your system from unwanted visitors. There are software firewalls that are part of the operating system, and the routers that are used with cable and DSL provide some firewall features. Another important security must is to ensure your operating system and applications are up to date with the latest security patches. Most applications have automatic updates, but this option must be enabled.

Today, part of the responsibility of owning and using a computer at home or work is to have a basic understanding of security and security threats. Without it, you could find yourself vulnerable.

Virtual Private Networks

In the mid-1990s Cisco, IBM, and Microsoft began working on a new technology known as *tunneling*. Essentially, the tunneling technology uses special protocols to create a point-to-point connection for data to be transported over a public network. *Virtual private networks (VPNs)* use tunneling to establish links over a public network such as the Internet or even a public switched telephone network (PSTN). VPNs are widely used in the business world to securely connect mobile users to the corporate network. With their help, the employees of a company can connect to the company network while they are traveling or when working from home.

The advantages of using a VPN link is that it can create a secure and economical connection between remote users and a corporate network. Without a VPN option, it may be necessary to install and maintain your own hardware to create such a link. A VPN allows you to use the hardware and software of the Internet to do the same thing. Figure 12.8 shows a visual overview of VPN connectivity.

FIGURE 12.8 VPN connectivity overview

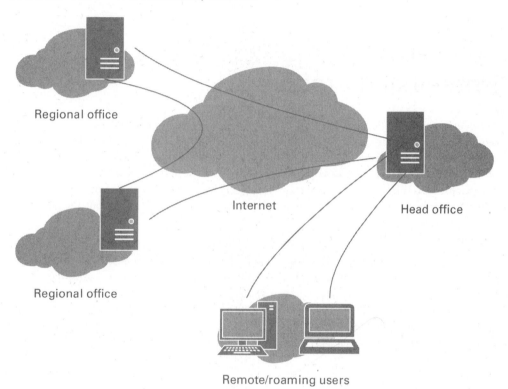

Other advantages offered by VPN connections are that they can be used to bypass region restrictions imposed by some websites or services (e.g. Netflix, Hulu), they provide better security than normal Internet connections, and they can be used to hide your real online identity.

Most operating system software today, including that on tablets and smartphones, has VPN capability built in. In addition to the client-side software required to establish a VPN, the following are all parts of establishing a VPN connection:

VPN Servers The VPN server is at one end of the connection and authenticates the client request to establish the VPN link.

VPN Clients   A VPN client can be any remote system such as a laptop, smartphone, tablet, or other device that has VPN client software installed.

Tunneling Protocols   As mentioned earlier, VPN connections use tunneling protocols to create the point-to-point link over a public network. The tunneling protocols include the Point-to-Point Tunneling Protocol (PPTP) and the Layer 2 Tunneling Protocol (L2TP).

Public WAN   The VPN link is established over the Internet.

Principles for Troubleshooting Networking Problems

Troubleshooting can be very complex, since hardware, software, protocols, and more combine to create a sea of settings, configurations, and switches. Despite the different approaches to troubleshooting and the complexity of technologies, some basic troubleshooting guidelines can be applied in most scenarios. Naturally, the exact approach to troubleshooting a situation will vary depending on many elements such as urgency, number of users affected, the type of problem, and many more, but the general guidelines apply.

So in a nutshell, here are five troubleshooting rules:

Rule #1: Get the Right Information   It may sound unusual, but some people start clicking around changing settings without really understanding the problem. Critical information can be gathered from computer users, system log files, other administrators, or error messages generated by the system. In your information gathering you are looking to answer several questions, including these:

- Who does the problem affect?
- What computers are affected?
- What was the computer doing at the time of failure?
- How often does the problem happen?
- What has been done in the past to try to fix the problem?

Answers to questions like these really help pinpoint the location of the error and help ensure an accurate and timely response to troubleshooting.

Rule #2: Keep It Simple   Networks, hardware, and software can be very complex, but the solution to most troubleshooting issues is often the simplest. If you are troubleshooting a situation where you cannot log onto the Internet at home, make sure that the cables are attached and check to see if the power is on at the wireless router before you try anything else. You may make the situation worse if you change settings or modify the system when what you really needed to do was plug something in.

Rule #3: Establish What Has Changed   Seldom does a computer stop working on its own. Often when you get into the troubleshooting you will find that an application was recently installed, a new device was added, something was uninstalled, or an upgrade was performed. The point is, if you can isolate a recent change of settings, either hardware or software, this is a great place to start.

Rule #4: Test the Results   It may happen that you fix something and leave before testing it or do not test thoroughly and the problem persists. It is really important to test a system or device to verify that the fix has worked and that in fact you have not made the situation worse.

Rule #5: Document the Solution   Documentation is as important as any of the other troubleshooting steps. If a problem happens once, it may happen again; the difference is, the next time the problem happens you can simply refer to your documentation and apply the fix. Unfortunately, proper documentation is very low on many troubleshooters' list of priorities.

So with some general guidelines, we can now look at some of the common tools you can use to troubleshoot systems.

Troubleshooting Network Problems with the Help of Windows Troubleshooting Tools

To make troubleshooting easier, Windows 7 includes a set of wizards that you can use to help fix all kinds of problems: programs that don't work well, problems with hardware, issues with the network and the Internet, and so on.

These wizards are found in the Control Panel and can be used by anyone. When a wizard runs, it checks for problems in the specific area you have chosen, and if problems are identified, it proposes solutions that can fix those problems. By following the recommendation of a troubleshooting wizard, you can actually fix many problems that may arise during everyday computing activities.

To help you learn how these troubleshooting wizards work, in Exercise 12.1 you will learn how to use the Internet Connections troubleshooting wizard that specializes in fixing problems that are related to Internet connectivity. Other wizards work in a similar manner.

EXERCISE 12.1

Using the Internet Connections Troubleshooting Wizard

1. Click Start, Control Panel, and then the Find And Fix Problems link found in the System And Security section (Figure 12.9).

FIGURE 12.9   The Find And Fix Problems link in the Control Panel

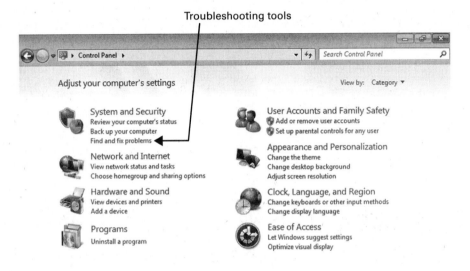

The list of available troubleshooting wizards is shown (Figure 12.10).

2. Click Network And Internet and then Internet Connections.

The troubleshooting wizard with the same name opens (Figure 12.11).

3. Click Next (Figure 12.11) and wait for the wizard to detect problems.

It will give you a list of suggestions.

FIGURE 12.10   The link to the Internet Connections troubleshooting wizard

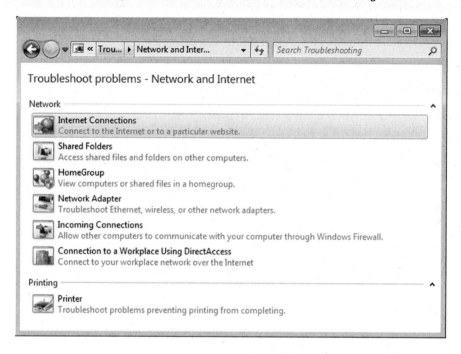

FIGURE 12.11   The Internet Connections troubleshooting wizard

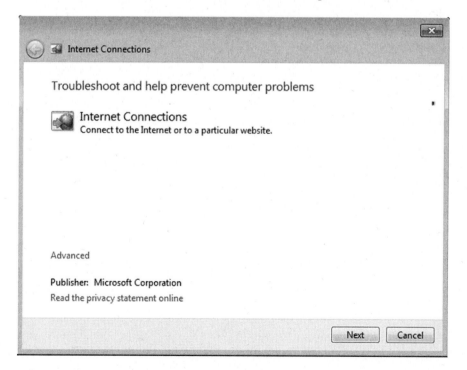

4. Click Troubleshoot My Connection To The Internet (Figure 12.12), and wait for the wizard to make its diagnostics and propose solutions.

FIGURE 12.12 Troubleshooting suggestions

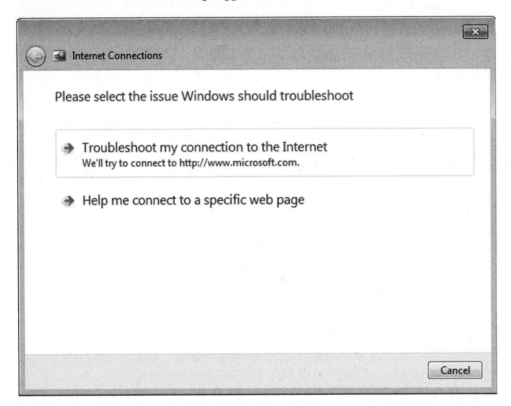

5. Follow the instructions proposed by the troubleshooting wizard and then click Check To See If The Problem Is Fixed (Figure 12.13).

FIGURE 12.13 Checking to see if the problem is fixed

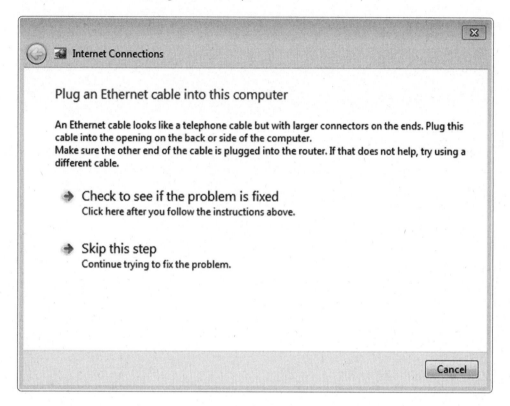

EXERCISE 12.1 *(continued)*

6. The troubleshooting wizard will verify whether the problem is fixed and show you a summary of its findings (Figure 12.14).

FIGURE 12.14   The summary shown by the Internet Connections troubleshooting wizard

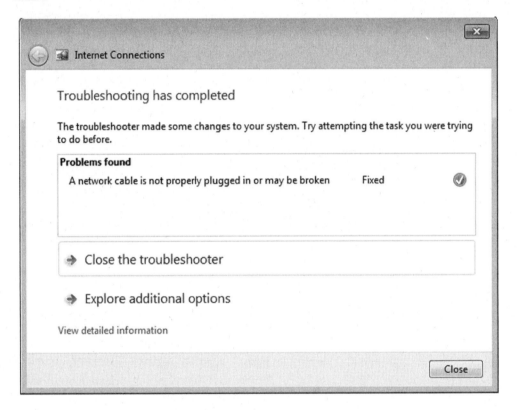

7. Click Close.

Troubleshooting Network Problems from the Command Prompt

When troubleshooting network and Internet-related problems, it is often necessary to view, test, and configure the TCP/IP configuration of the system. For that reason, a complete suite of tools is supplied with Windows client systems. Most of these tools are used from the command prompt. To access the command line in a Windows client system, click Start ➤ All Programs ➤ Accessories ➤ Command Prompt. Alternatively, you can click Start, type **cmd**, and press Enter on your keyboard. This will open the command prompt utility, as shown in Figure 12.15.

FIGURE 12.15 The command prompt

You may need many command-line tools to troubleshoot the network configuration. The following are three of the more common command tools used for troubleshooting TCP/IP.

Ping

Of all the tools discussed here, ping is perhaps the most used and the most useful. The ping tool allows you to test the connectivity between two devices on the network. When the ping command is issued, special packets called echo packets are generated and sent to the remote system. If the remote host is able to respond to the packets, it returns each of them, and the ping utility on the system that generated the query displays the amount of time, in milliseconds, that it took to complete the round-trip. You can see an example of the output from a successful ping command in Figure 12.16.

FIGURE 12.16   Running the ping tool

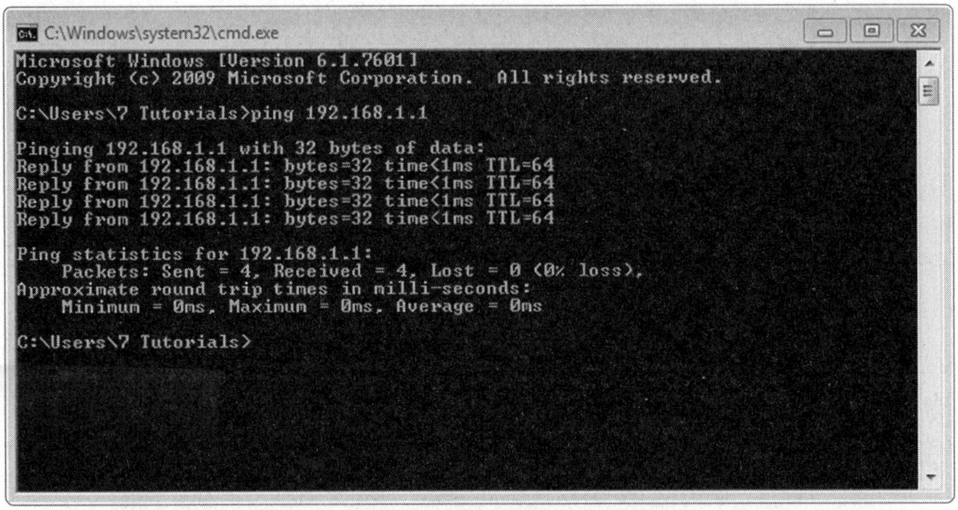

When using ping to locate a communication problem, there is a specific order in which to proceed. The following numbered steps define the process normally taken, but it is possible to skip straight to the last step and then, if that doesn't work, work your way back to determine the location of the problem.

1. ping the address of the local loopback.

    The local loopback is a special function built into the TCP/IP stack that allows it to be tested. It is basically the internal IP address of your computer. You can use any valid address in IP address range of 127.0.0.1–127.254.254.254 in your test, although 127.0.0.1 is most commonly used. If the ping of the local loopback is successful, it indicates that TCP/IP is loaded correctly on your computer and bound to the network interface properly. What it does not test is the physical network connectivity of the system because the loopback is a software function.

2. ping the IP address of the computer you are testing.

    It tests the connectivity between your computer and another computer on the network.

3. ping the IP address of the default gateway.

    As well as testing that the TCP/IP configuration of your system is valid, this tests the physical connectivity.

4. ping a host on a remote network.

Tracert

When you are unable to access a remote computer whether on a local network or on the Internet, one tool that can assist in determining where the problem lies is the `tracert` command. The function of `tracert` is to trace the path to the destination IP address and record the results. The `tracert` display shows the succession of IP routers used in the delivery of packets and how long the process took. You can also use it to trace the path to a website on the Web. Figure 12.17 shows the output of a `tracert` command.

FIGURE 12.17   Running the `tracert` command

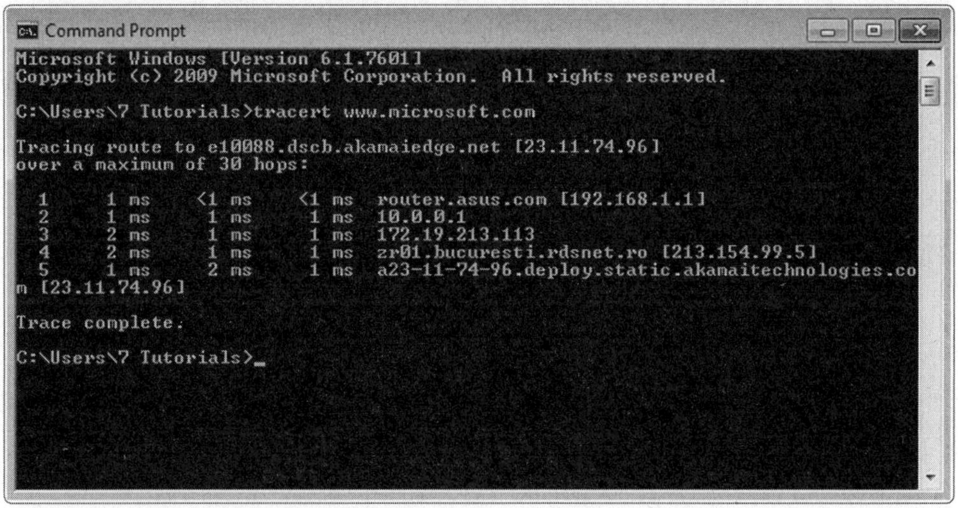

As far as troubleshooting with `tracert` is concerned, as the path to the destination IP address is traced, the command will display the last router that successfully forwarded the data packets. Such information is helpful in pinpointing where the communication failure is.

Ipconfig

The `ipconfig` command is the troubleshooter's main tool. `Ipconfig` is a Windows utility that is used to show the IP configuration of a machine on the network. The `ipconfig` command will display configuration information for all network cards installed within the system. Figure 12.18 shows the output screen from an ipconfig command.

FIGURE 12.18   Running the ipconfig command

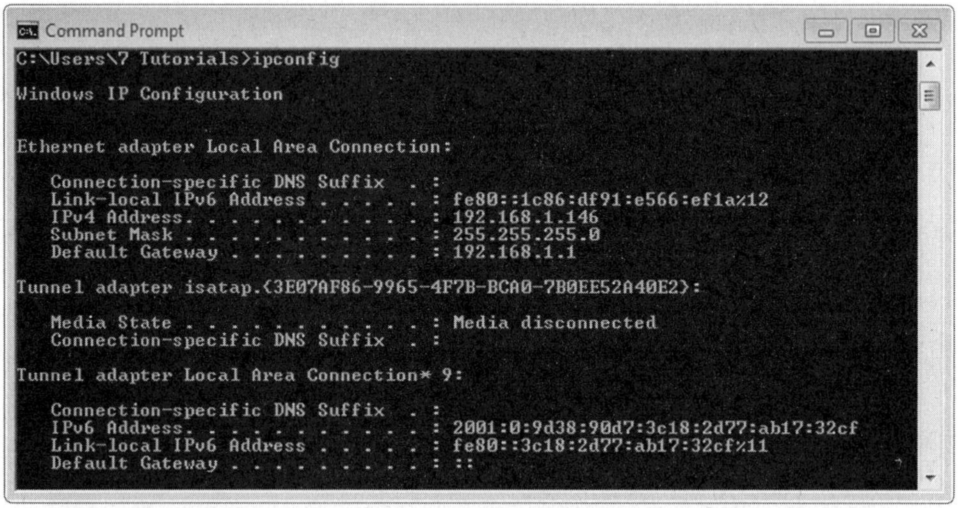

The information provided includes the IP address, subnet mask, current default gateway, MAC address, and more. The ipconfig command is often used with the /all switch, which provides additional information including the DNS configuration and the MAC address of the interface and whether DHCP is enabled.

All commands have a number of switches that can be used, but ipconfig has three very important ones for troubleshooting:

ipconfig /all   Used to review all TCP/IP information on a system

ipconfig /renew   Releases all TCP/IP information and then gets new DHCP information from the server

ipconfig /release   Releases all TCP/IP information

Table 12.5 summarizes these tools and others that are available for TCP/IP troubleshooting.

renew = DHCP

TABLE 12.5   TCP/IP troubleshooting utilities

Command-Line Utility	Function
ARP	Shows the Address Resolution Protocol table for the local system
ipconfig /all	Shows entire IP configuration information on a system
ping	Used to test connectivity between two devices on the network
route	Displays a copy of the local routing table for the system and provides the ability to modify the local routing table
netsh	Allows you to configure a computer's network remotely or locally
tracert	Tracks and displays the entire route between two systems

Summary

In this chapter we covered a lot of ground and explained concepts like LANs, WANs, IP addresses, VPNs, and others. While it may all seem very technical to you, the basics are simpler than you think, and you should not have any issues with learning them. Yes, computer networking is a very complex and advanced topic, but for the IC3 exam, you won't need to go into a lot of detail. What we have covered here is more than enough.

Security is very important in the world of networks, so we also showed the basics that you should keep in mind when securing a wireless network.

Then we discussed how speed is measured on the Internet, the factors that limit the speed of your Internet connection, and what to pay attention to when choosing an offer from an ISP for an Internet connection.

Finally, we discussed the basic troubleshooting tools that you can use to identify and solve problems with network and Internet connectivity. Some of them are easy to use and don't require any technical background from your side. Check them out, experiment with them, and learn how they work. They will surely come in handy at some point.

In the next chapter we will cover a friendlier topic that's less technical and a lot more fun: communicating over the Internet, using media like email, chat, and telepresence.

Exam Essentials

Understand LANs and WANS.   You should know the most common types of computer networks that you can encounter and what's different about them.

Know what an IP address is and what it does.   One of the most important concepts in computer networks is the IP address. You should know what it is, what it does, and how an IP address is assigned.

Learn the best practices for securing networks.   Security is very important in computer networks. You should learn the basics of securing a wireless network as well as how to secure networks in general with the help of firewalls and gateways.

Know how to measure the speed of your Internet connection.   Many ISPs promise fast Internet connections, but most of them are not as fast as advertised. You should know how speed is measured on the Internet as well as the factors that can limit the speed of your connection.

Know what a virtual private network is.   VPNs are widely used in business environments. You should know what they are and why they are useful.

Learn how to troubleshoot networking problems.   Even though you are not a network administrator or an IT professional, you can troubleshoot and fix basic problems that are related to network and Internet connectivity. You should learn the basic tools that are available in Windows and how you can use them to fix problems.

Key Terms

Before you take the exam, be certain you are familiar with the following terms:

802.11	Internet Protocol (IP)
Advanced Encryption Standard (AES)	Internet service provider (ISP)
authentication	IP address
bit	local area network (LAN)
broadband	plain old telephone service (POTS)
broadband Internet access	port
cloud	Service Set Identifier (SSID)
Counter Mode with Cipher Block Chaining Message Authentication Code Protocol (CCMP)	TCP/IP
dial-up	Temporal Key Integrity Protocol (TKIP)
Domain Name Service (DNS)	Transmission Control Protocol (TCP)
Dynamic Host Configuration Protocol (DHCP)	virtual private networks (VPNs)
firewalls	WEP
gateway	wide area networks (WANs)
Institute of Electrical and Electronics Engineers (IEEE)	wireless network
	WPA
	WPA2

Review Questions

1. Which of the following commands is used to display *all* of the IP configuration on a Windows system?

    A. ipconfig

    B. tracert

    C. ipconfig /all

    D. ping

2. What is the function of a VPN?

    A. Protect one network from another

    B. Encrypt data packets from the sending and receiving device

    C. Encrypt data packets from the receiving and sending device

    D. Create a point-to-point connection over a public network

3. What is result of blocking port 80 on a firewall?

    A. FTP is not available.

    B. HTTP and HTTPS are not available.

    C. HTTPS is not available.

    D. HTTP is not available.

4. How is IP configuration information assigned automatically?

    A. DNS

    B. DHCP   – IP config assigned automatically

    C. Subnet mask

    D. Gateway

5. During a troubleshooting procedure, you decide to ping Sybex.com and the IP address 208.215.179.132 is returned. What protocol manages this function?

    A. DNS

    B. DHCP

    C. Subnet mask

    D. tracert

6. You have just purchased a new wireless router and want to increase security. Which of the following offers the greatest level of security?

    A. TCP/IP

    B. WPA

    C. WEP

    D. WPA2

7. You are reviewing available wireless standards on your wireless router. Which of the following are valid 802.11 standards? (Choose all that apply.)

   A. 802.11ac

   B. 802.11cd

   C. 802.11t

   D. 802.11n

8. Which of the following are examples of LANs? (Choose all that apply.)

   A. A computer network on the floor of an office building

   B. The computer network of an international corporation

   C. The computer network in your house

   D. The Internet

9. Which troubleshooting wizard can help you diagnose and fix Internet connection problems?

   A. The Network Adapter troubleshooting wizard

   B. The Incoming Connections troubleshooting wizard

   C. The Internet Connections troubleshooting wizard

   D. The Shared Folders troubleshooting wizard

10. Which of the following are characteristics of broadband Internet access? (Choose all that apply.)

   A. An always-on Internet service

   B. An Internet connection with a maximum speed of either 56 Kbps or 128 Kbps

   C. Allows for bandwidth-intensive applications

   D. High-speed Internet access

Chapter

13

Communicating Online with Others

THE FOLLOWING IC3: LIVING ONLINE EXAM OBJECTIVES ARE COVERED IN THIS CHAPTER:

✓ **E-mail Communication**

- E-mail Account Settings
- Appropriate use of e-mail
- Managing e-mail communications

✓ **Real-Time-Communication**

- Text communication
- Audio Visual communication
- Telepresence (Social Media)

Now that you know what the Internet and the World Wide Web are, it is time to put them to good use. First, we will talk about email, what it is, and the basics of using it to communicate with others. We will also share some tips and tricks about how you could automate it and make your life easier in certain situations.

Then we will move on to other forms of online communication. First, we will show you how to communicate with others using text, with the help of technologies like SMS and chat services like Skype.

The beauty of the Internet is that you can also communicate with others using sound and video. With the right tools, you can easily turn your computer into a phone or a videoconferencing system. These subjects will also be covered in this chapter.

Finally, many people use social networks to keep in touch with friends, family, co-workers, and others. We will discuss the major social networks that are available today, how they can be useful, and how to protect your privacy when using them.

Sound like fun? Let's get started!

Creating and Securing Email Accounts

Electronic mail is a method of exchanging digital messages from an author to one or more recipients. This service is commonly referred to as *email* or *e-mail*. The storage and the delivery of email messages is handled by email servers that are specialized for this task. In order to send an email, you will need to have an email account registered with an email service. Email services are both public (for example, Gmail.com, Outlook.com, Yahoo.com) and private. Many businesses have their own internal email services that serve their employees and allow communication between them and with their business partners. An email address has the following format: username@domain name. One example is John.Smith@example.com, where John.Smith is the username, example.com is the domain name, and @ is a symbol for the word *at*. When creating an email account, you are asked to provide several details:

Your Name   This is the name that should be associated with your email account. If you are creating a business email account or a personal account that you want to use to communicate with others, you should use your real name. If you are using your email account only for subscribing to newsletters at several websites or for other miscellaneous uses, it is fine to provide a nickname or something else instead of your real name.

The Username   This is the name of the user account that you want to use. The username must be unique and not already chosen by other users of the same email service. You should try to use a username that represents you and is easily remembered by others.

The Password   You must have a password to authenticate to your email account. Short passwords are very easy to crack by hackers and security professionals. To keep your email account as safe as possible, you should use a password that contains at least eight characters and mixes letters with numbers and special characters like !, &, #, and so on. Also, you should use a mix of lowercase and uppercase letters.

Other Personal Details   Many email services ask for other personal details like your birthday, gender, mobile phone number, and other email addresses that you are using. This information may be used to identify you or to help you recover your password in case you forget it later on.

Password Recovery Information   Some email services ask you to select a method for recovering your password in case you forget it later on. Such methods include providing answers to more personal questions (for example, the name of your dog or the name of your school). You are asked to select the recovery method that you want to use before creating the email account and provide the necessary answers that will help you recover your password.

   In Figure 13.1 you can see the details that are asked when creating an email account with Gmail.com. As you can see, the email service automatically checks whether the username that you have provided is taken by others and returns the necessary warning, if applicable. Also, it analyzes the password that you have provided and lets you know whether your password is easy to guess, too short, or too weak. Always follow the recommendations that you receive, in order to be able to create an email account and generate a secure password for it.

FIGURE 13.1   Creating an email account with Gmail.com

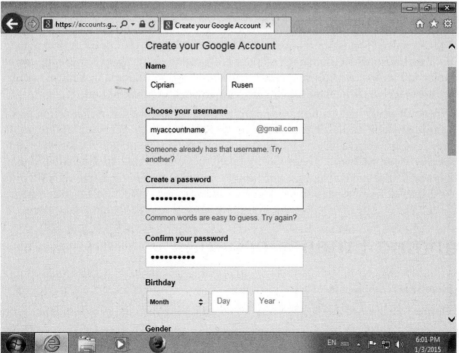

The username and the password are called *credentials*. They are the details that will be asked of you in order to authenticate to the email service that you are using.

There are three methods that you can use to increase the security of your email accounts:

- Create strong passwords.

  Strong passwords contain at least eight characters and mix letters with numbers and special characters like !, &, #, and so on. Here are a few examples of passwords that are both strong and easy to remember: This1sMyPa$$w0rd, HappyB1rthday, 1L0veCar$. As a general recommendation, do not use passwords that are easy to guess, like your birthday, your home address, your birthplace, and so on. Passwords should be long, memorable for you, and a mix of the types of characters mentioned earlier.

- Don't store your password in plain text and don't share it with others.

  Some people store their passwords in Microsoft Word documents or in text files on their computer. This practice is very insecure and makes it easy for others to access those files and learn your passwords. Instead, try to use professional services for storing, encrypting, and synchronizing passwords across computers and devices, like LastPass, RoboForm, 1Password, and others.

- Enable and use two-factor authentication when available.

  Two-factor authentication or *two-step verification* is a security process that involves two stages for verifying the identity of a person or entity that is trying to access a service of any kind (email, social networking, banking, and so on). This concept requires two or more of these three authentication factors: a knowledge factor, a possession factor, and an inherence factor.

  Traditional verification involves only one or two of the three factors mentioned earlier. For example, if you want to use a digital service like email, traditional verification involves knowing the username and the password. As we all know, knowledge can be stolen in a variety of ways, and people can learn both your username and password, use the same services as you do for all kinds of purposes, and pose as you.

  When using two-step verification, a third factor is added: the possession factor, usually your smartphone or mobile phone. This device is used for the second stage of verifying your identity. For example, when you sign in to your email account, you first provide your username and password. Then, you are asked to provide a time-based password that expires in 30 seconds. This password can be sent to your mobile phone via SMS or can be displayed by a mobile app like Google Authenticator or Microsoft Authenticator.

Sending Email Messages

Email messages consist of two major sections:

The Header   Each email message has one header, which is structured into the following fields:

   From   The email address and optionally the name of the author of the email message.

This field is automatically filled by the email service you are using with the details of your account.

To   The email address(es) and optionally name(s) of the message's recipient(s). You can send an email message to one or more recipients.

CC   The abbreviation means carbon copy. It indicates those who are to receive a copy of a message addressed primarily to another. The list of CCed recipients is visible to all other recipients of the message.

BCC   The abbreviation means blind carbon copy. This field is available for hidden notification. Recipients listed in the BCC field receive a copy of the message but are not shown any other recipients of the message, including other BCC recipients. By default, this field is hidden by email clients, but it can be enabled and used.

Subject   A brief summary of the topic of the message.

Date   The local time and date when the message was written. Most email clients fill this in automatically when sending the message. The recipient's client may then display the time in the format and time zone local to them.

The Body   This is the content of the message that you are sending, exactly the same as the body of a regular letter.

In Figure 13.2 you can see an example of an email message that's written and sent using Microsoft Outlook 2010. There you can see the standard fields that are shown by a typical email client: To, CC, Subject, and Body.

FIGURE 13.2   Writing an email message in Microsoft Outlook 2010

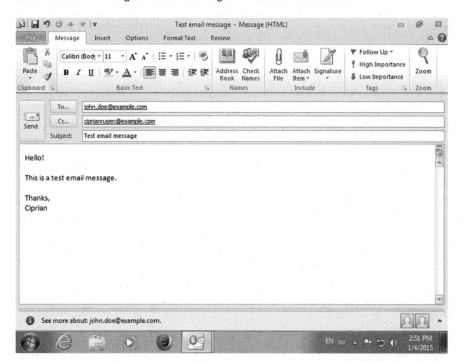

In Exercise 13.1 you will learn how to create and send a simple email message using Microsoft Outlook.

EXERCISE 13.1

Sending an Email Message in Microsoft Outlook

1. Click Start ➢ All Programs ➢ Microsoft Office ➢ Microsoft Outlook 2010.

2. Click the Home tab on the ribbon (Figure 13.3) and then the New E-mail button found in the New section.

FIGURE 13.3   The Home tab in Microsoft Outlook

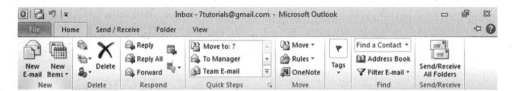

3. In the To field, complete the email address of a friend or family member.

4. In the Subject field, type the desired subject.

5. In the body area, type a message that you want to send to that person.

6. Click the Send button and wait for the email to be sent.

7. Close Microsoft Outlook.

Attaching Files to Email Massages

You can also attach one or more files to your email messages. This practice is widely used in business environments where co-workers and business partners exchange information by attaching presentations, documents, or Microsoft Excel worksheets.

In principle there are no restrictions as to how many files you can attach and how large they can be, but most email service providers implement various limitations. For example, many companies limit the size of email attachments to small files of up to 10 or 20 MB. Other email service providers do not allow users to attach executable files to their emails (with the extension .exe) because they can be used to distribute malware. In Figure 13.4 you can see an example of an email message with several files attached, in Microsoft Outlook 2010.

FIGURE 13.4 An email message with several files attached

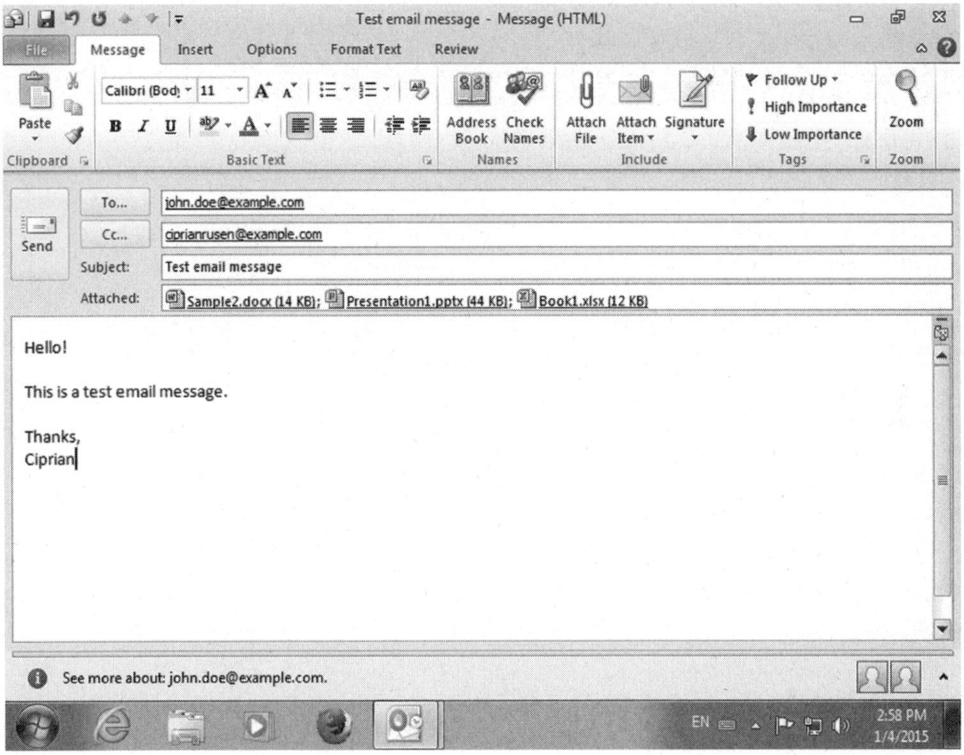

Building a Contacts List

In order to make it easier to keep track of the people you are emailing with, it is a good idea to build a contact list or address book. All email clients have the necessary features to build and maintain a contact list. When adding a new contact, you can store details like their name, email address, company, job title, phone numbers, and addresses. In Figure 13.5 you can see an example of a contact that's added into Microsoft Outlook 2010 and the fields of data that are available for a contact.

Creating a contact list with the people who you are emailing makes it easier to find them when you create a new email message and allows you to store and find information about them in one place. Contact lists are useful because they can be synchronized across devices. For example, if you have a Gmail.com email account and a smartphone with Android, your contacts are synchronized with your smartphone. Therefore, it is easy to find, call, or email people directly from your phone. The same is true for other platforms and email services. For example, Microsoft's Outlook.com email service and contact list are automatically synchronized with Windows Phone smartphones as well as Windows computers. Many companies synchronize a user's email account and contact list with their work phone and so on.

FIGURE 13.5 Creating a contact in Microsoft Outlook 2010

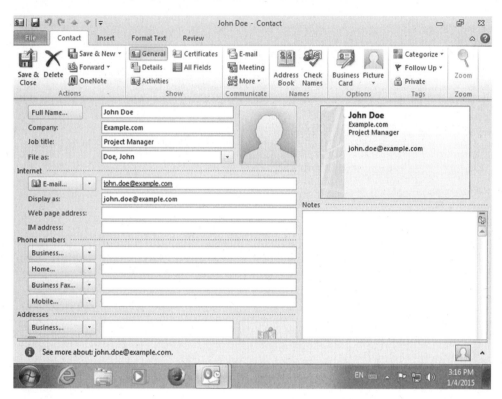

Many email services allow you to organize contacts into groups or create mailing lists. They can be useful when you need to send the same message to a large group of people. Instead of emailing each person individually or manually adding each person in the To field, you can type the group's name, and that message is sent to all the people who are part of that group.

When emailing a group of people, you should pay attention to whether the message should reach all the people who are part of it. If a message is not suitable to everyone in that group, it is best to spend the effort necessary to select only the email addresses of those people who are an appropriate target audience.

In Exercise 13.2 you will learn how to create a contact in Microsoft Outlook.

EXERCISE 13.2

Creating a Contact in Microsoft Outlook

1. Click Start ➢ All Programs ➢ Microsoft Office ➢ Microsoft Outlook 2010.

2. Click Contacts in the column on the left, just below Mail and Calendar.

3. Click the Home tab on the ribbon and then the New Contact button found in the New section, shown in Figure 13.6.

FIGURE 13.6   The buttons for creating new contacts and contact groups

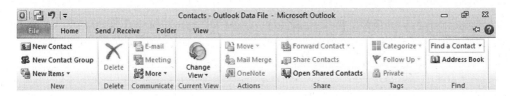

A window named Untitled - Contact appears, where you can add the details of your contact.

4. In the Full Name field (Figure 13.7) type the name of the person whom you want to add as a contact.

FIGURE 13.7   Creating a new contact in Microsoft Outlook

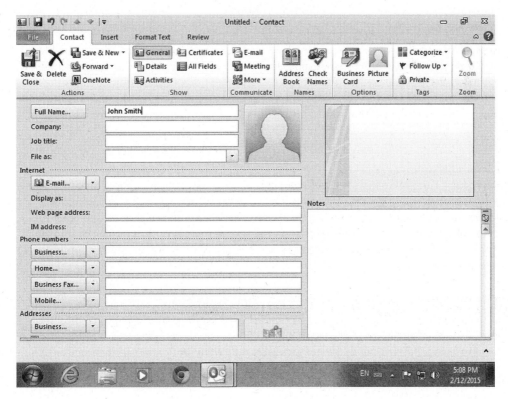

5. In the E-mail field, type the email address of that person.

6. Complete other details that you may consider important, like the company, job title, mobile number, and so on.

7. When finished adding all the details, look for the Actions section in the Contact tab of the ribbon and click the Save & Close button.

8. Notice that the new contact has been added. Close Microsoft Outlook.

Replying to and Forwarding Email Messages

Not all email messages require a reply, because you receive them just to be informed about something, without your having to take any action. If that is the case for one of the messages that you receive, simply close it or delete it. If further action is required, you have the following options:

Reply   You reply only to the sender of the message that you received (Figure 13.8). A new email message is created automatically with the same subject as the one used by the sender but prefixed by the term *RE:*. Also, the body of the reply includes the original message that was received from the sender as well as any other messages that were sent earlier in the same conversation. You can then type your message in the Body field, just above the original message. You can also choose to delete all the included text, so your email message isn't overloaded with information the recipient already has.

Reply All   This works the same as Reply with the difference that you reply to all the people who were included in the email distribution list, in the To and CC fields, including the sender of the message that you received. This option is useful when you need to reply to a conversation and include a whole group of people in that conversation. But be sure you really need to reply to everyone before you click Reply All. It's easy to annoy a lot of people very quickly.

Forward   This option allows you to resend an email message you received to a possibly different email address (Figure 13.9). A copy of the initial email message is created automatically with the same subject as the one used by the sender but prefixed by the term *FW:*. Also, the body of the email includes the original message that was received from the sender as well as any other messages that were sent earlier in the same conversation. You can then type a message in the Body field if desired, just above the original message.

FIGURE 13.8   Replying to an email message in Microsoft Outlook

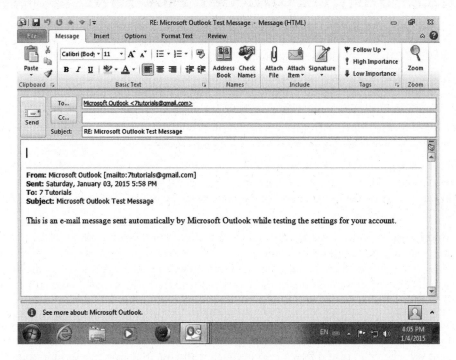

FIGURE 13.9   Forwarding an email message in Microsoft Outlook

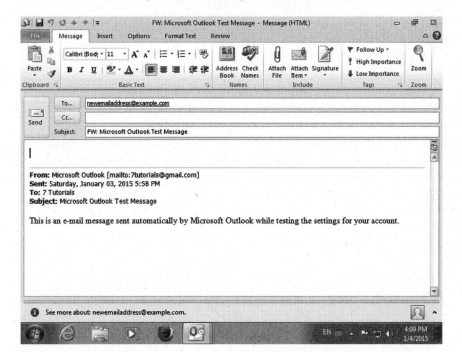

Automating Your Email Account

All email services offer several automation tools that can be useful when using your email account. These tools include the following:

Auto-responders   Each time you receive an email message you can have a reply sent automatically. This reply can be an Out of Office notice that's sent to inform people that you are away on vacation or on a business trip and you can't reply to their message right away. You can also use auto-responders to inform people that you no longer use some email account and that they should be writing to you at a new one.

Auto-forwarding   You can have your emails automatically forwarded to another email address. You can forward all of your new messages or just specific kinds of messages. You set this up by editing your email account's settings, and the procedure for doing this varies greatly among email services.

Signatures   You can attach a standard signature to all of your email messages. This signature can include anything from alternative contact details to pertinent job titles to company names, which help the recipient get in touch when emails are not responded to. You can also use professional signatures like a letterhead, signatures that show that you run a business (in some countries, you're required to do so), and so on.

An email signature shouldn't increase the length of your messages too much. Make it as short as possible (three lines is usually enough). The purpose of a signature is to let the recipient see who you are and how to get in touch with you. Make sure to include your name, your company and position, and other vital contact information.

In some European countries, laws dictate what items you must put in your email signature if you are a registered company. For example, UK law requires private and public limited companies to include the following: company number, address of registration, and VAT number.

You should avoid sharing your personal social media accounts (such as Twitter or Facebook), personal details like your home phone number or address, random quotes, or other details that are not useful to the recipients of your emails.

When setting an Out of Office reply, you should configure the time period during which it will be sent as an automated reply, as well as the subject and the body of the message. In order for the reply to be effective, you should specify when you will be out of the office, when you will be able to reply, how people can contact you in case of emergencies, and, if applicable, your stand-in for the period when you are away and how the recipient can contact them. In Figure 13.10 you can see an example of an Out of Office reply being set for the Gmail.com email service.

FIGURE 13.10   Setting an Out of Office reply in Gmail.com

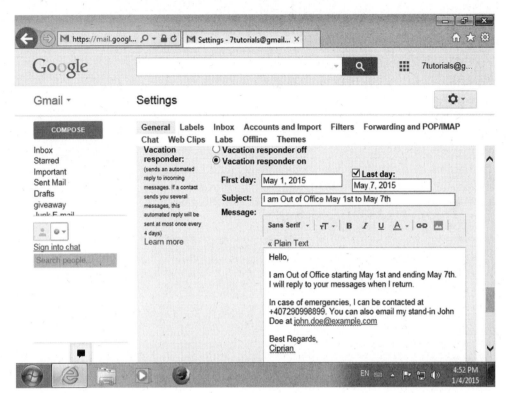

Organizing and Archiving Your Inbox

All email services and clients allow you to organize your email messages into folders. By default, you will encounter a folder named Inbox where all your received emails are stored, a Sent Mail folder where your sent messages are stored, and a Trash folder where your deleted messages are stored for a while. You will also find a folder named Spam or Junk where email spam is automatically stored when detected by the email service or the email client that you are using.

Email spam, also known as junk email or unsolicited bulk email, is a subset of electronic spam involving nearly identical messages sent to numerous recipients by email. Clicking links in spam email may send you to malicious websites that are hosting malware or to phishing websites that try to trick you into sharing important financial information like your credit card details. Spam email may also include attachments with infected files.

While most email services do a good job at filtering legitimate emails from email spam, there are times when legitimate emails are incorrectly marked as spam. That's why you should not forget to check the Spam folder from time to time and look for email messages that might not be spam. However, always be wary of opening the attachments of messages that are marked as spam, as well as clicking the links found in these messages.

In Figure 13.11 you can see an example of email folders displayed for a Gmail.com account that's accessed using Microsoft Outlook 2010.

FIGURE 13.11   Email folders in Microsoft Outlook

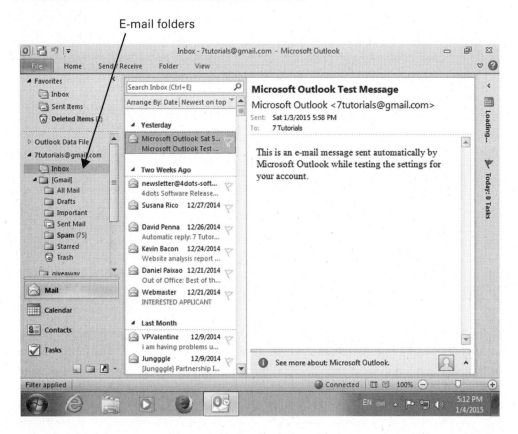

The standard number of folders that are available for an email account differ from service to service. However, you can always create your own custom folders and use them to better organize the messages that you are exchanging with others. Most email clients and services allow the use of folders for organizing your email.

When using email, especially in a business environment, you will encounter the term *email archiving*. This is the act of preserving and making searchable all the email messages that were sent and received by an individual. Email archiving tools capture the email content either directly from the email client used by the user or during transport. The messages are typically then stored on the computer's hard disk. The benefits of email archiving include the recovery of lost or accidentally deleted emails, accelerated audit response, preservation of the intellectual property contained in business email and its attachments, as well as an important discovery tool in the case of litigation or internal investigations (what happened when or who said what).

All email clients offer tools for archiving your email, according to a given set of rules. In Figure 13.12 you can see the options that are available for archiving your email in Microsoft Outlook 2010.

FIGURE 13.12   Archiving your email in Microsoft Outlook

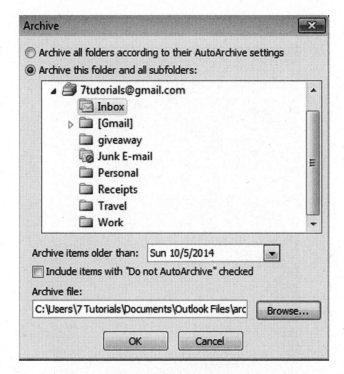

You can select the folders that are included in the archive, the rule used to archive email messages (emails that are older than a specified date), and the file where the archive is stored on your computer.

Communicating through Text Messages

Many people communicate a lot through text messages. They use not only email but also other ways of communication like SMS on their phones or chat clients on their computers.

The most widely used way of communicating through text messages is *Short Message Service (SMS)*—a text messaging service that is available on phones, the Web, and other mobile communication systems. It uses standardized communications protocols to allow devices to exchange short text messages. When sending an SMS message, you need to provide the number of the person you send it to and then write the actual message. One SMS can include up to 160 characters. If you send a message that's more than 160 characters, that message is split into as many SMS messages as needed in order to send it to the recipient. In Figure 13.13 you can see the fields that you must complete in order to send an SMS message on a Windows Phone smartphone.

FIGURE 13.13   Sending an SMS in Windows Phone

Another popular form of communication is *text messaging*. This is a type of online chat that offers real-time text transmission over the Internet. Short messages are typically transmitted bi-directionally between two parties, when each user chooses to complete a thought and click Send. More advanced instant messaging clients can add file transfer, clickable hyperlinks, voice, or video chat.

Instant messaging systems facilitate connections between specified known users, using a contact list also known as a buddy list or friend list. There are many chat services available worldwide, with new ones appearing every year. At the time of writing this book, the most popular chat services are the following:

Skype   An application that specializes in providing chat services using both text and video, as well as voice calls from computers, tablets, and mobile devices via the Internet to other devices or smartphones. Skype is available to download onto computers running Windows, Mac, or Linux, as well as Android, Blackberry, iOS, and Windows Phone smartphones and tablets. Much of the service is free, but users must have Skype Credit or a subscription to call landline or mobile numbers.

Google Hangouts   An instant messaging and video chat platform developed by Google. It replaces other messaging products that Google had implemented, including Google Talk and Google+ Messenger. In current versions of Android, Google Hangouts is the default application for text messaging. This service is available on Windows, Mac, Linux, Chrome OS, Android, and iOS.

Facebook Messenger   An instant messaging service and software application that provides text and voice communication. It is integrated with Facebook's web-based chat feature, and it is also available as a chat app for mobile platforms like Android, iOS, Windows Phone, and Blackberry. Messenger lets Facebook users chat with friends both on mobile and on the main website.

Each chat service and client application looks and works differently. However, some principles remain the same across all services and applications:

- Text messaging services require an Internet connection in order to work.
- You must have a user account registered with the chat service that you want to use. Just like with email, you need an account in order to authenticate yourself and chat with others.
- In most cases you can talk only with people who are in your contact lists and who have approved that they are your contacts. Very few text messaging services allow you to send messages to people who aren't listed as your friends or contacts.
- In order to chat with someone, you select that person's account, type your message, and click Send or press Enter on your keyboard.
- When that person reads your message, they can reply to you in real time.

Figure 13.14 shows the Skype window where you can send messages to a selected contact. The left side of the window contains the list of contacts that you have, and on the right, after selecting a person, you can send and receive text messages.

FIGURE 13.14 Sending a text message on Skype

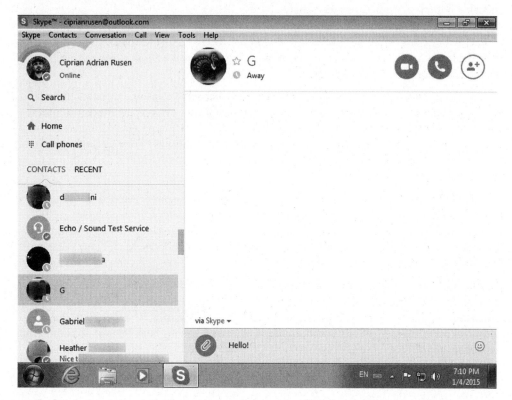

Communicating through Multimedia

A more modern form of communication is through the use of multimedia, which includes text, pictures, audio and video content. One of the most popular forms of communication through multimedia is *Multimedia Messaging Service (MMS)*. This is a standard way to send messages that include multimedia content to and from mobile phones. It extends the core SMS capability that allowed exchange of text messages only up to 160 characters in length by allowing users to use more characters in their messages and also add attachments to their messages.

The process for sending MMS messages is the same as for SMS messages, with the difference that you can write more text and attach files. If the receiver's handset is not MMS capable, the message is usually delivered to a web-based service from which the content can be viewed from a normal web browser. The URL for the content is usually sent to the receiver's phone in a normal text message. This behavior is usually known as the legacy experience since content can still be received by a phone number, even if the phone itself does not support MMS.

You can do audioconferencing as well as videoconferencing using specialized apps and services like Skype or Google Hangouts, which allow for videoconferencing between multiple users for free.

Each audio and videoconferencing service and client application looks and works differently. However, some principles remain the same across all services and applications:

- These services require an Internet connection in order to work.

- You need to have a user account registered with the service that you want to use. Just like with email, you need an account in order to authenticate yourself and talk with others.

- In most cases you can talk only with people who are in your contact lists and who have approved that they are your contacts. Very few services allow you to talk to people who aren't listed as your friends or contacts.

- In order to talk with someone, you select that person's account and press the Call button in order to start an audio conversation or the Video call button in order to start a video conversation.

- While talking with others, you can also send text messages, exchange files, and so on.

In Figure 13.15 you can see the Skype video chat window where you can have an audio and video conversation with another person. As you can see, the Skype window shares the video of the other person and hides the text chat window. However, you can also exchange text messages easily, send attachments, and so on, using the buttons that are available in the video chat window.

FIGURE 13.15   Having a video conversation on Skype

Most audio and video chat clients use *Voice over IP (VoIP)* for the delivery of voice communications and multimedia sessions. This is a group of technologies that work over Internet Protocol (IP) networks like the Internet. VoIP systems employ session control and signaling protocols to control the signaling, setup, and teardown of calls. The audio streams are transported over IP networks using special media delivery protocols that encode the voice, audio, and video with appropriate codecs. These codecs optimize the media stream based on application requirements and network bandwidth. VoIP is available on smartphones, personal computers, and many other devices with Internet access such as tablets, TVs, or gaming consoles.

Using Social Media and Social Networks

You may have heard the terms *social media* and *social networks*. You surely have heard about Facebook. What are these concepts, and why are they important?

Social media are computer-mediated tools that allow people to create, share, or exchange information, ideas, pictures, and videos in virtual communities and networks. These tools depend on mobile and web-based technologies to create highly interactive platforms through which individuals and communities share, co-create, discuss, and modify user-generated content.

Social-media technologies take on many different forms including magazines, Internet forums, weblogs, social blogs, microblogs, wikis, social networks, podcasts, social bookmarking, and more. The most popular technologies are social networks and blogs.

Social Networks

A *social network* is a platform where people can build social relationships with others who share interests, activities, backgrounds, or real-life connections. A social network service consists of a representation of each user (also known as a profile), their social links, and a variety of additional services.

Social network sites are web-based services that allow individuals to create a public profile, designate a list of users with whom to share connections, and view and cross the connections within the system. Social networking sites allow users to share ideas, pictures, posts, activities, events, and interests with people in their network.

The most popular social networks are Facebook, LinkedIn, and Twitter, with many more showing up on a regular basis. Even though they share many features and tools, they are different in the way they are used: Facebook is mostly for keeping in touch with family, friends, and acquaintances; LinkedIn is for keeping in touch with co-workers and other business professionals; while Twitter is a very public social network where you can exchange short messages of a maximum of 140 characters with just about anyone using Twitter.

You can do many things on a social network, from sharing your current status, having conversations with others, uploading pictures and videos, sharing links to interesting articles and blogs, and much more. The most basic of activities is sharing your status, and it is a very simple activity. Let's take Facebook as the first example. In Exercise 13.3 you'll learn how to update your status on this social network.

Updating Your Status on Facebook

1. Click Start ➤ All Programs ➤ Internet Explorer.

2. Type **facebook.com** in the Address bar and press Enter on your keyboard.

   Wait for Facebook to load.

3. Type the email address and password that you use for your Facebook account, and click Log In.

4. Once you're logged into Facebook, type a status in the Update Status field (Figure 13.16).

5. Click the button that says with whom you are sharing your status and select the group of people that you want to share this with (Public, Friends, and so on).

FIGURE 13.16   Updating your status on Facebook

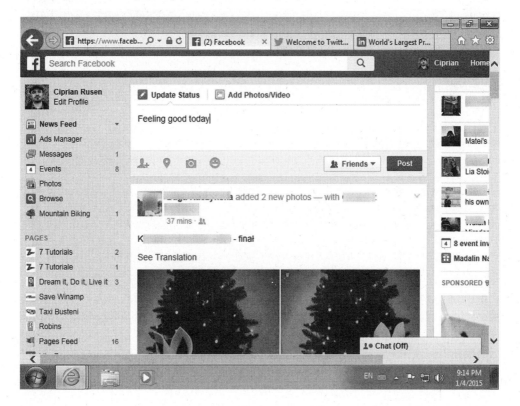

EXERCISE 13.3 *(continued)*

6. Click Post.

Notice that your Facebook status has been updated accordingly and only the people in the group that you have set can view it.

7. Sign out of Facebook and close Internet Explorer.

On Twitter, updating your status is done in a similar way: log into your account, and on the top of the Twitter window type your current status or message (Figure 13.17). Then, click the Tweet button.

FIGURE 13.17   Updating your status on Twitter

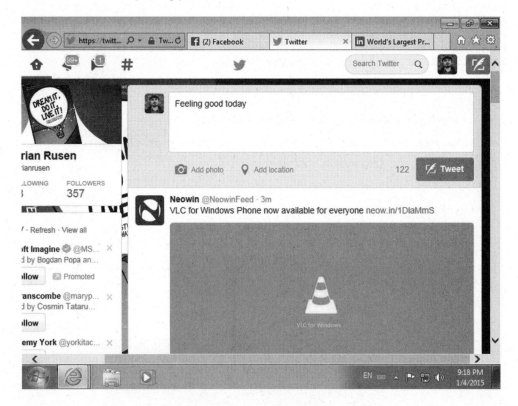

A similar process works for LinkedIn too: log in, and on the top of the window type your current status, choose with whom you want to share it, and click Share (Figure 13.18).

FIGURE 13.18   Updating your status on LinkedIn

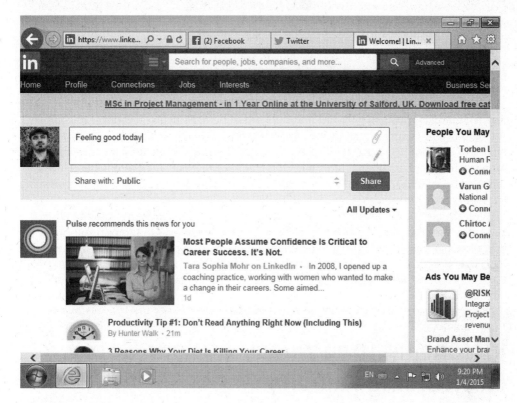

Special Social Networks

Some social networks serve specialized interests. A big one is LibraryThing (https://www.librarything.com/). It's for book lovers who want to catalog their libraries. By entering an ISBN or ASIN on the Add Books page, the site will look up the book and place it into your library catalog, complete with author, title, and publication details. You also have the option of adding custom tags to each book entry, such as fiction, mystery, history, and so on—as many as you like.

LibraryThing has experienced exponential growth in membership since its inception in 2005 and boasts that its members have cataloged more books than are in the Library of Congress. Going beyond cataloging books, the site also hosts a wide variety of discussion groups—some about books, of course, but also about ideas, history, sports, and even alcoholic beverages.

Another popular social network for book lovers is http://goodreads.com.

Blogs

A *blog* is a discussion or informational site published on the Web and consisting of posts typically displayed in reverse chronological order with the most recent post appearing first. Some blogs are the work of a single individual, while others are the work of a small group and often cover a single subject. Bloggers not only produce content to post on their blogs but also build social relations with their readers and other bloggers.

Many blogs provide commentary on a particular subject; others function as personal online diaries; still others function as online brand advertising of a particular individual or company. A blog generally combines text, images, and links to other blogs, web pages, and other media related to its topic. Readers generally have the ability to leave comments in an interactive format. Most blogs are primarily textual, although some focus on art, photographs, videos (known also as *vlogs*), music, and audio (podcasts). Microblogging is another type of blogging, featuring very short posts that can be read in just a couple of seconds.

With the help of modern technologies, nearly everyone can create a blog and publish content online, without requiring too much technical knowledge. On the Web you can find many free blogging tools that require minimal knowledge to set them up. With the help of tools like WordPress (`https://wordpress.com`), Tumblr (`https://www.tumblr.com`), or Blogger (`https://www.blogger.com`), anyone can create a personal blog in just a couple of minutes, for free.

Increasing the Privacy of Your Social Networking Activity

When using any social network, it is important to be aware of how and with whom you are sharing information, pictures, videos, and conversations. If you do not pay attention to your privacy, you risk sharing things that should be private with the wrong audience and that can end up causing you harm. That's why each social network provides the necessary tools to control whom you are sharing content with. These tools are generally not hard to find and they are easy to use.

When posting a status update on Facebook, you can easily select who should see your update. You can make the status update public, share it with only your friends, or share it with your friends but not your acquaintances, and so on. In Figure 13.19 you can see the privacy controls that were available on Facebook at the time this book was written.

Twitter has a very different approach to privacy because it was created as a public social network where it's easy to exchange information with people whom you do not necessarily know personally. That's why your posts are automatically posted as public. However, Twitter does offer some privacy controls that allow you to set whether others can tag you in photos, stop making your updates (tweets) public and have them visible only to people that you approve, specify whether you want your location added to your tweets, and indicate whether you want others to find you by using your email address. Figure 13.20 shows the privacy settings that were available on Twitter at the time this book was written.

FIGURE 13.19   Privacy controls on Facebook

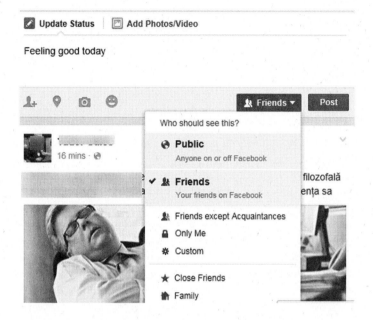

FIGURE 13.20   Privacy controls on Twitter

When sharing something on LinkedIn, you have very simple controls for configuring whom you are sharing with. By default, your posts are public, meaning that they can be seen by anyone. However, you can click Share With, and a drop-down list appears where you can select that you want to share your post only with your connections. In Figure 13.21 you can see the privacy controls that were available on LinkedIn at the time when this book was written.

FIGURE 13.21 Privacy controls on LinkedIn

To help you a bit more, here are a few recommendations that you should keep in mind when using social networks:

- Avoid sharing personal details like your home phone number or address, your credit card details, and so on.

- Never share your password with others.

- Keep an eye out for scams or people who try to scam you.

- Do not post details about others, including pictures and videos without their consent.

- Do not reveal your location publicly so that unwanted persons won't have access to this information.

- Don't post abusive content of any kind.

Summary

In this chapter we discussed how to communicate with others online. The most popular communication medium is email, so we started by explaining what it is and the basics of using it. You also learned some tips and tricks about automating certain aspects of your email account when required.

Then we moved to other forms of communications: SMS, chat services, MMS, and audio and videoconferencing. Technology makes it easy to communicate with others through several apps, services, and channels, so we covered the most important of them.

Finally, we shifted our focus to social media in general and social networks in particular. You learned what the major social networks are, what's different about them, and how to protect your privacy when posting content on them.

In the next chapter we will explain what it means to be a good digital citizen and how to communicate on the Internet. Then we will cover important concepts like licensing, intellectual property, piracy, copyrights, and so on.

Exam Essentials

Know how to use email.   Email is the most popular form of communication, especially in business environments. You should know what it is and how to use it.

Understand how to automate your email account.   Most email services offer useful tools to automate your account. You can create rules, set Out of Office notifications, and more. You should understand these features and how they are useful to you.

Learn how to use chat to communicate with others.   Another way of communicating with others is through chat services like Skype, Google Hangouts, or Facebook Messenger. You should learn the basics of using them.

Understand how to communicate with others through audio and videoconferencing.   With the help of technology, you can easily communicate with others through audio and video-conferencing. You should know the most important services that allow such forms of communication and the principles involved when using them.

Understand how to use social networks and how to protect your privacy on them.   Social media and social networks are another way we communicate with others on a daily basis. You should know what the major social networks are, how they differ, and the basics of protecting your privacy when using them.

Key Terms

Before you take the exam, be certain you are familiar with the following terms:

blog	social media
credentials	social network
email	text messaging
e-mail	two-factor authentication
email archiving	two-step verification
email spam	Voice over IP (VoIP)
Short Message Service (SMS)	Multimedia Messaging Service (MMS)

Review Questions

1. Which of the following are characteristics of email? (Choose all that apply.)

   A. Allows you to do video chat with others

   B. Allows you to exchange digital messages with others

   C. Requires a username and password in order to be used

   D. Requires you to provide the email address of the people that you want to send messages to

2. Which of the following are examples of strong passwords? (Choose all that apply.)

   A. 1234567

   B. hellokitty

   C. H3Ll0K1ttY

   D. Th1s1$Year2015

3. What does BCC mean when referring to email? (Choose all that apply.)

   A. A blind carbon copy

   B. A carbon copy

   C. Recipients listed in the BCC field receive a copy of the message but are not shown on any other recipient's copy, including other BCC recipients.

   D. Recipients listed in the BCC field receive a copy of the message and are shown on other recipients' copy.

4. Which fields of data are automatically populated by the email client or service when sending an email message? (Choose all that apply.)

   A. To

   B. Date

   C. Subject

   D. From

5. What happens when you use the Reply All button instead of Reply for sending a reply to an email message that you received?

   A. You reply only to the sender of the message.

   B. You reply to all the people who were included in the email distribution list, including the sender.

   C. You reply to yourself.

   D. You reply to everyone included in the email distribution list, excluding the sender.

6. What happens when you forward an email message? (Choose all that apply.)

   A. The subject of the forwarded message is prefixed by the term *RE:*.

   B. The subject of the forwarded message is prefixed by the term *FW:*.

   C. A new email message is created automatically.

   D. A copy of the email message is created automatically.

7. What should an Out of Office reply contain? (Choose all that apply.)

   A. How you can be reached in case of emergencies

   B. Who your stand-in is and how they can be reached

   C. Why you are out of office

   D. The time period when you are unavailable

8. Which of the following are characteristics of SMS? (Choose all that apply.)

   A. SMS stands for Short Message Service.

   B. An SMS can include up to 160 characters.

   C. SMS stands for Standard Message Service.

   D. An SMS can include up to 1000 characters.

9. Which of the following are examples of chat services/clients? (Choose all that apply.)

   A. LinkedIn

   B. Facebook Messenger

   C. Twitter

   D. Skype

10. Which of the following are examples of social media tools? (Choose all that apply.)

   A. Blogs

   B. Facebook

   C. OneDrive

   D. Internet forums

Chapter

14

Being a Responsible Digital Citizen

THE FOLLOWING IC3: LIVING ONLINE EXAM OBJECTIVES ARE COVERED IN THIS CHAPTER:

✓ **Communication Standards**

- Explain the difference between personal and professional communication and the importance of spelling and use of abbreviations in each type of communication.

- All capitals vs. standard capitalization

- Verbal vs. Written, Professional vs. Personal communication

- Explain the terms: Spamming, flaming, bullying and the harm that each can cause. Explain how they are not faceless, harmless electronic actions.

- Explain the terms Libel and Slander and the real life legal consequences of each.

✓ **Legal and Responsible Use of Computers**

- Explain what censorship is. Contrast its benefits and drawbacks.

- Explain what filtering is. Contrast its benefits and drawbacks.

- Explain Intellectual Property, its real value and the implications of its misuse.

- Explain Piracy, how to protect yourself from it and the ethical issues surrounding it.

- Explain what a copyright is, how it is obtained, the legal ramifications surrounding a copyright and its value to its holder.

- Licensing

- Explain what Creative Commons is, the licensing availability and legal issues surrounding it, as well as the benefits to the community.

Communication is part of everyday life, even more so in the digital era, where we have more communication devices and channels than at any time in our history. That's why it is important to get the basics right and understand the different forms of communication channels that are available and the do's and don'ts of each. In this chapter we will start by discussing the differences between personal and professional communication, both verbal and written, in the online world. We will also share examples and recommendations on the right way to communicate as well as some negative examples on how not to communicate.

In the second half of this chapter we will discuss intellectual property, copyrights, and licensing in the digital world. While the use of technology makes it easier than ever to get access to original works of all kinds, there are many ethical and legal matters to keep in mind. Also, piracy is a widespread problem that affects creators of original works all over the world. That's why it is important to understand concepts like copyright, digital rights management, and newer licensing models like Creative Commons.

Personal vs. Professional Communication

Personal communication can take place at any time, at any place, and on a variety of devices, such as a cellphone, tablet, or laptop. You can send instant messages, text, email, and even photos to friends and family as long as you have an Internet connection. How you speak with them often differs from how you are expected to speak to colleagues, supervisors, business partners, and customers. Personal communication depends on the reader of the message; for example, if the reader is a friend, then you can construct your message just as you would say it to them if they were standing right next to you. If you want your reader to think you are yelling or are very excited, then you can use all capital letters to express that, for example, "HEY MATE! I GOT THE JOB! THANKS FOR YOUR HELP, MAN!" Or another example could be writing to your son not to take the car or there will be trouble when you get home: "John: do NOT take the car. DO YOU HEAR ME? DO NOT TAKE THE CAR!!!!" This is parental "yelling" done through the use of capital letters and multiple exclamation marks. Also, good grammar may not be as important in your dialogue as in a professional environment.

You may speak with your friends using slang, abbreviations, and other forms of casual language. The widespread use of electronic communication through mobile phones and the Internet allowed for a marked rise in colloquial abbreviation. This is due largely to increasing popularity of textual communication services like Short Message Service (SMS), which supports message lengths of 160 characters at most. This brevity gave rise to an informal abbreviation scheme sometimes called *textese*, where 10 percent or more of the words in a typical message are abbreviated. More recently Twitter began driving abbreviation use with 140-character message limits, making textese even more popular.

Professional communication, however, is neither as simple nor as spontaneous or emotive as using all capital letters and multiple exclamation marks. Business or professional audiences expect a certain level of reserve, decorum, and courtesy as conveyed through the medium and structure chosen (an email as opposed to an instant message), the tone and mechanics used (informal or formal), and the level of detail provided in the message. A colleague will expect some kind of acknowledgment to the previous message as a way to prepare them for what this new email message relates to. This is called *bridging information*. Here's an example:

> Thanks for requesting more information about our travel reimbursement policy, Jane. This policy was recently changed, so here is the most current information you will need to assist you as you complete your expense report.

This is a courteous way to acknowledge the request, personalize the message, and provide the answer to the question that may have been asked informally in the hallway or formally via voicemail or email. The form and the content of the message follow the rules of grammar, spelling, mechanics, punctuation, and overall stylistic expectations of courtesy and clarity.

Abbreviations may be used in a professional communication but mostly when referring to academic or professional titles like Dr. for Doctor, Prof. for Professor, and so on. In more conservative professional environments, abbreviations might be mandatory when communicating with others.

Unlike personal communication, in professional environments textese is not accepted as an appropriate way of communicating with others, and you should avoid it as much as possible.

The Pitfall of Mixing Friends and Business Associates

Social networks represent a challenge for many people in terms of how and what they should be communicating when using them. For example, on Facebook you might have as friends both close friends and family as well as co-workers and business partners. If you are very personal in your updates and you use textese, for example, that may be fine with your friends, but it might not be acceptable with your business partners, and this may damage your image as a professional. That's why when you post on social networks, you should always use the tools that are available for sharing posts and content, and you should filter who can see what. For example, you should not keep your real friends and your co-workers in the same group.

If you are a heavy LinkedIn user, you should always use the standards of professional communication because this social network is designed for business professionals who expect a certain standard from you. Twitter, on the other hand, is a very public social network. Yes, textese is allowed and expected on Twitter due to its enforced brevity, but you should be careful about what kind of content you post. If it is not suitable for anyone in the world to see it, then you should not post it.

Verbal vs. Written Communication

Spoken or verbal communication reflects your personality and the type of relationship shared with the receiver of your message or audience. How you speak is typically more colloquial than how you are expected to write at work, so your *tone* must fit the expectations of the audience. Vocal inflections, facial expressions, and body language add to the overall delivery and resulting interpretation of the spoken message by the audience.

Written communication, however, is faceless, so what you write needs to be as clear as possible. If it is not, the message may be misinterpreted as you being rude or even insubordinate. *Emoticons* (symbolic facial expressions expressed through smiley faces made with a colon and a right parenthesis, for example) can be helpful, but even these can be misinterpreted, so use emoticons with caution and only if you know your audience is aware what each emoticon means. ☺ Unless you know your audience appreciates these, limit their use to personal communications, which includes only social media, personal texting, and personal email. Always remember that what you write online can potentially last forever, so present your best self at all times.

Professional communication also exists in verbal or written forms, and knowing your audience's expectations and preferences is also essential for effective communication. Verbal communication includes giving an oral presentation, for example, and professional written communication ranges from writing simple emails to creating more complex research reports and informal and formal proposals.

The most effective form of communication to use depends on the context and the purpose of your message. For instance, written communication works better for giving long directions, while verbal communication works better for obtaining direct feedback from your audience. When deciding how to communicate with others, always think about your purpose, which form of communication is more effective in achieving it, and which form of communication is preferred by the person or the people you are about to communicate with.

Inappropriate Ways of Communicating Online

Just like in real life, there are also many inappropriate ways of communicating online. Here are some things that you should avoid doing.

Spamming   *Spamming* is the act of sending unsolicited messages to others, especially advertising and self-promotion. On a personal level, some people use their personal email accounts to spam friends with unsolicited updates about what they do, promote their personal blogs, or send presentations and other materials that the recipients don't need or are not interested it, without their consent. On a business level, some companies use spam as a method of blatant self-promotion and send unsolicited advertising materials to people all over the world, without their consent.

Spamming can be done through all kinds of media, from email to instant messaging clients, to forums, to social networks, and so on. While spam is used because it has some degree of success and very low costs, you should avoid being a spammer. First of all, it creates a bad personal and/or business image that may do you more harm than good. Second, in some countries it is illegal, and spam may cause you legal problems.

Flaming   *Flaming* is a hostile, insulting interaction between users on the Internet, often involving the use of profanity. This is mostly encountered in the context of Internet forums, chat, email, and online games. Flaming is mostly the result of the discussion of heated issues such as politics, religion, and sports but can also be provoked by seemingly trivial differences like what character you and your team want to play in an online game.

There are also people who do deliberate flaming, as opposed to flaming as a result of emotional discussions. These individuals are referred to as flamers, and they specialize in starting heated, insulting interactions with others. For example, a common way of flaming someone is to pick on incorrect spelling and grammatical mistakes. Flamers may try to impugn their opponents' intelligence by highlighting their errors in grammar or spelling.

Bullying   *Bullying* is not new form of negative behavior, but in the modern era it has moved to the digital world. As you know, bullying is the activity of repeated, aggressive behavior intended to hurt another person. Bullying can be physical (hitting, punching, or kicking), verbal (name-calling or taunting), relational (destroying peer acceptance and friendships), and cyberbullying (using electronic means to harm others).

Unlike other forms, cyberbullying can go undetected because of a lack of parental/authoritative supervision. Because bullies can pose as someone else, they can remain anonymous. Cyberbullying includes but is not limited to abuse using email, instant messaging, text messaging, websites, social networking sites, and so on.

Libel and Slander   Other forms of inappropriate ways of communication are *libel* and *slander*. They are similar in the sense that they represent the communication of a false statement that harms the reputation of a person or an entity. They are generally irrational, unprovoked criticism that has little or no factual basis and whose only aim is the defamation of another. Slander is the spoken type of defamation, while libel is defamation made on printed media like newspapers and magazines, images, or the Web. Obviously, just because you have a personal blog or a Facebook profile, it doesn't mean that it is acceptable to libel others, and you should be mindful of what you communicate.

Censorship and Filters in the Digital World

International human rights law covering freedom of speech now extends to the Internet. This means that communications must not be interfered with in any way, either by employers or governments or even Internet service providers themselves, for example. The United Nations holds freedom of speech as a fundamental human right, allowing every individual to participate in public discourse without fear of reprisal. *Censorship* results when access to the Internet is denied or curtailed in any way as well as when any unauthorized editorial activity changes or deletes someone's writing or transmissions.

Governments that manipulate the Internet's infrastructure or force its intermediaries for the sole purpose of censoring information before it has a chance to be transmitted are attempting to control who has access to that information as a way to mitigate intercultural conflict or sociopolitical unrest. One example of this is China's Great Firewall, which filters all the Internet traffic going in and out of China and also monitors Internet access of individuals. Other governments may be more reactive in that an offense must be committed first before punitive actions result. In Figure 14.1 you can see a world map with Internet censorship and surveillance by country, published by Wikipedia in 2014, based on data from the OpenNet Initiative and Reporters Without Borders.

FIGURE 14.1   Internet censorship and surveillance by country

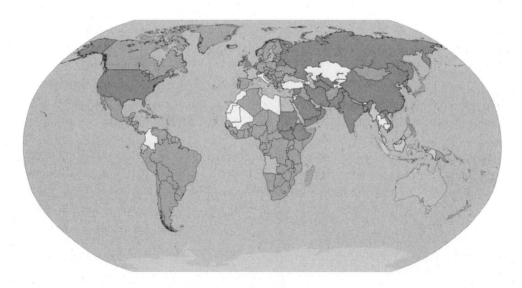

Figure 14.2 gives you information on how each country is classified in the previous figure.

FIGURE 14.2   The legend for Figure 14.1

Internet censorship and surveillance by country[1][2][3][4]

■ Pervasive	■ Changing situation
□ Substantial	■ Little or none
□ Selective	■ Not classified/No data

In the absence of governmental controls, companies have instead become the moral arbiters of portions of the Internet; for example, YouTube has Community Guidelines, which prevents hate speech from being spread, and this includes anything deemed to be devaluing of any human being and/or glamorizing crime and injustice. Google and Bing (Microsoft's search engine) similarly try to prevent sexually explicit material from being returned in any of their searches by using the same SafeSearch technology.

Although the freedom of speech that the Internet enables so quickly can thereby promote democracy, it can also challenge cultural, political, and religious norms, thereby provoking social and political unrest. In many countries, if what is posted incites hatred, then the writer can be charged with hate speech offenses.

In the United States, freedom of speech is covered most robustly by the First Amendment to the U.S. Constitution; however, many countries do not enjoy similar protections. As a result, private worldwide organizations, such as the World Wide Web Consortium (W3C), the Internet Engineering Task Force (IETF), and the Internet Corporation for Assigned Names and Numbers (ICANN), have developed to govern the Internet, to protect freedom of speech, and also to prevent the proliferation of hate propaganda. Because the Internet enables global communications at a speed and low cost never seen before, any specific international law will need to protect freedom of speech with the UN's Universal Declaration of Human Rights as its foundation. Currently, the Internet does fall under traditional media and its protections and limitations under international law, but international law cannot be used to control social media companies or to force any country to censor online content or speech originating from within its borders.

In order to censor content on the Internet, *filters* have been designed. They are programs designed to screen any content deemed inappropriate or illegal for its end users. They do this by checking the origin of the content against a rubric of rules designed by the programmer, usually in response to a government request. Such filters should catch materials that depict the exploitation of children, for example, as well as malware or viruses. They are usually part of a firewall or proxy server, and some filters can report what has been filtered and who requested it. Filters can also be soft, in that automatic warning pages are issued instead of blocked access, and blocked access can still be overridden by an administrator.

The obvious benefits of filtering include that it can be used to catch pedophiles and track down pornographers and proponents of violence and cruelty to animals and people. Parents can also exercise more control over what their children may be exposed to on their home computing devices using parental control products, which make extensive use of filtering technologies. Further, when applied to email, filters act as spam monitors. However, a drawback is that, when used inappropriately, filters can hinder one's freedom to access information on any given subject.

Intellectual Property, Copyright, Licensing, and Piracy

Within the relatively new information economy, *intellectual property* has taken on a new importance. It refers to knowledge and creative ideas or expressions that are protected by copyright, patent, trademark, industrial design rights, or trade secret laws. Intellectual property rights are themselves a form of property, called intangible property. Such material must not be imitated, diluted, or infringed upon in any way.

Examples of intellectual property within the digital marketplace include software, formulas, songs, stories, essays, movies, art work of all kinds, and so on. Websites that provide intellectual property assets, particularly for knowledge-intensive and high-innovation areas, offer more value to the user than those that do not. However, the widespread downloading and distribution of intellectual property, such as music and movie sharing, have forced lawmakers to keep up with the times by extending laws to the Internet. Australia and the United States have each passed laws to cover intellectual property on the Internet, but enforcing the laws presents unique challenges. For example, even though the United States has its Digital Millennium Copyright Act of 1998 (DMCA) codified as section 1201 of the Copyright Act, the law has acted more to stifle many legitimate activities such as security research and free speech than to mitigate piracy. Fair use is also circumscribed in that a user may legally make copies for personal use of a movie on DVD, for example, but physically cannot because of movie companies using encryption that prevents any copying at all.

Under the larger area of intellectual property law, industrial property refers broadly to inventions, and *copyright* refers primarily to literary and artistic creations, including computer programs and electronic databases. A copyright gives the creator exclusive rights to it, usually for a limited time. The copyright does not cover ideas and information themselves but the form or the manner in which they are expressed in the marketplace. Countries that have signed onto the Berne Convention for the Protection of Literary and Artistic Works treaty agree that such creations include books, pamphlets, and other writings as well as drawings, photographs, music, dance, plays, and so on. Although computer programs and multimedia productions are not specifically listed, the Berne Convention treaty still includes such newer items under Article 2. While a creator has copyright protection automatically, it is better to file for copyright protection if violations seem likely, so that the copyright can be used also as an effective protection tool against piracy. In the United States, for example, the electronic U.S. Copyright Office (eCO) provides an online application form at `http://www.copyright.gov/eco/` for a small processing fee.

Avoiding Piracy

Intellectual property laws and copyrights exist to protect creators from theft or copyright infringement. On the Internet it is very easy to distribute copyrighted work without the creator's consent and without the creator receiving any benefit from their original work. The whole phenomenon of copyright infringement is known as *piracy*, and it has a very large negative impact on content creators of all kinds, from independent authors to software developers to the movie and music industries. The reasons why people choose to pirate works that are protected by intellectual property laws are many and varied. Some of the most important are these:

Pricing   This is a valid problem especially in less-developed countries where people don't earn enough money and can't pay for products at the price requested by legitimate sellers.

Unavailability   This problem plagues many industries but especially the movie and the music industries. For example, in many countries there are no legitimate services for renting and viewing movies, similar to Netflix in the United States. Because people don't have easy access to the newest movies, they may revert to the use of piracy to get access to the movies they are interested in.

Usefulness   Some products include annoying copy protection systems that restrict legitimate use. Others include irritating advertisements and disclaimers that cannot be skipped, making the user experience less desirable than when using pirated versions of the same products.

Videos, music, online games, and software are the usual booty for online pirates. Piracy laws protect content creators from losing money on sales that have been redirected because their product has been stolen and given away either for free or for a fee to the pirate. The main problem with piracy laws is enforcement, but antipiracy software, antipiracy campaigns, and antipiracy reporting systems have been instrumental in charges being laid against online pirates. In the United States, this means up to five years in prison and fines up to $250,000. Even if the pirated booty was given away for free, civil penalties can add up to thousands of dollars in fines.

To prevent being charged with piracy, do not share or resell any copyrighted material, such as movies, music, games, and software. To do so is to steal from the content creator's potential earnings. If you are unclear about whether something online is protected, familiarize yourself with your country's intellectual property and copyright laws. Also, you should not be using websites that distribute copyrighted works for free. Use legitimate sources instead. For example, if you don't want to purchase lots of music CDs, you can pay a monthly subscription fee to a legitimate music-streaming service like Spotify or Deezer and listen to the music that interests you at any time. You can also buy music from dedicated services such as iTunes, Google Play Music, or Amazon Prime Music.

To counter online piracy of copyrighted materials, *digital rights management (DRM)* has been adopted as a solution. DRM is a class of technologies used by hardware manufacturers, publishers, copyright holders, and individuals with the intent of controlling the use of digital content and devices after their sale. DRM can be used to control the copying of a work, its execution, viewing, printing, or altering, depending on the product and the intent of its creator. For example, when you buy a DVD of a video game or a movie, that DVD is protected by DRM so that you can't make unauthorized copies of it and give it to others or sell it without the creator's consent.

Creative Commons: A Less Restrictive Form of Licensing

We have talked extensively about licensing both in this chapter and also in Chapter 3, "Understanding Software." If there's one takeaway from all these discussions, it is that licensing is a complex and nuanced subject, which sometimes can be very restrictive on legitimate users of a copyrighted product. As a response to these issues, Creative Commons, a U.S. non-profit corporation founded in 2001, decided to create its own licensing system that allows the free distribution of an otherwise copyrighted work.

This license is used when the creator wants to give people the right to share, use, and build upon their work. Creative Commons provides the creator flexibility (for example, to allow only noncommercial uses of their own work) and protects the people who use or redistribute the work from concerns of copyright infringement as long as they abide by the conditions that are specified in the license by which the creator distributes the work.

There are four types of Creative Commons conditions that you can use to create your own license:

Attribution Licensees may copy, distribute, display, and perform the work and make derivative works based on it only if they give the licensor the credits in the manner specified.

Share-Alike Licensees may distribute derivative works only under a license identical to the license that governs the original work.

Noncommercial Licensees may copy, distribute, display, and perform the work and make derivative works based on it only for noncommercial purposes.

No Derivative Works Licensees may copy, distribute, display, and perform only verbatim copies of the work, not derivative works based on it.

You can learn more about Creative Commons and create your own licenses by going to https://creativecommons.org/.

There are several positive aspects to using Creative Commons licenses, the most important being the fact that they are easy to create, understand, and use. Second, they are generally recognized as legitimate licenses in many countries around the world. Thus, they are widely used online on many websites and blogs, with many content creators choosing to protect their work using Creative Commons.

Summary

In this chapter we discussed what it means to communicate correctly in the digital world. As in real life, you should always pay attention to the context you are in, the people you are talking to, and the tools that you have available. While some norms work well in personal communication, they may not apply to professional communication and vice versa. That's why we have shown you the basics of what it means to communicate effectively in the digital world, as well as a few do's and don'ts that you should keep in mind.

Also, knowing the communication tools that are available and how to use them goes a long way in communicating effectively with others. Don't hesitate to use them to your advantage.

Finally, when using a computer or a mobile device, you will use products that are protected by intellectual property laws, ranging from hardware to software to original content like music, movies, games, and so on. It is very important to be mindful of copyrights and licenses and to use products responsibly, from legitimate sellers and not from online pirates. This will not only benefit the creators of the products that you are using but also protect you from legal issues.

In the next chapter we will discuss security and how to stay safe when online. We will also show you how to correctly use a computer from a health standpoint. You will learn how things like posture, lighting, the position of your chair, and other factors may negatively affect your health in the long term, if you don't pay attention to them.

Exam Essentials

Know the differences between personal and professional communication. Professional communication has different standards from personal communication. You should be aware of them and apply them in your work.

Understand how you should not communicate online. Just like in real life, there are inappropriate ways of communicating online. You should know what they are and avoid using them.

Understand censorship and filtering. Censorship is a real problem that affects people all over the world. Filtering technologies are also used to block access to certain types of content online. You should know the basics about these concepts and how they can affect you.

Learn what intellectual property and copyright are. Original works and content that you find on the Internet are usually protected by intellectual property laws and copyrights. You should know what these concepts are and how they impact the way you use original products and content online.

Learn about piracy and its negative effects. You should know what piracy is, its negative effects on content creators and users, and how to protect yourself from it.

Key Terms

Before you take the exam, be certain you are familiar with the following terms:

bullying	intellectual property
censorship	libel
copyright	piracy
digital rights management (DRM)	slander
filters	spamming
flaming	textese

Review Questions

1. On which occasion would it be acceptable to type your message in all capital letters?

   A. Resume to a potential employer

   B. Text message to a friend

   C. Email communication to your supervisor

   D. An important email to fellow colleagues

2. Which of the following are examples of spam? (Choose all that apply.)

   A. Sending an unsolicited email about your product to a distribution list with a large number of people

   B. Sending an SMS about your upcoming product launch to a large number of people, without their prior consent

   C. Advertising your product on your company's blog

   D. Posting a photo with yourself on Facebook

3. Why does tone matter in professional communications?

   A. It meets the expectations of the audience.

   B. It does not matter at all.

   C. Tone determines if copyright is needed.

   D. Tone may allow filters not to work.

4. What are symbolic facial expressions like ☺ called?

   A. Filters

   B. Digital licenses

   C. Emoticons

   D. Short messages

5. Where are emoticons typically acceptable to use?

   A. Formal progress reports

   B. Informal proposals

   C. Personal communications

   D. Cover letters

6. Which of the following are examples of censorship? (Choose all that apply.)

   A. Creative Commons

   B. Parental controls

   C. Bandwidth

   D. Government-blocked websites

7. What do DRM technologies try to control? (Choose all that apply.)

    A. The copying of a work

    B. Spam attacks

    C. The altering of a work

    D. Censorship

8. What is the term for knowledge and creative ideas or expressions that have commercial value and are protected either by copyright, patent, trademark, industrial design rights, or trade secret laws?

    A. Copyright

    B. Intellectual property

    C. Digital licenses

    D. Piracy

9. What is Creative Commons? (Choose all that apply.)

    A. A license used when the creator gives people the right to share, use, and build upon their work

    B. A license used when the creator doesn't give people the right to share, use, and build upon their work

    C. A flexible kind of license that protects only the people who use or redistribute the work

    D. A flexible type of license that protects the people who use or redistribute the work from concerns of copyright infringement as long as they abide by the conditions that are specified in the license

10. What is it called if you make copies of a movie to sell online without the permission of the creator?

    A. Piracy

    B. Fraud

    C. Censorship

    D. Digital license

Chapter

15

Maintaining Your Health and Safety While Using Computers

THE FOLLOWING IC3: LIVING ONLINE EXAM OBJECTIVES ARE COVERED IN THIS CHAPTER:

✓ **Secure Online Communication or Activity**

- Identity Protection

  - Explain how to completely remove data from hard drives, portable memory, digital devices.

  - Explain how to secure the data on your computer and keep it updated by backing up data to other sources – cloud, backup hard drives.

  - Describe how to use protection programs and the value of these services. Also describe the harm that can come from not using these products and services.

✓ **Ergonomics**

- Explain and demonstrate proper ergonomics. Problems that come from improper ergonomics in relation to monitor height and angle.

- Explain and demonstrate proper ergonomics. Problems that come from improper ergonomics in relation to mouse and keyboard shapes and use.

- Explain the ergonomics around proper chair height and settings, arms, lumbar support, etc.

- Explain the issues around poor lighting, short term and long term eye problems.

- Explain the physical issues surrounding poor body posture, especially with prolonged time in the same position(s).

In this chapter we will start by discussing how to protect both your identity and your data when you are online. On the Internet you expose yourself to many threats and perils. People may try to trick you into sharing personal details about yourself like your home address, while some may try to steal your financial data like your credit card number. Others may try to make you a victim of a hoax and purchase things you do not need or simply give them money while promising you an unbelievable return on your "investment." In order to keep yourself as safe as possible, you should learn and apply several principles that will help you in most situations. Also, knowing how to keep your computer secure goes a long way toward having a good computing experience, without exposing yourself to problems that can be avoided, like virus infections.

Finally, you should pay attention to your own health. Prolonged and incorrect computer use may cause health problems. We are going to offer several recommendations for creating an ergonomic workspace and how to use the computer so that you don't negatively affect your health. You will also learn about several ailments that are common to computer users, so that you can recognize them and take action in case you start having health issues caused by prolonged computer use.

Protecting Your Identity and Your Data

Protecting your identity and your data involves many important choices. First, you should know several principles for protecting your identity online. Then, you should know how to keep the data on your computer as safe as possible.

When you use the Internet and browse the Web, it is important to know, apply, and use several principles that will help you protect your identity:

- Use different passwords.

  You should use a different password for every website and service that you are accessing online. Over the years, you will end up using lots of websites and you will have many accounts, which may prove difficult to manage on your own. To help you keep track of all your passwords, it is best to use a password manager like LastPass, RoboForm, 1Password, or other similar service.

- Use strong passwords.

  In Chapter 13, "Communicating Online with Others," we talked in detail about using strong passwords for your email accounts and what makes a password strong. This is another area where a password manager can help you generate unique strong passwords for each website and service that you are using on the Internet.

- Share personal details only with people you know.

  You should avoid turning personal details into public information. Share things like your email address or home address only with people you know. Also, avoid sharing financial details like your credit card number with anyone other than your family.

- Use a secondary email address for less-important online activities.

  Ideally, you should not use your personal email address for things like signing up to newsletters, forums, and online communities of any kind. It is best to use a secondary email address for these activities. That's because hackers have an easier time hacking into less-known websites and communities, which may not benefit from the same security that a big company like Facebook does. It is easy enough for them to steal your email address from an online forum and then hack into your email account if you have a weak password.

- Purchase items online only from websites that use secure connections.

  Avoid buying merchandise from websites that do not use the Hypertext Transfer Protocol Secure (HTTPS), which encrypts the data that you are sending. Transfers that take place without using a secure connection are easily intercepted, and your financial details can be stolen without you realizing it has happened. HTTPS provides authentication and encryption. It protects against man-in-the-middle attacks, eavesdropping, and tampering with the data that is being sent.

- Use the privacy settings available on the social networks that you are using.

  In Chapter 13 we talked about social networks and the fact that they offer tools and settings for protecting your privacy. Don't hesitate to use them, and make sure that your social networking activity is not public and easily accessible to anyone.

- Regularly check your bank statements.

  You should check your banks statements regularly and look for purchases that were not made by you. If a hacker manages to steal your credit card details, they may be trying to use that information to purchase things online without your approval.

- Pay attention to what you click on or to whom you reply.

  If you are contacted by people you don't know, about some crazy offer that's too good to be true, then most likely they are trying to scam you. Also, pay attention to whom you reply via email or social networks like Facebook. If something feels dodgy, then it most probably is, and you should listen to your instincts. Also, don't click every link you receive from others or all the ads that you see online. Some links and ads are a form of spam and take you to websites that are trying to make you pay for something that you should not be buying or, even worse, trying steal your personal and financial data.

No matter how careful you are, there's no guarantee that others won't manage to steal your identity, portions of it, or some of your personal data and misuse it. However, if you apply these principles, you can protect yourself quite well and limit your chances of being the victim of an online scam or hoax.

Keeping your personal data safe is another aspect that you should pay attention to. On your business laptop or desktop, most probably your employer has enabled encryption using solutions like *BitLocker*—the encryption tool that's built into Windows. Encryption is very important because, should your computer be stolen, others will have a very difficult time accessing the data found on it. While encryption is not foolproof and data can be decrypted, the whole process is so complex and resource intensive that most people won't be able to do anything with the data stored on an encrypted computer. If you have very important personal data on your computers at home, you may also want to enable encryption so that it is protected if someone else gets unauthorized access to your computer.

Another aspect of keeping your data safe involves having a backup system in place. In Chapter 4, "Troubleshooting Problems with Your Computer," we discussed the principles involved in creating your own backup system and how to use the built-in Backup and Restore tool that's available in Windows. If you don't like the tools that are available in Windows, you can find many other products that were developed by other companies. Don't hesitate to try them out and choose the one that works best for you. When your computer crashes, your backup system will be very handy in recovering your data and making sure that you lose as little as possible.

Removing Data from Your Computer

In Windows, in order to delete a file or folder, you first select it and then press the Delete key on your keyboard. Alternatively, you right-click it and select Delete from the context menu. When you do this, a prompt is shown asking for your confirmation to delete that file or folder (Figure 15.1). Click Yes and the item is deleted.

FIGURE 15.1   The Delete Folder prompt

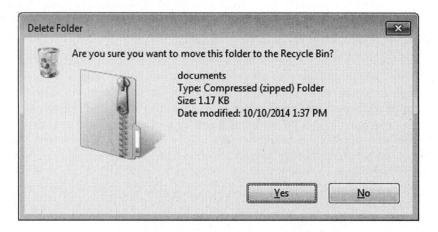

However, it is not deleted for good. It is only moved to a special area named the *Recycle Bin*. This is the place where the references to your deleted files and folders are kept. Physically, your deleted items still occupy the same location on the hard disk. You just can't use them or open them when they are in the Recycle Bin. Windows keeps track of where they came from, so you can restore them if you want to. Each partition of your hard drive has a Recycle Bin, but the fun thing is all the files you delete appear in this one folder with the Recycle Bin icon on your Desktop, shown in Figure 15.2.

FIGURE 15.2   The Recycle Bin shortcut on the Desktop

When you double-click the Recycle Bin shortcut, you can view all the files and folders that were deleted on your computer (Figure 15.3). You can select any of them and restore them to their original location, or you can empty the Recycle Bin and delete all the references to your deleted items. This is done by clicking the Empty The Recycle Bin button at the top of the Recycle Bin window and making the necessary confirmations.

As long as deleted files are found in the Recycle Bin, they continue to take up space on your computer. If you want that space freed up, then you should empty the Recycle Bin so that the space they occupy is unlocked by Windows and used for saving other files on your computer.

FIGURE 15.3 Viewing the contents of the Recycle Bin

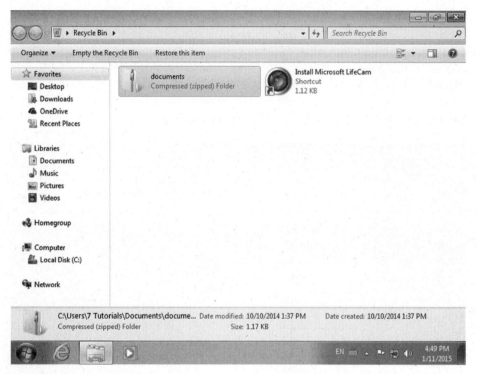

If you want to remove a file or folder without having it move to the Recycle Bin and automatically free the space it uses, you should select it in Windows Explorer and then press Shift+Delete on your keyboard. You are then asked if you are sure you want to permanently delete this file (Figure 15.4). Click Yes and the file is deleted for good, without being moved to the Recycle Bin.

FIGURE 15.4 Deleting a file in Windows

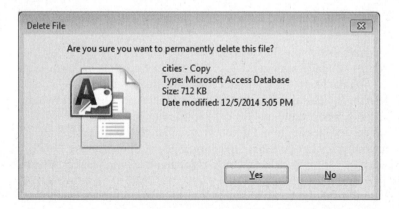

If you then open the Recycle Bin, you will notice that the file you removed with Shift+Delete is not available.

The trouble with deleting files in Windows and any other operating system is that even though you use Shift+Delete, files still remain physically on your computer's hard disk. Yes, the references to them are deleted and they cannot be recovered without using special data-recovery tools like Recuva (http://www.piriform.com/recuva). However, if no files are written on top of them, in the space that they used to physically occupy on the hard disk, they can be easily recovered with appropriate tools.

In order for a file to be completely deleted from your hard disk and completely unrecoverable, you must overwrite the part of the drive containing the data from that file a dozen times with the contents of other files. This is difficult for a computer user to do, and operating systems don't tend to include tools for complete data wiping. That's why a whole niche exists of software applications that specialize in complete data wiping. There are plenty of tools available, both free and commercial. One of the most popular ones is CCleaner Free (http://www.piriform.com/ccleaner). It is a complex application that specializes in finding and removing unnecessary files that take up space on your computer (Figure 15.5). It is also capable of wiping the free space that's available on your computer so that all the data that used to be on it can no longer be recovered.

FIGURE 15.5   The CCleaner Free application

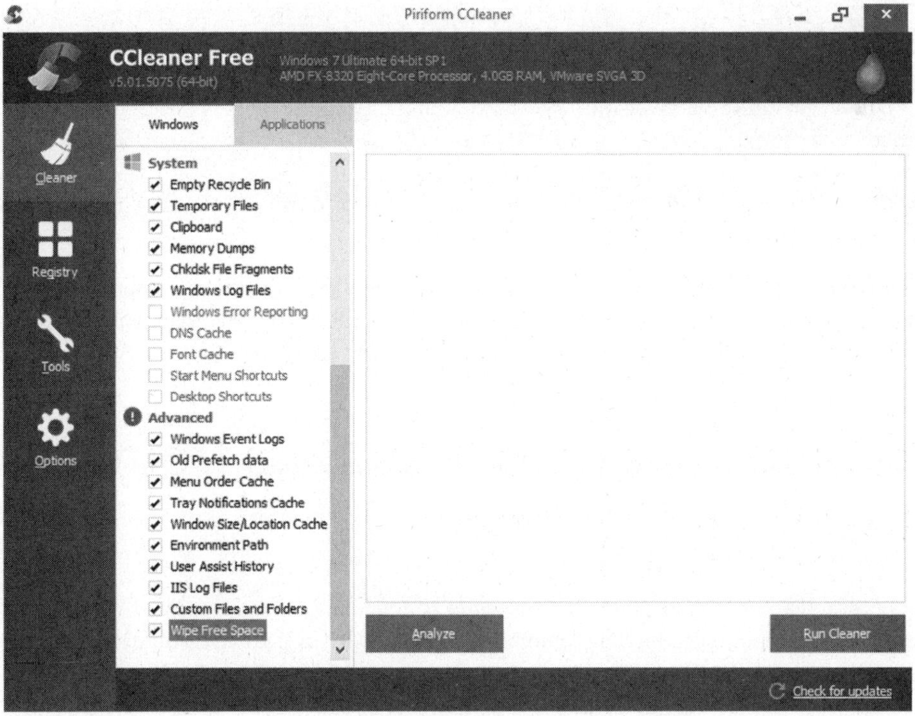

Another popular tool is File Shredder (`http://www.fileshredder.org`). This application deletes files and folders in a way that makes them unrecoverable, not even with specialized software (Figure 15.6).

FIGURE 15.6   The File Shredder application

While removing data in a way that makes it unrecoverable by others is important in business environments that work with classified information, you may also want to use similar tools on your personal computers when removing sensitive data.

Keeping Your Computer Safe from Threats and Malware

A good practice for having a safe computing experience on a Windows PC is to keep Windows Update enabled and running automatically in the background at all times. In Chapter 1 we discussed the benefits of having your operating system and applications up to date. Also, we showed you how Windows Update helps in having a safe experience and the reasons why you should have it always enabled. Don't hesitate to go through that chapter again and review the section on software and system updates.

Modern operating systems like Windows offer some security tools such as antivirus and firewall protection, but they may not be enough in today's complex technological landscape. That's why it is a good practice to invest in commercial security products like antivirus or Internet security suites. An antivirus actively monitors what is going on with a computer, and if it detects any unusual activity, it blocks it or it informs the user. Antivirus software also regularly scans your computer for malware, and if it finds any infected files, it removes them.

There are also more complex security products called Internet security suites. They include the protection modules offered by antivirus products, as well as firewall protection and other advanced features like ad blockers, virtual keyboards that cannot be intercepted by keyloggers, safe browsing modes for performing protected financial transactions online, and others. To learn more about malware, its potential negative impact, and how to protect yourself from it, don't hesitate to read the section "Protecting Yourself from Malware" from Chapter 3.

The Ergonomics of Using the Computer in a Healthy Way

People all over the world spend a lot of time in front of computers. We use them at work, while on the road, and also at home. Some people may end up spending more than eight hours a day in front of a computer. Because of that, it is very important to pay attention to how you sit in front of a computer and how much you do it.

It is essential to have a workspace that is well organized and arranged so that you have the correct position when using the computer. Also, you should keep an eye on your posture, and don't forget to take breaks on a regular basis. Here are a few things to consider when working in front of a computer and arranging your workspace:

- Use an ergonomic chair that's optimized for computer use.

  When you choose a chair for sitting in front of a computer, you should make sure that it has the following elements: a comfortable cushion to sit on, arm rests for when you aren't typing, the ability to swivel or roll around, adjustable seat height so that you can match the chair to the height of the desk, adjustable back rest height, and lumbar support. The lumbar support is very important because our backs are slightly curved inward, meaning that the chair's back shouldn't be directly vertical. It should support your lower back by coming forward (Figure 15.7).

FIGURE 15.7   Lumbar support (on the right) versus missing lumbar support (on the left)

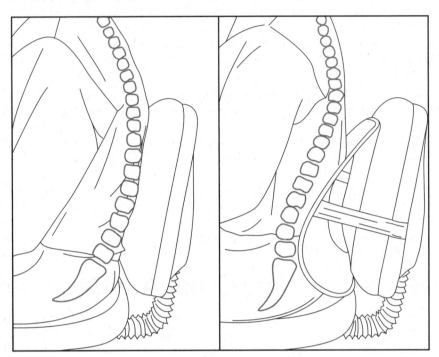

- Place your keyboard and mouse close together.

  You should position the mouse and keyboard as close together as possible. When positioning the keyboard, pay attention to the keys, not the keyboard. You want the B key to be positioned directly in front of you, in the center of the desk.

- Position the top of the computer's monitor at eye level.

  This will help you avoid tilting your head forward or back, which would stress your neck and shoulder muscles when sitting in front of the computer. You can place your monitor on top of the computer if you need to raise it up to meet this height requirement, or you could manipulate your chair up or down accordingly. With a monitor that is larger than 20 inches (50.8 cm), consider positioning the top of your monitor 3 inches (7.6 cm) above eye level. Also, the screen should be at least 20 inches (50 cm) from your eyes.

- Pay attention to your posture.

  You want to be sitting up, with your back about a 100-degree angle to your legs. Keep your elbows close to your body and your wrists straight. Also, try to keep your shoulders and back relaxed. Your keyboard should be at a level where you don't need to use the armrests.

- Protect your eyes.

  In order to do this, you should first eliminate glare on the monitor. While some monitors can tilt, many can't, and you're likely going to have to solve this problem with strategic lighting placement instead of monitor tweaks.

Another common problem that's related to prolonged computer use is eyestrain. If you experience dizziness, headache, lightheadedness, or twitching/spasms around your eyes, you're likely suffering from eyestrain. Tired or irritated eyes, burning eyes when closed, headache, and even nausea are indications as well. The problem is that most people who experience these symptoms shrug them off as a hard day at the office. Instead, pay attention to the signals your body is sending you and do something about it.

Consider taking frequent breaks. There's rule called *20-20-20* that was made to help people protect their eyes in office environments that involve a lot of sitting in front of the computer. The rule says that for every 20 minutes you spend staring at the computer, you should spend 20 seconds looking at objects 20 feet away—or at least far enough away that your eyes aren't working to focus. While most of us can't get up from the computer every half hour while we work, it is important to stop for a few minutes and do something that doesn't involve looking at the screen. Go get a glass of water, or just do a lap around your cubicle, or talk to a colleague. Your eyes will thank you.

Common Problems That Are Generated by Incorrect Computer Use and Posture

It doesn't matter how ergonomic your desk may be, you still need to be mindful of your body when you work or you'll never reap the benefits of your properly set-up workspace. For example, if you don't pay attention to your posture and you slouch in front of the computer, over a period of time this may have a long-lasting impact upon your posture. Developing and maintaining the correct habits can go a long way in avoiding chronic pains associated with poor posture.

Long-term computer users may also suffer from *repetitive strain injury (RSI)*, which is a common condition where pain and other symptoms occur in an area of the body that has done repetitive tasks, such as the arms or the hands. It is usually related to a task or occupation, but leisure activities can also be a cause, including sports overuse. Unlike a normal strain following a sudden injury, symptoms of RSI can persist well beyond the time it would take symptoms of a normal strain to ease. The main cause is frequent and repetitive movements of a part of the body, for example, typing, using a computer mouse a lot, and so on.

Other factors may contribute, such as poor posture while doing the movement, using excessive force to perform the task, and not taking enough breaks from the task. Some research suggests that psychosocial workplace factors (like stress) can also contribute to RSI. Symptoms in the affected area can include pain, tightness, dull ache, throbbing, numbness, or tingling. The symptoms tend to develop gradually. At first the symptoms may occur only while you do the repetitive task and ease off when you rest. In time the symptoms can be present all the time but tend to be made worse by doing the repetitive task. If you have these symptoms, you should see a doctor. The earlier the problem is recognized and dealt with, the better the outcome.

Summary

An important part of being a digital citizen who uses the Web and the Internet on a daily basis is knowing how to protect yourself. Many people will try to learn personal and financial information about you in order to use it for all kinds of malicious activities. Others may try to extort money from you through numerous means, including computer viruses. Knowing and applying the basics about how to protect yourself when online will do you a world of good. That's why you should follow the recommendations that we shared at the beginning of this chapter.

Unfortunately, when we use computers we tend to ignore things like good posture, setting up our workspace so that we have the correct body position when working on the computer, and so on. That's why, in this chapter, we have given you several recommendations for setting up your workspace correctly and maintaining good posture in front of the computer. Using these recommendations will go a long way toward avoiding health issues caused by long-term computer use.

Finally, we also discussed the most common health issues that are experienced by computer users so that you can recognize them in case you start suffering from them and can take corrective action as early as possible.

In the next chapter we will discuss the use of search engines on the Web, how to find the information that you need, finding trusted sources, and more.

Exam Essentials

Understand how to protect yourself when online.   Know and apply the principles we shared for protecting your identity when online.

Know how to remove data from your computer.   You should know how deletion works, how to delete files from your computer, and the tools that you can use to make sure that your deleted data is no longer recoverable.

Learn how to set up your workspace correctly.   In order to avoid health problems, you should learn how to set up your workspace, position your computer, use the correct posture, and so on. This will help you avoid health problems caused by incorrect computer use.

Know common health problems caused by incorrect computer use.   Know the common health problems that are caused by incorrect computer use so that you recognize them early and take action, in case you have similar issues.

Key Terms

Before you take the exam, be certain you are familiar with the following terms:

20-20-20   Recycle Bin

BitLocker   repetitive strain injury (RSI)

Review Questions

1. Which of the following are examples of what not to do when online? (Choose all that apply.)

   A. Use the same password for all your email accounts.

   B. Share your home address publicly on Facebook or Internet forums.

   C. Use passwords of eight characters or more, which include both lowercase and uppercase letters as well as numbers and symbols.

   D. Reply to emails from people you don't know, promising an incredible deal.

2. Which of the following are good recommendations for protecting your financial data? (Choose all that apply.)

   A. Make purchases only on websites that use HTTPS.

   B. Make purchases when connected to public wireless networks.

   C. Purchase online only things that you like.

   D. Don't share your credit card details with others online.

3. Which of the following are examples of protecting the data on your computer? (Choose all that apply.)

   A. Using a strong password for your user account

   B. Using encryption tools like BitLocker

   C. Creating a backup system with Backup and Restore

   D. Deleting the data on your computer

4. What happens when you select a file, press Delete on your keyboard, and confirm that you want to delete the file? (Choose all that apply.)

   A. The file is removed from your computer.

   B. The file can no longer be recovered.

   C. The file remains on your hard disk, using up disk space.

   D. The file is moved to the Recycle Bin, where you can recover it if needed.

5. Which of the following are characteristics of the Recycle Bin? (Choose all that apply.)

   A. A place where Windows stores recovered files

   B. A place where Windows stores references to deleted files and folders

   C. A folder from where you can recover deleted files

   D. A folder used for recycling files

6. How do you delete a file without moving it to the Recycle Bin?

    A. Select the file and press Delete on your keyboard.

    B. Right-click the file and then click Delete.

    C. Select the file and press Shift+Delete on your keyboard.

    D. Select the file and press Ctrl+Delete on your keyboard.

7. Which of the following are ways of completely removing a file from your computer so that it can no longer be recovered? (Choose all that apply.)

    A. Select the file and press Shift+Delete on your keyboard.

    B. Select the file, press Shift+Delete on your keyboard, and overwrite that part of the drive a dozen of times with the contents of other files.

    C. Use an application like CCleaner or File Shredder to wipe the free space on your hard disk several times so that deleted data is no longer recoverable.

    D. Empty the Recycle Bin.

8. Which of the following are characteristics of an ergonomic chair? (Choose all that apply.)

    A. It is black and it looks great.

    B. It has a comfortable cushion.

    C. It has lumbar support.

    D. It has adjustable height and back rest height.

9. How should you position the computer monitor on your desk? (Choose all that apply.)

    A. Position it at eye level.

    B. Place it directly on your desk.

    C. If the computer measures 20 inches or more, position the top of it 3 inches above eye level.

    D. Place it at least 20 inches from your eyes.

10. What does the 20-20-20 rule stand for?

    A. For every 20 days spent working on a computer, take 20 days off doing 20 things that do not involve using a computer.

    B. For every 20 minutes spent staring at the computer, spend 20 seconds looking at 20 objects.

    C. For every 20 minutes spent staring at the computer, spend 20 minutes taking a break.

    D. For every 20 minutes spent staring at the computer, spend 20 seconds looking at objects 20 feet away.

Chapter

16

Searching the World Wide Web

THE FOLLOWING IC3: LIVING ONLINE EXAM OBJECTIVES ARE COVERED IN THIS CHAPTER:

✓ **Using Search Engines**

- Explain how to use search engines to acquire information. The value of the resources available on the internet.

- Demonstrate how to use search engines to answer questions and solve problems by using good search terms to get specific information from reputable sources.

✓ **Evaluate Search Results**

- Forums

    - Explain the value and problems with internet forums.

- Explain that ads are paid messages from companies that want to interest you in their products. Messages are not necessarily factual.

- Explain that sponsored links are a form of advertising and not to be relied on as an informational resource.

- Explain that a knowledge base is a collection of data around a particular subject. Include examples like Help menus available from software and hard good manufacturers.

- Explain how to determine the validity of various sources, including but not limited to domain names/domain, published journals, government sites and documents vs. forums, blogs, personal websites.

- Explain that articles can be both factual and made up. Articles are created for a number of reasons including, reviews of products that may or may not have been given to the reviewer, personal opinion, or well researched documenting of fact.

✓ **Using Advanced Features of Search Engines**

- Search types

We have arrived at the last chapter of this book, and it's time to talk about finding information online. The Web is a huge place that's growing every day. Finding information online can be a challenge, even if you are using a good search engine like Google or Bing. That's why we will show you how to make effective searches online and how to create more advanced queries using things like symbols and operators so that you can find what you need more easily. We will also show you how to search for files online, not just information. As you will see, the procedure involved when searching for files is not that different from searching for information.

Toward the end of the chapter we will discuss concepts like online advertisement and the most common forms of advertising that are found on the Web. We will also show how you can block many ads that you find online.

Finally, we will talk about finding information on Internet forums and knowledge bases. Then, we will share some principles that you can use to validate the information that you find online to make sure that it is as complete and as accurate as possible.

Using Search Engines to Find Information Online

One of the most common ways of finding information online is through the use of a *search engine*. This is a software system in a web browser that is designed to search for information on the Web. In order to use a search engine, you need to type what you want to learn, press Enter, and then review the results that are displayed. Search results can be a mix of web pages, images, videos, and other types of files and information.

The first search engine that appeared on the Web was the W3Catalog, which was released on September 1993. It was a very primitive engine that periodically mirrored pages that existed on the Web at that time and rewrote them into a standard format that could be used for performing searches and finding information. Since then, many search engines have been created, and today's most important engines are Google, Baidu (it serves only China), Bing, and Yahoo!.

In order to use a search engine, you must visit its page and then type what you want to find. You can type a word or more, a full sentence, or a question describing what you are looking for. As you type, search engines make suggestions for popular keywords that are used by others, which may help you fine-tune your search. When you have finished typing, press Enter and review the list of results. Generally, for each search result, you are shown a title, the URL of the page, and a small description.

In Exercise 16.1 you will learn how to make a simple search using Google.

EXERCISE 16.1

Searching the Web Using Google

1. Click the Internet Explorer shortcut on the Windows taskbar.

2. In the Address bar at the top of the Internet Explorer window, type **google.com** and press Enter on your keyboard (Figure 16.1).

FIGURE 16.1   Typing google.com in Internet Explorer's Address bar

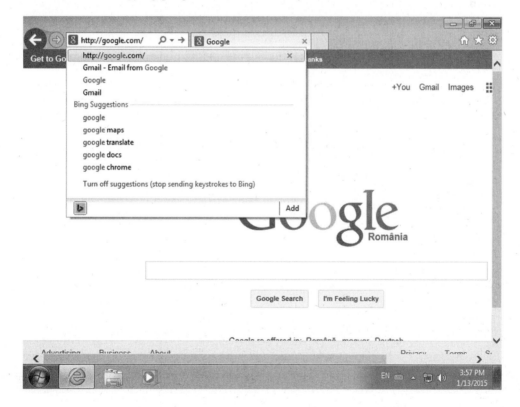

3. Type **windows 7 tutorials** as the key words for your search (Figure 16.2).

Notice how Google automatically suggests other popular key words to fine-tune your search and automatically loads search results that are appropriate to the key words that you are using.

FIGURE 16.2 Searching for windows 7 tutorials on Google

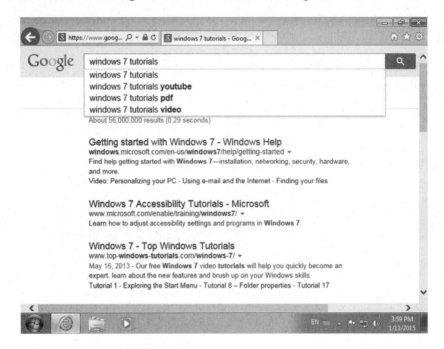

4. When finished typing, press Enter on your keyboard.

5. Look at the information displayed for each search result.

6. Click the first search result that is displayed by Google.

7. Close Internet Explorer.

We mentioned earlier that there are many search engines available on the Web. To familiarize you with the concept of making simple web searches, Exercise 16.2 will share how to make a search using Bing, Microsoft's search engine.

EXERCISE 16.2

Searching the Web Using Bing

1. Click the Internet Explorer shortcut on the Windows taskbar.

2. In the Address bar at the top of the Internet Explorer window, type **bing.com** and press Enter on your keyboard (Figure 16.3).

3. Type **windows 7 tutorials** as the key words for your search (Figure 16.4).

FIGURE 16.3   Typing bing.com in Internet Explorer's Address bar

FIGURE 16.4   Searching for windows 7 tutorials on Bing

EXERCISE 16.2 *(continued)*

Notice how Bing automatically suggests other popular key words to fine-tune your search.

4.   When finished typing, press Enter on your keyboard.

5.   Look at the information displayed for each search result.

6.   Click the first search result that is displayed by Bing.

7.   Close Internet Explorer.

As you can see from these two simple exercises, the way search engines function is very similar. Yes, they look different and sometimes display different search results, but the process for finding information is the same.

Performing Advanced Searches Using Symbols and Search Operators

Very few people know that modern search engines allow you to create advanced searches using symbols or search operators, which allow you to get very specific results. Since Google is the most popular search engine, let's take a look at what symbols you can use and what they do when making a search:

+ (plus sign)   Search for Google+ pages or blood types. Examples: **+Chrome** and **AB+.**

@   Find social tags. Example: **@ciprianrusen** returns my Twitter account.

$ Find prices. Example: **Samsung $400.**

Find popular hashtags for trending topics on social networks like Twitter. Example: **#blackfriday.**

- (minus sign)   It can be used to remove words or to connect words. When you use a dash before a word or a site, it excludes results that include that word or site. This is useful for words with multiple meanings, like Jaguar the car brand and jaguar the animal. Examples: **jaguar speed -car** and **dogs -site:wikipedia.org.** When the dash is in between multiple words, the search engine will know the words are strongly connected. Example: **two-year-old cat.**

_ (underscore)   Connect two words like **quick_sort.** Your search results will find this pair of words either linked together (quicksort) or connected by an underscore (quick_sort).

" " (quotes)   When you put a word or phrase in quotes, the results will include only pages with the same words in the same order as what's inside the quotes. Example: **"Not everyone can become a great artist, but a great artist can come from anywhere."**

* (asterisk)   Add an asterisk as a placeholder for any unknown or wildcard terms. Use with quotation marks to find variations of that exact phrase or to remember words in the middle of a phrase. Example: **"a * saved is a * earned."**

.. (two dots)   Separate numbers by two periods without spaces (..) to see results that contain numbers in a given range of things like dates, prices, and measurements. Example: **smartphone $100..$200.**

Some of the symbols mentioned in the list also work on other search engines like Bing in the same way, while others do not.

Earlier, we mentioned the term *search operators*. They are words that can be added to searches to help narrow down your results. Here are the search operators that work with most search engines:

site   Get results from certain sites or domains. For example, you can find all mentions of *football* on the CNN website by typing **football site:cnn.com.**

link   Find pages that link to a certain page. For example, you can find all the pages that link to wikipedia.org by typing **link:wikipedia.org.**

related   Find sites that are similar to a URL you already know. If you search for related sites to the nytimes.com, you'll find other news publication sites you may be interested in. Example: **related:nytimes.com.**

OR   If you want to search for pages that may have just one of several words, include OR between the words. Without the OR, your results would typically show only pages that match both terms. Example: **Olympics location 2016 OR 2020.**

info   Get information about a URL, including the cached version of the page, similar pages, and pages that link to the site. Example: **info:microsoft.com.**

When you search using operators that include a colon (:), don't add any spaces between the operator and your search terms. For example, a search for **site:microsoft.com** will work, but **site: microsoft.com** will not. OR is the only exception to this rule.

Searching for Files Online

You can also search for files online. For example, you may want to find pictures of a certain person like a movie star, or you may want to find the video of a hit from your favorite band, or you may want to find the latest album of a band you like. All this is possible with the help of search engines.

When you make a search, your results are split by type into several tabs: Web, Images, News, Videos, Maps, and so on. Let's assume that you are working on a paper and you need to find information about the American president Barack Obama. At first, when you type his name, you get a list of web pages that are talking about him. If you click the Images tab, you'll get a gallery with pictures of him and his family (Figure 16.5). If you click the Videos tab, you'll get a list of videos with Barack Obama.

FIGURE 16.5   Searching for pictures of Barack Obama

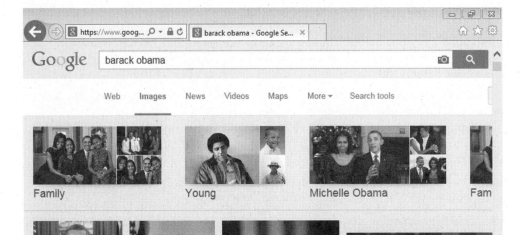

If you are interested in finding only a specific type of files, like pictures or videos, you can also use websites that are specialized databases of that type of files. For example, https:// www.flickr.com/ is one of the world's largest databases of pictures and images taken by people all over the world (Figure 16.6). You can use it not only to publish and store your own pictures but also to find pictures made by others. You type the keywords that you are interested in and press Enter, and then you will get access to thousands of pictures that are representative for your search.

If you are looking for video content, YouTube and Vimeo are some of the best locations on the Web. Visit https://www.youtube.com/ or https://vimeo.com/ and search for the videos that interest you (Figure 16.7). Many artists launch their official videos for their songs on YouTube, and you can use this website to stay up to date with their work. You can also find how-to guides, movie trailers, and all kinds of video content. The principles that you use for searching video content on these websites are the same as those used by search engines.

FIGURE 16.6   A screenshot of Flickr.com

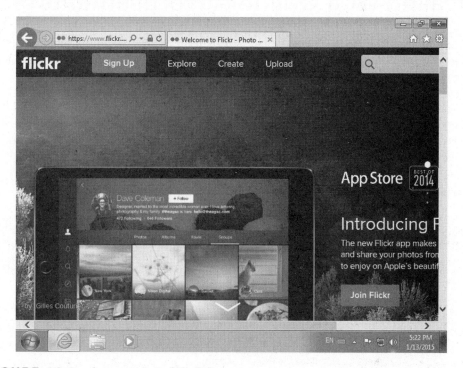

FIGURE 16.7   A screenshot of YouTube

Dealing with Online Advertisements

We see ads every day: on the subway, in airports, in train stations, on streets, and also on TV. As soon as the Web gained in popularity and number of users, ads also moved online. They take many forms and shapes, and you encounter them on almost every website.

For starters, you encounter ads and sponsored links when using a search engine like Google or Bing (Figure 16.8). For example, if you search for "buy a computer," you will first see a long list of search results that are ads or sponsored links. These results are marked with the word *Ad*, and they are presented differently when compared to search results that are not paid for by a company or another organization.

FIGURE 16.8 Ads displayed by Google when searching online

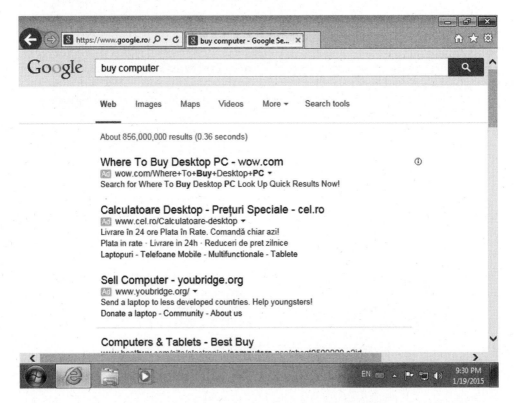

While clicking ads returned by a search engine will take you to relevant web pages, they are not necessarily the best result for your search. In the end they are commercial offerings that are sponsored by a certain company. The best offer may be found on another site that did not pay for a sponsored link to show up in your search results. That's why it is best to scroll down a bit and also check some of the unsponsored results that are returned.

Another form of advertising that's often encountered on the Web is sponsored posts. Some websites correctly highlight these posts as being sponsored while others do not. Sponsored posts can be informational articles that present a product or service made by a company, or they can be one of their special offers. They tend to present what is being sold in a flattering manner in order to convince the reader or the viewer to buy. It is best to take sponsored posts with a grain of salt and document your results from other sources before purchasing what is being sold.

Another popular format for advertising is the *web banner* or *banner ad*. This is basically an advertisement that is embedded into a web page. Web banners are used to attract traffic to the website of the advertiser. Web banners function the same way as traditional advertisements: notifying consumers of the product or service and presenting reasons why the consumer should choose the product in question. When the advertiser detects that a web user has visited the advertiser's site from the content site by clicking the banner ad, the advertiser sends the content provider a small amount of money. This is a very common monetization method used by websites around the world.

Banner ads come in all kinds of shapes and sizes, which are optimized for the web page that is viewed and the size of the display the user is using. Unfortunately, many websites choose to add so many web banners on their web pages that users find them highly frustrating. As a result, ad blockers have been created. They can be manually installed by users so that banners are automatically blocked when browsing the Web. The most popular ad blocker is Adblock Plus (`https://adblockplus.org/`). It works with all web browsers, and it can be easily installed and used by anyone.

Unfortunately there's also a downside to using ad blockers—they are so effective that they cause financial problems to the websites that are using ad banners as a way of financing their work. If everyone were to use ad blockers when browsing the Web, many websites would go bankrupt and would not be able to generate revenue from their work.

A good principle for using products like Adblock Plus is to enable it only for those websites that overuse banner ads and provide a bad user experience because of them. Disable it for those websites that provide a good user experience and valuable content.

Finding Valuable Information on Internet Forums and Knowledge Bases

When you search for solutions to all kinds of problems, especially those that are computer related, you will often find great information in more unusual places like Internet forums and knowledge bases.

An *Internet forum* or *message board* is a discussion site where people can hold conversations in the form of posted messages. These messages are automatically stored and displayed by the site in a conversation-like format. Forums have a specific jargon associated with them. For example, a single conversation is called a *thread*, or topic. A forum can contain a number of *subforums*, each of which may have several topics. Within a forum's topic, each new discussion started is a thread, and it can be replied to by any number of people. Depending on the forum's settings, users can be anonymous or have to register and then subsequently log in to post messages. On most forums, users do not have to log in to read existing messages.

Forums tend to be specialized based on interests; whatever your heart desires, there's probably a forum dedicated to it. Many companies tend to use forums in order to provide support to their customers. For example, Microsoft uses their Microsoft Answers forums (http://answers.microsoft.com) to provide support to customers using products like Windows, Microsoft Office, and so on. If you are having issues with any of their products, all you have to do is to register an account, log in, and post your questions.

However, when posting on Internet forums, be mindful of the basic communication rules that were shared in Chapter 14. Be polite, don't flame other users, and describe your problem(s) as clearly and as completely as possible so that you get to the desired resolution as soon as possible.

A *knowledge base* is a way of storing complex data about a computer system or product in a structured format that's easily accessible to a computer user. Knowledge bases can be found both on the Web in the form of websites that are created to store data about a product or on your computer in the form of help files that are installed by the applications that you are using. Their main purpose is to help users understand how to use a product when they cannot figure it out on their own. For example, when you use any Microsoft Office application, if you press F1 on your keyboard, you will access its Help documentation (Figure 16.9). You can search for what you are trying to do with that application, and Help will return information from its database. The Help from Microsoft Office is a knowledge base. Many other applications have similar knowledge bases, and they can generally be accessed by pressing F1 on your keyboard.

FIGURE 16.9   The Help for Microsoft Word

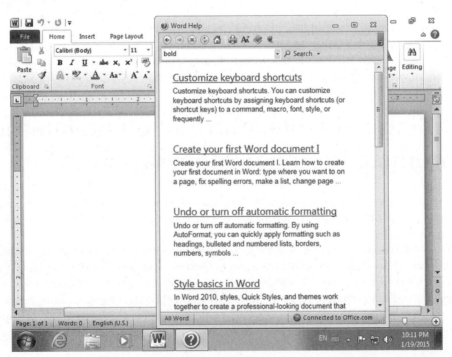

Some software manufacturers have moved their knowledge bases online. Therefore, when you press F1 on your keyboard, a website loads with the complete documentation that is available for their product.

Evaluating the Information That You Find on the Web

When browsing the Web, you will find tons of information. Knowing whether an item is true or false can be quite a challenge. Also, some information might be incomplete, or it may present the perspective and the interests of a certain group and ignore the others. Just like news channels on TV, many websites present information in a way that represents the interests of a certain group or entity, while few will be truly neutral and present all facts from an impartial perspective.

So, who do you believe on the Web? That's a tough question to ask, and nobody can answer it with 100 percent accuracy. But, to help you out, let's share a couple of principles that will certainly be useful:

- Don't read news just from one source.

  Try to follow more than one news site that covers similar subjects. This way you will have more information and you will receive more than one perspective on the topics that interest you.

- Read more than one review of the same product.

  Reviews online can be legitimate but also paid or fake. For example, many companies buy positive reviews on less-reputable websites that try to fool people into buying certain products or services. Some small websites without many resources publish fake reviews without having access to the product that they are reviewing. They make up reviews based on user comments found online, the description, and the specifications of the product they pretend to be reviewing. That's why it is best to read more than one review of the same product before purchasing it and to check reviews on more reputable websites that have a history of publishing relevant reviews.

- Many articles online are jokes or satire.

  There are many websites that publish news and articles in a professional format, which are actually satire. *The Onion* (http://www.theonion.com/) is a very popular example of this type of website. *The Onion*'s articles comment on current events, both real and fictional. It parodies traditional news websites with stories, editorials, op-ed pieces, and interviews, using a traditional news website layout and editorial voice. Its humor often depends on presenting mundane, everyday events as newsworthy, surreal, or alarming.

  Before believing a certain news article from an unknown source, don't hesitate to do a quick background check and see whether that website is actually publishing satire or fake news or real news and facts. A good place to check on the truth or falsehood of a story is Snopes.com.

- User-generated content is fun but not necessarily true.

  You will find plenty of websites with user-generated content, like 9GAG (http://9gag.com/). On such websites, anyone can upload and share user-generated images, videos, or articles. The content is promoted based on its popularity and the votes it receives from other users, and you'll often find such content being shared on social networks like Facebook. While this type of content may be very entertaining, it doesn't mean that it is true, so be wary of taking data from these websites as fact.

- Value data from official sources more than data from random blogs and forums.

  Yes, you may find individuals who have great information on a certain subject, and they publish it online on their blog or on a forum where they are active. But as a general rule, data shared by individuals online may not always be accurate, complete, or true. Depending on what you are looking for, try to also get data from official sources like published journals, government sites, research institutes, and so on. Compare the data that you get and the different views that you find, and you will have a more accurate interpretation of the subject that interests you.

Summary

We have covered a lot of ground together since the start of this study guide. In this final chapter we showed you how to find information and files using search engines like Google or Bing. You learned how to make a basic search and also how to build more advanced search queries that help you find more specific things on the Web.

Then, we talked about the many forms of advertising that you encounter on the Web, how they work, and how to block banner ads when there are too many of them.

Lastly, we discussed finding information from Internet forums and knowledge bases and how to evaluate the information that you find online. Remember, using more than one source is always the way to go.

Exam Essentials

Know how to use a search engine.   Know how to find information and files using a search engine like Google or Bing.

Learn how to perform advanced searches.   With the help of symbols and operators you can fine-tune your searches so that you are more effective in finding the information that you are interested in.

Know the most common types of online advertising.   When browsing the Web, you will encounter many forms of advertising, ranging from ads to sponsored links, sponsored posts, and banner ads. You should know what they are and what their purpose is.

Know what forums and knowledge bases are.   You should know what forums and knowledge bases are and how they can be useful to you when solving problems.

Understand how to evaluate the information found on the Web.   The Web is filled with information of all kinds. You should understand and use several basic principles that will help you evaluate the accuracy of the information that you find on the Web.

Key Terms

Before you take the exam, be certain you are familiar with the following terms:

banner ad	search engine
Internet forum	search operators
knowledge base	web banner
message board	

Review Questions

1. What is a search engine?

    A. A software system that is designed to search for information on the Web

    B. A way to search for information on your computer

    C. A computer program that you install to find files on your computer

    D. A software system that is designed to search for information in your email account

2. Which of the following are search engines? (Choose all that apply.)

    A. Facebook

    B. Google

    C. Bing

    D. Yahoo!

3. Which of the following information is displayed for each search result when searching on Google or Bing? (Choose all that apply.)

    A. The title

    B. The color

    C. The URL

    D. The description

4. Which of the following symbols can be used to make searches on Google? (Choose all that apply.)

    A. $

    B. \

    C. ^

    D. " "

5. What is the correct use of the * (asterisk) symbol when making a search on Google or Bing?

    A. Add it to put a word or phrase in quotes.

    B. Add it as tool to find prices.

    C. Add it as a placeholder for any unknown or wildcard terms.

    D. Add it to find trending topics on social networks like Twitter.

6. What are search operators in the context of search engines?

    A. Words that can be added to searches to increase the number of search results

    B. Words that can be added to searches to make the search more complex

    C. Words that can be added to searches to find prices online

    D. Words that can be added to searches to help narrow down your results

7. What does the site: search operator do?

   A. Gets results on a certain subject

   B. Gets results from a certain site or domain

   C. Excludes results from a certain site or domain

   D. Helps you find prices on a certain domain

8. Which of the following are characteristics of a banner ad? (Choose all that apply.)

   A. An advertisement that is embedded into a web page

   B. An advertisement that is embedded into a website

   C. A tool to attract traffic to the website of an advertiser

   D. A tool to reduce the traffic of the website of an advertiser

9. Which of the following are characteristics of a message board? (Choose all that apply.)

   A. It's a site where people can create, share, and vote on user-generated content.

   B. It's a discussion site where people can hold conversations in the form of posted messages.

   C. It's a site where messages are displayed in a conversation-like format.

   D. Each new discussion started is called a thread and can be replied to by any number of people.

10. What is a knowledge base? (Choose all that apply.)

   A. A way of storing complex data about a product in a structured format

   B. A way of finding information online

   C. A way of storing complex data in an unstructured format

   D. A way of storing complex data about a product in a format that's accessible to users

Appendixes

Appendix A

Answers to Review Questions

Chapter 1: Understanding Operating Systems

1. C. Operating systems are the middleman between the hardware of the computer, the user, and the software applications that are installed. The operating system always takes the input from the user, translates it into commands for the hardware, and returns the result.

2. A, D. Windows and Android are operating systems. Microsoft Office is an application that must be installed on top of the operating system. Hardware is the collection of the physical elements that constitute a computer.

3. B, C. When you lock your computer or switch users, the computing session is paused, and your applications and files remain open. You do not have to save your work because you are not ending the session. If you opt to log off the computer, your session is ended. Also, if you shut down the computer, the computer is turned off, and your session has ended.

4. B, D. When you cut something and then paste it, the item is moved. If you were to copy it instead, the item would not be moved, but a copy of it would be created. There is no specific Move command, but if you right-click and drag a folder from one area of the hard drive to another, Move Here is an option after you drop the item.

5. A, C, D. When using Windows Explorer, you can learn the file type of each file when you are using the Content, Tiles, and Details views. The List view displays a list with all your files, without any additional information.

6. A. Ctrl+C is the shortcut for Copy; Ctrl+X is the shortcut for Cut; Ctrl+V is the shortcut for Paste; Ctrl+P is the shortcut for printing a document.

7. A, B, D. The Magnifier is a tool available from the Accessibility Center that enables you to zoom in on what is showing on the screen. You can decrease the screen resolution to make everything larger, while increasing it would make everything smaller. You can also opt to make text and other items larger from the Display window.

8. C. The only place where you can go to customize both the Desktop background and the theme used by Windows is Start ➤ Control Panel ➤ Appearance And Personalization ➤ Personalization. The other options take you to panels where you can customize other items.

9. D. Only administrators are allowed to make changes that affect all users of the computer and create other users.

10. D. Read is the permission that offers access to a file but does not allow any alteration to it. Read/Write allows access and editing. View and Delete are not valid permissions.

Chapter 2: Understanding Hardware

1. A, C. RAM and the CPU are housed inside the computer and are thus internal hardware. A mouse and a printer are connected externally so they are external hardware or peripherals.

2. A, C, D. RAM is the only type of volatile memory in this list. It loses all its stored data when powered off. SSDs, DVDs, and USB flash drives do not lose their data when powered off.

3. B, C. The speakers and the webcam are generally connected to a desktop computer and are not found inside the case of the computer. They are peripherals.

4. A, B. A monitor shows the visual output of the computer. Speakers output sound. A microphone accepts data, so it's an input device. A keyboard accepts keystrokes, so it is also an input device.

5. D. Servers tend to have very powerful hardware, which requires more energy than other computers. They are used to provide all kinds of specialized services to other computers.

6. B. One byte contains 8 bits (or 8 bits make up 1 byte).

7. A. A byte represents a single letter. It would take many bytes to represent a picture or a video. You do not have to group 8 bytes together to represent something; 1 byte will suffice.

8. C. RAM is denoted in GBs. GHz and MHz are used with the CPU; MB is too small a measure. Note that in the past MB was used as a unit of measure for RAM, but now it comes in GBs.

9. D. The Performance tab offers graphs to represent usage history. The Processes and Services tabs do not offer graphs. Resource Monitor is a button on the Performance tab and is also an application.

10. B. One hertz is one computing cycle per second or one computer instruction per second. The only correct answer is B. The other answers are incorrect.

Chapter 3: Understanding Software

1. B. System requirements describe the hardware components or other software resources that need to be present on the computer where you want to use an application.

2. A, D. Typical application installations allow users to change the installation folder and specify which shortcuts they want installed.

3. C. You can start the removal process for any of your installed applications by clicking Start ➢ Control Panel ➢ Uninstall A Program. There you will see a list of all your installed applications, and you can remove any of them.

4. A, C. EULA stands for end-user license agreement, and it is the contract between the company that published the software that you want to use and you, the user.

5. B, D. GPL (GNU General Public License) and MIT are the most commonly used open-source licenses. Freeware and shareware are proprietary licenses.

6. C, D. A and B are characteristics of databases, whereas C and D are characteristics of spreadsheets and spreadsheet programs like Microsoft Excel.

7. A. While both word processing programs and desktop publishing programs can work with text and images, word processing programs specialize in creating written documents, whereas desktop publishing programs specialize in creating materials that are comparable to traditional typography and printing.

8. B, C. Microsoft PowerPoint and LibreOffice Impress are similar programs that can be used to create presentations.

9. A, B, D. Installing an antivirus program is the only action listed that you can take that does not increase the amount of free space available on your computer's hard disk.

10. D. A, B, and C are harmful activities that can be performed by all kinds of malware. What separates a virus from other types of malware is its capacity to replicate itself.

Chapter 4: Troubleshooting Problems with Your Computer

1. D. Windows Compatibility Center is a website where you can check whether an application is compatible with your version of Windows.

2. C. Task Manager is the tool that you can use to learn the status of your running applications and close those that are no longer responding to your commands.

3. A, B, D. Booting into Safe Mode is the only thing that doesn't prevent malware infections.

4. A, C. Safe Mode is a way of loading Windows with only the barest essentials that are required for it to run, which allows users to troubleshoot and fix problems that cannot be solved when loading Windows normally.

5. B, D. Microsoft Answers is an online community where you can get help from Microsoft employees, technical experts, and other users. Fix It Solution Center is a portal created by Microsoft where you can find solutions to many Windows-related problems.

6. A, B, D. Dust doesn't cause monitors to stop displaying the image on the screen. All the other possible causes do.

7. B, C. You should install a driver on your computer only if it was made for the exact hardware component that you are using and only if it is compatible with the version of the operating system you are using.

8. A, C, D. B is the only answer that doesn't describe a characteristic of the BIOS.

9. B, C. If you have a backup system in place, you can easily recover your data when your computer crashes or gets stolen.

10. A, B, C. Cloud storage solutions do not impose a time limit for recovering your data. All other options are characteristics of cloud storage solutions.

Chapter 5: Exploring Common Application Features in Microsoft Office

1. C, D. C and D are the only answers that describe the complete and correct procedure for opening a Microsoft Word document on your computer.

2. A. The main difference between Save and Save As is that Save As saves a copy of your document and your latest changes.

3. B. Ctrl+A selects the contents of the entire document.

4. A, D. As the name implies, the Spelling and Grammar tool only checks the spelling and the grammar of your file.

5. A, B, D. When you hide a column from a table, that column is no longer visible, but its data is still stored in your file. Also, if data from that column was used in one or more charts, its data will no longer be included in those charts until you unhide it.

6. B, C. Ctrl+V is the keyboard shortcut for Paste. There is no Undo option in the File menu.

7. D. Non-adjacent cells are cells that are not located in the same column or row. Selecting several non-adjacent cells is done using the Ctrl key on your keyboard and the mouse.

8. A, C. The printing settings are accessed by clicking File and then Print or by pressing Ctrl+P on your keyboard.

9. B. B is the only answer that describes all the formatting characteristics that can be changed using a style. The other answers are incomplete or incorrect in their characterization of styles.

10. C. Crop is the only tool that allows you to remove the outer parts of an image. The others only allow you to change the way it is positioned or sized. Print allows you to print your files and not edit them in any way.

Chapter 6: Using Microsoft Word

1. B, C. You can change and improve the spacing of your documents using Styles or the Line and Paragraph Spacing tool.

2. D. Ctrl+R is the keyboard shortcut for Align Text Right.

3. A. Microsoft Word allows you to organize the text in up to three columns per page.

4. A, D. The margins of a document say how much blank space there is around the edges of a page and define how much text and graphics fit on a page.

5. A, C, D. The ruler is a measurement tool that allows you to align text, graphics, tables, and other elements in your documents.

6. B, C. An indent is the distance or the number of blank spaces that are used to move a line of text or a paragraph away from the left or right margin of the page.

7. C. The Increase Indent and Decrease Indent tools are found by clicking the Home tab on the ribbon and going to the Paragraph section.

8. A. When you press Tab on your keyboard while creating a Microsoft Word document, the insertion point for the text is moved ½ inch to the right.

9. A, C. Lists with text can be sorted in Microsoft Word using ascending or descending alphabetical order.

10. C. A merged cell is two or more table cells located in the same row or column that are combined into a single cell.

Chapter 7: Using Microsoft Excel

1. A, D. A workbook is a Microsoft Excel file that contains one or more worksheets.

2. B. Many people incorrectly refer to spreadsheets as Microsoft Excel files. A spreadsheet is an application that is used for organizing, analyzing, and storing data in tabular form.

3. A. You can change a row's height by following the procedure detailed in answer A. All the other ways are incorrect.

4. B, C. The tools for increasing the font size of a cell are found on the Home tab on the ribbon, in the Font section. There you can use both the Increase Font Size button and the Font Size drop-down list.

5. A. The number formats are applied to the way data is displayed in Microsoft Excel but not to how the data is numbered, how calculations and formulas are used, or how it is added into graphs.

6. D. One way of changing the format of a cell to Number is to right-click it, click Format Cells, and then select Number in the Format Cells window. Click OK to apply your setting.

7. C. You can filter only one or more columns of data in Microsoft Excel.

8. A, B. In Microsoft Excel, you will find all the options for filtering and sorting data using one of these two ways: click the Home tab, go to the Editing section, and click Sort & Filter, or click the Data tab and use the appropriate buttons in the Sort & Filter section.

9. C. In Microsoft Excel, you can enter a formula by selecting the cell where you want to insert it and then typing = followed by the numbers (or constants), math operators, cell references, and functions that make up the formula.

10. B. The buttons for adding charts and graphs into Microsoft Excel are always found on the Insert tab on the ribbon, in the Charts section.

Chapter 8: Using Microsoft PowerPoint

1. B. A slide is a single page of a presentation that is created with presentation software like Microsoft PowerPoint.

2. A, D. A slide show is a collection of slides or a series of images, graphics, text, and other multimedia content presented on a projection screen or a computer display, one after the other.

3. C. The slide pane is the area on the left side of the Microsoft PowerPoint window where you can select slides and change their order.

4. A, D. There are two ways of deleting a slide: you select it and then press Delete on your keyboard, or you right-click it and then click Delete Slide.

5. D. Applying a new theme changes major visual design details like the effects applied to titles and text, the way tables and charts are displayed, the layouts and backgrounds of your slides, and so on. You can apply a new theme to your presentation by using the ribbon. Click Design, go to the Themes section, and click the theme that you want to apply.

6. B, C. The options for changing the layout of a slide are found by going to the Home tab on the ribbon and clicking the Slide Layout button in the Slides section or by right-clicking the slide, selecting Layout, and then selecting one of the available layouts.

7. D. The only complete procedure is the following: click the Insert tab on the ribbon, look for the Illustrations section, click Chart, and then click the desired shape. Then, click inside the slide where you want to add the shape.

8. A, C. You can create the chart directly in your presentation using the tools that are available in Microsoft PowerPoint using the procedure from answer A, or you can copy a chart made in a Microsoft Excel file and paste it into your presentation.

9. A, B, C. Animations are applied to all the elements of a slide (title, text, pictures, tablets, charts, and so on) but not to the transitions between slides.

10. B, C. You can view your presentation as a slide show by pressing F5 on your keyboard or by going to the Slide Show tab on the ribbon and clicking the From Beginning button, in the Start Slide Show.

Chapter 9: Using Microsoft Access

1. B, D. Databases are organized collections of data. Databases are organized in tables, which are a means of arranging data in rows and columns.

2. A, B, C. Tables are a way of arranging data in rows and columns. Rows are also called *records* whereas the columns are also called *fields*. A table can have a set number of columns and any number of rows.

3. C, D. A query is a request for data results, for action on data, or for both.

4. A, C, D. Reports are a way of viewing, formatting, and summarizing information from a Microsoft Access database.

5. A, C. You can access the Find And Replace dialog by pressing Ctrl+F on your keyboard or by clicking the Find button in the Found section in the Home tab of the ribbon.

6. B. You can run a query stored in a database by double-clicking its name in the Navigation Pane.

7. C. You can run a report stored in a database by double-clicking its name in the Navigation Pane.

8. B, C. Sources for reports can be tables or queries but not both at the same time.

9. C. You can view the data found inside a table by double-clicking the table name in the Navigation Pane.

10. A. The Report Wizard helps users create simple, customized reports in a visual way.

Chapter 10: Collaborating with Others When Working in Microsoft Office

1. C. The New Comment button is found on the Review tab of the ribbon, in the Comments section. This path applies to Microsoft Word, Microsoft Excel, and Microsoft PowerPoint.

2. A. In Microsoft Word, comments are displayed by default in a separate column, on the right side of the document.

3. B. In order to quickly jump to the previous comment, click the Review tab on the ribbon and then the Previous Comment button found in the Comments section.

4. B. You activate the Track Changes feature in Microsoft Word by going to the Review tab on the ribbon and clicking the Track Changes button in the Tracking section.

5. D. You accept the current change and move to the next one by clicking the Review tab on the ribbon and then the Accept And Move To Next button in the Changes section.

6. A, B, D. Good practices to keep in mind when sending emails at work with file attachments are the following: avoid sending emails with attachments to large email lists because unauthorized parties might get access to confidential data; do not send emails with large files or many files attached because you might break the rules imposed by the network administrator; respect your company's policies for sharing your work documents with other people.

7. A, D. Cloud computing is a form of computing in which large groups of remote servers are networked to allow centralized data storage and online access to computer services or resources. It focuses on maximizing the effectiveness of the shared resources.

8. A, C, D. Cloud computing has multiple advantages, including lowering costs, reducing environmental damage, reducing the power consumption, and so on.

9. B, D. Network attached storage solutions are specialized storage devices that are connected to the company network that allow the storage of files for all or a group of the users in that company.

10. B, C. OneDrive and Google Drive are two cloud storage solutions: the first made by Microsoft and the second made by Google.

Chapter 11: Using the Internet

1. B, D. The Internet is the global network of interconnected networks that use standardized communication protocols to exchange data and information between them. In a simpler manner, it is also considered the physical network of computers and devices (smartphones, tablets, and so on) all over the world.

2. C. WWW stands for World Wide Web.

3. A, D. The World Wide Web is a system of websites connected by links. It is a part of the Internet but not the entire Internet.

4. A, B. URL stands for Uniform Resource Locator, and it is the address of a website or a web page on the WWW.

5. B, D. A web browser is an application that displays a web page on a computer or mobile device. The first web browser was called WorldWideWeb, to suggest that it is software that is used to navigate websites and web pages that are found on the World Wide Web.

6. C. A hyperlink is a reference to data that can be accessed by clicking it.

7. A, B. Posting your pictures on Facebook or a video on YouTube are the only examples listed here of performing an upload of data.

8. D. The homepage is the web page that is loaded each time you open a web browser.

9. B. The browsing history is a complete log of the websites and web pages that you have visited in a web browser.

10. C. A plug-in or an add-on is a software component that adds a specific feature to a web browser and enables it to do more.

Chapter 12: Understanding Networking and Its Most Important Concepts

1. C. In a Windows network environment, the `ipconfig` command with the `/all` switch is used to view all IP configuration information of a system.

2. D. A VPN uses tunneling protocols to create a secure point-to-point connection over a public network such as the Internet.

3. D. Each protocol within the protocol suite is associated with a specific port. If that port is blocked, then the associated service will be unavailable. The HTTP service uses port 80, and if this port is blocked on a firewall, HTTP and web services will not be available.

4. B. A DHCP server is used to automatically assign TCP/IP information to a client system. This includes the IP address, the subnet mask, and the default gateway.

5. A. DNS is responsible for translating hostnames to IP addresses. Pinging the hostname returns the IP address associated with Sybex.com.

6. D. Securely setting up a wireless router or access point involves configuring the security protocols used. WEP was the original wireless security protocol but proved ineffective as tools were created that could easily get around WEP security. WPA followed WEP and increased security using TKIP. Today, WPA2 is commonly used for security, and it increases the security over WPA.

7. A, D. The IEEE specifies the 802.11 wireless standards. Under this designation there are a number of specifications that you may see on an AP, including 802.11a, 802.11b, 802.11g, 802.11n, and 802.11ac.

8. A, C. LANs are the computer network from the floor of an office building and the computer network in your house.

9. C. Windows offers several troubleshooting wizards for solving network and Internet-related problems. The one that helps you solve Internet connection problems is named Internet Connections.

10. A, C, D. Broadband is a form of high-speed Internet access, with maximum speeds that go beyond the 128 Kbps provided by dial-up connections. Broadband is largely an always-on Internet service that allows for bandwidth-intensive applications.

Chapter 13: Communicating Online with Others

1. B, C, D. Email is a method of exchanging digital messages with others. In order to use email you must have a registered username and password, and you need to provide the email address of the people whom you want to communicate with through this medium.

2. C, D. C and D are strong passwords because they contain at least eight characters and mix letters with numbers and special characters.

3. A, C. BCC means blind carbon copy. This field is available for hidden notification, and recipients listed in the BCC field receive a copy of the message but are not shown on any other recipient's copy, including other BCC recipients.

4. B, D. To and Subject are fields that you have to fill in yourself. Date and From are automatically populated by the email client or the email service that you are using.

5. B. When using Reply All, you reply to all the people who were included in the email distribution list, in the To and CC fields, including the sender of the message that you received. This option is useful when you need to reply to a conversation and include a whole group of people in that conversation.

6. B, D. When using Forward, a copy of the initial email message is created automatically with the same subject as the one used by the sender but prefixed by the term *FW:*. Also, the body of the email includes the original message that was received from the sender as well as any other messages that were sent earlier in the same conversation.

7. A, B, D. In order for the reply to be effective, you should specify when you will be out of office, when you will be able to reply, how people can contact you in case of emergencies, and, if applicable, who your stand-in is for the period when you are away and how the recipient can contact them.

8. A, B. SMS means Short Message Service, and one message can include up to 160 characters.

9. B, D. Facebook Messenger and Skype are examples of very popular chat clients.

10. A, B, D. Social media tools can take many forms, including blogs, social networks like Facebook, or Internet forums. OneDrive is a cloud storage solution provided by Microsoft.

Chapter 14: Being a Responsible Digital Citizen

1. B. Using all capital letters is interpreted by readers as excitement or yelling, depending on the context, so it is best to avoid such stylistic decisions in professional communications.

2. A, B. Spamming is the act of sending unsolicited messages to others, especially advertising and self-promotion. It applies to all kinds of media, including email and SMS.

3. A. Professional audiences expect courtesy and cultural sensitivity, and this is achieved through the tone the writer sets by the words they choose.

4. C. Emoticons help to share the emotion that accompanies a statement.

5. C. Emoticons help readers process the emotion that goes along with the sentence but are typically used in only personal communications, such as texting, social media postings, and email. Professional communications achieve tone through accurate and emotionally appropriate diction.

6. B, D. Censorship can take the form of blocked access, filtering of certain types of sites, and filtering with a firewall against any site that uses certain key words. Parental controls are solutions that censor access to content based on rules set by the parents.

7. A, C. DRM technologies can be used to control many things, including the copying of a work or its altering.

8. B. Intellectual property refers to knowledge and creative ideas or expressions that have commercial value and are protected either by copyright, patent, trademark, industrial design rights, or trade secret laws.

9. A, D. Creative Commons is used when the creator wants to give people the right to share, use, and build upon their work. Creative Commons provides the creator flexibility and protects the people who use or redistribute the work from concerns of copyright infringement as long as they abide by the conditions that are specified in the license by which the creator distributes the work.

10. A. Piracy is also known as copyright infringement, and it is a criminal offense in most countries.

Chapter 15: Maintaining Your Health and Safety While Using Computers

1. **A, B, D.** When online, you should not use the same password on all your email accounts, share your home address publicly on the Internet, or reply to people you don't know, who promise you incredible deals.

2. **A, D.** When making purchases online, you should avoid websites that do not use HTTPS, which encrypts the data that is sent between you and the website where you make the purchase. Also, you should not share your credit card details with others online.

3. **B, C.** You can protect your data by encrypting it with solutions like BitLocker, which makes it hard for others to access it and use it, and by setting up your own backup system with tools like Backup and Restore.

4. **C, D.** When you delete a file using this method, the file remains on your computer, and it continues to take up disk space. Its reference is moved to the Recycle Bin, where it can be recovered later on and you can resume using it.

5. **B, C.** Recycle Bin is a folder where the references to your deleted files and folders are kept. You can use the Recycle Bin to view a list of your deleted items and recover any of them.

6. **C.** You delete a file without moving it to the Recycle Bin by selecting it and then pressing Shift+Delete on your keyboard.

7. **B, C.** You completely wipe a file so that it is no longer recoverable by deleting it with Shift+Delete and rewriting the space it took on the disk several times with data from other files. Also, you can use specialized applications like CCleaner or File Shredder, which help you remove a file forever.

8. **B, C, D.** An ergonomic chair should have many characteristics, including but not limited to a comfortable cushion, lumbar support, adjustable height, and adjustable back rest height.

9. **A, C, D.** The best practices for positioning the computer monitor on a desk are the following: position it at eye level unless it measures 20 inches or more, in which case you should position the top of it 3 inches above eye level. Also, you should place it on the desk at least 20 inches from your eyes.

10. **D.** The rule says that for every 20 minutes you spend staring at the computer, you should spend 20 seconds looking at objects 20 feet away—or at least far enough away that your eyes aren't working to focus.

Chapter 16: Searching the World Wide Web

1. A. A search engine is a software system that is designed to search for information on the Web.

2. B, C, D. Google, Bing, and Yahoo! are search engines. Facebook is a social network.

3. A, C, D. For each search result, a search engine like Google and Bing will display the title, the URL of the page, and a small description.

4. A, D. $ can be used to find prices, and " " (quotes) are used to put a word or phrase in quotes. The results of using quotes will include only pages with the same words in the same order as what's inside the quotes.

5. C. The asterisk acts as a placeholder for any unknown or wildcard terms.

6. D. Search operators are words that can be added to searches to help narrow down your results.

7. B. The search operator site: gets results from certain sites or domains.

8. A, C. The banner ad or web banner is an advertisement that is embedded into a web page. Web banners are used to attract traffic to the website of the advertiser.

9. B, C, D. An Internet forum or message board is a discussion site where people can hold conversations in the form of posted messages. These messages are automatically stored and displayed by the site in a conversation-like format. Within a forum's topic, each new discussion started is called a thread and can be replied to by any number of people.

10. A, D. A knowledge base is a way of storing complex data about a computer system or product in a structured format that's easily accessible to a computer user.

Appendix B

Using the Practice Files

This appendix lists the practice files that accompany the book. The information is organized by module and chapter for easy reference. You can find all practice files online, in the "Other Study Tools" section of the interactive learning environment that was created for this book. Before going through all the exercises that are offered, please register and download all the practice files.

IC3—Module 1: Computing Fundamentals

Part I

Chapter	Practice Files
Chapter 1: Understanding Operating Systems	None
Chapter 2: Understanding Hardware	None
Chapter 3: Understanding Software	documents.zip
Chapter 4: Troubleshooting Problems with Your Computer	None

IC3—Module 2: Key Applications

Part II

Chapter	Practice Files
Chapter 5: Exploring Common Application Features in Microsoft Office	Presentation1.pptx
	Sample1.docx
	Sample2.docx
	Book1.xlsx
	Picture1.jpg
Chapter 6: Using Microsoft Word	Sample1.docx
	Sample3.docx
	Sample4.docx
	Sample5.docx
	Sample6.docx
	Sample7.docx
Chapter 7: Using Microsoft Excel	Book1.xlsx
	Book2.xlsx
	Book3.xlsx
	Book4.xlsx
	Book5.xlsx
	Book6.xlsx
	Book7.xlsx
Chapter 8: Using Microsoft PowerPoint	Presentation2.pptx
	Book7.xlsx
	Presentation3.pptx
	Movie1.wmv
	Presentation4.pptx
Chapter 9: Using Microsoft Access	cities.accdb
Chapter 10: Collaborating with Others When Working in Microsoft Office	Sample1.docx
	Presentation3.pptx
	Sample8.docx
	Sample9.docx

IC3—Module 3: Living Online

Part III

Chapter	Practice Files
Chapter 11: Using the Internet	None
Chapter 12: Understanding Networking and Its Most Important Concepts	None
Chapter 13: Communicating Online with Others	None
Chapter 14: Being a Responsible Digital Citizen	None
Chapter 15: Maintaining Your Health and Safety While Using Computers	None
Chapter 16: Searching the World Wide Web	None

Index

Note to the Reader: Throughout this index **boldfaced** page numbers indicate primary discussions of a topic. *Italicized* page numbers indicate illustrations.

Free Online Learning Environment

Register on Sybex.com to gain access to the free online interactive learning environment and test bank to help you study for your IC3 Internet and Computing Core Certification Global Standard 4 exam.

The online test bank includes:

- Assessment Test to help you focus your study to specific objectives

- Chapter Tests to reinforce what you learned

- Practice Exams to test your knowledge of the material

- Electronic Flashcards to reinforce your learning and provide last-minute test prep before the exam

- Searchable Glossary to give you instant access to the key terms you'll need to know for the exam

- Practice Files for you to use in chapter exercises and activities

Go to `http://sybextestbanks.wiley.com` to register and gain access to this comprehensive study tool package.